ARIS & PHILLIPS HISPANIC CLASSICS

GUILLÉN DE CASTRO

The Force of Habit
La fuerza de la costumbre

Edited with Introduction and Notes by

Melissa Reneé Machit

Translated by

Kathleen Jeffs

LIVERPOOL UNIVERSITY PRESS

First published 2019 by
Liverpool University Press
4 Cambridge Street
Liverpool
L69 7ZU

www.liverpooluniversitypress.co.uk

Copyright © 2019 Melissa Reneé Machit and Kathleen Jeffs

The right of M. R. Machit and K. Jeffs to be identified as the authors of this book has been asserted by them in accordance with the Copyright, Designs and Patents Act 1988.

All rights reserved. No part of this book may be reproduced, stored in a retrieval system, or transmitted, in any form or by any means, electronic, mechanical, photocopying, recording, or otherwise, without the prior written permission of the publisher.

British Library Cataloguing-in-Publication data
A British Library CIP record is available

ISBN 978-1-78694-144-2 hardback
ISBN 978-1-78694-145-9 paperback

Performance rights for K. Jeffs's translation of The Force of Habit can be arranged by contacting the author at jeffs@gonzaga.edu or by writing to:

Dr. Kathleen Jeffs
Department of Theatre and Dance
Gonzaga University
502 E. Boone Ave.
Spokane, WA 99258-0022
USA

Typeset by Tara Evans

Printed in Poland by BooksFactory.co.uk

Cover image: Photo by Ross Mulhausen, University of Puget Sound.

Para Elliot y Ayla, pedazos de mis entrañas

M. M.

For Jonathan Thacker

K. J.

CONTENTS

Acknowledgements	vii
Introduction	1
Biography of Guillén de Castro	1
Plot Summary	8
Textual History	12
The Present Edition	14
The *Editio Princeps* and Manuscripts	16
Editorial Methods	21
Metrical Analysis	22
Critical Essay. Bad Habits: Gender Made and Remade in *La fuerza de la costumbre*	24
Introduction: *La fuerza de la costumbre*, The Power of Habit	24
I Cross-Dressing in Spanish Golden Age Theater	28
II Masculine Perfection: Theorized and Performed	34
III Gender Trouble in *La fuerza de la costumbre*	47
Dressing Up as 'Oneself'	55
IV Gen(i)us and Gen(d)eration: the Conceits and Conceptions of Paternal *ingenio* in *La fuerza de la costumbre*	58
In the Name of the Father: Félix's Transition	64
Genre Trouble: Hipólita Unmade	71
Conclusion	84
Bibliography	85
Translator's Note	94
Illustrations	96
La fuerza de la costumbre / The Force of Habit	109
Index of Variants	325

ACKNOWLEDGEMENTS

This project began as my doctoral dissertation at Harvard University. I am sincerely grateful to have had the insightful guidance of Mary Malcolm Gaylord, Meg Greer, Luis Girón Negrón, and Dian Fox, an incredible group of scholars, on the minutiae and big picture questions of this edition. Harvard University's Department of Romance Languages and Literatures and the Dudley House Graduate Student Council supported the project with summer grants, which made it possible for me to pore over the manuscripts and early print editions of *La fuerza de la costumbre* at the Biblioteca Nacional in Madrid. Kathleen Jeffs offered fresh eyes and new perspectives on the edition. I would also like to thank my husband Dan and my parents for their enduring support, and my children, for making everything brighter.

Melissa Reneé Machit

I am grateful to the following people who played a role in bringing this play to life in English and in performance: Guy Jeffs, Jonathan Thacker, Tyler Fisher, Clare Litt, Melissa Machit, Ben Gunter, Susan Paun de Garcia, Harley Erdman, Rick Davis, Janine Kehlenbach, Jason Price, Suzanne Morrison, and the ATHE reading cast, Erin Fitzgerald, Patrick Ostrander, Sara Romersberger and the Gonzaga University cast and crew, Sara Freeman, Hannah Ferguson, and the University of Puget Sound cast and crew.

Kathleen Jeffs

INTRODUCTION

Biography of Guillén de Castro

Guillén de Castro lived a life of arms and letters, serving as a captain of the Valencian Coast Guard, participating in literary circles (known as *academias*) and winning poetry contests, taking a post as governor of Scigliano, a province in southern Italy, deporting Moors banished from Valencia to North Africa, and living at the court in Madrid where the rich and powerful funded his literary endeavors. Born in Valencia in 1569, Guillén de Castro was baptized in the parochial church of San Martín on November 4 of the same year (Juliá Martínez 1925–1927 I, vii). He was the first child of Francisco de Castro and Castellana Bellvís, who had been married in the same church just a year prior, on October 24, 1568 (Martí Grajales 1927). William E. Wilson claims that local legends purported that he was related on his father's side to Laín Calvo, the grandfather of Rodrigo Ruy Díaz de Vivar, the Cid Campeador, and that he was a descendent of King John I of Aragon via his mother's family (Wilson 1973, 13). Francisco and Castellana had three more children: Juan (b. 1570), Francisco (b. 1572) and a daughter, Magdalena (b. 1578).

Valencia was famed for its refined and sophisticated culture in the sixteenth and seventeenth centuries. Strong literary and cultural ties with Italy enriched the city, which was teeming with poets, dramatists, and literary activity. Francisco Tárrega mentions Guillén de Castro in *El prado de Valencia*, in which he describes the grand wedding of don Francisco de Palafox to doña Lucrecia de Moncada, which took place on September 14th of 1590 in Valencia's Plaza Mayor (Luciano García Lorenzo 1976, 14).[1] Near the middle of the 240 lines Tárrega dedicates to his description of the festivities and the finely dressed Valencian nobles in attendance, he records the presence of Guillén de Castro, who would have been 20 or 21 years old at the time:

> De plata negro, grave y muy gallardo,
> con don Guillén de Castro al lado izquierdo,
> don Villarich Carroz y don Luís Pardo,
> entró don Juan, su padre, alegre y cuerdo.

---

1 It is possible that the character Pedro de Moncada in *La fuerza de la costumbre* was named for this family, particularly since he comes from Valencia, according to Costanza's description (I. 37–40; 45).

[In black silver, solemn and very handsome,
with Sir Guillén de Castro on his left,
Sir Villarich Carroz and Sir Luis Pardo,
Sir Juan, their father, entered, happy and wise.][2]
(1985, v. 2120-2123)

The young poet surely attended many such grand events of Valencia's noble class.

On March 11, 1592 Guillén de Castro, now twenty-two years old, presented a few poems under the penname 'Secreto' ['Secret'] at his *academia*, called 'La academia de los nocturnos' ['The Nocturnal Academy'], in which he was an active participant throughout the early 1590s (Juliá Martínez I, viii–ix). This literary society met on Wednesday nights to discuss poetry and present their own poems and compositions. The meetings were held most often in the palace of Gaspar Mercader, the founder of the *Academia*, who went by the pseudonym 'Relámpago' ['Lightning']. Guillén de Castro not only presented poems at the *Academia*, but also three Discourses: the 'Discurso contra la confiança' ['A Discourse Against Trust'] on Wednesday, October 6th, 1593, 'Discurso como a de grangear vn galán a una dama' ['A Discourse on How a Young Man Should Win A Lady'] the following week, on October 13th, 1593, and a 'Discurso alabando el secreto del amor' ['A Discourse Praising Secrecy in Matters of Love'] on December 23rd, 1592.[3] These Discourses range from a serious tone to a more raunchy one – the 'Discurso como a de grangear vn galán a una dama', for example, gives instructions tailored to find favor with women of six different categories: *Donçellas* (maidens), *Casadas* (married women), *Viudas* (widows), *Monjas* (nuns), *Beatas* (pious women) and *Solteras* (single women). This Discourse and its scandalous topic show us a different side of the young author's wit. The Discourses are quite entertaining and, if taken to represent the author's beliefs, revealing with regards to the young Guillén de Castro's thoughts on amorous affairs. He paints women as fickle and corruptible at best, and outright dangerous to man's well being at worst.[4]

---

2   Quotes have been translated by the editors unless otherwise noted.
3   The text presented by Juliá Martínez does not give a year for this 'Discurso', but given that the *Academia de los nocturnos* met on Wednesday nights, this 'Discurso' must have been presented in 1592. The 'Discursos' are found in Juliá Martínez's edition of Castro's *Obras completas* [*Complete Works*], 1925–1927 III, pp. 573–589.
4   In the Discourse on trust, he charges that women are the ones "de quien más devríamos guardarnos, pues sabemos quantas vidas cuesta el averse fiado dellas" ["from whom we

Guillén de Castro's own troubles in love may have provided inspiration for this bitter perspective. He was involved in an amorous dispute with a woman named Helena Fenollar which went to court in 1593, registered in the Valencian 'Indice de Procesos matrimoniales, jactancias y divorcios desde 1400 hasta 1642' ['Index of Marital Cases, Complaints and Divorces From 1400 to 1642'], though the details of the case are unclear (Juliá Martínez I, x). This entry in the registry likely indicates that Guillén de Castro and Helena Fenollar either divorced or broke a legal promise of marriage (Oleza 1997, xii).

Though Guillén de Castro was born into a noble family, he did not inherit the kind of wealth that his fellow *Nocturnos* possessed. His grandfather, don Beltrán de Castro, was the first in his family to be granted a title of nobility. Charles V, Holy Roman Emperor, granted don Beltrán the title in 1542 for his service in the Americas (Oleza 1997, x). Originally from Cuenca, don Beltrán de Castro relocated to Valencia in 1547, where he married Juana Palafox, a member of the established Valencian nobility. Thus, Guillén de Castro had a title, and family lineage on his mother's side which gave him access to the wealthy and powerful aristocracy of Valencia, but it was necessary for him to use these connections to earn a living.

From 1593 until about 1600 he served as a captain of the Coast Guard, which patrolled the coast on horseback in search of Moors and pirates trying to land on Valencian shores (Juliá Martínez I, ix). On December 17th, 1595, he and doña Marquesa Girón de Rebolledo were married. This marriage would prove short-lived and only produced one child, a daughter born in 1596. According to the baptism records of the parish church of San Esteban, this daughter was given a great many names: Juana, Ana, María, Francisca, Jacinta and Castellana (Juliá Martínez I, x). We can infer that Guillén de Castro was already a widower by 1600 from Gaspar Mercader's pastoral novel, *El prado de Valencia* [*The Fields of Valencia*], published in 1600, in which he refers to the death of his friend Guillén de Castro's

---

[men] should protect ourselves the most; since we already know how many lives have been lost due to trusting them"] (Juliá Martínez III, 575). He opens the Discourse on winning the favor of women by lamenting the fact that ultimately it will come down to a matter of luck, since woman's inconstant nature is unintelligible to man: "sólo dios puede torçer su naturaleza tan inclinada a mudanças" ["only God can bend her nature, so inclined to changes of heart"] (Juliá Martínez III, 583). In order to win the favor of maidens, for example, he instructs the young man that he "procure andar muy galán y bien compuesto" ["try to go around very dressed up and put together"] (Juliá Martínez III, 584), because young women are only interested in the superficial qualities of men and do not look past a man's appearance.

wife through Guillén's pastoral pseudonym, Lisardo, who loses his beloved 'Belisa' (1907, cvii; 155). Doña Castellana Bellvís, Guillén de Castro's mother, died on December 22, 1597, and was buried the following day at Nuestra Señora de la Merced (Juliá Martínez I, x), meaning that Guillén de Castro lost both his wife and mother within the span of just a few years. There is no mention after this time of Guillén de Castro's young daughter, suggesting that she did not live to adulthood. One consolation during this time of great loss may have been the presence of Lope de Vega in Valencia from 1595–1597; the already famous playwright and friend of Guillén de Castro took refuge in Valencia during his banishment from Madrid. Though Lope took part in the extensive royal festivities for the wedding of Felipe III with Margaret of Austria in 1599, it appears that Guillén de Castro chose not to attend the ceremonies (Juliá Martínez I, x–xi).

Guillén continued to seek the favor and protection of the aristocracy, and in 1601 he was employed as the *procurador general* [solicitor general] of Carlos de Borja, Duke of Gandía, an influential Spanish grandee. Nothing is known about Guillén de Castro's fate for the next six years. 1607 found the poet living abroad, serving as governor of Scigliano, a province and township in Naples, Italy, by appointment of the Count of Benavente, Viceroy of the kingdom of Naples (García Lorenzo 1976, 17). It is unclear how long he lived there, but he had probably arrived before 1604; legal documents processed in Valencia and Denia prove that Guillén was back in Spain by December of 1609 (Juliá Martínez I, xii). He had probably been in Spain since the summer of 1609, since the Neapolitan fleet had been dispatched to Mallorca and Valencia in August of that year. Under the command of the Count of Benavente's son, don Diego Pimentel, the eighteen-galley fleet was charged with the massive deportation of the *moriscos*, moors, who had been banished from Spain. Castro participated in the mission until its completion in November of 1610.

Guillén de Castro did not return to Italy with the fleet, however. Around this time, the poet suffered a lung malady which rendered him too ill to travel and forced him to ask for a leave of one year without pay from the Viceroy of Naples so that he could recover at home. Joan Oleza quotes the 1613 medical records written by Dr. Melchor de Villena, *catedrático* of the University of Valencia: "tuvo poco años ha una grande enfermedad de hechar sangre del pecho [...] en grande cantidad, que le tuvo en peligro grande de su vida, y después acá ha tenido otros accidentes y tiene al presente una destilación al pecho por la qual se purga todos los años [...] Para todo lo qual le es muy contraria la mar" ["A few years ago he suffered a serious illness which caused significant bleeding in his chest, which put his life in great danger, and here, after that, he has had other problems and at present has fluid in his chest which must be purged every year. On account of all of this the sea is very bad for his health"] (quoted in Oleza 1997, xiii). Though he survived the illness, he was not well enough to resume his post as governor of Scigliano, and in 1611 the Viceroy of Naples appointed someone else to the position. His lungs were left very weak, and his doctor recommended that he not travel by sea, nor live in humid climates (Wilson 1973, 14; Juliá Martínez I, xii). According to Otis Green's 'New Documents for the Biography of Guillén de Castro y Bellvís', he was eventually able to return to Italy from 1613 to summer of 1616 (1933).

Throughout his domestic and international service, Guillén de Castro continued to be involved in literary endeavors. In 1602, he won a poetic joust, the 'Justa poética celebrada en loor de San Raymundo de Peñafort' ['Poetic Joust Celebrated in Honor of Saint Raymond of Peñafort'], in which he was praised for his *estanzas*.[5] In 1608, his plays *El caballero bobo* [*The Foolish Gentleman*] and *El amor constante* [*Constant Love*] were published in the volume, *Doze comedias famosas de quatro poetas naturales de la insigne y coronada ciudad de Valencia* [*Twelve Famous Comedies by Four Poets Native to the Distinguished and Honored City of Valencia*] alongside plays by the other well-known Valencian playwrights, Francisco Tárrega (known in Spanish as 'el canónigo Tárrega'), Gaspar Aguilar and Miguel Beneyto (Juliá Martínez I, xii). It could be because of the publication of these plays or Castro's participation in poetic contests that Miguel de Cervantes came across Castro's writing before either of his collections of plays was published – Cervantes mentions Guillén de Castro in his *Viaje del Parnaso* [*Journey to Parnassus*], published in 1614. Upon his return to Valencia in 1616, Castro tried to revive the rich Valencian literary culture of his youth by founding an *academia* called 'Los montañeses del Parnaso' ['The Dwellers of Mt. Parnassus'] (Oleza 1997, xiv). The Academy did not last long; this failure could have motivated the dramatist to leave Valencia for the lively intellectual climes of the Court in Madrid.

In 1618, Guillén de Castro borrowed 2600 reals from his neighbor, Vicente Ferrer, to finance the publication by Felipe Mey of the *Primera parte de las obras de don Guillem de Castro* [*First Part of the Works of Don Guillén de Castro*] (Juliá Martínez I, xiii). Oleza posits that the Valencian was preparing

---

5 Francisco Tárrega was one of the three judges for this event (Juliá Martínez I, xi).

for his arrival in Madrid by having proof-in-hand of his dramatic credentials, and furthermore was hoping to live off their sale. The move to court was financially risky since Castro financed it entirely on loans. Before departing from Valencia, he authorized Jerónimo de Herrera to sell 900 copies of the *Primera parte* in January of 1619, the same month in which the poet arrived in Madrid. The sales of these volumes were to be put towards the money he owed Ferrer and two other acquaintances from whom Castro borrowed another 660 reals after arriving in Madrid.

The Valencian playwright's bold plan bore fruit rather quickly. He found his much-needed patron in don Juan Téllez Girón, Marqués de Peñafiel and firstborn son of Pedro Girón, Duke of Osuna (Juliá Martínez I, xiii–xiv). The Marquis gave him a black slave, whom he sold for 1000 reals on February 10th, 1619 (xiii). The following year, the Duke's son granted him a *cortijo*, an estate where he was allowed to live and keep the profits from the cultivation of the land. He also received an annual stipend of three thousand *maravedís*. The Duke of Osuna himself endorsed his son's gift on account of "los muchos y buenos servicios que don Guillén de Castro nos ha hecho al Marqués de Peñafiel, mi hijo, y a mí, y por los que espero que nos hará, y para que mejor pueda sustentarse conforme a la calidad de su persona" ["...the many and good services that Mr. Guillén de Castro has done for my son, the Marquis of Peñafiel, and me, and for those which I hope he will do for us in the future, and so that he may better provide for himself in accordance with the quality of his person"] (quoted in Juliá Martínez I, xiv).

Financially, life seems to have been slightly more stable for him during this time, though even such consistent support did not rescue him entirely from debt. However, the state of his affairs did allow him to sign the profit from his estate over to his sister, doña Magdalena, now unhappily married to don Melchor Figuerola, on July 5, 1620. Either he was finally financially stable due to the support of the Duke and Marquis or he was spending beyond his means. The second possibility seems more likely given that in February of 1623 he mortgaged his estate to pay a merchant for 35 yards of fabric (Juliá Martínez I, xv).

Guillén remarried with the help of the Marquis at the age of 57, to one of the Duchess's ladies-in-waiting, Ángela María Salgado (Oleza 1997, xvii). The support of the Marquis and Duke continued to foster Guillén de Castro's dramatic and poetic success in the 1620s. He participated in (and won) poetic jousts, saw plays such as *Las mocedades del Cid* [*The Youthful Deeds of the Cid*] and *Dido y Eneas* [*Dido and Aeneas*] become hits, and was praised by some of the most important literary figures of his day, including Lope de Vega, Baltasar Gracián and Pérez de Montalbán.

In 1621 Castro published the *Primera parte* a second time, again in the printing house of Felipe Mey in Valencia, this time dedicating the collection to Doña Marcela de Vega Carpio, Lope de Vega's daughter. The 1621 volume contains the following curious accusation: "Un mercader de libros, más curioso que cortés, estando yo ausente, sin mi licencia imprimió estas doze Comedias, añadiendo a sus yerros los del Impressor." ["A bookseller, more self-interested than courteous, printed these twelve comedias without my permission while I was away, adding to his mistakes those of the printer."] Close examination of the two editions has shown that they are, in fact, identical in every detail aside from the first leaf. Furthermore, both editions were done by Felipe Mey, the very well-known Valencian printer not only of the 1618 edition that Guillén de Castro himself commissioned, but also the 1608 *Doze comedias famosas de quatro poetas naturales de la insigne y coronada ciudad de Valencia*. Therefore, it is evident that for some reason, Guillén de Castro invented this pretext for the 1621 reissue of his *Primera parte*. Juliá Martínez proposes that this may have been a stunt to sell more copies, while William E. Wilson argues in his biography, *Guillén de Castro* that the playwright may have reissued the volume in order to add the dedication to Lope's daughter (1973, 15). A subtle though possibly revealing change between the 1618 and 1621 editions suggests another possibility: the first reads 'PRIMERA PARTE / DE LAS COMEDIAS / DE DON GUILLEM DE CASTRO / NATURAL DE LA CIUDAD DE VALENCIA', whereas the second reads simply 'PRIMERA PARTE / DE LAS COMEDIAS / DE DON GUILLEM DE CASTRO'. This change may represent an attempt to shift from an off-center Valencian identity to a more broadly Spanish persona, that of a court poet and playwright, as Castro was seeking patronage and acclaim in Madrid from 1618 onward.

In 1624 Guillén de Castro was embroiled in another scandal: he was denounced by a man from Menorca, Rafael Sierra, for allegedly contracting an assassin to kill a nobleman. King Felipe IV instructed the investigators to look into the matter "procediendo con mucho recato, porque en caso que no hubiere fundamento no se note con la voz que podría resultar la persona de don Guillén" ["proceeding very cautiously, so that in case it is groundless, no voice shall be raised against Don Guillén"] (Juliá Martínez I, xv). Juan Jerónimo Montañés was a suspicious figure who had caused some trouble in Valencia and had been accused of plotting to assassinate a nobleman, and Castro was rumored to be implicated in the plot. In the end, no evidence was found and the Council of Aragón did not pursue the case against Guillén, though they did send Montañés to Menorca to be punished (García Lorenzo 1976, 19).

The *Segunda parte de las obras de don Guillem de Castro* [*Second Part of the Works of don Guillén de Castro*] was published in Valencia in 1625, this time by Miguel Sorolla. Guillén went to his native city for the publication, but returned to Madrid shortly thereafter. Throughout the last years of his life, he fought frequently with his father-in-law, Francisco Salgado, about money and access to Ángela's maternal inheritance (Juliá Martínez I, xvi). These personal troubles may explain the strangely bitter and irreverent tone of the 'Al letor' ['Note to the reader'] of the 1625 *Segunda parte*: "No quiero llamarte discreto, ni sabio, porque tal vez podra ser que no lo seas, ni lisongearte quiero tampoco, con la comun civilidad de llamarte piadoso; pues si sabes, no tengo mis cosas tan levantadas de punto, que te causen embidia, y dexes por esso de alaballas." ["I do not want to call you discreet, nor wise, because perhaps it may be that you are not, nor do I want to flatter you with the common civility of calling you pious; for, if you know, I do not have my affairs in such order as to cause you envy, therefore please do not praise them."] Here, the playwright seems to openly mock his reader, as well as paint himself in a negative light.

On July 28, 1631, Guillén de Castro died in Madrid at the age of 62. Perhaps his campaign of negative publicity against himself worked: it was believed for years that he died penniless, and was given a pauper's burial. However, his will contains an inventory of his belongings (see Juliá Martínez I, p. xviii–xxii for the complete inventory), and this list is not one befitting a *pícaro*.

Plot Summary

La fuerza de la costumbre opens with Costanza's announcement to her son, Félix, that his father, Pedro de Moncada, and sister, Hipólita, are arriving from Flanders after a twenty-year separation. In the 180 lines that follow, Costanza presents her son (and the audience) with a detailed family history. She describes her childhood with her brother, her courtship and secret wedding to Pedro, against her father's wishes, and explains that Pedro was forced to flee Zaragoza with their infant daughter after killing Costanza's brother, while Costanza was pregnant with their son, Félix.

After this exposition, Pedro arrives with Hipólita, who has grown up fighting by her father's side in the war in Flanders and has returned home a fierce soldier. She is accustomed to living as a man; her father introduces her to her mother and brother as a "gallardo mancebo" ["handsome young man"] (I. 235).[6] Félix, who was born after Pedro's departure and therefore raised by Costanza, still wears long dress and has not learned any of the manly arts, but rather has adopted effeminate traits and skills from his mother. The main action of the play depicts the process of re-educating Hipólita and Félix in the gender that corresponds to their physical sex.

The play's structure more or less follows Lope de Vega's prescription for the organization of a *comedia* in the *Arte nuevo de hacer comedias en este tiempo* [*New Art of Writing Plays at This Time*]: "En el acto primero, ponga el caso, / en el segundo enlace los sucesos, / de suerte que hasta el medio del tercero / apenas juzgue nadie en lo que para" (1998, v. 298–301) ["Set the situation in Act One, / and in Act Two so complicate the plot / that hardly anyone can tell before / the middle of Act Three how it will end" (trans. Victor Dixon, 2009)]. In the first Act, all main characters are introduced, and the challenges of resolving the situation are established. Castro builds tension and comedic opportunity by staging the rambunctious failure of all of the initial strategies for fixing Hipólita's and Félix's gender trouble. Pedro orders the children to change into clothes which correspond to their newly assigned genders, then transfers Hipólita's sword to Félix's belt (I. 556–558); the first of many symbolic and material attempts to reassign the gender roles. Hipólita bids her sword a reluctant farewell in four melancholic *décimas* (I. 561–600), complying with Lope's prosodic prescription for complaints.[7]

From this point on, Castro alternates episodes of Félix's and Hipólita's unsatisfactory gender performances, which sometimes overlap with one another (for example, Félix interrupts Hipólita's sewing lesson and tries to help her, and Hipólita's *brío* [manly spirit] leads to her fierce intervention in her brother's sword-fighting lesson). One of these episodes of interwoven failed gender performances occurs when a street brawl spills into the house. Hipólita, horrified that her brother cowers near Costanza instead of fighting

---

[6] All citations will give Act number and line number. The English translation of *La fuerza de la costumbre* from this volume is presented alongside Spanish quotes. Where a literal translation is needed, this deviation from the text is indicated by the abbreviation, 'lit.'.
[7] Lope de Vega, *Arte nuevo* (1998), v. 307: "Las décimas son buenas para las quejas" ["The *décima* is suited to complaints"] (trans. Dixon, 2009).

by their father's side to defend the home, unsheathes her sword from her brother's belt and fends off the intruders.

This fray introduces the children's respective love interests (and gender models) to the stage. Hipólita discovers Luis, a handsome local man, at the end of her sword, and the two become enamored of one another; meanwhile Leonor, Luis's sister, immediately captures the attention of Félix. Luis and Leonor stand in contrast to Hipólita and Félix in their perfect embodiment of their respective masculinity and femininity. Luis balances bravery and physical skill with shrewdness and respect; his beautiful sister Leonor sings enchantingly and skillfully charms and manipulates men. The two sibling pairs maintain a complex relationship with each other. Luis and Leonor serve as both models to imitate (Hipólita-Leonor, Félix-Luis) and motivators of change by way of heterosexual attraction (Hipólita-Luis, Félix-Leonor). Furthermore, as the de Moncada children begin to perform their new genders more successfully, their future brother and sister-in-law serve important friendship roles, such as Luis accompanying Félix to fight Otavio in Act III, or Leonor teaching Hipólita how to provoke jealousy in the men by 'accidentally' dropping gloves and sleeve cuffs from the balcony to the ground below near the end of Act II.

In Act II, tension mounts as Hipólita and Félix continue to give unsuccessful gender performances, portrayed mainly through exaggerated, boisterous action. The tone of Act II and the second half of Act I is a blend of over-the-top gender farce (surely a crowd-pleaser Castro would want to exploit to the fullest extent) and the more serious escalating urgency for Félix to assume his masculine role. Pedro's threats against his son increase in violence as Félix repeatedly proves unable to rescue his own and his family's honor from the ruin that his effeminacy threatens. Even the audience within the play finds the siblings' incongruent gender performances extremely amusing. Act II opens by presenting the family as a spectacle, as Otavio, Marcelo and other onlookers gawk at their odd hybridity:

> Otavio: ¿No es extremo peregrino
> los contrapuestos hermanos?
> ¡Causa admiración el verlo!
> Marcelo: Es notable cosa el ver,
> él pareciendo mujer,
> y ella no acertando a serlo.

[Otavio: Aren't the cross-dressed siblings
a rare sight to behold?
Marcelo: They're quite shocking to look at.
It's an extremely odd thing to see,
he seeming so like a woman,
and she not knowing how to be one.]
(II. 55–60)

These gossip sessions reveal the increasingly high stakes of Félix's and Hipólita's transitions due to the public nature of their judgment, heightening the urgency of their transformation.

Hipólita continues to abhor the femininity being forced upon her, even after many lessons in sewing, wearing *chapines* [women's shoes] and shawls, and sitting and talking like a woman: "Reniego / de quien me puso a mujer," ["I disown / the one who made me a woman,"] she laments (II. 221a–222). Félix fares even worse, giving such a miserable performance at his sword-fighting lesson that his sister attacks and almost kills the hired *maestro de armas*, swordfighting instructor, in defense of her brother's honor. Otavio, a rival suitor, humiliates Félix in front of his sister and Leonor by snatching a *prenda*, a treasured garment, Leonor's glove, from his hand. Act II closes with the gender transition underway but far from complete, and with Félix's honor seriously in question.

Hipólita's and Félix's plotlines in Act III build to a climax in which deception and jealousy lead to acts of violence that will finally complete their respective transitions to their new genders. Félix plans his revenge on Otavio with his father, Luis, and the Captain, who all implore Félix, after such a grave humiliation, to either assert his manliness or hope to be killed by Otavio (III. 1–197). Félix at last challenges his rival when Leonor awakens his jealousy by granting Otavio the disputed glove (III. 470–561); Félix cuts Otavio's face, recovers Leonor's glove from his hat, and triumphantly brings Otavio's sword to Leonor (III. 696–747).

Meanwhile, the servant Galván takes vengeance on Hipólita for her humiliating assault on his nose by telling her that Luis has been deceiving her and has already married Marcelo's (imaginary) sister (III. 262a–375). In cloak-and-dagger style, Hipólita storms off to avenge this supposed betrayal with her sword, wearing male dress and a mask. This duel scene ends with Luis tricking Hipólita into moving their fight behind an 'olmedo' ['poplar grove'], boasting, "y allí verás que soy hombre / para más de una mujer" ["There you will see that I am man enough / for one who is more than a woman"] (III.

674–675). When she returns home, Hipólita recounts to her mother that during this duel Luis immobilized her sword and raped her when she slipped on the wet grass. Hipólita reports to her mother that this event has completed her transition to womanhood: "desde entonces soy mujer" ["since that moment I am a woman"] (III. 865). Though both Luis (alluding to the act before it takes place) and Hipólita (describing it to her mother after the fact) refer to the sexual initiation as a violent act, Hipólita does not lament or complain, but rather portrays it as an eye-opening event which has revealed her true nature. The Captain returns to the house and narrates Félix's success to Costanza and Pedro, who happily and proudly welcome their children back into the home and arrange the marriages of Luis to Hipólita and Félix to Leonor.

Textual History

Guillén de Castro's *La fuerza de la costumbre* was first published by Miguel Sorolla in 1625 in Valencia as the ninth of twelve plays of the *Segunda Parte de las comedias de don Guillem de Castro*.[8] Had the *Segunda parte* been published in Madrid, its publication would have narrowly missed the ten-year prohibition on publishing plays from the *Consejo de Castilla* (Council of Castile), convened by Felipe II. On March 6, 1625, the *Junta de Reformación* [Reformation Council] made the recommendation to the Council of Castile to stop granting publication licenses for plays and *novellas*, due to the negative influence such texts were believed to have on the young people of Spain.[9] It is possible that Castro returned to Valencia to publish this volume in order to avoid complications with publication in Madrid. The 'Aprobación' [Approval] was granted by Fray Lamberto Novella on

---

8   The other *comedias* in this volume are: 1. *El engañarse engañando* [*The Fooler Fooled*], 2. *El mejor esposo* [*The Best Spouse*], 3. *Los enemigos hermanos* [*The Enemy Brothers*], 4. *Cuánto se estima el honor* [*Honor's Worth*], 5. *El Narciso en su opinión* [*The Narcissist*], 6. *La verdad averiguada, y engañoso casamiento* [*The Truth Found Out, and Misleading Marriage*], 7. *La justicia en la piedad* [*Justice in Piety*], 8. *El pretender con pobreza* [*Poor Intentions*], 10. *El vicio en los extremos* [*Vice in Extremes*], 11. *La fuerza de la sangre* [*The Power of Blood*], and 12. *Dido y Eneas* [*Dido and Aeneas*].

9   Jaime Moll quotes the official ruling of the *Junta de Reformación*: "Y porque se ha reconocido el daño de imprimir libros de comedias, nouelas ni otros deste género, por el que blandamente hacen a las costumbres de la jubentud, se consulte a su Majestad ordene al Consejo que en ninguna manera se dé licencia para imprimirlos" ["And in recognition of the damage done by printing books of comedies, novels, or other such works, since they make our young people's habits soft, it is suggested that his Majesty instruct the Council that in no way should they grant license to print them"] (1974, pp. 97–103).

December 20th, 1624, and the license for the *Segunda parte*, granted by Don Martín de Funes, Vicar General of the Archbishopric of Valencia, is dated February 7th, 1625, in Valencia.

The *Segunda parte* is one continuous volume, unlike the *Primera parte de las obras de Guillem de Castro*, which was published as a series of *suelta*s, independent plays with their own pagination. Two copies of the printed 1625 *Segunda parte* are housed at the Biblioteca Nacional de España in Madrid, one at the Biblioteca Palacio Real in Madrid, and one at the Bibliothèque Nationale de France in Paris. The Biblioteca Nacional holds three hand-copied manuscripts of *La fuerza de la costumbre*, two of which originate from the library of the Dukes of Osuna, and one from the library of Agustín Durán. A fourth manuscript is held at the Biblioteca Palatina in Parma, Italy. Only the texts held at the Spanish libraries, the Biblioteca Nacional and the Biblioteca Palacio Real, were consulted for this study.

The *Primera parte* contains *Las mocedades del Cid* [*The Youthful Deeds of the Cid*], currently Guillén de Castro's most widely read play, which draws from the ballad tradition to dramatise the youth of Spain's epic hero. Castro frequently based plays on material borrowed from the *romancero* (other ballad-based plays include *El conde Alarcos* [*The Count of Alarcos*], *El nacimiento de Montesinos* [*The Birth of Montesinos*], and *El conde de Irlos* [*The Count of Irlos*]); he also uses mythology and historical chronicles (mythology: *Progne y Filomena* [*Procne and Philomena*], *El Narciso en su opinión*, *Dido y Eneas*; chronicles: *La humildad soberbia* [*Humble Pride*]) and works by his contemporaries, particularly Cervantes (*Don Quixote de la Mancha*, *La fuerza de la sangre* [*The Power of Blood*], *El curioso impertinente* [*The Foolish Curious One*]). *La fuerza de la costumbre*, however, fits into none of these categories. The plot is either based on an unknown source, possibly an Italian *novella*, given the prominence of Italian literature in Valencia in Castro's time, or is an invention of the author. This play is most appropriately grouped with Castro's *comedias de costumbres*, comedies of manners, such as *Los mal casados de Valencia* [*Unhappily Married in Valencia*], though it also contains some elements of the *capa y espada*, cloak and dagger, genre.

The date of composition of this play remains unknown, nor is there any known performance history. Courtney Bruerton, whose dating of Castro's *comedias* is the most persuasive to date, argues that *La fuerza de la costumbre* was written before 1620, probably between 1610–1615 (1944). Juliá Martínez also proposes that *La fuerza de la costumbre* was written in the second decade of the seventeenth century; his chronology places *La fuerza de la costumbre* after *El Narciso en su opinión* (1925–1927 III). Juliá Martínez assigns dates to Castro's plays based on themes, character names, and plot types, since Castro's works rarely give internal evidence of dates of composition. Bruerton used a very different method in his chronology, dating the plays based on metrical analysis.

There have been few subsequent editions of *La fuerza de la costumbre*. Castro's comedy appears in Ramón de Mesonero Romanos's 1857 collection, *Dramáticos contemporáneos a Lope de Vega* [*Dramatists Contemporary with Lope de Vega*], vol. 1, and in the third volume of Eduardo Juliá Martínez's *Obras de don Guillén de Castro y Bellvis*, published in 1925–1927.[10]

The Present Edition
Seventeenth-century witnesses of La fuerza de la costumbre
(and abbreviations)
EDITIO PRINCEPS
P   Heading: SEGUNDA PARTE / DE LAS COMEDIAS / DE DON GUILLEM / DE CASTRO. / DIRIGIDAS A DOÑA ANA / Maria Figuerola y de Castro. / El titulo de las Comedias se vera en la / segunda hoja. / Año 1625. / CON LICENCIA, / En Valencia, Por Miguel Sorolla, junto a la / Vniuersidad. / Vendense en la misma Emprenta.

P_1 Biblioteca Nacional de España: U/6740 (microfiche: R.MICRO/27446). As the Biblioteca Nacional's catalogue states, this copy of the princeps edition is deteriorating in some areas where problems with the ink make the text illegible (see, for example, pp. 411–14).

P_2 Biblioteca Nacional de España: R/14699 (R.MICRO/4070). This volume has been cropped smaller than P_1; in fact the first line of the title page ("Segunda parte") has been cut off. The words "De la casa de Castro en Huesca ciudad de Aragon" have been hand written on the title page. The image of the shield at the end of the 'Al Letor' is slightly different in P_2: it appears that someone modified the design by adding lines in pen by hand to the printed design.

P_3 Biblioteca Palacio Real de Madrid: VIII/1120. "Vazquez de Acuña" is written on the title page. Other handwriting on this page is illegible.

---

10   Joan Oleza published the first volume of his edition of Guillén de Castro's *Obras completas* [*Complete Works*] in 1997 (Madrid: Fundación José Antonio de Castro), but subsequent volumes have yet to be released.

Notes: In this volume the pages are misnumbered from pp. 207–21; these pages are marked 107–21. At page 222, the numbering corrects to the 200s. Analysis of the three copies available in Madrid revealed identical printings. The Biblioteca Palacio Real volume VIII/5365 contains one play from the 1625 *Segunda parte de las comedias* (*El mejor esposo*), and thus will appear in a catalog search for the *Segunda parte*, but does not contain *La fuerza de la costumbre*.

MANUSCRIPTS

A Biblioteca Nacional de España: MSS/15623. 49 folios. Early 17th century. Was acquired by the Biblioteca Nacional from the library of the Dukes of Osuna. Heading: "Comedia dela fuerça dela costumbre / salen· doña costaza ·y don felis destudian / te –". First and last lines: "Donf que nobedades son estas" (f. 1r) / "la fuerça de la costumbre" (f. 49v).

B Biblioteca Nacional de España: MSS/17064. 28 folios; two blank, unnumbered folios between Act I and Act II.[11] Early 17th century. Also originates from the library of the Dukes of Osuna. Heading: 2COMEDIA Famossa de la / # Fuerça de la costumbre =". First and last lines: "d. felix. Que nouedades son estas" (f. 1r) / "la fuerça de la costumbre" (f. 28v).

C Biblioteca Nacional de España: MSS/15370. 49 folios. Early 17th century. Copied by two hands which alternate. From the library of Agustín Durán, purchased by the Biblioteca Nacional in 1865. Heading: "La fuersa de la costumbre primera jornada / felis y costansa solos d· guillen de castro2. First and last lines: "felis/ que nouedades son estas" (f. 2r)/ "la fuersa de la costumbre" (f. 49v). A colophon at the end of the work reads: "Escribio la osorio, y es suya a pesar de uellacos."

D (Not consulted.) Biblioteca Palatina Parma. CC* IV 28033 Vol. 76, V. 2.

Nineteenth- and Twentieth-Century Editions

MR *Dramáticos contemporáneos a Lope de Vega: colección escogida y ordenada, con un discurso, apuntes biográficos y críticos de los autores, noticias bibliográficas y catálogos, por don Ramon de Mesonero Romanos*. Biblioteca de autores españoles, desde la formacion del

---

11 The 10th and 11th leaves of the first quire were left blank and were not numbered by the Biblioteca Nacional. I follow the Biblioteca Nacional's numbering of the folios when referring to this manuscript.

lenguaje hasta nuestros dias. Edited by Ramón de Mesonero Romanos. Tomo I. Madrid: M. Rivadeneyra, 1857; pp. 347–366.

J Obras de Don Guillén de Castro y Bellvis. Real Academia Española Biblioteca Selecta de Clasicos Españoles. Edited by Eduardo Juliá Martínez (JM). Tomo III. Madrid: Real Academia Española, 1927; pp. 39–76.

The *Editio Princeps* and Manuscripts

The three manuscripts offer notable variants from the text of the 1625 *editio princeps*. There is no clear relationship between the four versions, except that the *princeps* contains the greatest total number of lines (each manuscript is missing some lines, though not necessarily the same ones). Given that A, B and C vary quite a bit from one another, and yet all lack certain passages (particularly from Act III[12]), I believe that the manuscripts pre-date the *princeps*, and that Guillén de Castro made final revisions to the play before the 1625 print publication, with most new material appearing in Act III.

A was likely a copy of an earlier version of the play, given the number of missing lines (about 424, with 34 of these missing lines added in by the second hand in the margins) and other differences with the text of P. Inés does not appear in this text at all, and Marcelo and Otavio are reversed as speakers in their entire conversation at the beginning of Act II. The main hand copied folios 1r–47v, and a second hand made corrections throughout the text, added some missing passages in the margin (16 lines on f. 8r, 8 on f. 10r, and 10 on f. 12v), and copied the last 110 lines of the play on f. 48r–49v. Unfortunately, on many folios the outermost edge of this additional text was lost, likely during a rebinding and trimming of the volume. In some cases, lines have been copied into the margin that are in fact present in the original text, such as line 721 on folio 12v. Given the corrections and additions of text, it is likely that the second hand copied from a later and/or more complete source than that of the first hand, since the second hand's text coincides more with P. Notwithstanding this increase in agreement between the second hand and P, there are still enough variants to suggest that the second hand did not copy directly from P. There is further evidence that the two hands of A copied from different sources at the transition between the two hands in Act III. After line III. 893, the last line on folio 47v and the final verse written in the main hand is crossed out. The crossed out line

---

12 All manuscripts lack the following 76 lines: I. 522a; III. 262c; 277b–333a; 791–794; 852–863; 962–963.

reads: "pero apenas alli ubieron llegado". The second hand begins f. 48r with a different version of the line which coincides with all other witnesses: "pero por esconderme arodillado." Thus it is evident that the second hand used a different source text which had more in common with all other manuscript and print sources.

The colophon "fin desta jornada / alabado sea el ssantisimo sacramento / amen" closes both Acts I and II, though no colophon appears at the end of the play.

B is a careful copy written in one hand with relatively few missing lines, particularly in Acts I and II. Of the 141 lines absent in B, 124 of those are from Act III, and 56 of those lines are the conversation between Inés and Hipólita in Act III (277b–333a), which is not present in any of the manuscript witnesses. Many of the omissions are just a line or two (as opposed to long passages), especially in Acts I and II. This manuscript contains many stage directions that do not appear in A or C, though they are not always worded the same way as P. In fact, in some cases B presents stage directions that are absent in P. B has some lines that follow P but are divided differently (See Index of Variants, Act II. 1b–2 and 45 for examples). B seems to be the most careful and complete of the manuscripts. One odd feature of the volume is that, though it does not coincide with A very closely in Acts I and II, it shares many variants with A in Act III, especially between lines III. 200–980, in which the two witnesses share almost all omitted lines and many other variants.

The end of each Act is announced as follows: Act I: "fin de la Pmr^a Jornada"; Act II: "fin de la 2a / Jornada"; Act III: "Fin". Juliá Martínez's claim that this manuscript was copied by Jacinto Cordero appears to be unfounded, given that comparison of the hand of B revealed no similarities to Jacinto Cordero's handwriting.[13]

The most notable feature of manuscript C is the alternation of the two hands which copy the text. The first hand copies f.2r–f.5v, f.8v–f.10v, f.12v–f.25r, f.28r–f.28v, f.30v–f.36r, f.38v–f.40r, and f.41v–f.49v; the second hand copies f.6r–f.8v, f.10v–f.12v, f.25r–f.28r, f.28v–f.30v, f.36r–f.38v, f.40r–f.41v. A third hand makes minor corrections throughout the text; generally these

---

[13] "El otro manuscrito, que también procede de la misma Biblioteca, al parecer es de mano de Jacinto Cordero" ["The other manuscript, which is from the same library, seems to be copied by Jacinto Cordero"] (1925–1927 III, x). See the Manos Teatrales Database of Theatrical Manuscripts directed by Margaret R. Greer at http://manosteatrales.org/ for images of manuscripts copied by Jacinto Cordero. The database also contains images of A, B, and C.

corrections do not correspond with any other known source (for examples, see Index of Variants lines I. 4; 6; 12; 20a, etc.). In fact, many of these corrections change words that would have otherwise agreed with the other witnesses, suggesting that this corrector made these modifications based on his own preferences, rather than copying from another source (unlike the case of the corrections in A). In some cases these corrections do not make sense, as in the case of line II. 371, in which the first hand shared P's reading, "Pedros, Guillenes, Ramones" and the third hand crossed out "Pedros" and wrote "pardos". The colophons, by Act, are as follows: Act I: "fin de la primera jornada / laus deo et m^e" (bordered by 2 small flourishes on right and left); Act II: "fin de la segunda laus deo et m^e" (rubric below); Act III: "finis laus deo et ^{me} / escribio la osorio y es suya a pesar de uellacos" (rubric below). Despite the mention of Osorio, neither hand of C matches the hand of the well-known *autor de comedias*, Osorio.

Although Juliá Martínez posits that this is a copy of A (he claims that they share errata and missing verses), a close analysis reveals that this is highly unlikely since C presents lines that are consistent with B and P but omitted in A, and A lacks twice as many lines as C.[14] They also both have errata and missing lines not present in the other text, suggesting that neither is a copy of the other. Furthermore, while A and B correspond closely in Act III, C does not follow the same patterns, suggesting a textual lineage at least a few degrees removed. It appears that Juliá Martínez copied Paz y Melia's information about the manuscript, because he repeats Paz y Melia's mistaken number of folios (listed in these two sources as 28 leaves, though there are 49).

It is difficult to establish a clear relationship or lineage among the three manuscript sources. I believe that the three manuscripts were copied before the 1625 publication or were based on texts that were, and that they were based on an unknown source text. Some variants and omitted lines that are shared by all manuscripts suggest that revisions were made to the play before publication, with the heaviest alterations being made to Act III. For example, all manuscripts lack the conversation between Inés and Hipólita in Act III (277b–333a), and share two replacement lines, with a slight variant in C: "Galván: no te acierto hablar / Hipólita: ¿Qué traes, amigo?" In C the first

---

14   "Procedente de la Biblioteca de Durán es el manuscrito que parece hecho sobre el 15623, pues tiene casi las mismas erratas y la misma falta de versos" ["Coming from the Library of Durán is the manuscript that seems to be based on the 15623, because it has almost the same errata and the same missing verses"] (Juliá Martínez III, x).

of these two lines reads "gal / no se como asierte ablar." Manuscripts A and C lack the character of Inés entirely. She appears briefly in B and appears in the list of characters. In B her only spoken lines are in Act II, 529–31; modified 533–35; 619a. A, B and C share the following missing lines: I. 522a, III. 262c (Inés), 277b–333a (Inés), 791–4, 852–63, 962–3. This information reveals more about the history of P than about the manuscripts; it seems that Guillén de Castro heavily edited Act III before the 1625 publication, leading to these common variants in all manuscript sources, which were likely based on earlier, pre-revision sources.

A stemma has not been possible because of the fact that there is no pattern of overlap between the manuscripts that is sustained throughout the whole text. In lieu of a stemma, I have charted omitted lines by act and performed a statistical analysis to demonstrate that the correlations among the manuscripts do not follow a stable pattern from which one could derive a stemma (Table 1).

As can be seen in the charts of omitted lines, A and C share some variants throughout Acts I and II, although they also present many unshared variants. B shares very few omitted lines with A or C in Acts I and II. Of the 108 omitted lines in Act I in A, B shares only one, and then omits 4 lines not omitted in A. In Act II, A omits 107 lines, only 4 of which are also omitted in B. However, B suddenly follows A rather closely in Act III: of A's 189 missing lines, B is missing 123. This sudden similarity is surprising given that A and B share so few variants in Acts I and II. They are clearly not copies of the same source text, given that they are so different for such a large percentage of the play. The one conclusion that can be definitely stated is that their versions of Act III are very similar (a 0.77 correlation is extremely high), and thus likely share ancestry for Act III. C has less in common with A in this Act than it did in the first two Acts, meaning that C's Act III comes from a different branch, although C overlaps with A much more in Acts I and II.

20 Introduction

Table 1. Line Omissions by Act

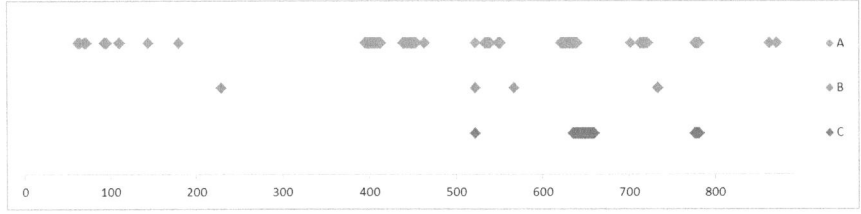

Act I Statistical correlations:
A–B   0.02
B–C   0.06
A–C   0.16

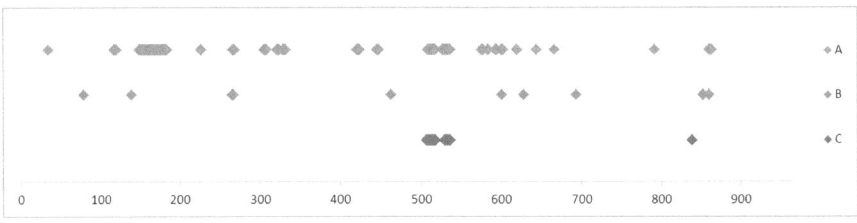

Act II Statistical correlations:
A–B   0.08
B–C   -0.02
A–C   0.38

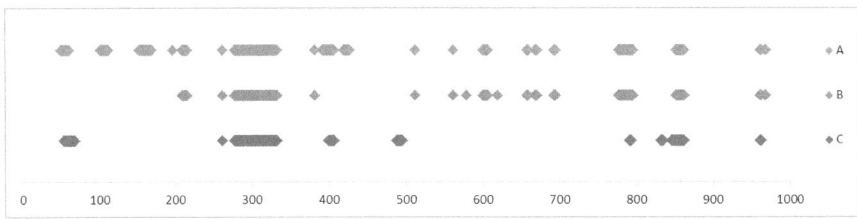

Act III Statistical correlations: Total correlations:
A–B   0.77   A–B   0.50
B–C   0.57   B–C   0.46
A–C   0.55   A–C   0.42

Editorial Methods

Since Guillén de Castro oversaw the printing of both volumes of his plays and there are no known author-autographed manuscripts, P has been used as the base text for the present edition (P_1 was transcribed first, then P_2 and P_3 were checked against the transcription of P_1, with no variants found). P is a quality edition complete with punctuation, stage directions, and few errata. All modifications to P's source text, including printing errors, will be noted on the page with a footnote (+), and the relevant versions of the line(s) from the manuscripts will be listed for comparison. This edition has modernized the text of P following current standards for accents and spelling as set by the Real Academia Española, except in cases where this would change the sound of word, such as 'agora', 'monstros', or 'decilla'. All abbreviations have been resolved. I have altered the capitalization of words such as 'Misa', 'Iglesia', 'Galán', 'Cruz'," 'Rey Cristiano', 'Caballero', 'Evangelios', 'Oriente', and 'santo Patrón'. Some unnecessary spaces have been corrected, for example, 'a parte', 'a dios', etc. I have also modified punctuation to shorten long sentences and clarify meaning. I have replaced question and exclamation marks in P with other punctuation when the original punctuation did not seem appropriate. Square brackets indicate the addition of text that was not present in P. If this text comes from one of the manuscripts, a textual note on the page will explain which source gave that reading. In some cases the manuscripts presented helpful stage directions that clarified the action of the play; manuscript B in particular offered many useful stage directions. If there is no note following a square bracket, I have added the text to clarify meaning, as in Act III 967–969.

While explanatory notes will appear after the line number of the passage in question, notes concerning textual issues will be indicated by the symbol (+). All variants from the manuscripts are collected in the Index of Variants. Spelling differences are not listed in the variants unless they change the meaning, sound or syllable count of the word. All variants other than those mentioned above will be indicated.

The annotations are intended to orient the reader to the language, historical and cultural contexts, and literary antecedents of *La fuerza de la costumbre*, and are aimed at scholars and students alike. Specifically, the notes will clarify vocabulary that is either no longer in use or has changed in meaning since the 17th century, present relevant historical information and explain cultural customs and beliefs.

Metrical Analysis

The 2857 lines of *La fuerza de la costumbre* are written almost entirely in Castilian verse forms, including *romance*, *redondillas*, *quintillas* and a few *décimas*. There are two short sections that use Italianate forms: eleven *octavas reales* near the end of Act III, and five stanzas of a modified *estrofa alirada* with rhyme in aBabBccDD, where 'DD' is a refrain.[15] This predominance of Spanish verse is in keeping with Guillén de Castro's preference for Spanish verse throughout his career.[16]

The relative percentages of *redondillas* and *romance* support the theory that this play was written later in Castro's body of work, probably in the 1610s. Over the course of his career, Castro employed the *redondilla* more than any other verse form. As in the case of Lope de Vega, however, Castro's use of the *redondilla* decreased as the *romance* was used more heavily. Bruerton uses this metrical evolution to divide Castro's plays into two time periods, those written prior to 1613 and those written between 1613–1624 (the period in which Guillén de Castro composed *La fuerza de la costumbre*).[17]

---

15 Navarro Tomás' *Métrica española* [*Spanish Meter*] defines the *estrofa alirada* as aBabBcC, which most closely resembles this mix of heptasyllables and hendecasyllables. In *Guillén de Castro*, Wilson defines the *lira* as a six-line strophe of heptasyllables and endecasyllables with 3 rhymes. He finds eleven forms of this strophe, the most common being aBabCC, abbacC, AabBCC and AbbAcC (1973, 42). Bruerton defines this verse as a *canción*, not a *lira* (1944, 112). The same 8-line *canción* structure is found in *Las mocedades del Cid I*, Act I, v. 518–541 (1944, 123; Castro 1996).

16 According to Bruerton, the play with the lowest percentage of Spanish meter is *El mejor esposo* (74.5%), and the highest are *Los mal casados de Valencia* and *Don Quijote de la Mancha*, written entirely in Spanish verse.

17 Bruerton performs a detailed analysis of all of Castro's verse forms, using Lope de Vega as parallel to judge when innovations and changes in metric trends were likely to have occurred (1944, 101–102).

Introduction 23

Table 2. Verse Forms and Percentages by Act

Total lines:	Act I: 892		Act II: 964		Act III: 1001		Total: 2857	
Redondilla	352	(39.5%)	492	(51%)	719	(72%)	1563	(55%)
Romance	440	(49%)	226	(23%)	154	(15%)	820	(29%)
Quintilla			220	(23%)			220	(8%)
Décima	100	(11%)					100	(3.5%)
Octava real					88	(9%)	88	(3%)
Estrofa alirada					40	(4%)	40	(1.4%)

Verse Forms by Act

Act I
1–198   Romance (a–a)
199–362   Redondillas
363–472   Romance (i–a)
473–560   Redondillas
561–660   Décimas
661–760   Redondillas
761–892   Romance (e–e)

Act II
1–492   Redondillas
493–502   Quintillas
503–518   Canción[20]
519–628   Romance (o–o)
629–848   Quintillas
849–964   Romance (ó)

Act III
1–375   Redondillas[18]
376–415   Estrofa alirada
416–759[19] Redondillas
760–865   Romance (é)
866–953   Octavas reales
954–1001   Romance (u–e)

---

18   This number does not divide by four because of a three line stanza at v. 285–287. This appears to be an oversight on the part of the poet, since continuity of the plot is maintained (there does not appear to be a line missing) and line 284 rhymes with both v. 281 and v. 287. Castro seems to have counted v. 284 as both the end of the preceding stanza and the beginning of the next one.
19   Hipólita's prose letter to Luis has been marked as line 451a since it does not form part of the rhyme scheme of the play, and thus should not be counted as a 'line'.
20   The *canción* consists of 12 lines of *romance* in é, followed by a quatrain: AabB (11-7-7-11).

CRITICAL ESSAY
BAD HABITS: GENDER MADE AND REMADE IN *LA FUERZA DE LA COSTUMBRE*

Introduction: *La fuerza de la costumbre*, The Power of Habit

> Fuertemente es poderosa;
> más que papas, más que reyes;
> divinas y humanas leyes
> puede hacer.
>
> [It is strong and powerful;
> more than popes, more than kings;
> it can make divine
> and human laws.]
> (Otavio on 'costumbre' ['habit'], lit., II. 65–68a)

La fuerza de la costumbre examines the force exerted by habit and practice in the cultivation of 'natural' abilities and virtues. It also examines the methods by which problematic but deeply habituated identities, namely Hipólita's masculinity and Félix's effeminacy, can be forcibly reconstructed. According to Aristotle, moral virtues "are engendered in us neither by nor contrary to nature; we are constituted by nature to receive them, but their full development in us is due to habit" (2004, 31). Actualizing one's natural abilities requires careful training and attention to proper action. Aristotle's theory underlies the entire premise of the play: that education and the cultivation of habits, leads to success (or failure) in assuming one's 'natural' role. In the *Nichomachean Ethics*, Aristotle emphasizes the importance of developing good habits early, because potential can only be activated by exercising and habituating virtue: "So it is a matter of no little importance what sort of habits we form from the earliest age – it makes a vast difference, or rather all the difference in the world" (2004, 32). The title, *La fuerza de la costumbre*, alludes to Aristotle's argument for the power of habit; yet it also raises other questions. While 'fuerza' certainly means 'power', or 'force', it can also mean 'the act of forcing';[21] bringing another set of

---

21 The second definition of 'fuerza' listed in the *Diccionario de Autoridades* of 1791

meanings into view. 'La fuerza de la costumbre' could mean the forcing, commanding, by some agent, of one's habits. The characters of *La fuerza de la costumbre* employ various methods and strategies in order to correct Hipólita and Félix's gender inversion (see plot summary for a review of how this comes about). The *comedia* does not often show child-rearing, and still less often does it depict so directly the teaching of gender, yet this pair of siblings receives a lifetime's worth of lessons about gender and behavior in the course of a few days.

Gender trouble abounds within the theatrical world of *La fuerza de la costumbre*: a female-born child raised as a man successfully passes in a world of men for most of her life, but ultimately is transformed into a woman as an adult. Her brother, whose mother intentionally inhibits his interest in masculine activities and confines him to the domestic feminine realm, develops no manliness at all during his adolescence, and yet as an adult he is molded from an effeminate, neutered figure into a man. In the world of these 2857 lines, gender is surprisingly fluid, as the line(s) that divide women from men are crossed multiple times. Gender emerges as a socially constructed, rather than inherent trait. Though the play does not dictate gender based on sex[22] and allows for multiple instances of change of

---

reads: "El acto de obligar á alguno á que dé asenso, ó haga alguna cosa" ["The act of forcing anyone to give assent, or to do something"].

22 Both 'sex' and 'gender' are terms that invoke symbolic and discursive force. Though the sex/gender distinction can be helpful in separating physiological gender features from psychic gender, this quickly becomes a slippery slope, as Laquer (1990), Butler (1993; 2006), Fausto-Sterling (2000; 2012) and Salamon (2010), among others, have asserted. Fausto-Sterling implores her reader not "to lose sight of the fact that our debates about the body's biology are always simultaneously moral, ethical, and political debates about social and political equality and the possibility for change" (2000, 255). Thus, I understand both 'sex' and 'gender' to be subject to discourses of power and cultural paradigms. By referring to the 'body' or 'physical sex' I do not mean to reinforce linguistic structures that hold the body as having a truth which precedes the symbolic force of discourse. In spite of this, it is necessary to refer to such a distinction in the analysis of *La fuerza de la costumbre* because the play examines exactly this question – what is the relationship of the body, anatomical sex, to what we can call 'gender', which is psychic or social expression of gender norms? Because the text in fact relies on the imagined sex of characters' bodies to foreground questions of aptitude and behavior, I will refer to their sex, while acknowledging it as a discursive category, doubly so in the context of a work of fiction. Though these are fictional characters and therefore do not possess physical anatomy, I will refer to their 'birth sex' as an equivalent of biological sex, given that Costanza specifically mentions each child's sex ("Una niña salió a luz" ["a little girl was born"] (I. 113); "él es […] mi don Félix" ["he is […] my Don Félix"]) (I. 275).

gender, there is no freedom for subjects to choose the gender that they feel suits them. Instead, there is an extreme external control of gender identity and performance, exerted in particular by the father; thus Hipólita's and Félix's genders are shaped under duress and threat of violence. The handful of critics who have written on this play see love as the force which brings the siblings' genders into alignment with their declared birth sex, despite the fact that the definitive assumption of the newly assigned gender role is brought about, in both cases, by violence.[23] Though this play capitalizes on the popularity

---

23 Juliá Martínez dedicates three pages to this play and the sources he consulted for his edition in the 'Observaciones preliminares' to the third volume of his *Obras de don Guillén de Castro y Bellvis*. He calls it a "curiosa comedia [...] en la que se plantea el problema de la educación como medio de contrarrestar la costumbre" ["an odd comedy, in which is shown the problem of education as a way of countering habit"] (1925–1927 III, x). Melveena McKendrick examines Hipólita in her study of the *mujer varonil*, *Woman and Society in Golden-Age Spanish Drama*, asserting that the "heroine fits into no stereotyped pattern" (1974, 98–102). McKendrick calls the play "one of the most charming comedies the *siglo de oro* produced." Her analysis focuses on Pedro's fierce daughter and the conditions of her transformation to womanhood, in which "Hipólita is revealed as the puppet of convention which most of us are; having learnt to dance to one tune, she has to unlearn it and be taught to keep time with another" (100). Jonathan Thacker dedicates fifteen pages to an excellent study of the play in his book, *Role-Play and the World as Stage in the Comedia* in which he proposes that the individual in the *comedia* develops itself out of role-play, and that members of the public, in turn, learn to construct their own 'selves' by watching and imitating others (2002, 12). He contends that *La fuerza de la costumbre* "demonstrates the theatrical nature of social life by showing the efficacy of the nuclear family in rehearsing and perpetuating role-models" (34). In his view, "Hipólita is transformed through 'seduction' and Félix metamorphosed through love" (30). Kathleen Jeffs sketches the ways in which this play undermines the idea that there is an original order which can be restored by the givens of biology, and analyzes the arc of the characters' gender transformation in the article 'Gender Politics in Guillén de Castro's *La fuerza de la costumbre*' (2011). She also discusses how a director might problematize the play's ending, specifically Hipólita's transformation, which she sees as far from complete at the end of the play. In the article, 'The Power of Transformation in Guillén de Castro's *El caballero bobo* (1595–1605) and *La fuerza de la costumbre* (1610–1615): Translation and Performance', Jeffs starts from perspectives of performance of the play, from which she delves deeper into core issues of gender, identity and transformation (2015). This is the only work of Guillén de Castro's mentioned by Baltasar Gracián in the *Agudeza y arte de ingenio* [*The Art of Wordly Wisdom*]: "*La fuerza de la costumbre* de Don Guillén de Castro, por la bizarria del verso, y por la invencion merece el inmortal laurel" (2001 II, 138) ["*The Force of Habit* by Don Guillén de Castro, for the wonder of the verse, and for inventiveness, deserves the immortal laurel"]. In his book on the Valencian playwright, Luciano García Lorenzo does not analyze this play, though he calls it "una de las mejores comedias de Guillén" ["one of the best plays by Guillén"] by way of introduction to Gracián's praise of the work (1976). William E. Wilson quotes *La fuerza de*

of cross-dressing plots, here core identities themselves are manipulated and rearranged; its characters violate gender borders at a deeper level than in the woman-dressed-as-man scenario. Félix and Hipólita's forced imitations and internalizations of genders different than those originally imprinted on them in their childhoods points to an underlying preoccupation with and curiosity about gender and identity categories in general. *La fuerza de la costumbre*'s toying with gender makes great fun of a serious cultural anxiety about the instability of gender/sex categories by depicting seemingly fixed categories as malleable, constructed and unstable, disrupting the supposed self-evident truth of the categories themselves.

---

la costumbre throughout the chapter of his book on 'Guillén de Castro and the Spanish Code of Honor', though he does not refer to the play by name, nor does he explore the theme of honor in the context of the play itself (1973, 47–61). John Loftis and Sarah Taddeo have written comparative studies of *La fuerza de la costumbre* and the English adaptation, *Love's Cure, or the Martial Maid* (Loftis 1999; Taddeo 1993), and the play is mentioned in Greer (2004, 246) and Valverde (1981, 81).

I. Cross-Dressing in Spanish Golden Age Theater

La fuerza de la costumbre engages with the dramatic tradition of female characters taking the stage in male garb, a tradition that had been commonplace for decades when the play was composed. Lope de Vega references the crowd-pleasing effect of the plots that dressed women as men in the *Arte nuevo de hacer comedias en este tiempo*, written in c. 1608,[24] a pleasure produced in no small part by the sight of women's legs in revealing tights, instead of the traditional full-length skirts. The most common transvestite plot involves a female character dressing as a man in order to resolve a problem that she cannot negotiate from within her female role. Rosaura in Calderón de la Barca's *La vida es sueño* [*Life is a Dream*] (published 1635), for example, travels to Poland dressed as a man in order to confront Astolfo, the prince, who abandoned her after taking her virginity. Tirso de Molina's 1615 *Don Gil de las calzas verdes* [*Don Gil of the Green Breeches*] presents many twists and turns of mistaken identity. The scorned woman, Juana, follows Martín, the man who had promised to marry her, to Madrid in male garb to obstruct Martín from pursuing the hand of Inés, a wealthier woman. Juana steals her fiance's alias, 'Don Gil', (173–176), and begins to court Inés herself; she also invents a third identity, 'Elvira'. In Guillén de Castro's play about the miseries of married life, *Los mal casados de Valencia* (published 1618), Don Álvaro asks his mistress, Elvira, to dress as a page so that she can travel with him to the home which, as Elvira soon discovers, he shares with his wife. Lope de Vega's *La prueba de los ingenios* [*The Test of Wits*], written between 1612 and 1613 (1997, 41–42), adds an interesting twist to the *mujer varonil* [manly woman] tradition, when Florela follows her lover, Alejandro, who has left her after a promise of marriage, to the Duchy of Ferrara, under the pseudonym, 'Diana'. Once she has secured the friendship of the Duchess, Laura, Florela/Diana creates a masculine persona, 'Félix', in order to court Laura and prevent Alejandro from winning her favor. This verbal cross-dressing creates a great deal of confusion for Laura, who sends Finea, a servant, to ascertain Florela/Diana/Félix's gender, so that she can know with certainty if her love for 'him' is

---

24 "Las damas no desdigan de su nombre, / y si mudaren traje, sea de modo / que pueda perdonarse, porque suele / el disfraz varonil agradar mucho" (1998, v. 280–283) ["Don't let your ladies be unladylike, / and if they should disguise themselves as men, / since such cross-dressing never fails to please, / ensure they do in ways that may be excused" (2009, v. 280–283)].

acceptable. Order is restored, as usual, with the abandonment of the alias(es), heterosexual marriages, and Florela's honor restored. Cross-dressed siblings appear in Ángela de Azevedo's *comedia de enredo* [comedy of intrigue], *El muerto disimulado* [*Feigned Death*], in which Lisarda travels to Lisbon as 'Lisardo' to seek retribution for the death of her brother, Clarindo, only to fall in love with his 'killer', don Álvaro, who 'murdered' Clarindo out of jealousy over his love interest, Jacinta; Clarindo is however, still alive, but he is disguised as 'Clara', a medicine peddler, in order to gain access to the house of his love interest, Jacinta. Although there are significantly fewer instances of male transvestism in Spanish Golden Age theater, those that exist frequently involve a man dressing as a woman in order to gain special access to a woman he aims to woo, as in the case of Clarindo in Azevedo's play. In Calderón's *Las manos blancas no ofenden* [*White Hands Do Not Offend*], 'César' becomes 'Célia' in order to woo a woman of desirable wealth and social status. Class is also a factor in the acceptability of male cross-dressing: the servant Castaño in Sor Juana's *Los empeños de una casa* [*The House of Trials*] dons female clothing so as not to be recognized, but being a servant and *gracioso* [comic servant] he is not subject to the same demands of comportment as the nobility, making his cross-dressing less of a threat to the social order.[25]

Examples from other genres abound as well: some of the best-known cross-dressers of the sixteenth century are those of Montemayor's *La Diana*. Cervantes presents various transvestite characters in both volumes of *El ingenioso hidalgo don Quijote de la Mancha* (Dorotea, Claudia Jerónima, the cross-dressed children of Diego de la Llana); Teodosia and Leocadia both take on male personas in order to confront their lover, Marco Antonio in Cervantes' *Novela Ejemplar* [*Exemplary Novel*], *Las dos doncellas* [*The Two Damsels*]. Carmen Bravo-Villasante's 1955 (2nd edition 1976) *La mujer vestida de hombre en el teatro español (siglos XVI–XVII)* distinguishes between two main types of the *mujer vestida de hombre* [woman dressed as man], the *mujer enamorada* [woman in love] and the *heroica-guerrera* [heroic warrior woman]. Bravo-Villasante argues that the trope makes its way onto the Spanish stage via Italian models, such as Marfisa and Bradamante of Ariosto's *Orlando furioso*, though figures from Greek mythology, such as the Amazons, also influence the development of Spanish characters (1976, 11–31). B. B. Ashcom and Melveena McKendrick disagree with Bravo-

---

25 For more on male cross-dressing, see Sidney Donnell's study of the topic: *Feminizing the Enemy: Imperial Spain, Transvestite Drama, and the Crisis of Masculinity* (2003).

Villasante's claim that the primary influences on these types, especially the woman warrior, are Italian, arguing that they have deeper roots in classical literature and mythology, although McKendrick concedes that the 'female page' (Bravo-Villasante's *mujer enamorada*, the most common woman-disguised-as-man figure of the Spanish stage) is undoubtedly an Italian contribution (Ashcom 1960; McKendrick 1974, 308–309).[26] Bravo-Villasante sees a simultaneous adoption of the Italian female page figure in Spain in drama and the novel, in Lope de Rueda's *Los engañados* [*The Deceived*] (an adaptation of the Italian play *Gl'Ingannati*, about cross-dressed twins) and Montemayor's *La Diana* (1976, 11–31).

While the sight of women dressed as men on stage continued to draw audiences to the *corrales*, it inflamed moralists, clerics and legislators, causing great controversy over who should be allowed to act and in what clothing. Allowing women to take the stage, even dressed as women was seen as problematic, and was banned by the Council of Castile in 1596. The Council overturned this decision with the reopening of the theaters in 1600. Despite concerns about potentially dangerous influences on the chastity of the audience if they witnessed female actors, women were ultimately allowed to act due to the fear of the effeminacy inherent in allowing men or boys to play female roles.[27] Ursula Heise compares the socio-political motives for the differing Spanish and English policies toward female actors and boy actors playing women's parts, claiming that England's anxiety about the

---

26 For more on these types and their history, see Ashcom, Bravo-Villasante, Romera-Navarro, and McKendrick. Melveena McKendrick argues for a new critical approach to the topic in the 1974 volume, *Woman and Society in the Spanish Drama of the Golden Age: A Study of the 'Mujer Varonil'*. This impressive survey affirms the importance of the *mujer varonil* figure to feminist readings of Golden Age drama, opening the typology of the *mujer varonil* to include far more variations than just the *mujer vestida de hombre*, substantiated with copious examples.

27 The Carmelite Friar José de Jesús María dedicates an entire chapter of his book on the virtue of chastity (*Primera parte de las excelencias de la virtud de la Castidad*, [*First Part of the Excellence of the Virtue of Chastity*] published in 1601) to the immorality of theatrical practices that he sees as destructive to "la honestidad de la república" ["the chastity of the republic"], arguing that "los teatros son templos del demonio, y los comediantes sus ministros" ["theaters are temples of the devil, and actors are their ministers"]. The Friar continues, "Es cosa, sin duda, que las comedias, como agora se representan, son cuchillos de la castidad, incentivo de torpezas, seminario de vicios, fuente de disolución; estrago de todos los estados, corrupción de las costumbres, destruyción de las virtudes" ["It is without a doubt the case that plays, as they are performed these days, are as knives to chastity, a lure to slovenliness, a seminary of vices, a source of dissolution; a rot to all states, a corruption of customs, destroyer of virtues"] (quoted in Cotarelo y Mori 1904, 368).

behavior of wives, mothers and daughters overpowered its concerns about homosexuality, while the Spaniards' deep preoccupation with the behavior of women was ultimately subjugated to the nation's overwhelming fear of emasculation and increasing Inquisitorial concern over sodomy throughout the sixteenth century (1992). Heise describes the Spanish anxiety over the risks to masculinity of seeing women on stage:

> This almost hysterical preoccupation with the effeminizing influence of the theater reveals a deep apprehension that female sexuality, which finds a space of its own in the free social intercourse of the actors and actresses, the performance of love plays and the adoption of male disguise, might ultimately not only de-humanize the male spectators by turning them into beasts or dogs but also emasculate them. The assumption seems to be that when the male is confronted with unconcealed, un-covered femininity, he reacts not by asserting his difference but by imitating and adjusting to the female. There is, then, something fundamentally unstable about the male self, which can only keep itself from lapsing into the identity of its sexual other by depriving her of a full expression of what is specifically her own. Theatre, opening up at least temporarily a space for such expression, thus threatens the sexual differentiation on which the nation bases its own identification. (1992, 369)

The contagious effeminizing and lewd influence of women on stage was still preferable to allowing boys to dress as women, which would be far too suggestive of the *pecado nefando* ['sodomy', lit. 'horrible sin'] (1992, 362–65). Moralists warned that allowing boys in dresses to take the stage would create such an emasculated population that Spain would no longer be capable of defending itself militarily. This idea may have its origins in Plato's *Republic*, which cautions against men dressing as women on stage, and generally against any departure from any individual's given social role, in order to maintain the militia class (1998, 91–95). Due to these concerns, the Council of Castile in 1600 declares that it is preferable and allowable for women to play female roles on stage, given certain restrictions:

> Y porque asimismo dicen que no deben representar mugeres, porque en actos tan públicos con su desenvoltura provocan á pecado, y que si en lugar dellas entraren muchachos en hábito de muger, no vayan con afeite ó compostura deshonesta, parece al Consejo que es de mucho menos inconveniente, que mugeres representen, que muchachos en hábito de mugeres aunque no se afeiten, como no sea en hábito y figura de hombres andando en las compañías de las comedias con sus maridos ó padres.

[And also because they also say that women should not act, because in such public acts their exposure leads to sin, and that if instead they have boys dress in the women's clothes, that they should not be allowed to act or look unchaste, it seems to the Council that it is far less problematic for women to play the parts than for boys to act the parts of women, even if they do not shave, as long as the women do not take on male clothing or characters, and provided that they are accompanied by their husbands or fathers in the theater company.]

(quoted in Cotarelo y Mori 1904, 164)

The Council viewed female actors not as an ideal solution, but rather as the lesser of two evils: the nation's *hombría*, manliness, should be preserved above all else.

Although the Council attempted to prohibit female actresses from taking the stage in male attire, the number of theatrical plots involving women dressing as men on stage only continued to increase in the seventeenth century. This was particularly problematic for conservative legislators because female actresses dressed in tight breeches were seen as even more attractive than when dressed in feminine attire, possessing deep powers of seduction. The Bible forbids women from wearing men's clothing and viceversa (Deuteronomy 22:5). Friar José de Jesús María denounces those who would dare ask the king to allow women to take the stage in male attire:

Fuerte cosa es que á un Rey cristiano y tan justo le pidan que permita una cosa tan vedada y detestable por leyes divinas y humanas, como es que la mujer se vista en traje de hombre. Si representar la mujer en su propio hábito pone en tanto peligro la castidad de los que la miran, ¿qué hará si representa en traje de hombre, siendo uso tan lascivo y ocasionado para encender los corazones en mortal concupiscencia?

[It is quite a thing to request that such a just and Christian King permit an illicit and loathsome thing forbidden by divine and human laws, which is that a woman dress herself in a man's clothing. If a woman acting in a play dressed in women's clothes puts at such risk the chastity of those who look upon her, what will happen if she acts in men's attire, which is lascivious and kindles mortal concupiscence in their hearts?]

(Quoted in Cotarelo y Mori 1904, 381)

Juan Luis Vives ridicules women who would dare dress as men in his 1523 treatise, *On the Education of the Christian Woman*:

I do not think I need to advise a woman against putting on men's clothing and attire. To do so would be a clear sign of a masculine audacity and astonishing impudence in a woman's heart. In the distinction of dress, modesty is preserved, which is the parent and guardian of chastity, and we must harken to the Lord's prohibition in these words of Deuteronomy: "A woman shall not wear a man's clothing nor shall a man put on a woman's clothing for whoever does this is an abomination to God."

(2000, 108–109)

Despite these objections, playwrights continued to invent gender-bending plots, making the woman-disguised-as-man scenario an extremely common and familiar delight to seventeenth-century audiences.

II. Masculine Perfection: Theorized and Performed

> Es género más perfeto,
> y así es más apetecible
> el nuestro.
>
> [Our gender is the more perfect
> of the two, and therefore is more
> desirable.]
> (Otavio, II. 649–651a)

The decision to allow women to act instead of putting men in feminizing roles is directly connected to Spanish conceptions of masculinity and honor. It is necessary to trace the relative value of masculinity, and relatively lower value placed on femininity, to analyze *La fuerza de la costumbre*, as well as the general allure of female actresses in men's clothing. Early modern Spanish society believed that men were, by nature, more perfect than women; in fact 'woman' was defined, even biologically, as an imperfect version of man. As Otavio's comment shows, it was a commonplace that masculinity was the more perfect form, while the feminine form implied imperfection and weakness. In *The Book of the Courtier* (published in Italy in 1528, and translated into Spanish by Juan Boscán in 1534), signor Gasparo refutes the Magnifico Giuliano's (much better received) Platonic conception of women as men's equals, arguing that "very learned men have written that, since nature always intends and plans to make things most perfect, she would constantly bring forth men if she could; and that when a woman is born, it is a defect or mistake of nature, and contrary to what she would wish to do: as is seen too in the case of one who is born blind, or lame, or with some other defect" (Castiglione 2002, 156). Gasparo invokes the Aristotelian view that "man is as the form and woman as the matter; and therefore, just as the form is more perfect than the matter – nay, gives it its being – so man is far more perfect than woman" (Castiglione 2002, 158).

Juan Huarte de San Juan's 1575 medical treatise, *Examen de ingenios para las ciencias* [*The Examination of Men's Wits*], posits a theory of man's intelligence and aptitude for various professions and arts (and woman's lack of these capacities) based on his revisions of classical philosophy's theory of the four humors. He also gives an account of how to produce male children and raise them to be most capable of contributing to the republic; in his view, these biological principles are paramount to the health of the nation. In this theory, each person's humoral temperament is dictated by their personal balance of the four opposing elements of heat, cold, moisture and dryness. The intersection of the wet–dry and hot–cool axes gives rise to the four humors, each of which has an accompanying personality profile: heat and dryness create an excess of bile and a choleric disposition, a cool and dry composition indicates a melancholic nature, heat with wetness makes for a sanguine disposition, and the phlegmatic disposition is cold and wet. Huarte argues against writers of antiquity such as Aristotle and Galen on the point that a balance of the four elements was the ideal state, affirming instead that, although all men are afflicted by their imbalances,[28] the positive aspect of these imperfections is that they enhance different kinds of *ingenio* (wit/ intelligence) (1989, 179–80). Thus, the universal pathology of imbalance benefits man's intelligence and abilities: "De manera que hay destemplanza y enfermedad determinada para cierto género de sabiduría, y repugnante para las demás; y, así, es necesario que el hombre sepa qué enfermedad es la suya y qué destemplanza, y a qué ciencia corresponde en particular (que es el tema de este libro)" ["Therefore, there are imbalances and diseases which foster certain kinds of wisdom, while poorly suiting others; and thus, it is necessary for man to know which illness and distemper is his own, and which science in particular this will correspond to (which is the subject of this book)"] (179).

The crux of Huarte's *Examen* is the definition of the faculties of the rational soul, three forms of intelligence, and their accompanying talents and aptitudes: *entendimiento*, understanding, *imaginativa*,[29] imagination, and *memoria*, memory. *Entendimiento*, the most prized form of intelligence, stands opposite memory on the dry–wet axis, where *entendimiento* results from dryness, while moisture facilitates memory, the lowest of the faculties of the rational soul. The quality of heat gives rise to imagination, and coldness impedes the development of intelligence altogether.[30] A man of

---

28   Huarte takes this idea of man's universal illness from Democrates and Hippocrates (174–76), and then follows the Scholastics in the application of this idea the suffering of man after the explusion from the Garden of Eden (177; 180–81).
29   Huarte replaces the Scholastics' 'will' with '*imaginativa*', which angered some readers and censors (see Serés' Introduction, p. 113). As Serés explains, Huarte's concept of 'imagination' constitutes a reinstatement of the Aristotelian model, rather than a departure from it, since Aristotle does not include the will in his theory of the three faculties of intellect: memory/sense perception, imagination, and intellect (96–99).
30   Huarte's views on the effects of coldness are inconsistent, and will be explored further below.

entendimiento (caused by a dry nature) will excel in theology, theoretical medicine, dialectics, natural and moral philosophy, and the study and practice of law, though he will never master handwriting, foreign languages, or public speaking (395; 400–402; 407). Huarte assigns a wide range of abilities to *imaginativa*: poetry, music, painting, drawing, governing, writing (both handwriting and authoring fiction), prayer, preaching/public speaking, comedic ability, the practice of medicine, physical ability, military skill, mathematics, astrology, engineering and invention; people of this sort are risk takers, impulsive, daring, do not seek agreement or approval from others, and often suffer from a touch of madness (395–96; 403–10; 267). Memory is the least valued because it is a purely passive intelligence, lacking the ability to create anything, and capable only of absorbing information via sense perception and retaining it. This intellect instills natural facility with grammar, languages, theoretical jurisprudence, positive theology, cosmography and arithmetic (395; 397–400).

From the opening sentence of his treatise, in the Preface addressed to King Felipe II, Huarte underscores the political valences of his project. He emphasizes in particular the importance to the republic that each man perform only the function that he is biologically predisposed to[31]:

> Para que las obras de los artífices tuviesen la perfección que convenía al uso de la república, me pareció, Católica Real Majestad, que se había de establecer una ley: que el carpintero no hiciese obra tocante al oficio del labrador, ni el tejedor del arquitecto, ni el jusrisperito curase, ni el médico abogase; sino que cada uno ejercitase sola aquel arte para la cual tenía talento natural, y dejase las demás.

> [In order that works of ingenuity have the perfection that will benefit the needs of the republic, it seems to me, Catholic Royal Majesty, that a law should be established: that the carpenter not do the work pertaining to the skills of the farmer, nor the weaver that of the architect, nor should the legal mind practice medicine, nor the doctor practice law; but rather each person should perform only the art for which he has a natural talent, and should leave the others aside.]

(149)

Reproduction carries political consequences as well, as men of *ingenio* beget other men of *ingenio*, strengthening the nation (601). Huarte excuses

---

31 See Serés' introduction for an in-depth discussion of the political aims of the *Examen de ingenios* (29–42).

himself for discussing shameful matters like genitals and sex on account of the nationalist interests which take precedence over modesty, "porque reducir a arte perfecta la manera que se ha de tener para que los hombres salgan de ingenio muy delicado es una de las cosas que la república más ha menester" ["because boiling down to a perfect art the method of ensuring that men possess delicate wit is one of the things most crucial to the republic"] (607).

This appropriation of (man's) intellect and reproductive lineage for political purposes is unabashedly gendered: only men are capable of attaining (and reproducing) the *ingenio* so critical to the health of the nation, whereas the female intellect is inherently feeble in Huarte's model due to its cold and wet nature, which is only good for making women docile and fertile.[32] Female *nature* simply does not allow intelligence in this theory: "...la compostura natural que la mujer tiene en el celebro no es capaz de mucho ingenio ni de mucha sabiduría" ["...the natural composition of woman's brain is not capable of much wit, nor wisdom"] (163).[33] He argues that women are also incapable of prudence or discipline, and are 'naturally' repulsed by intellectual tasks: "Pero, quedando la mujer en su disposición natural, todo género de letras y sabiduría es repugnante a su ingenio. Por donde la Iglesia católica con gran razón tiene prohibido que ninguna mujer pueda predicar ni confesar ni enseñar; porque su sexo no admite prudencia ni disciplina" ["But, to a woman left to her natural state, all manner of letters and knowledge is repugnant to her intelligence. Which is why the Catholic Church with good reason has prohibited women from preaching, confessing, or teaching, because her sex does not allow prudence or discipline"] (615).[34] Accordingly, Huarte locates women on the corner of the humoral chart that manifests the fewest intellectual capacities, although depending on the degree of cold and

---

[32] In the 1594 edition's Chapter VIII, he states that cold destroys all abilities, from digestion, to sperm production, to motor skills, to reasoning (327). He takes issue with Aristotle's argument that cold enhances intelligence (328–329; 352), although he is not entirely consistent in this view. (María de Zayas exploits this inconsistency in her preface to the *Novelas amorosas y ejemplares*; See Margaret Rich Greer, *María de Zayas Tells Baroque Tales of Love and the Cruelty of Men*, pp. 64–72.) He also gives a devastating statement about humidity: "De la humidad, es dificultoso saber qué diferencia de ingenio pueda nacer, pues tanto contradice a la facultad racional" ["As for humidity, it is difficult to know what sort of wit can be born from it, since it is so contrary to the rational faculty"] (334).

[33] In his book on the ideal woman/wife, *La perfecta casada*, Fray Luis de León also references women's moral and intellectual inferiorities, though he encourages women to use virtue to overcome them (1999, 32).

[34] Georgina Dopico-Black details critics' attempts to explain Sor Juana's intelligence as a product of biological abnormality and androgyny, even into the twentieth century (2001).

moisture, it is possible for some women to attain some intellectual capacity (he cites the biblical examples of Judith and Deborah, 615).

Men who lose their testicles, which for Huarte are the seat of the humors, will also find their intellectual abilities castrated:

> Cuánto daño haga al hombre privarle de estas partes, aunque pequeñas, no serán menester muchas razones para probarlo. Pues vemos por experiencia que luego se le cae el vello y la barba; y la voz gruesa y abultada se le vuelve delgada; y con esto pierde las fuerzas y el calor natural, y queda de peor condición y más mísera que si fuera mujer.
>
> [The extent of the damage done to a man when deprived of these parts, though they are but small, will not need much said about it to be evident. For we see from experience that soon his hair and beard fall out; and his deep, resonant voice becomes thin; and with this he loses his strength and natural heat, and is of worse condition and more wretched than if he were a woman.]

(619)

A man's intelligence prior to castration has no bearing on the intellectual capacities he will possess after, because it is equivalent to a cerebral injury: "…si antes que capasen al hombre, tenía mucho ingenio y habilidad, después de cortados los testículos lo viene a perder como si en el mismo celebro hubiera recibido alguna notable lesion" ["…if, prior to castration, the man possessed great wit and ability, after his testicles are cut he will start to lose it, as if he had suffered a serious injury in his brain itself"] (619–20).

Castration was not the only way to alter gender, however. Intrinsic to the 'one-sex' model of gender, which held that men and women possessed the same anatomy formed either internally or externally, was a certain degree of instability of anatomical sex. Huarte argues that men and women have the same anatomy, with the only difference being an external manifestation of genitalia (caused by heat in the womb) or an internal genitalia formation (due to a cooler womb). The vagina and cervix correspond to the penis, and the testicles to the ovaries, although he would not have used these terms since female anatomy was not ascribed separate terms in the sixteenth century:

> Y es que el hombre, aunque nos parece de la compostura que vemos, no difiere de la mujer, según dice Galeno, más que en tener los miembros genitales fuera del cuerpo. Porque si hacemos anatomía de una doncella hallaremos que tiene dentro de sí dos testículos, dos vasos seminarios, y el útero con la mesma compostura que el miebro viril sin faltarle ninguna delineación. Y de

tal manera es esto verdad, que si acabando Naturaleza de fabricar un hombre perfecto, le quisiese convertir en mujer, no tenía otro trabajo más que tornarle adentro los instrumentos de la generación; y, si hecha mujer, quisiese volverla en varón, con arrojarle el útero y los testículos fuera, no había más que hacer. Esto muchas veces le ha acontecido a Naturaleza, así estando la criatura en el cuerpo como fuera; de lo cual están llenas las historias, sino que algunos han pensado que era fabuloso viendo que los poetas lo traían entre las manos. Pero realmente pasa así[.]

[And it is the case that the man (although he appears to be composed of what we see), does not differ from the woman, according to Galen, other than that his genital members are outside the body. For if we take the anatomy of a young woman we shall find that she has within herself two testicles, two seminal vesicles, and the uterus has the same composition as the penis, without a single detail missing. And this is true to such a degree that, once Nature has finished making a perfect man, and then wanted to change him into a woman, the only task required would be to put the reproductive parts back on the inside; and if having made a woman, Nature wanted to make her a man, there would be nothing more to do than to move the womb and testicles back to the outside; that is all. This has often happened in Nature, regardless of the form the body has taken; history is full of examples, but some have thought that it was make-believe, since it was in the hands of the poets. But it really happens like this.]

(608)[35]

The one-sex model contains an inherent hierarchy, in which woman is a less perfectly formed man, as Gasparo argues in Book III of *The Book of the Courtier* (Castiglione 2002).[36] Another consequence of this theory was that gender could change depending on conditions: Huarte hypothesizes that babies can change gender *in utero* due to an excess of cold or heat. If a fetus was female for the first month or two of pregnancy, but then had his/her genitalia externalized due to an excess of heat (a process he calls 'transmutación' ['transmutation']), "se conoce después claramente en ciertos movimientos que tiene, indecentes al sexo viril: mujeriles, mariosos, la voz

---

35 Huarte also mentions that the one-sex view is somewhat controversial, "el vulgo está en ella muy descuidado" ["the public is very suspicious about it"] (608).
36 In *Making Sex: Body and Gender from the Greeks to Freud*, Thomas Laqueur posits that the one-sex model renders 'gender' the given, and 'sex' the cultural category (1990, 8). It also links sex to power and social rank, given that "*man* is the measure of all things, and woman does not exist as an ontologically distinct category" (62).

blanda y melosa; son los tales inclinados a hacer obras de mujeres, y caen ordinariamente en el pecado nefando" ["it is clearly recognized later in certain movements he makes, indecent to the virile sex: womanish, foppish, a soft and sweet voice; these are the type who are inclined to do woman's work, and typically fall into sodomy"] (1989, 609). This example and its mannish woman counterpart aim to demonstrate how what we currently call 'sex' could come to disagree with gendered behavior, as well as the connection between mal-formed gender and homosexuality. Huarte reports that gender/sex can also change spontaeously later in life.[37] Thus, while Huarte is absolutist about masculinity as the intellectually superior human form, a certain fluidity of sex/gender is also inherent in his theory.

This view of masculinity as a higher form allowed for some instances of socially condoned transvestism or gender transition. Valerie Hotchkiss investigates stories of female nuns and saints dressing as men after Christian conversion throughout the middle ages.[38] Though cross-dressing was officially prohibited by the church (as well as the government and society at large), the transgressions Hotchkiss investigates were permitted by the church because maleness was seen as a higher moral state, and therefore a woman dressing as a man after a profound religious experience symbolized the transformational power of Christianity.[39] A female could live a more

---

37 "Y que se hayan vuelto mujeres en hombres después de nacidas, ya no se espanta el vulgo de oírlo; porque fuera de lo que cuentan por verdad muchos antiguos, es cosa que ha acontecido en España muy pocos años ha. Y lo que muestra la experiencia no admite disputas ni argumentos" ["And that women have turned into men after being born, the public is not surprised to hear; because apart from that which is believed to be true by many ancients, it is something that has happened recently in Spain. And what is proved by experience does not allow for disputes or arguments"] (609).

38 Hotchkiss cites over 30 examples of this phenomenon from medieval hagiographic literature (1996, 15–27). See also Sabrina Petra Ramet (1996) and Dekker and van de Pol (1989).

39 Friar José de Jesús María is outraged by attempts to validate stage cross-dressing with the stories of female saints who wore male clothing: "Y si en las historias eclesiásticas se lee de algunas mujeres que usaron de este hábito, no fué para ser vistas, sino para estar encubiertas; no para salir al tablado á ser ocasión de culpas, sino para esconderse y hacer más fácilmente penitencia de las que habían cometido; [...] no es razón que se traiga en consecuencia de cosas tan feas y detestables, como son las acciones lascivas de los comediantes, ni hay para qué autorizar sus vicios é insolencias con las virtudes heroicas de las vírgenes sagradas" ["And if ecclesiastic history tells of some women who used this dress, it was not to be seen, but rather to be covered up; not to go out to the stage to be the occasion for sin, but rather to hide themselves away and more easily do penitence for the sins they had committed; [...] this should not be used as a justification for such ugly, detestable acts, such as the lascivious

perfected (asexual) life as a male, given that the soteriological project of the church is progress and perfection of the soul, while a male would likely not be permitted to live in an inherently inferior state, that of the female, because this would constitute corruption of divine perfection.

Where this moral impunity was not preserved, however, cross-dressing was seen as a depraved act, punishable by law. During the summer of 1587 in Ocaña, Eleno/a de Céspedes was tried for sodomy, bigamy/contempt for the sacrament of marriage, and consorting with the devil, only a year and a half after being declared legally male and thus, permitted to marry a woman, by the court of Toledo (Burshatin 1996, 105–12). In his/her defense, Eleno claimed to be a hermaphrodite who developed a penis after giving birth to a son when s/he was sixteen years old, at which time s/he began living as a man and became a doctor (Burshatin 1996, 111). As part of the legal verification of his/her sex for the Ocaña trial, Eleno/a was probed with fingers and a candle, and declared by the midwives and doctors who performed the examination to be female and a 'virgin' (Burshatin 1996, 106); this after nine doctors and midwives had examined Eleno/a and pronounced him/her male before his wedding to María del Caño in 1586 (Vollendorf 2005, 17). On account of the court's doctors' declaration that s/he was and had always been female, not a hermaphrodite, Eleno/a was sentenced to 200 lashes and 10 years of imprisonment for the crime of bigamy (Burshatin 1996, 118). Though the court investigated Eleno/a for sodomy, according to Burshatin, "the tribunal opted in the end for ruling only on the least 'messy' and most strictly procedural aspects of the case" (1999, 424). The accusation was that Eleno/a had married María without a certificate proving that Eleno/a had been widowed by Christóval Lombardo, to whom Eleno/a had been married when she was sixteen. As Burshatin and Vollendorf have pointed out, de Céspedes' status of mulatto and former slave likely made the court less inclined to accept him/her into their ranks of men.

Lisa Vollendorf recounts the remarkable case of doña Magdalena Muñoz, who reportedly sprouted a penis while carrying a heavy load of grain (2005, 11). After having his/her new genitalia inspected by two priests and confirmed as definitively male, Muñoz's father was called to retrieve him/her from the convent where s/he had been living. One of the priests involved in the case documented the father's happiness at having a son and heir (12).

Catalina/Alonso/Antonio de Erauso, the 'Lieutenant Nun', Renaissance

---

conduct of actors, nor is there any reason to authorize their vices and insolent behavior with the heroic virtues of the sacred virgins"] (quoted in Cotarelo y Mori 1904, 381).

Spain's most famous transgender figure, was ultimately granted permission from the Pope to live as a man.[40] As a teenager, he ran away from the convent where he was to take orders as a nun, and fashioned a male outfit from his habit (Perry 1999, 397). From that point forward, he dressed and lived as a man, under the name Alonso Díaz Ramírez de Guzmán, and made his way to the Americas where he worked for a merchant, enlisted with the military multiple times, was engaged to two women at once, gambled, survived duels (some of which he instigated), and became known for his prowess in battle. The rank of *alférez*, 'lieutenant', was granted to him when he rescued his company's flag from the Araucanian warriors against whom the Spaniards were fighting in Chile (Perry 1999, 401). He returned to Spain after confessing to a bishop that he was a woman while thinking he was on his deathbed. In 1625 he petitioned the crown to receive the soldier's pension he had earned for his military service (Mendieta 2009, 24–26). The Spanish crown honored his request, and eventually Erauso received permission from the Pope to dress in male attire, as long as he promised to abstain from sexual activity and marriage. His virginity was critical to having these petitions granted, as he was able to present himself as asexual and emphasize his desire to live as a man in order to serve the crown (Mendieta 2009, 170).

Erauso obtained permission to continue living as a man because he appealed to the ideals of masculine perfection; however such a situation in the reverse would not have been afforded the same consideration. According to Mary Elizabeth Perry, the popular seventeenth-century 'manly women', such as Catalina de Erauso, "reassured people concerned about the numbers of men who left Spain for the New World, allowing them to believe that the country had not 'feminized' and consequently gone to the dogs" (1990, 134). Whereas Eleno/a tried to defend him/herself with medical explanations of his/her gender fluidity which failed due to the lack of the phallus, Catalina/Antonio confessed to having a female body, while claiming to have been inspired to live as a man for reasons of a moral calling, that of serving Spain in its pursuits of empire (Velasco 2000, 46–49). Stories of cross-dressing as an achievement of a higher state ultimately reinforce the patriarchal hierarchy which holds men as supreme. Thus, while a manly woman could serve her country, as Erauso was ultimately allowed to do, a womanly

---

40 Although many scholars continue to refer to Erauso using feminine pronouns, I use only male pronouns in his case in order to respect his preference and the gender with which he identified based on the documentation of Erauso's petitions to both state and church law to have a male gender identity.

man represented an intolerable degradation of the valor of a nation facing challenges to the perception of its strength around the globe. The importance of masculinity to this society likely informs *La fuerza de la costumbre*'s careful treatment of Félix's gender identity. Though Félix and Hipólita appear to be in parallel situations, a closer look reveals the limits of the play's willingness to undermine masculinity. While Hipólita expresses a fully formed masculinity, Félix's effeminacy is more ambiguous. Hipólita arrives home dressed as a man, whereas Félix is dressed, not as a woman *per se*, but rather as a child or a priest. Pedro assumes, upon seeing his son's long robes, that he must be interested in an ecclesiastical profession: "Hijo, ¡sucesos extraños!, / mas teniendo ya veinte años, / ¿hábito largo, y ¿por qué? / ¿Es devoción bien fundada? / ¿Quiere ser de iglesia?" ["Son, this is strange, / for you are now twenty years old, / yet you're in this long dress? Why? / Is this some kind of devotion? / Does he intend to join the church?"] (I. 280–284).[41] Though Pedro's question certainly hints at an accusation of effeminacy, Félix's performance is not exactly that of 'woman', but rather one of an 'effeminate man'.[42] This imbalance evidences the privileged place of masculinity in Spanish society. Whereas Félix's effeminacy puts his life and the family name at risk, Hipólita's masculinity, while problematic, mesmerizes the men of the town and is a source of quiet pride for her father. Furthermore, by emphatically attributing Félix's lack of masculinity to unnatural habits forced upon him by Costanza, Castro leaves the door open for Félix's 'true nature' to be restored (this will be explored further in section IV). Castro does not push Félix's gender further into the feminine realm because this move would threaten the social order much more than Hipólita's manliness, which could arguably be condoned for purposes ranging from nationalistic to those of entertainment.

Félix threatens his family's honor more than Hipólita does, since he fails to occupy the privileged masculine role; worse yet, his failures are public, putting the entire family's honor in question. Julian Pitt-Rivers' *The Fate of Shechem*, a study of honor in Spanish society, analyzes the interrelation of honor and masculinity, and the way honor operates within

---

41 Marjorie Garber maintains that priests "were in many ways equated with women in medieval society" in *Vested Interests: Cross-dressing and Cultural Anxiety* (1992, 218).
42 The playwrights who adapt Guillén de Castro's play do not share his hesitance to feminize a man: the English adaptation of *La fuerza de la costumbre*, Beaumont and Fletcher's *Love's Cure, or, The Martial Maid* makes both children equally gender crossed: Eugenia raises Lucio, their son, as a daughter in order to protect him from Vitelli, her husband's rival and enemy.

family structures. Pitt-Rivers examines the need for external affirmation in order for honor to have any social meaning (1997, 1–13). In *De la edad conflictiva*, Américo Castro argues that honor was an obsession of sixteenth- and seventeenth-century Spanish society due to the concern over *limpieza de sangre*, lineage free of Moorish and Jewish blood (1976, 33). Though Félix possesses 'vertical' honor, the honor associated with lineage and social hierarchy, his lack of masculinity damages his 'horizontal' honor, that of reputation, which, according to Gustavo Correa, "descansaba por entero en la opinión que los demás tuvieran de la persona" ["rested entirely on the opinion that others held of the person"] (1958, 101).[43]

Womanish men not only shamed themselves, but also threatened society as a whole. As Spain's massive empire suffered bankruptcy, defeat, social unrest and famine in the latter half of the sixteenth century, Spain's prominence and grandeur seemed less unassailable than it had in the previous period of wealth and domination. This period of crisis and decline inspired both nostalgia over Spain's earlier heroic past and also disquietude about its current *flojedad*, weakness, and effeminacy, which were blamed for this change in national fortune, as José Antonio Maravall has shown (1975, 92–95). Maravall quotes multiple seventeenth-century outcries against this effeminacy, including that of Fray Francisco de León in 1635, who claimed that the nation's problems had their origins in "los hombres convertidos en mujeres, de soldados en afeminados" ["men turned into women, and soldiers into effeminate men"] (1975, 94).[44] The servant Caramanchel in Tirso's *Don Gil de las calzas verdes* expresses his abhorrence of womanish men and references the legal consequences for tainted masculinity (which is what he takes Doña Juana for after thinking her to be a man, and then seeing her dressed as a woman):

> Azotes dan en España
> por menos que eso. ¿Quién vio
> un hembri-macho, que afrenta
> a su linaje?

---

43 Among the numerous important contributions to the study of honor on the Spanish stage, those which have been most helpful to the present work are those of Dunn (1960), Jones (1958; 1965), D. Larson (1977), and McKendrick (2002).

44 For more on the fear of effeminacy, see Cartagena Calderón (2008), Perry (1990), Donnell (2003), Velasco (2006), and Milligan and Tylus (2010), which includes excellent articles on the 'masculinity crisis' of the seventeenth century by Fox, Vélez Quiñones, and Cartagena Calderón.

[…]
Amo, o ama,
despídome: haga cuenta.
No quiero señor con saya
y calzas, hombre y mujer;
que querréis en mí tener
juntos lacayo y lacaya.
No más amo hermafrodita;
que comer carne y pescado
a un tiempo, no es aprobado.

[But here in Spain a person will
Be flogged for less. What are you called?
Man-woman? A hermaphrodite?
What about your reputation?
[…]
Well, master-mistress, that's your lot.
Whatever you may be, or not,
Farewell. Let's have the reckoning.
I won't serve someone who can swing
From breeches to a petticoat,
Or else my own identity
Would have to wander as you do,
And be both bloke and housemaid too.
No more hermaphrodites for me.
A dish that should be made of meat
But turns out to be fish? No, sir.][45]
(1969, III. 651–654a; 655b–663)

The Spanish uneasiness over effeminacy likely motivated the author's decision to instill Félix with a less fully articulated femininity than Hipólita's cohesive masculinity. It also explains why, despite this difference in degree of expression of the 'problematic' gender, the pressure to change exerted on Félix is fervent and more severe. Although Hipólita's gender incongruence is problematic, it does not shame the family (or the republic) in the same way that Félix's effeminacy does. Furthermore, Hipólita has the backing of a long lineage of epic and mythological warrior women, as well as saints,

---

45 O'Brien, Sean trans. *Don Gil of the Green Breeches* by Tirso de Molina. Unpublished production script, 2013, p. 122–123.

who have found 'higher' status in masculine roles. Her name associates her with the legendary female warriors, the Amazons; according to Greek mythology, Hipólita (in English, Hippolyta or Hippolyte) was the daughter of the god of war, Ares, and the Queen of the Amazons. Félix's character has primarily negative connotations and antecedents. Particularly in the political context of the seventeenth century, Félix's gender non-conformity poses a greater threat to social hierarchy and familial honor than that of his sister.

III. Gender Trouble in *La fuerza de la costumbre*

> Es notable cosa el ver,
> él pareciendo mujer,
> y ella no acertando a serlo.
> Ni al uno viene la espada,
> ni al otro el manto le viene.
>
> [It's an extremely odd thing to see,
> he seeming so like a woman,
> and she not knowing how to be one.
> One can't handle the sword,
> and the other can't master the shawl.]
> (Marcelo, II. 58–62)

These words, spoken by Marcelo, show the amusement produced by Hipólita and Félix's failures to convincingly embody and perform the genders their father assigned them in Act I. At this point in the play, sex, gender and their signs are jumbled and confused in this pair of siblings. Marcelo specifically emphasizes failure here, by using negation instead of positive statements ("ella no acertando;" "ni ... ni...") with the exception of line 59, "él pareciendo mujer," which in itself is a negation of manhood. Félix and Hipólita's inability to 'pass' as men or women threatens their legibility, and thus their status as social subjects, confirming Judith Butler's argument that the "citation of the gender norm is necessary in order to qualify as a 'one,' to become viable as a 'one,' where subject formation is dependent on the prior operation of legitimating gender norms" (1993, 177). Hipólita and Félix's illegibility as gendered subjects threatens the modalities of hierarchy and identification which had moral, legal and personal ramifications.

In the *Republic*, Plato argues against acting and allowing people to play multiple parts, first, because "it's impossible for a single individual to play lots of roles as successfully as he plays a single role" (1998, 90), and because they may adopt the behavior they represent, diverting them from their nature and purpose (91–95). In his prohibition of women wearing men's clothing in *The Education of a Christian Woman*, Juan Luis Vives demands that 'natural' differences be made visible in outward signs, such as clothing, and argues that one who is 'ambiguous' in dress is an abomination:

> Nature made a sharp distinction of sexes in the bodies of living things. If we cover the body and divert the attention of those we meet from that natural

distinction by means of a suitable covering, as is proper, we must see to it that our clothes give visible sign of that distinction and do not obscure what nature has clearly marked. Therefore, one who is ambiguous in dress is justly called abominable by the Lord, since he is attempting something that is contrary to the laws of nature, which would give rise to many perils in human society. But no woman attempts such a thing unless she has already cast off her chastity together with her sense of modesty.

(2000, 109)

In the *Arte nuevo*, Lope de Vega makes similar demands (though in the realm of the composition and performance of plays) for correspondence between characters' status (political, class, gender, etc.) and his or her speech and actions (1998, v. 246–312). Marjorie Garber demonstrates that the sumptuary laws in Renaissance England attempted to regulate clothing in order to ensure definitive legibility of a person's class, gender and social station: "The ideal scenario – from the point of view of the regulators – was one in which a person's social station, social role, gender and other indicators of identity in the world could be read, without ambiguity or uncertainty. The threat to this legibility was 'confusion'" (1992, 26).[46] Plato, Aristotle, Huarte,[47] Lope de Vega, Vives – these are just a few of the voices demanding integration of the "self" with both its outward signs and with behavior. Though this rule was not always followed (as demonstrated by Catalina/Antonio de Erauso), the strict moral ideal was for the subject's body to accurately portray signs of identity and its place within a hierarchy. Ironically, in *La fuerza de la costumbre* it is when Félix and Hipólita attempt to bring their exterior gender signs into conformity with their assigned genders (their supposed 'original' sex/gender) that they become completely illegible.

Before delving deeper into the social demands of gender performance and legibility, it is necessary to establish the ways in which *La fuerza de la costumbre* engages with and departs from the *mujer vestida de hombre* trope of Spanish Golden Age theater. Most heroines of transvestite theater appropriate the signs of masculinity 1) voluntarily (even if coerced by circumstance), 2) as adults, and 3) as a *disguise*, while maintaining an underlying identity that

---

46 See also Perry, *Gender and Disorder in Early Modern Seville* (1990, Chapter 2, 'Virgins, Martyrs, and the Necessary Evil', pp. 33–52).
47 Huarte, building on Plato and Aristotle, opens the first 'Proemio' of the *Examen de ingenios para las ciencias* with this idea of the political importance of each man serving a singular purpose (1989, 149–51).

they will return to once their problem has been resolved.[48] In all of the cross-dressing plots catalogued in M. Romera-Navarro's article, 'Las disfrazadas de varón en la comedia' ['Women Disguised as Men in the comedia'], the characters disguise themselves voluntarily, frequently due to complications in a love story and/or a (consensual or non-consensual) sexual encounter:

> Hagamos el catálogo: ocultar su vergüenza y deshonor, huyendo a los montes, eludir la justicia de un hermano vengador de su honra, o satisfacer el agravio hecho a su honor, cuando no escapar de un centinela que quiere forzarla; otras mujeres, para libertar al esposo, visitar a una reina injustamente en prisión y defender mejor su causa, para socorrer a su galán, o acompañarle en el destierro, para sólo llevar un mensaje; algunas por ocultar su identidad y acompañar al amante, o por celos y desconfianza de su galán; muchas para perseguir al infiel que las ha engañado o para restaurar su perdido honor, y otra pequeña legión para realizar sus planes amorosos.
>
> [Let us make the catalogue: to hide her shame and dishonor by fleeing to the mountains, avoiding the punishment of a brother avenging his honor, or to avenge a grievance done to one's honor, to escape a guard who attempts rape; other women, to free a spouse, to visit an unjustly imprisoned queen to better defend her cause, to assist a suitor, or to accompany him in exile, or just to bring a message; some do it to conceal their identity and accompany a lover, or for jealousy and distrust of their beloved; many do it to pursue an unfaithful man who has deceived them or to restore their lost honor, and another small legion do it to carry out their plans for love.]
>
> (1934, 273)

The above-mentioned story lines ascribe a certain degree of agency and intentionality to their cross-dressed protagonists. By contrast, Hipólita's and Félix's gender trouble begins in childhood, at life's earliest stages; they do not choose their childhood gender any more than a newborn baby pronounced 'boy' or 'girl' does.

Whereas in other cross-dressing plots the disguise is usually motivated by a transgression, either committed by the cross-dresser or inflicted on her, the de Moncada siblings have to change their identities (twice, in fact), as a result of their parents' problematic marriage, which was mysteriously

---

48 The most common outcome of cross-dressing in theater is that the transvestite character forsakes the disguise by the end of the play. However, this may be less consistent in other genres. See Barbara Fuchs study of transvestism in *Don Quijote*, which examines episodes in which the previous gender identity is not fully restored (1996).

opposed by Costanza's father, Juan de Urrea, "por su condición extraña" ["because of his strange condition"] (I. 98). Costanza and Pedro marry in secret, attempting to circumvent Juan de Urrea's disapproval. This secrecy inadvertently leads to the death of Costanza's brother, who attacks Pedro thinking he is an intruder and subsecuently dies at Pedro's hand. Pedro flees Spain to avoid the retribution Costanza's father was entitled to pursue; Costanza takes refuge with an aunt and her father disowns her, vowing never to pardon Pedro. Hipólita and Félix's gender trouble can be read as a consequence of a marriage not entirely condoned by social and paternal order. The gender each child performs at the beginning of Act I is the product of the imitation and influence of their respective parental models. It is Costanza and Pedro who instigate this first gender crossing, not the children themselves; Pedro for the purposes of hiding Hipólita's sex from the other men in the war camp where she grows up in Flanders, and Costanza in order to keep her only remaining family member, her son, by her side and out of harm's way (I. 247–254; 285–294). The siblings' genders are *formed*, rather than *masked*, by the actions of their parents.[49] The back-story of this play puts in question how gender is formed and developed in children, and how gender interacts with the process of maturation. This is altogether different from the plots described by Romera-Navarro.

The non-voluntary nature of both the first instance of gender formation (the one that does not conform to the children's declared birth sex), as well as that of the change they are asked to perform as adults, is a critical element to *La fuerza de la costumbre*'s treatment of gender, which is shown to be constructed, heavily regulated, and violently imposed. Judith Butler's *Gender Trouble* articulates the performative nature of gender as both a creation and tool of a kind of regulatory power. Butler argues that gender is not an inherent phenomenon which manifests itself from within a person. Rather than a 'natural' or 'innate' identity given at birth, gender is a set of performances and imitations which depend on cultural requirements:

---

49   Early childhood, according to Huarte, is an extremely impressionable time in which children absorb habits and knowledge with ease owing to the abundance of moisture inherent in this age: "…acontesce en los muchachos, que por la mucha humidad que tienen en el celebro son faltos de entendimiento, y muy memoriosos por la gran blandura del celebro, en el cual, por razón de la humidad, hacen las especies y figuras, que vienen de fuera, gran compresión, fácil, profunda y bien figurada" ["what happens with youths is that, on account of the high humidity in their brains they lack knowledge but have very good memories, due to the malleability of their brains, in which, because of the moisture, they comprehend categories and figures that are presented to them with ease, depth and precision"] (1989, 339).

Gender ought not to be construed as a stable identity or locus of agency from which various acts follow; rather, gender is an identity tenuously constituted in time, instituted in an exterior space through a *stylized repetition of acts*. This formulation moves the conception of gender off the ground of a substantial model of identity to one that requires a conception of gender as a constituted social temporality.

(2006, 191)

The circumstances of being raised as a boy by her father in the masculine space of a war camp have dictated that the "stylized repetition of acts" that Hipólita has adopted as her own are those pertaining to masculinity. Both of Hipólita's instances of gender formation, first as a male-gendered soldier in the war camp, and later as a female-gendered Spanish lady, daughter and wife, are produced not as a choice or conscious desire, but rather in response to social (and as will be discussed in section IV) specifically paternal demands. Now, returning to the third point: most cross-dressers of the Golden Age Spanish stage use masculinity as a disguise which affords them the subject position necessary to achieve their desired ends. Barbara Fuchs draws a helpful distinction between 'romance transvestism' and 'androgyny': "If transvestism is occasional, contingent and inherently unstable, androgyny is near-permanent, absolute and often ends only with death" (1996, 19).[50] The type most frequently taken up by the Spanish playwrights is the former, the 'romance tranvestite'. In most cases, clothing is sufficient to create a new persona, and most cross-dressed characters 'pass' without trouble, as do most disguised characters in comedy.[51] Despite the disguise, generally these characters continue to think of themselves as women. For example, while Juana, the protagonist of Tirso de Molina's *Don Gil de las calzas verdes* is dressed as a man, she still thinks of herself as female, as does Quintana, who is in on her ploy.[52] Eva Mendieta argues that gender switching and 'passing' are more feasible in the one-sex model, which grants clothing high value in establishing an individual's gender. If both sexes possess the same anatomy, she concludes, gender is inherently staged and clothing holds great transformative power (2009, 173).

---

50 Bravo-Villasante makes a similar distinction between "la mujer enamorada" ["the woman in love"] and "la heroica-guerrera" ["the heroic warrior woman"] (1976, 13).
51 Romera-Navarro points out that the *mujer vestida de hombre* is almost never recognized as such (1934, 276).
52 See, for example, the opening scene, I. 1–250.

Clothing does not wield this masking power in *La fuerza de la costumbre*. The central conceit of Castro's play is the portrayal of a woman *being* a man; not disguised as one (at least not in her mind), but rather fully embodying and performing masculinity, regardless of clothing. Similarly, he shows a man who doesn't have a clue how to be manly; Félix's impotence invalidates the signs his masculine clothing attempts to invoke. Thus, *La fuerza de la costumbre* moves beyond the trope of stagey transvestism by showing even more complex manipulations of gender than a stable gender identity in disguise. The misguided embodiment of an already habituated but 'incorrect' gender occasions a unique plot in which failures of gender performance are at odds with the assumed 'sex' (and, presumably, the sex of the actors who would portray the characters). Pedro attempts to invoke the power of clothing normally granted in romance transvestism when he orders Félix and Hipólita to exchange garments (I. 335–338): "Quedaré con esperanza / de trocar con el vestido / las costumbres que ha tenido" [lit. "I will remain hopeful / that we can change his habits / by changing his clothes"] (I. 339–341). In spite of Pedro's invocation, the superficial application of clothing does not allow Félix or Hipólita to 'pass' in a given gender performance; instead it turns them into illegible hybrids, out of compliance with dimorphic gender requirements, as Marcelo's commentary in the opening of Act II shows. This failure to occupy a position in the binary must be corrected to restore the social order: to borrow from Arthur Brittan, "a person without gender identity is [...] not fully human" (1989, 28).

The fact that Félix and Hipólita have been raised in the gender which does not correspond to their 'birth sex' means that after Pedro commands them to trade their clothing, they are both cross-dressing in what would seem to be their 'natural' gender. Hipólita, who clearly falls more in line with the model of the androgynous warrior woman than the 'romance transvestite', was not simply disguised as a boy by her father, but rather was educated in a way that cultivated masculine virtue in her through habituation, as Aristotle prescribed.[53] The fact that Hipólita begins the play expressing a male identity – not that of a woman dressed up as a man – complicates the question of cross-dressing.[54] If Hipólita's gender is masculine, her adoption of female

---

53   Aristotle emphasizes the importance of habits and right actions in the cultivation of virtue in *The Nichomachean Ethics*. The philosopher contends that one learns a given skill by doing it; virtue is acquired through the repeated performance of intentional virtuous acts (2004, 31–39).
54   Hipólita is fearful and reluctant to become a 'woman': in Act I, Pedro admonishes her,

dress is in fact the cross-dressing she performs. With the exceptions of her first appearance on stage and the scene in Act III in which she confronts Luis dressed as a man, Hipólita acts as a female-bodied, male gendered man, all while dressed in women's clothing.[55]

Félix is never seen on stage in explicitly female clothing, though the long robe he wears in the first scene marks him as effeminate. The humor in Félix's case originates in his discomfort in his new male clothing and his inability to project a masculine persona while being outwardly dressed for the part. Félix's comic value emanates from his repeated, failed attempts to match sex and gender, a failure only emphasized by male clothing. While Garber and Butler have argued that drag/transvestism/cross-dressing denaturalizes sex and gender signs that are often assumed to be innate and fixed,[56] *La fuerza de la costumbre* shows that failures of performance can also destabilize these categories. Similarly, the brutal consequences of the failure to replicate the required gender performances reveal the force and violence through which gender is enforced. Félix and Hipólita's inability to match sex, gender, and performance denaturalizes gender signs from gender, and gender from sex, such that the imitative and performative elements of these categories are brought to light.

Between the initial exchange of clothing in Act I and the successful adoption of the new assigned genders in Act III, Hipólita and Félix's gender identities become extremely complex, allowing the play to produce humor by way of raucous action and colossal failures of gender performance. There is a

---

saying "Tente, mujer," ["stop, woman,"] to which she replies "El nombre me ha reportado, / afrentoso para mí."["That name holds me back, / I despise it"] (I. 740b–742).

55   A similar situation occurs in Juan Pérez de Montalbán's play (written after *La fuerza de la costumbre*) about the life of Catalina de Erauso, *La monja Alférez*, when Guzmán/Catalina arrives at court, trying to play the part of a lady.

56   Marjorie Garber: "If transvestism offers a critique of binary sex and gender distinctions, it is not because it simply makes such distinctions reversible but because it denaturalizes, destabilizes, and defamiliarizes sex and gender *signs*" (1992, 147). In *Gender Trouble*, Butler theorizes that "Indeed, part of the pleasure, the giddiness of the [drag] performance is in the recognition of a radical contingency in the relation between sex and gender in the face of cultural configurations of causal unities that are regularly assumed to be natural and necessary" (2006, 187). In *Bodies That Matter*, Butler specifies that drag shows the implicit involvement in regimes of power associated with social categories and norms, but is not necessarily subversive of these. What it does reveal is, in some sense, how subjects are constituted: "drag is subversive to the extent that it reflects on the imitative structure by which hegemonic gender is itself produced and disputes heterosexuality's claim on naturalness and originality" (1993, 85).

double crossing of the gender binary that might be called criss-cross-dressing. Let us dissect the layers of Hipólita's gender: Hipólita's 'birth sex' is female, but she develops a masculine gender identity because of her upbringing with her father. This masculinity constitutes the first cross-gender performance (described in I. 231–270; Pedro's 'creation' of Hipólita will be analyzed in Section IV). Layered over her masculine gender identity are female clothing and an (often half-hearted) attempt to perform femininity – the second gender crossing, an imposed gender performance that aligns with her sex but contradicts her habituated gender. Even when wearing a dress, Hipólita bucks the feminine category in behavior and attitude; her performance is unmistakably masculine. Her exaggerated cursing, manly gait, and absolute rejection of the feminine role in fact make her performance *more* theatrically masculine. She fails to suppress the well-practiced masculine *bravado*. For example, watching her brother's miserable performance at his fencing lesson, she can't help but shout and jeer at his flaccid weapon from the sidelines: "¡No te retires, hermano! / ¡Jesús, qué espada tan floja!" ["Don't draw back, brother. / Jesus, what a limp sword!"] (II. 337–338). Hipólita understands herself to be performing femininity (albeit begrudgingly), but the audience would delight in this contradictory performance, the (failed) feminine superimposed over the exaggeratedly masculine; a hyperbolic incongruence.

This criss-cross-dressing further denaturalizes the signs of gender by drawing a distinction between clothing/appearance and performance. Both the amusement produced by the illegible, conflicting gender performances (shown, for example, in Marcelo's observations) and the violence and force with which it is corrected show the simultaneous anxiety about and fascination with the possibility of variability within seemingly determined categories. As Garber argues, the figure of the transvestite seduces at the same time that it threatens the very identity of the 'self':

> Renaissance antitheatricalists, in their debates about gender, cross-dressing, and the stage, articulated deep-seated anxieties about the possibility that identity was not fixed, that there was no underlying 'self' at all, and that therefore identities had to be zealously and jealously safeguarded. […] The transvestite in this scenario is both terrifying and seductive precisely because s/he incarnates and emblematizes the disruptive element that intervenes, signaling not just another category crisis, but – much more disquietingly – a crisis of 'category' itself.

(1992, 32)

Huarte exposes this anxiety in his discussion of spontaneous sex changes (see Section II). Hipólita shows this category crisis and lack of underlying 'self' by having greater legibility, and thus a more acceptable social status, when living 'as a man' than she does when she attempts to comply with the feminine gender that her body supposedly mandates. As Costanza tells Hipólita in Act II, appearances are of the utmost importance ("Mas ya no basta en el mundo / limpieza de corazón, / pues juzga por lo exterior / y éste ha de ser ejemplar" ["Still, it isn't enough anymore / to just have a pure heart in this world, / as you will be judged by what is visible / therefore this must be exemplary"] (II. 211–214)).

Dressing Up as 'Oneself'
The dislocation of any 'natural' (not in the sense of biologically determined, but rather unintentional, unaffected) performance highlights the acting inherent in any successful social performance. Butler posits that drag is an allegory of heterosexuality that brings into relief the "understated, taken-for-granted quality of heterosexual performativity" (1993, 181). The amount of teaching and other intervention required to bring Félix and Hipólita's gender performances in line with the socially mandated order implicates the other characters in the meta-theatrics of gender. These characters not only teach gender, but they enforce and regulate it, revealing their own consciousness of its performative and imitative elements. Lionel Abel argues that meta-theatrical works

> are theatre pieces about life seen as already theatricalized. By this I mean that the persons appearing on the stage in these plays are there not simply because they were caught by the playwright in dramatic postures as a camera might catch them, but because they themselves knew they were dramatic before the playwright took note of them. What dramatized them originally? Myth, legend, past literature, they themselves. They represent to the playwright the effect of dramatic imagination before he has begun to exercise his own; on the other hand, unlike figures in tragedy, they are aware of their own theatricality.
> (2003, 134)

In this play, all of the characters' genders are shown to be performative and hyperbolic, bordering on caricature. Masculinity is exaggerated, not only by Hipólita, but also by Luis (see, for example II. 895–909), Pedro (I. 748b–752), and the Captain (III. 938–945). The Captain reportedly kills multiple lawmen without legal consequence (and boasts about it); Pedro chases Félix with his sword unsheathed, threatening to kill him; Otavio mocks Félix's impotence with his sword. Femininity is exaggerated as well – Leonor faints and 'drops' her glove at convenient times; Costanza frets about Félix's lack of *destreza* [skill]. As Garber asserts with regard to cross-dressing in Shakespeare, "Transvestite theater recognizes that *all* of the figures onstage are impersonators. The notion that there has to be a naturalness to the sign is exactly what great theater puts in question. In other words, there is no ground of Shakespeare that is not already cross-dressed" (1992, 40). In his article on the semiotics of theater, Umberto Eco argues that "it is not theatre that is able to imitate life; it is social life that is designed as a continuous performance and, because of this, there is a link between theatre and life" (1977, 113). *In La fuerza de la costumbre*, even the gender-conforming characters are shown to be caricatures and rehearsals of various trite masculine and feminine roles. According to Abel, the characters of meta-theater also dramatize one another.[57] All of the teachers in *La fuerza de la costumbre* become the authors, prompters and directors, scripting and blocking various aspects of Félix and Hipólita's performances. They personify the constraint, force and threat which Butler posits as central to the reproduction of norms that constitute the subject (1993, 60).

These metatheatrical elements give the reader or audience a behind-the-scenes look at the social processes which require citation of gender norms for the legitimization of social subjects. The gender binary and its supposed naturalness are revealed to be functions of a patriarchal structure whose principal aim is to replicate itself. Although Castro tidies up Hipólita and Félix's genders by ending the play with heterosexual marriages and leaves the siblings supposedly giving corrected gender performances, the puppet strings involved in the presentation of masculinity and femininity continue to show. The essentially constructed nature of the categories itself, the dominance of habit, the role of imitation and models in the determination of gender have been revealed. Garber, like Butler, argues that drag reveals the illusory nature of gender categories: "It is epistemologically intolerable to many people – including many literary and cultural critics – that the ground should be figure. That gender exists only in representation. But this

---

57 Abel cites *Hamlet* as an example of this kind of inter-character dramatization: "there is hardly a scene in the whole work in which some character in not trying to dramatize another. Almost every important character acts at some moment like a playwright, employing a playwright's consciousness of drama to impose a certain posture or attitude on another" (2003, 119).

is the subversive secret of transvestism, that the body is not the ground, but the figure" (1992, 374). Thacker argues that Castro almost performs such a destabilization, but then corrects it:

> The possibility that with the right education any role is available to any individual is one which has the potential to undermine a hierarchy which peddles the myth of one sex being superior to another. However, Castro is not ultimately interested in maintaining the social dislocation he has portrayed, but explores instead the comic side of the relocation of the elements that have broken free from the norm.
>
> (2002, 27)

This is in part true, but I believe that the more important dislocation is that of any 'natural' or 'original' identity free from the social power structures. The resolution in marriages is completely in keeping with the theatrical mode; what is revealing here is not the outcome, but what occurs during the period of destabilization. The audience or reader is invited to laugh at these two characters who have each learned to play the role opposite of the one the gender/sex system dictates for them, but one wonders how much anxiety or uneasiness would accompany this laughter. While I agree with Thacker that the play shows gender as socially constructed, I do not agree that *La fuerza de la costumbre* undermines the gender hierarchy. Masculinity continues to occupy a position of greater worth in the binary, and Hipólita and Felix's transitions only reinforce the greater relative value and importance of masculinity. What is undermined is the supposed 'naturalness' of masculinity and femininity, not the hierarchy that values one over the other. A challenging feature of *La fuerza de la costumbre* is the simultaneous depiction of gender as malleable and unstable alongside unwavering dedication to an androcentric gender hierarchy.

IV. Gen(i)us and Gen(d)eration: the Conceits and Conceptions of Paternal *ingenio* in *La fuerza de la costumbre*

> Desde que el pecho dejó,
> si no el ser, le mudé el nombre,
> y con pensamientos de hombre
> el hábito se vistió.
>
> [lit. Since she left the breast,
> I changed her name, if not her whole being,
> and with the mind of a man,
> she put on male attire.]
>   (I. 247–250)

> Y es, en efeto, gallina.
> Siendo Moncada, ¡por Dios!,
> que es una cosa inaudita.
> Menester será volvelle
> su naturaleza misma.
> Pondré fuego en sus acciones,
> hirviendo la sangre mía
> en sus venas y en su pecho.
> Será honrada, pues es limpia,
> o sacarésela toda.
>
> [He is, in short, a chicken.
> And for a Moncada, by God,
> this is unheard of.
> It will be necessary to change him
> back to his own nature.
> I will put a fire under his actions;
> boiling my own blood
> in his veins and in his heart.
> It will be honoured, for it is pure,
> or I will shed it all myself.]
>   (I. 460–469)

As the first of the quotations above shows, when Pedro began the process of masculinizing his daughter, he granted himself the power and authority to alter not only her clothing and appearance, but also her name, thoughts (*pensamiento*) and being (*ser*). He alters her very nature, and his fecund masculinity bears fruit in the figure of Hipólita, who, upon her return to Spain, embodies the ideals of masculinity bestowed upon her by her father. In the passage in which he describes Hipólita's upbringing and the inception of her manhood (I. 231–270), he repeatedly emphasizes the fact that he did this by making her an extension of himself. When Costanza asks who the 'boy' is, Pedro replies: "Deste tronco es un renuevo, / mas ya para vos venía / bien sobrescrito el papel" ["He's a chip off the old block all right, / but he is an image of you which I have / written over with quite new material"] (I. 238–240). Avoiding gendered language, Pedro reveals that this is their child by calling her a "bud" or "sprout" from his "[tree] trunk", a product of his (male) family tree, even though the child was originally destined to blossom in the image of her mother; which is to say, she was supposed to be a woman. (In her reply, Costanza still makes a claim to Hipólita even though Pedro has in some sense cut her out of the family tree for the moment: "Un retrato miro en él / de lo que yo ser solía" [lit. "He is the very picture of / who I used to be."] (I. 241–242). It is interesting that, while saying that she sees herself in 'him', she refers to Hipólita using a male pronoun.)

Moving from botanical to bellicose metaphors of bodily extensions, Pedro recounts their constant proximity by comparing Hipólita to his sword: "y como si fuera espada / nunca la perdí del lado" ["and just as if she were my sword, / I have kept her always at my side"] (I. 253–254). Pedro compares Hipólita to his tool for attack and defense, the most powerful symbol of manhood and honor throughout *La fuerza de la costumbre*. As he tells Félix when placing Hipólita's sword at his side later in Act I, "Es la espada, al lado asida, / en el que tiene valor, / un respeto del honor / y un resguardo de la vida" ["The sword, at a man's side, / is where his valour is, / a sign of his honour / and a safeguard of his life"] (I. 611–614). By raising Hipólita "como si fuera espada," Pedro equates her with his own honor and valor, as well as his military prowess. Hipólita, raised as an extension of her father in the midst of battle, has witnessed, imitated and perfected her father's skill with the sword and other weapons. Pedro continues to articulate his view of Hipólita as his creation, of her as a branch of his own tree, in his comparison of how they fight: "pues pelea, yo lo fío, / y como yo se aventura, / si no con tan gran cordura, / a lo menos con más brío" ["She fights and attacks / just like I do, I tell you, / if not with as much wisdom, / at least with more manly spirit"] (I. 263–266). Pedro seems to delight in seeing himself mirrored in this warrior woman who has adopted every manly trait her father asked her to learn; Hipólita, literally and figuratively weaponized by him (I. 255–256), stands as a reflection of Pedro's own *hombría*. In fact he compares her to Spain's epic hero, the Cid, a figure who represents the ideal of epic Spanish manliness and military skill (I. 259–260).

His power to inscribe masculinity is so great that she lives and passes as a man, even in her own and her father's minds. He introduces her to Costanza as a "gallardo mancebo", a "handsome young man", and refers to her using a mixture of masculine and feminine adjectives and pronouns, as he begins here her transition to the feminine realm (though "leísmo" aids Pedro in largely avoiding gendered words in his description of Hipólita's education (I. 247–270), he uses the following gendered words: "desenfadado" (I. 251), "la" (I. 254), "gallardo mancebo" (I. 235); Costanza also vascilates: "él" (I. 241), "hija" (I. 244), "vestida" (I. 245b)). Characters outside of the family affirm Pedro's valor as mirrored in Hipólita; after Hipólita attacks Luis, Pedro introduces her as his daughter, to which Luis replies "En el valor lo parece" ["She takes after you in valour"] (I. 861–862). The fact that Hipólita's masculinity is fully developed (within the epic context) is problematic in so far as she is not 'biologically' male, but at the same time it is a testament to the potency of Pedro's masculinity. Pedro clearly has the power to inscribe her with a readable status as social subject, which his daughter is very successful in performing.

In *La fuerza de la costumbre*, Guillén de Castro not only explores how gender is formed and changed, but also stages a public test of the generative power of masculinity, and examines the power of paternal authority to exert creative and constitutive force in the family. At the time this play was written, it was believed that the father conferred the soul upon his offspring, while the mother contributed the body (Laquer 1990, 30). Juan Luis Vives also puts forth the idea of paternal prominence in conception: "Nature produced few sterile men, but many women, according to a wise plan of creation, because male sterility is a greater harm than female, *since the power of propagation lies more in the man than in the woman*" (2000, 267, emphasis mine). Thus, the father's seed was more determinative of the nature of his progeny.[58] According to Huarte, defective children will be

---

58 Laquer summarizes Galen and Aristotle's views on this issue: "For Galen too each parent contributes something that shapes and vivifies matter, but he insists that the female parent's seed is less powerful, less 'informing', than the male parent's because of the very nature of the female. To be female *means* to have weaker seed, seed incapable of engendering" (1990, 40); "Males, in Aristotle's account, produce *sperma*, which is the efficient cause in

born to men whose semen does not have the right humoral balance: "...si la simiente humana es de mala sustancia y no tiene el temperamento que conviene, hace el ánima vegetativa mil disparates" ["if the human seed is of poor substance and does not possess the required temperament, it will cause a thousand problems in the vegetative soul"] (1989, 295). He goes on to explain how divine perfection was only granted to the first men God created, since he made them himself, but that since then reproduction has occurred due to secondary causes and thus replicates human imperfection:

> Solos los primeros hombres que hubo en el mundo dice Platón que los hizo Dios; pero los demás nacieron por el discurso de las causas segundas, las cuales, si están bien ordenadas, hace el ánima vegetativa muy bien sus obras, y si no concurren como conviene, produce mil disparates.
>
> [Only the first men who existed in the world were created by God, according to Plato; but the others were born through the unfolding of secondary causes, which, if they are in good order, make a vegetative soul which functions well, and if they do not coincide as they should, they produce a thousand absurd results.]
>
> (1989, 295–296)

Parents bestow their imbalances and imperfections on their children: "...la enfermedad que tienen los padres al tiempo del engendrar, esa misma (dicen los médicos) sacan sus hijos después de nacidos" ["...a disease carried by the parents at the time of conception, will be seen (say the doctors) in the children after they are born"] (1989, 178).[59] Judeo-Christian doctrine holds that, though divine creation is perfect, man is the cause of imperfection after the fall (Genesis 3:17–19). Huarte applies this concept to reproductive biology here, warning that since human defects are transmuted across generations, men must take care with their own physiology, lest they produce problematic, ugly and/or improperly formed offspring.

---

generation, and females do not. Females provide instead the *catamenia*, which is the material cause and thus of an entirely different nature" (41).

59 Huarte gives the example of Adam, who produced Cain as a direct result of his suffering and discomfort after the expulsion from the Garden of Eden: "Y con tal destemplanza conoció a su mujer y engendró tan mal hombre como Caín, de tan mal ingenio, malicioso, soberbio, duro, áspero, desvergonzado, envidioso, indevoto y mal acondicionado. Y, así, comenzó a comunicar a sus descendientes esta mala salud y desorden" ["And with this imbalance, he lay with his wife and engendered such a bad man as Cain, of such poor intelligence, vicious, prideful, harsh, surly, shameless, envious, undevout, and of poor condition. And, then, this poor health and disorder began to pass to his descendents"] (1989, 178).

There are two critical points here for the analysis of paternal creation in *La fuerza de la costumbre*. First, Huarte sets up a parallel between God's power of creation and that of the father, who replicates the act of creation within his own family, albeit on a much smaller scale and lacking in divine perfection. The second is that Huarte's model holds the father, his nature, and in turn his seed responsible, as the secondary 'creator', of imperfect offspring. Georgina Dopico-Black examines the role of the woman's body as a 'transcoder' of male discourses and anxieties in early modern Spain in *Perfect Wives, Other Women* (2001). In a similar manner in *La fuerza de la costumbre*, the bodies of offspring (male, female, and everything in between) become sites of interpretation. Given the belief which held sway from antiquity until the Enlightenment that fathers had greater biological influence over children than their mothers, Hipólita and Félix's gender incongruities put Pedro's masculinity and its fertility up for examination.

Pedro's capacity to engender men is not only a biological issue, however; *La fuerza de la costumbre*'s twisted backstory creates a situation in which the test of Pedro's biology/lineage is also a test of his *wit*. Pedro takes pride in his account of how he 'created' Hipólita as a man, and seems fascinated and intrigued by the challenge of reversing the genders of his offspring (I. 319–341); he enjoys being in the role of the 'creator' within his family, possessing the authority and ability to name and rename, to construct and deconstruct his subjects. Pedro takes on the role of author of his family, and his 'authority' as a man and as a father, gives him the right (and obligation) to form his children in a way that upholds his honor and that of his ancestors. The words 'author' and 'authority' derive from the Latin *augere*, meaning to increase, originate or promote; the *OED* traces the word 'author' through a Middle English meaning of "a person who invents or causes something"; the first definition of 'authority' in the *OED* reads "the power or right to give orders, make decisions, and enforce obedience". Thus, the ideas of creation, invention, power, authority, and enforcement are entangled etymologically.

Acts of biological reproduction and intellectual production are frequently linked in Huarte's *Examen de ingenios*, in language itself (concept/conception, creativity/creation, genius/generation, *poeisis*, to name a few) not to mention in literature's most famous brain child ("hijo del entendimiento"), Miguel de Cervantes' Don Quijote.[60] Huarte connects *ingenio* with engendering: "Y esto

---

60 Miguel de Cervantes employs this metaphor in the prologue of the first volume of *El ingenioso hidalgo don Quijote de la Mancha*: "Desocupado lector: sin juramento me podrás creer que quisiera que este libro, como hijo del entendimiento, fuera el más hermoso, el más

baste en cuanto al nombre *ingenio*, el cual desciende de este verbo *ingenero*, que quiere decir engendrar dentro de sí una figura entera y verdadera que represente al vivo la naturaleza del sujeto cuya es la ciencia que se aprende" ["And that is enough about the term wit, which comes from the word engineer, which means to engender within oneself a complete and true figure which brings to life the nature of the subject which pertains to the science being studied"] (1989, 193–94, italics from original). Semen was associated with the brain, resulting in the theory that "conception is for the male to have an idea, an artistic or artisanal conception, in the brain-uterus of the female" (Laquer 42).[61] Establishing this link between the biological and the intellectual is essential to the aims of Huarte's *Examen de ingenios*, since maximizing the potential of the faculties of the rational soul is predicated on proper reproduction and humoral nature. *Entendimiento*, the highest form of Huartean wit, "tiene virtud y fuerzas naturales de producir y parir dentro de sí un hijo, al cual llaman los filósofos naturales *noticia* o *concepto*" ["has natural virtue and strength to produce and birth offspring within itself, which the natural philosophers call *knowledge* or *concepts*"] (188). The reproductive independence of *entendimiento*, which inseminates and then gives birth to itself, means that this faculty can generate "hijos y nietos" ["children and grandchildren"] without the influence of an 'other' (187–188). Laquer investigates the political and intellectual implications of fatherhood in the one-sex model, concluding that "being male and being a father, having what it takes to produce the more powerful seed, is the ascendancy of the mind over the senses, of order over disorder, legitimacy over illegitimacy. Thus the inability of women to conceive within themselves becomes an instance – among many other things – of the relative weakness of her mind" (1990, 58–62; 59). Valeria Finucci's *The Manly Masquerade: Masculinity, Paternity and Castration in the Italian Renaissance* argues that, because paternity could not be confirmed in the same way that maternity could, "the issue of who contributed what was important, not because it was biological but because it was political: woman needed to be postulated inferior and man as superior,

---

gallardo y más discreto que pudiera imaginarse. Pero no he podido yo contravenir al orden de naturaleza; que en ella cada cosa engendra su semejante" ["Idle reader: thou mayest believe me without any oath that I would this book, as it is the child of my brain, were the fairest, gayest, and cleverest that could be imagined. But I could not counteract Nature's law that everything shall beget its like…"] (1997, 50; 2001, 11).
61 Early medical philosophers postulated that "sperm, a foam much like the froth on the sea, was first refined out of blood; it passed to the brain; from the brain it made its way back through the spinal marrow, the kidneys, the testicles, and into the penis" (Laquer 1990, 35).

no matter what a scientific investigation might prove" (2003, 12); in order to maintain the political force of paternity, "legal and philosophical practices provided whatever links were missing in the medical and religious discourses on reproduction" (2003, 28). In this gender hierarchy, the father has a great deal more to prove in the procreative act; questions of biological generation are bound up with those of intellectual creation, authority and virility.

In this context, the masculinity issues of both of his children (in Hipólita, too masculine, and in Félix, not masculine enough) are public reflections of Pedro's masculinity and honor. Within the world of his family, Pedro is the inscriber of souls, of social subjects, and the men he succeeds or fails to sire are the screen onto which the signs of his own masculinity are projected for all of society to see. Just as the stakes are imbalanced for Hipólita and Félix in their gender transitions, Costanza and Pedro's creative abilities are not put to an equal test. When Pedro declares his intention to "hacer, / para que el mundo se asombre, / vos una mujer de un hombre, / yo un hombre de una mujer" [lit. "make, / for the amazement of the world, / you a woman from a man, / and I a man from a woman"] (I. 332–334), he proclaims himself as engaged in an act of *poeisis*, of creation. Although in this passage he assigns Costanza the parallel task of making "una mujer de un hombre" ["a woman from a man"] (I. 333), masculinity and femininity do not carry the same stakes, as has been shown, nor do they have an equal power of creation in the seventeenth-century medical and philosophical framework. The feminine role in this case is not to *make* anything, but to unmake, to weaken, to emasculate the father's hyper-masculine creation. In all of Costanza's coaching and teaching of Hipólita, she never refers to herself as engaged in an act of creation.

In the Name of the Father: Félix's Transition
Pedro has already tested the potency of his masculinity to replicate itself by raising Hipólita to be an exemplary soldier, but Félix presents a still greater examination: now Pedro must engender a son with the weight of habit and twenty years of effeminizing upbringing working against him. Costanza's role in Félix's effeminacy is both a challenge to Pedro, in that she has instilled bad habits in Félix, and a protection of the de Moncada masculinity, in so far as Costanza provides an 'other' who can be blamed for training Félix's 'natural' masculinity out of him. Pedro's anxious questioning of the Tutor about Félix's 'nature' implies that this problem may have been altogether unsolvable if Félix's 'true nature' were the root cause of his effeminacy:

> ...dime tú, que le has criado,
> si el quedar así encogido
> don Félix, mi hijo, ¿ha sido
> naturaleza o cuidado?
>   ¿Nace de su mismo ser
> lo que en él su madre ha hecho?
> ¿Tiene valor en el pecho
> que revienta sin querer?
>   ¿Por qué pasión se lastima?
> ¿De qué temores se espanta?
> ¿Qué pensamientos levanta?
> ¿Con qué inclinación se anima?
>   Y di verdad.
>
> [You tell me, since you raised him,
> if these cowardly qualities
> in Don Félix, my son, are due to
> his nature or her choice?
> Does it have roots in his own nature,
> the way his mother has made him?
> Has he any valour in his heart
> that bursts out unexpectedly?
> By what passion is he stirred?
> What frightens him?
> What does he think about?
> What interests excite him?
> And tell the truth.]
>
> (I. 351–363a)

This uneasy investigation into Félix's potential for masculinity is informed by the legal, patriotic and moral consequences of effeminacy in Spanish society, both for Félix as an individual and for the father as his creator. The tutor confirms that Félix had shown, as a young child, "señales [...] / de caballeroso brío" ["signs / of a noble nature"] but that Costanza changed him through the power of habit (I. 379–394). The text's insistence on the mother's intentional interference in the development of Félix's masculinity protects Pedro's masculine lineage, meaning that the son's aberration is not judged to be the result of Pedro's failing, at least not in a direct biological/ seminal sense. Vives cautions widows against raising their own children, especially without the help of a surrogate father-figure, since the overindulgence to which mothers are prone is known to engender morally corrupt children when left unchecked by a masculine influence.[62] Costanza admits to 'shackling' Félix with long garments: "nunca su ánimo dispuse / a que mudara el vestido, / y el hábito largo ha sido / grillos que a los pies le puse" ["I never encouraged him to / dress like an adult, / and this long habit has been like / shackles I have placed on his feet"] (I. 295–299). The mention of the "grillos" further supports the idea that Félix's effeminacy was imposed in order to contradict his nature. The female influence on children can be dangerous, even rendering a child unlovable as an adult according to Vives: "Therefore, much more depends on the mother in the formation of the children's character than one would think. She can make them either very good or very bad" (2000, 270; 275). Pedro calls Costanza "causadora desta afrenta" ["the cause of this outrage"] (II. 893), and accuses her of having "infected" their son, equating Félix's effeminacy with contagious physical malady: "es contagioso este mal, / y vos se lo habéis pegado" ["this malady is contagious, / and it is you who has infected him"] (II. 411–412).[63]

Three changes are made to initiate this transformation: 1) clothing (I. 311–315; 335–341), 2) the transfer of the sword (I. 327–328), and 3) proximity to Pedro (I. 323–326; this mirrors his masculinization of Hipólita, I. 253–254). In addition to these symbolic and biological invocations of masculinity, Pedro also appeals to the authority of his lineage: "que la casa de Moncada / no consiente hombres mujeres" ["for the House of Moncada / does not allow any girly men"] (I. 329–330). The sword carries great symbolic power in *La fuerza de la costumbre* (and was a symbol and authenticator of lineage via the chivalric tradition, taken up in other plays such as *La vida es sueño*).

---

62 Juan Luis Vives has the following views on widows as mothers: "We often see it happen that those brought up by a widow are less obedient than they should be to those to whom they owe obedience, spoiled by the excessive indulgence of the widow. Thus, the expression 'a widow's child' has become a proverb among many peoples, especially our own. It is used of young men who are badly brought up, of corrupt, insolent youths who lead a morally depraved life. I should counsel a widow to place the care of the upbringing of her children upon some virtuous and sensible man, for, out of blind love, she thinks she is treating her children too severely, even when she is far too lenient with them" (2000, 315).
63 In Renaissance Italy, women were seen as carriers of disease, especially during menstruation (Finucci 2003, 22); effeminate men and those accused of sodomy were, according to Perry, even kept separate from other prisoners in the Royal Prison of Seville for fear that they could infect others (1990, 123–24).

In this play, masculine honor and valor are defined by the sword and a man's ability to maneuver it;[64] this is shown in masculine characters' use of the phallic tool, in Félix's martial impotence, and Hipólita's unabashed brandishing of her weapon.[65] Félix has two failed attempts at sword-wielding in Act II, the fencing lesson (II. 268–404), and the altercation with Otavio (II. 784–803), both of which are followed by violent and damnatory rebukes by Pedro. Though this is not a 'wife murder' play, many parallel concerns surface within Pedro's relationship with his son. The father reminds his son of the gravity of the situation: "Hijo mío, ten valor; / mira que en peligro pones / nuestra honra" ["My son, be brave; / you must see that you put all our / honour at risk"] (II. 465–467a). It is unacceptable to Pedro that the masculinity he was endowed with by his ancestors should come to be perverted in his offspring, the product of his seed:

> ¿Qué vileza te acobarda?
> ¿Qué cobardía te vence?
> ¿Tú eres Moncada, y ordenas
> vilezas con que me afrentes?
> ¿No sabes por qué vertientes
> llegó mi sangre a tus venas?
> ¿No has visto en tantos papeles
> dónde y cómo está fundada
> la gran casa de Moncada,
> que tiene por chapiteles
> que compiten con el sol,
> tantos Hugos y Gastones,
> Pedros, Guillenes, Ramones,
> honra del suelo Español?
> Siendo tal, mucho me aflijo
> de que tú, con afrentarte,

---

64 For example, Pedro invokes his public honor when he boasts to Leonor and Luis that his "sword" is respected in Italy, Flanders and France (I. 763–767).
65 Luis refers to both Hipólita and Félix as swords: talking about Hipólita, he says "es como la misma espada" [lit. "She is like the sword itself"] (II. 105). He uses the sword as a symbol of Félix's strenth in lineage when asked what he thinks of Félix: "Eso dejo a la esperanza / del tiempo, que aunque criado / entre regalos tan mal, / él es de tan buen metal / que lucirá bien templado" ["That one I leave to the hope / of passing time, for though he was raised / spoiled by such poor playthings, / he is of such good metal that he will / ultimately shine when polished"] (II. 128–132).

la derribes por la parte
que yo la sustento, hijo.

[What baseness makes you such a coward?
What cowardice overcomes you?
You are a Moncada, yet you dare
affront me with this base behaviour?
Do you not know that the blood
of our ancestors runs in your veins?
Have you not read all our histories
and learned where and how
the great house of Moncada was founded,
whose spires rise up
to compete with the sun,
men such as the Hugos and Gastons,
Pedros, Guilléns, Ramóns,
the honour of the Spanish land?
With this in mind, it afflicts me
that you, bringing shame on yourself,
tear down our great house
just as I am trying to build it up, son.]
(II. 359–376)

Instead of being a sprout from Pedro's tree as Hipólita was, Félix's effeminacy threatens to uproot Pedro's masculinity entirely. The genesis of the de Moncada line is stressed with the list of names. The lack of *hombría* threatens not only the individual, but the family as well: Pedro fumes, "Que el quedar sin heredero / será menos daño en mí / que ver esta mengua en ti" [lit. "To be left without an heir / will be less harmful to me / than seeing this stain in you"] (II. 389–391).

This test of paternal authority and fecundity is met with various attempts by the father to doctor his inadequate progeny: "Si salgo / buen maestro, no haré poco" ["If I teach him a lesson, it will be no small feat"] (II.579b–580); "Ya vale la industria mía" [lit. "My cunning is starting to pay off"] (II. 589); "Si yo curo cobardías / seré médico famoso" ["If I can cure cowardice, / I could be a famous doctor"] (II. 627–628). Pedro has a minor success in extracting the desired performance from Félix when he sets a trap to force Félix to defend himself (II. 471–485a; 538–591), but soon after, Félix's stunted virility is publicly exposed and mocked by Otavio:

Félix:	Dicha he tenido.
Otavio:	A venir yo sin espada,
	dicha, y grande, hubiera sido.
	(Quítasele de las manos.)
Félix:	Mira que soy...
	(Quiere meter mano DON FÉLIX y no puede.)
Otavio:	Eres nada,
	y esta prenda yo la quiero.
Félix:	¡Espera!
Otavio:	Harás maravillas.
Félix:	No puedo...
Hipólita:	¡Oh, vil caballero!
Otavio:	Ten envainado el acero
	y trata de hacer vainillas,
	o lleva siempre un criado
	que tire para poder
	sacalla; mas he pensado
	que el valor debe de ser
	el que tienes envainado.
Félix:	No puedo...
Otavio:	En pudiendo acuda,
	amigo, a herirme con ella;
	mas no podrá, pues sin duda
	tendrá espada tan doncella
	vergüenza de andar desnuda.
[Félix:	It's my good fortune.
Otavio:	If I had come here without my sword,
	it would have been your greatest fortune.
	(He snatches it from his hands.)
Félix:	See here that I am...
	(He tries to draw his sword, but cannot do it.)
Otavio:	You are nothing,
	and this is the prize that I want.
Félix:	Wait!
Otavio:	I'm sure you'll do something amazing.
Félix:	I cannot...
Hipólita:	Oh, unworthy gentleman!

Otavio:	Keep your sword in its scabbard and go back to your knitting, or bring a servant everywhere with you who can get it out for you; I've always thought that courage is what you've got stuck there in that sheath.
Félix:	I cannot…
Otavio:	If you can, then do it, my friend, wound me with it; but you will not, for doubtless such a shy, maidenly sword will be ashamed to be seen naked.] (II. 785b–803)

Otavio's negation of Félix's being ("Eres nada"), confirmed by Félix's own admissions ("No puedo […] No puedo,") forces Félix either to definitively become a man or, as Pedro suggests, to sacrifice his life to salvage the honor of the family (II. 923–928). By effeminizing Félix's phallus and verbally castrating him, Otavio calls into question whether Pedro's child is a son or a eunuch. The exasperated father exclaims, "¡Vive Dios que he de sacarte / cuanta sangre tienes mía!" ["By God, I'll spill whatever blood / of mine is in your veins!"] (II. 847–848). Pedro's threats of a violent blood-letting of his son if he is unable to assume his masculine role anticipate Gutierre's obsession with finding a medical cure for his honor, resulting in the bleeding to death of his wife, Mencía, in Calderón's *El médico de su honra* [*The Physician of his Honor*] (1637). Hipólita's virile lust for her sword further shames her brother, as his failure arouses her *brío* and commands her to rectify this problem on her brother's behalf (although she is impeded in doing so by her mother, Leonor, and Pedro (II. 860–872)).

Félix's defeat of Otavio and capture of his sword in Act III win him recognition as a man; he avenges the public exposure of his "espada doncella" ["virginal sword"], by taking possession of his detractor's phallic symbol, thereby proving his own. He reiterates Otavio's insult as a way of tricking him into a more isolated area, so that his bashful sword won't feel "ashamed of being naked" (III. 715); he warns his rival that the period of his sword's celibacy is now over, when Otavio mocks his sword's 'virginity':

Otavio:	Grande la debe tener;
	que es muy doncella sospecho.
Félix:	Yo confío que en tu pecho
	ha de dejallo de ser.
[Otavio:	It must be big;
	though I suspect it may be a virgin.
Félix:	I'm confident that she won't be after she
	thrusts into your chest.]

(III. 716–719)

Félix bolsters his newfound manliness by killing a bailiff who tries to arrest him. The Captain serves the important role of bearing witness to the birth of Félix's honor: for his honor to be fully restored and socially validated, it has to be voiced by a witness, a member of the public body in which reputation rests.[66] Félix further publicizes his newfound masculinity and honor by returning Leonor's glove to her in the presence of other men; the additional gifts of Otavio's sword and hat broadcast his redemption through the defeat of the rival who mocked him. Félix's being is finally transformed, and he is accepted into the paternal body: "Entra agora en mis entrañas" [(lit.) "Enter now into my entrails"] (III. 958). Pedro has successful inscribed a legible masculine subject, and with 'help' from Luis, Hipólita has ceased to defy the binary, adopting the feminine role. As the father, Pedro takes responsibility for this: "Su naturaleza misma / volver a mis hijos pude," ["To their own nature / I changed my children back"] now that his paternity, authority and honor have been reinstated (III. 994–995). Pedro's ability to sire men has been doubly proven.

Genre Trouble: Hipólita Unmade

Hipólita's change in genre causes almost as much trouble as her gender transition; in fact one could argue that her change in setting causes the gender trouble, as she had achieved subject status as a soldier in the epic world she was raised in, and it is the change of context that renders her masculinity unacceptable. While there are literary precedents for warrior women, how does this figure translate into the urban setting, into the realm of courtly love, of Petrarchan poetics, once Hipólita returns to Zaragoza? A particularly provocative manifestation of Hipólita's genre/gender trouble

---

66 See Pitt-Rivers: "Honour […] is only irrevocably committed by attitudes expressed in the presence of witnesses, the representatives of public opinion" (1977, 6–7).

is her response to courtly love tropes. Her negative reaction to the poetics of courtship shows that she rejects both the feminine role of inspiring and receiving those poetic tributes, and also rejects the male role that produces them. While fighting with Luis during the street brawl in Act I, he counts her beauty among her weapons, invoking Petrarch's "dolce et amata mia nemica" ("My sweet and beloved enemy", Sonnet 254, v. 2) motif:

> Tente, señora, ¡por Dios!
> No me mates, rendireme;
> que aunque con la espada tiras,
> pero con los ojos hieres,
> con mucha ventaja riñes.
> [...]
> Ya me ha muerto tu hermosura,
> pero ha sido dulcemente.
>
> [Wait, my lady, by God!
> Do not kill me, I will surrender;
> though you strike with the sword
> you wound with the eyes;
> you fight with a great advantage.
> [...]
> Your beauty has killed me
> but it has been a sweet death.]
> (I. 783–787; 793–794)[67]

However, these praises irritate Hipólita: "Deja dulzuras aparte, / que me cansan y me ofenden, / y riñe sin cortesías" ["Leave these sweetnesses aside, / for they tire me and offend me, / and fight without flattery"] (I. 795–797). Hipólita refocuses their exchange on the physical fighting, and attempts to obstruct the metaphorical hijacking of the language of her domain, battle.

---

67 Sonnet 61 of Petrarch's *Canzoniere* is exemplary of the contradiction of the "sweet pain" of love as battle or injury that Luis is invoking: "Benedetto sia 'l giorno e 'l mese et l'anno / el la stagione e' l tempo et l'ora e 'l punto / e 'l bel paese e 'l loco ov' io fui giunto / da' duo begli occhi che legato m'ànno; / et benedetto il primo dolce affanno / ch'i' ebbi ad esser con Amor congiunto, / et l'arco e le saette ond' i' fui punto, / et le piaghe che 'nfin al cor mi vanno" (v. 1–8); "Oh blessèd be the day, the month, the year, / the season and the time, the hour, the instant, / the gracious countryside, the place where I / was struck by those two lovely eyes that bound me; / and blessèd be the first sweet agony / I felt when I found myself bound to Love, / the bow and all the arrows that have pierced me, / the wounds that reach the bottom of my heart" (Petrarch/Musa 1999, pp. 96–97).

She rebuffs love rhetoric again with Marcelo and Otavio's advances in Act II:

Marcelo:	Pienso que amanece agora.
Otavio:	Soles son luces tan bellas.
Hipólita:	¡Qué cansada está el aurora, el sol, la luna y estrellas destos requiebros, señora!
[Marcelo:	Dawn is breaking now.
Otavio:	Two suns radiate beautiful light.
Hipólita:	How tired are the dawn, the sun, the moon, and the stars of these blandishments, my lady!]

(II. 669–673)

This rejection of the Petrarchan poetics of love does not go unnoticed; Marcelo and Otavio joke about the difficulty of a courtship in which gentle words are useless, and the love object only responds to *desafíos*, challenges to violence.

Otavio:	Si la hablas tiernamente, no responderá jamás.
Marcelo:	Si no es que la desafío, ¿qué he de hacer?
[Otavio:	If you try to sweet talk her, she'll never speak to you again.
Marcelo:	If not to challenge her to a fight, what else can I do?]

(II. 682–685)

When Luis and Marcelo fight over her fallen cuff, she retorts "Si es mío, ¿qué hacéis los dos?" ["If it's mine, what are you two doing?"] (II. 779), clearly misunderstanding or rejecting the concept of "dulces prendas" ["sweet spoils"] of courtly love lyric.[68] These exchanges appear to confuse and anger her; she resents the rhetorical appropriation of combat motifs for romantic pursuits. Hipólita uses the vocabulary of battle in a very literal way, yet she is made by Castro to enact the metaphors and tropes she rejects. Guillén de Castro toys with the literary paradox erected by the male courtly love rhetoric, which on one hand empowers woman as a quasi-warrior, and on the other woos the

---

68 See Garcilaso de la Vega, Sonnet X (2001, v. 1).

silent woman with uncharacteristically gentle words from men. *La fuerza de la costumbre* exploits the overlap of these discourses to comedic effect: Marcelo and Otavio joke with Luis about the bodily dangers of his new love, which "ha entrado / con gentiles cuchilladas" [(lit.) "has entered / with pleasant stabs"] (II. 21b–22). (The joke also hints at the threat of effeminization Hipólita poses to Luis, via the references to penetration.) Luis maintains the play on the bellicose metaphor in his response, claiming that in his skirmish with Hipólita he surrendered his soul as the spoils of battle: "pero sus divinos ojos / hicieron más sangre en mí /que la espada, a quien rendí /toda el alma por despojos" ["but her divine eyes / have shed more of my blood / than her sword, to which I yielded / my entire soul as the spoils of love"] (II. 25–28).[69]

There is a queer flavor to the instant attraction between Hipólita and Luis, Félix and Leonor, well before the de Moncada siblings have begun to convincingly perform their newly assigned genders.[70] Hipólita falls in love with Luis by testing his skill with the sword, while still performing a largely masculine identity: "Prueba conmigo la espada / que con los demás valiente / se ha mostrado" ["Test me with the sword / that has proven its valour / with the others"] (I. 773–775b). *La fuerza de la costumbre* shows a "woman" falling in love with a man via masculine codes of evaluation. Hipólita measures Luis against the values of her epic heritage; her discourse about Luis is homoerotic as she praises the traits of 'her own' gender, masculinity, in him. Luis's attraction to her is less overtly homoerotic given his more skilled deployment of the rhetoric of courtly love, the fact that he has the supposed 'truth' of her female 'birth sex' on his side, and the early modern cultural fascination with masculine women. Hipólita, however, claims to her mother that she sees Luis through the eyes of a man, not with the 'cares' of a woman, and is drawn to him for his valor and honorable demeanor:

---

69 Compare to Petrarch 133: "Dagli occhi vostri uscio 'l colpo mortale / contra cui non mi val tempo né loco; / da voi sola procede (et parvi un gioco) / il sole e 'l foco e 'l vento ond' io son tale. / I pensier son saette, e 'l viso un sole, / e 'l desir foco; e 'nseme con quest'arme / mi punge Amor, m'abbaglia et mi destrugge" (v. 5–11); "From out your eyes there came the mortal blow / against which time and place are of no use; from you alone there comes (you take it lightly) / the sun, fire, and wind that make me such. / Your thoughts are arrows and your face a sun, / desire, fire: with these arms all at once / Love pierces me, he dazzles and melts me" (Petrarch/ Musa 1999, 218–219).

70 Although the issue of homoerotic desire caused by cross-dressing plots had been dismissed as insignificant by critics (such as McKendrick (1974) and Bravo-Villlasante (1976)) for many years, that tide has shifted since Bradbury's article on the topic (1982). Since then, further studies have emerged, including Stroud (1991; 2007), Fothergill-Payne (2000), and Velasco (2000).

> Como le vi tan valiente,
> tan cortés y tan honrado...
>> vile barrer una calle
>> de hombres con tal destreza,
>> tanto brío y fortaleza,
>> que aficionaba el miralle.
>> Vile a mi padre tener
>> tan hidalga cortesía;
>> vile de la espada mía
>> defenderse y no ofender.
>> Cobrele afición, y así
>> quise miralle mejor,
>> porque es imán el valor,
>> a lo menos para mí;
>>> *mas no, por Dios, con cuidado*
>>> *de mujer.*
>
> [Because I saw that he was valiant,
> so courteous and so honourable...
> I saw him clear a street
> full of men with such skill,
> so much spirit and strength,
> I had to just stare at him in awe.
> I saw him treat my father
> with such noble courtesy; I saw
> him defend himself from my sword
> without a single offence to me.
> I have come to admire him, and so
> I wanted to take a closer look,
> because valour is a magnet,
> at least for me; *but never,*
> *by God, did I look at him the way*
> *a woman would.*]
>> (II. 187–202a, emphasis mine)

She sketches his male exemplarity, ("cortés", "honrado", "brío y fortaleza", "espada", "valor"), which she had occasion to scrutinize when she challenged him (as a man) and he responded in an ideal (male) way. Though her mother (and the audience/reader) may see it differently, she sees herself as an equal to Luis; in a relationship of 'like to like'. She admits to admiration and attraction, but claims that these reactions are rooted in her masculinity. In Act III, Luis forces Hipólita to confront her difference, invalidating her claim to be a woman "only in name".[71] After Galván and Inés trick her into believing that Luis has betrayed and made a fool of her by marrying another woman, Hipólita ambushes Luis, disguised as a man. At this point, she crosses a genre boundary by becoming a hybrid of the warrior she was raised as and the typical seventeenth-century stage transvestite, the *mujer vestida de hombre*, who disguises herself as a man to resolve a love-story gone awry; this is the first and only instance of 'stage transvestism' in the whole play. As Bravo-Villasante argues, part of the male attraction to the figure of the manly warrior woman could be the hope of one day coming to dominate her.[72] Luis takes this unwarranted attack (he has been completely faithful to her) as the occasion to strip Hipólita of her volatile masculinity once and for all. He code-switches as well, still speaking through the language of battle, but now with real intention to dominate his future wife. He first hints at his purpose in his designation of the weapons for the duel: "serán / estas mismas que traemos" ["let's / use those that we carry with us"] (III. 664–665); then openly states his desire to assert his masculinity through force and violence: "Y allí verás que soy hombre / para más de una mujer. / Has de probar, vive Dios, / de mis fuerzas los extremos" ["There you will see that I am man enough / for one who is more than a woman; / You will taste, by God, / the full force of my strength"] (III. 674–677). Hipólita and Luis are seen heading toward Luis' chosen location for the duel, both acknowledging that Luis has some kind of trick up his sleeve.[73]

---

71 At the beginning of the duel, Hipólita boasts: "y allí que tengo has de ver / de mujer no más del nombre" ["and there you will see / that only in name am I a woman"] (III. 672–673).
72 "El porqué de esta admiración y entusiasmo que el hombre siente por la mujer heroica y guerrera, vestida varonilmente, quizá resida en el pensamiento secreto e íntimo de suponer un día vencida por ellos la arrogancia de la heroína y sometido su independiente y libre espíritu" ["The cause of this admiration and enthusiasm that man feels for the heroic warrior woman, dressed as a man, perhaps resides in the secret and intimate thought of imagining, some day, the arrogance of the heroine conquered, and her independent and free spirit subdued"] (1976, 22).
73 They both reference the imminent trick in a series of alternating asides: "Hipólita: (*Aparte*) Él me engaña, ya lo veo, / pero no lo quiero ver. / Luis: (*Aparte*) Ella se deja llevar / de mi engañosa corriente. / Hipólita: (*Aparte*) Engaña discretamente / el que se deja engañar" ["HIPÓLITA: (*Aside*) He is deceiving me, I see that, / but I do not want to see it. / LUIS: (*Aside*) She lets herself be carried away / in the swift current of my deceit. / HIPÓLITA: (*Aside*) One can deceive discreetly / by allowing oneself to be deceived"] (III. 682–687).

The next time Hipólita appears on stage, it is "de mujer" ["as a woman"] (III. 770), walking with "lead feet" (III. 769).[74] She confesses the details of her transformation to her mother:

> Forcejamos un gran rato,
> cada uno por vencer;
> mas es jabón en la yerba
> el rocío; resbalé,
> y dando traspiés, caí
> de mi enemigo a los pies.
> Y aun esto no fuera nada,
> pero después de caer
> hizo, ¡ay, madre!, cierta cosa,
> que nunca la imaginé.
> Revolviome toda el alma
> y mudome todo el ser,
> diciendo, 'para que vea,
> pues, es mujer, que lo es.'
> Creí con tal desengaño
> que lo soy, y ya no sé
> sino llorar tiernamente
> su ausencia; quiérole bien,
> y en efeto, madre mía,
> desde entonces soy mujer.

> [We wrestled for a long time,
> each one the victor in turns;
> but the grass was slippery as soap
> from the dew; I slipped,
> and stumbled, I fell,
> at the feet of my enemy.
> And as if that were not enough,
> right after I fell
> he did, oh mother, something,
> that I never could have imagined.

---

74 This reverses the typical order of the cross-dressing plots, in which women frequently disguise themselves as men *after* sexual initiation. Pitt-Rivers goes so far as to say that dishonored women *become* men: "The parable could not be clearer: a woman stripped of her honour becomes a man. Her honour restored, she reverts to her true sex" (1977, 45).

He stirred my soul,
and changed my whole being,
saying, 'let the one
who is a woman see that she is.'
I understood, I saw so clearly
that I am, and now I do not know
how to do other than weep tenderly
and miss him; I love him so well,
and so, my mother,
since that moment I am a woman.]
(III. 846–865)

Luis asserts his manly power over Hipólita and brings about her betrayal of her own masculinity by defeating her in combat, knocking her to the ground and then raping her. This conquest of Hipólita's sword and body is the definitive emasculating act which causes her to renounce the phallus. I strongly disagree with McKendrick that "love effects this transformation and it cannot be deterred or deceived by upbringing" (1974, 102). She sees love as "the essence of femininity," arguing that "Guillén de Castro differs from other seventeenth-century dramatists only in his realistic inclusion of the precipitating power of sex" (102). This is, however, not an act of love, but rather of violence and dominance. At this point, the play takes a dark ideological turn, by indicating that this non-consensual sex act has the power to cause Hipólita not only to put down her weapons, but also to unlearn how to use them, and to adopt a position of fear, pain, and physical weakness. By making Hipólita aware of her supposed anatomical inferiority or vulnerability, Luis asserts the dominance of 'true' phallic masculinity and forces her to assume the sexually inferior position assigned to women by seventeenth century society. As her future husband, it is in his interest and purview to do so.

Through the sexual conquest, Luis revokes Hipólita's claim to the power of the epic figure which was bestowed upon her by her upbringing as a soldier; he remakes her gender and genre. Laquer explains that in Roman culture, the passive, penetrated party in male homosexual intercourse was shamed, effeminized, while the penetrating partner's masculinity was not at risk (1990, 53). This defeat and penetration emasculate Hipólita, invalidating her claim to masculinity; such an event would have been shameful to any 'man' within this hierarchy of gender. While Iphis is turned into a boy on his wedding night, restoring hetero-normative order just in time for marriage and sex (Ovid 2004, IX. 666–797), Hipólita is 'turned into a woman' at a moment that would have emasculated her regardless of her sex.[75] If she were a man, this would be the moment of *pecado nefando*, sodomy, for which the Inquisition burned people alive.[76] The undoing of her manhood occurs through the act that would have most threatened hetero-sexual law, invalidating her masculine gender just in time to validate her as a citizen (woman) protected by the law.[77]

Luis undoes Pedro's creation and remakes Hipólita as a woman, finally casting Pedro's masculinity out of her, while replacing the loss by inserting himself into the family as husband and son-in-law. This competition of masculinities between Pedro and Luis in the figure of Hipólita is resolved by the wedding, which permanently links Pedro and Luis, and ascribes to each man the honor of the other's lineage.[78] The body of the woman, in this scenario, becomes a discursive field in which questions of power, hierarchy and social affiliation are resolved.

In the case of Eleno/a de Céspedes, the Inquisition went to great lengths to enforce conformity of the body to the social position, and the lack of the virile member definitively precluded Eleno/a from placing him/herself in the category of 'man'. Vollendorf sees in the court's punishment of Eleno/a a prohibition of self-fashioning: "Up against the living example of the defendant, who successfully negotiated female and male identities for more than forty years, the Inquisition denied that identity was negotiable, particularly for individuals who appropriated the benefits of the dominant ethnicity, class, religion, or sex" (2005, 27). Burshatin argues that in the Eleno/a case,

> The central question shifted to one of discursive affiliation. The issue was not whether a woman could turn into a hermaphrodite, but who would

---

75 See, for example, Huarte (1989, 609) and Perry (1990, 126–127) on the connection between effeminacy and homosexuality.
76 Perry has studied the fervor with which sodomites were prosecuted (1990, 123–127), finding that sodomy was an almost exclusively male crime, with the implication that "the real crime of sodomy was not in ejaculating nonprocreatively, nor in the use of the anus, but in requiring a male to play the passive 'female' role and in violating the physical integrity of a male recipient's body. In this view, females only could be receptacles for semen, their biological integrity 'naturally' inviting this invasion of their inner physical space" (125).
77 Catalina/Antonio de Erauso was only granted the right to continue dressing as a man on the condition that he refrain from sexual contact with members of either sex, and in order to achieve this allowance, he had to have his virginity verified by the church and the King (Mendieta 2009, 167).
78 Gayle Rubin's analysis of the role of women in kinship structures is helpful here: "If it is women who are being transacted, then it is the men who give and take them who are linked, the woman being a conduit of a relationship rather than a partner to it" (1997, 37).

write the cultural program within which 'the biology of sexual difference is embedded' (Laquer 19). The Inquisitors and their experts asserted the privilege of patriarchy when they denied that Eleno's body contained any evidence that the internal male organs have appeared in the past.

(1999, 450).

A similar question of authority over the 'cultural program' is at play in Hipólita's case. Hipólita's verbal claims to masculinity are invalidated in Guillén de Castro's drama, just as Eleno/a's assertion of masculinity was refuted by the court of Toledo when s/he was determined to be lacking a phallus. Luis is the enforcer of the patriarchal power that has the authority to reconstitute Hipólita as 'woman'.

After Hipólita's violent sexual initiation, she renounces the phallus: "Ya me espanta un arcabuz, / ya para mí no ha de haber / tratar en cosas de acero" ["Now I am frightened of a harquebus; / I shall no longer / deal with things of steel"] (III. 782–784) and exchanges it for the feminine symbol of virginal blood: "ya me duele, si me pica / la punta de un alfiler, / y si hay sangre, será cierto / el desmayarme después" ["Now it hurts me if I prick / my finger with a pin, / and if there is blood, I will certainly / faint right away"] (III. 786–789). Rape leading to transformation has classical antecedents; Marcia Welles cites fifty rapes or "sexual extortions" in Ovid's *Metamorphoses*: "The poet's landscapes of sylvan beauty provide the setting for terrifying pursuit – both venatic and erotic – and death, either literal or by metamorphosis into a non-human form. Places of refuge become sites of violence" (2000, 1). Hipólita describes her new state as a 'death' and loss of the soul, now reproducing the tropes she had previously rejected:

> Madre, ¡mis ojos me han muerto!
> ¡Atrevimiento cruel!
> A don Luis inclinados,
> tanto dellos me fié
> que por ellos llevó el alma.
>
> [Mother, my eyes have killed me!
> Cruel daring!
> They inclined toward Don Luis,
> I trusted them so completely that
> he took my soul out through them.]
> (III. 806–810)

This recalls Luis' poetic "loss of soul" at II. 25–28, but also has a more literal ring of defeat. Though it is surprising to a modern reader that this act cause Hipólita to love Luis even more, Renaissance concepts of gender support such a view. In his discussion of perfection in women and men in *The Book of the Courtier*, Signor Gasparo argues that a woman continues to love her first lover (whereas a man comes to hate his) "because in such an act the woman takes on perfection from the man, and the man imperfections from the woman; and that everyone naturally loves what makes him perfect" (Castiglione 2002, 159). In many cases, retribution for rape called for the attacker to marry the victim. Thus, as harsh and violent as this 'corrective' rape may be, it fulfills the Renaissance belief that women achieved greater perfection by being subjects of men.

The Iberian poetic tradition plays a crucial role in the passage in which Hipólita discusses her sexual subjugation and gender/genre transformation with her mother. Hipólita tells Costanza that Luis gained the upper hand by tricking her into moving their fight to behind an "alameda", where she slips on the dewy grass. She describes a setting rich with features of the *locus amoenus* typical of lyric poetry of the medieval Iberian and classical traditions:

> Y en un ameno pradillo
> donde el sol no pudo arder
> por las sombras que le hacían
> dos álamos y un laurel,
> con tantas pintadas flores,
> que al más curioso vergel
> causarle pudiera envidia;
> [...]
> Allí, madre, allí atrevidos,
> que todo amante lo es,
> sacamos las dos espadas.
>
> [And in a secluded meadow
> where even the sun could not shine
> through the shadows made by
> two poplars and a laurel,
> with so many ful flowers,
> that even the most splendid orchard
> would be driven to envy;
> [...]

There, mother, there, daringly,
for every lover is daring,
both of us drew our swords.]
(III. 820–826; 836–838)

Hipólita's poetic confession to her mother, as well as the idyllic setting she describes, invoke the space of the medieval *cantigas d'amigo*, the space of sexuality and sexual initiation in the gallego-portuguese lyric tradition. The frequent exclamations of "Ay, ¡madre!", "¡Madre de los ojos míos!", "Madre mía", which punctuate the narrative of Hipólita's introduction to sexuality unequivocally invoke this tradition.[79] Hipólita's entrance into this poetic space thus represents a return to an Iberian literary tradition, an undoing of her foreign/unnatural (both in location, Flanders, and in social role, male soldier) upbringing. She recounts the events to her mother in *romance* with rhyme in é, a native Spanish verse form which, according to Mary M. Gaylord, carried the weight of poetic truth in Golden Age theater.[80] Gaylord identifies songs from the popular tradition as particularly steeped in sexuality: "Traditional songs codify mountains, rivers, flora, fauna, and the routines of rural life (washing, harvesting, milling) into a language of natural love that celebrates sexual passion as part of nature's cycles of fertility and renewal" (2006, 81). In echoing the *cantigas d'amigo* and traditional Spanish songs, Hipólita speaks through Iberian poetic archetypal voices for women (specifically, young daughters) to announce her return to her native country and biological gender. There is also a biblical resonance to the passage, from the Song of Songs: "Who is that coming up from the wilderness, / leaning upon her beloved? / Under the apple tree I awakened you. / There your mother was in travail with you, / there she who bore you was in travail" (Song of Solomon 8:5). This intertext invokes themes of sexual awakening, rebirth and homecoming.[81]

---

79 See Margit Frenk's anthology, *Lírica española de tipo popular*; for example, Gil Vicente's "Donde vindes, filha" (2004, 85), Pero Meogo's "Digades, filha, mia filha velida" (52), and Juan Vásquez's "No me firáis, madre" (102), examples of the tradition in which daughters confess their sexual awakenings to their mothers, in some cases in a dialogue with the mother.
80 Mary Gaylord argues that "[t]he *romance* offers a privileged window onto the competition among *polimetría*'s diverse codes for the most coveted dramatic roles: vehicles of poetic truth and poetic justice" (2006, 82).
81 The translation in the Vulgate Bible adds another theme, that of the corruption or violation of the mother: "sub arbore malo suscitavi te ibi corrupta est mater tua ibi violata est senetrix tue;" in his translation of the Song of Songs from Hebrew into Spanish, Fray Luis mentions the change in the Latin version and translates it as: "Allí fue violada la que te parió, allí fue corrompida tu madre" ["There the one who gave birth to you was violated,

Through Félix and Hipólita's gender transformations, violence is shown to be a crucial element of the sex/gender system. Almost all scholarship on *La fuerza de la costumbre* sees love as the force that ultimately undoes Félix and Hipólita's 'inappropriate' gender habits. McKendrick claims that "love effects this transformation and it cannot be deterred or deceived by upbringing" (1974, 102). Thacker's view is similar: "As well as appealing directly to both siblings to change their roles to something more appropriate to the society in which they live, the patriarchal representatives of the play hope that they can leave the misfits to a certain extent to the pulls of their natural heterosexual inclinations. Hipólita is transformed through 'seduction' and Félix metamorphosed through love" (2002, 30). Certainly, the platonic conception of love as a purifying force which aids the soul in connecting with divine beauty, knowledge and happiness underlies and reinforces the play's depiction of Félix and Hipólita's transitions. However, while love for Leonor and Luis awakens previously unknown virtues in Félix and Hipólita, it also falls short of bringing about the desired permanent change. In *La fuerza de la costumbre*, it is through violence, specifically sexual violence, that the children come to correctly perform the gender mandated for them by the social order. Juliá Martínez cites love as the primary force in the play, though he acknowledges the role of violence: "El amor sigue siendo el móvil de todas las acciones; pero en esta comedia es en la que con mayor ahinco se proclaman las excelencias de la bravura. Es cierto que en lo más íntimo lo que se pregona es la ventaja de la valentía sobre el afeminamiento en el hombre. Y recurre a esa violencia cuando la pasión amorosa encuentra el dique de los celos" ["Love continues to be the motivator of the action; but it is in this comedy that, with the most zeal, what is proclaimed is the advantage of fierceness. It is true that, at the most intimate level, what is proclaimed is the victory of bravery over the feminization of man. And this violence is resorted to when amorous passion comes up against the obstacle of jealousy"] (III, xi). Thacker seems to acknowledge this, even if only partially, when he describes the sex act as "sexual conquest" (32), as Luis "dominating and possessing her body" (33), but he also repeatedly refers to it as a scene of "seduction" (30, 33) and "love" (31). The sword/phallus defines gender, and to comply with their new genders, each sibling has to change their relationship to the male weapon. Hipólita is castrated through defeat in battle, leading to the subjugation of her body to her husband and her disavowal of masculinity. Félix loses his phallic virginity when he

---

there your mother was corrupted"] (1999, 161).

stains his blade with Otavio's blood, returning to his family and future wife carrying the rival's symbols of masculinity. Violence and lawlessness form an integral part of the construction of masculinity in this work.

Conclusion
La fuerza de la costumbre upholds male supremacy in the gender hierarchy, even while showing that gender is not a fixed category. In this play, 'woman' is a dirty word, (as Galván's joke at II. 414 indicates). The degree of feminism one attributes to this play correlates directly to the degree to which one sees Hipólita as a man or a woman when the play starts. In a sense, the play upholds the Huartean misogynist view that gender dictates capabilities, since Hipólita is stripped of her skill once she assumes the feminine role and Félix is not seen as a man until he learns how to perform masculinity. Changes in sex/gender are not outside the realm of possibility in Huarte's theory (due to the instability in the one-sex model discussed by Laquer), as shown by his discussion of cases of *in utero* gender/sex switching, the effects of castration in men, and spontaneous sex changes in adults. *La fuerza de la costumbre* explores and pushes on the limits of Huarte's theory, on the edge of disproving his misogynistic claims by showing that a daughter can be raised as a boy with the right training and influences, and demonstrating the possibilities for mismatches of gender and body that he posits as plausible exceptions to the rule. *La fuerza de la costumbre* and Huarte's *Examen de ingenios* are both fundamentally essentialist about gender, if not about sex. The play's gender bending signals an anxiety about this lack of stability of masculinity, which was particularly poignant in the milieu of Spanish decline and 'masculinity crisis' in the seventeenth century.

BIBLIOGRAPHY

Abel, Lionel. *Tragedy and Metatheatre: Essays on Dramatic Form.* New York: Holmes and Meier, 2003.
Alpern, Hymen. 'A Note on Guillén de Castro'. *Modern Language Notes* 41, no. 6 (June 1926): 391–92.
Antonucci, Fausta. 'Una nota sobre la fortuna de Guillén de Castro: Secuencias de *La fuerza de la costumbre* en *La batalla de Pavía* de Cristóbal de Monroy y Silva'. *Rivista di Filologia e Letterature Ispaniche* 6 (2003): 315–26.
Ariosto, Lodovico. *Orlando furioso.* Edited by Lanfranco Caretti. 2 vols. First published 1966. Torino: Einaudi, 1992. Translated by David R. Slavitt as *Orlando Furioso: A New Verse Translation* (Cambridge: The Belknap Press of Harvard University Press, 2009).
Aristotle. *The Nicomachean Ethics.* Translated by J. A. K. Thomson, revised and annotated by Hugh Tredennick. London: Penguin Group, 2004.
Ashcom, B. B. 'Concerning "La mujer en hábito de hombre" in the *Comedia*'. *Hispanic Review* 28, no. 1 (1960): 43–62.
Azevedo, Ángela de. *El muerto disimulado.* In *Women's Acts: Plays by Women Dramatists of Spain's Golden Age.* Edited by Teresa Scott Soufas, 91–132. Lexington: University Press of Kentucky, 1997.
Beaumont, Francis, and John Fletcher. *Love's Cure; or, The Martial Maid.* Edited by George Walton Williams. In *The Dramatic Works in the Beaumont and Fletcher Canon*, Vol. 3, edited by Fredson Bowers, 1–112. Cambridge: Cambridge University Press, 1976.
Bass, Laura R. and Margaret R. Greer (eds). *Approaches to Teaching Early Modern Spanish Drama.* New York: Modern Language Association of America, 2006.
Bernis, Carmen. *Indumentaria española en tiempos de Carlos V.* Madrid: Instituto Diego Velázquez, del Consejo Superior de Investigaciones Científicas, 1962.
Bernis, Carmen. *Trajes y modas en la España de los Reyes Católicos.* 2 vols. Madrid: Instituto Diego Velázquez, del Consejo Superior de Investigaciones Científicas, 1978.
Blackmore, Josiah, and Gregory S. Hutcheson (eds). *Queer Iberia: Sexualities, Cultures, and Crossings from the Middle Ages to the Renaissance.* Durham: Duke University Press, 1999.
Bradbury, Gail. 'Irregular Sexuality in the Spanish "Comedia"'. *The Modern Language Review* 76, no. 3 (1982): 566–80.
Bravo-Villasante, Carmen. *La mujer vestida de hombre en el teatro español: siglos XVI–XVII.* 2nd edn. Madrid: Sociedad General Española de Librería, 1976.
Brittan, Arthur. *Masculinity and Power.* Oxford: Basil Blackwell, 1989.

Bruerton, Courtney. 'The Chronology of the Comedias of Guillén de Castro'. *Hispanic Review* 12, no. 2 (April 1944): 89–151.
Burshatin, Israel. 'Elena Alias Eleno: Genders, Sexuality and "Race" in the Mirror of Natural History in Sixteenth-Century Spain'. In *Gender Reversals and Gender Cultures: Anthropological and Historical Perspectives*. Edited by Sabrina Petra Ramet, 105–22. London: Routledge, 1996.
Burshatin, Israel. 'Written on the Body: Slave or Hermaphrodite in Sixteenth-Century Spain'. In *Queer Iberia: Sexualities, Cultures, and Crossings from the Middle Ages to the Renaissance*. Edited by Josiah Blackmore and Gregory S. Hutcheson, 420–56. Durham: Duke University Press, 1999.
Butler, Judith. *Bodies That Matter: On the Discursive Limits of 'Sex'*. New York: Routledge, 1993.
Butler, Judith. *Gender Trouble: Feminism and the Subversion of Identity*. 2nd edn. 1999. Reprint, New York: Routledge, 2006.
Calderón de la Barca, Pedro. *Las manos blancas no ofenden: dos textos de una comedia*. Edited by Ángel Martínez Blasco. Kassel: Reichenberger, 1995.
Calderón de la Barca, Pedro. *El médico de su honra*. Edited by D. W. Cruickshank. Madrid: Castalia, 1989. Translated by Dian Fox and Donald Hindley as *The Physician of his Honour* (2nd edn by Dian Fox, Oxford: Oxbow, 2007).
Calderón de la Barca, Pedro. *La vida es sueño*. Edited by Ciriaco Morón. Madrid: Cátedra, 2006.
Calderón de la Barca, Pedro. *No hay burlas con el amor*. Translated by Don Cruickshank and Seán Page as *Love Is No Laughing Matter*. Warminster: Aris and Phillips, 1994.
Cartagena Calderón, José Reinaldo. *Masculinidades en obras: el drama de la hombría en la España imperial*. Newark: Juan de la Cuesta, 2008.
Cartagena Calderón, José Reinaldo. 'Of Pretty Fops and Spectacular Sodomites: *El lindo don Diego* and the Performance of Effeminacy in Early Modern Spain'. In *The Poetics of Masculinity in Early Modern Italy and Spain*. Edited by Gerry Milligan and Jane Tylus, 317–49. Toronto: Centre for Reformation and Renaissance Studies, 2010.
Castiglione, Baldesar. *The Book of the Courtier*. Edited by Daniel Javitch. Translated by Charles Singleton. New York: Norton, 2002.
Castro, Américo. *De la edad conflictiva: crisis de la cultura española en el siglo XVII*. 4th edn. Madrid: Taurus, 1976.
Castro, Guillén de. *Comedias selectas*. Edited by Luis Guarner. Barcelona: Iberia, 1961.
Castro, Guillén de. *El curioso impertinente*. Edited by Christiane Faliu-Lacourt and María-Luisa Lobato. Kassel: Edition Reichenberger, 1991.
Castro, Guillén de. *Los mal casados de Valencia*. Edited by Luciano García Lorenzo. Madrid: Castalia, 1976.

Castro, Guillén de. *Las mocedades del Cid*. Edited by Stefano Arata. Introductory essay by Aurora Egido. Barcelona: Crítica, 1996.

Castro, Guillén de. *Obras completas*. Edited by Juan Oleza. Madrid: Fundación José Antonio de Castro, 1997.

Castro, Guillén de. *Obras de Don Guillén de Castro y Bellvis*. Edited by Eduardo Juliá Martínez. 3 vols. Madrid: Real Academia Española, 1925–1927.

Cervantes Saavedra, Miguel de. *Don Quijote de la Mancha*. Edited by Florencio Sevilla Arroyo and Elena Varela Merino. 2 vols. Madrid: Castalia, 1997.

Cervantes Saavedra, Miguel de. *The Ingenious Hidalgo Don Quixote de la Mancha*. Translated by John Rutherford. New York: Penguin Books, 2001.

Cervantes Saavedra, Miguel de. *Novelas ejemplares*. Edited by Jorge García López. Barcelona: Crítica, 2001.

Cervantes Saavedra, Miguel de. *Viaje del Parnaso*. Edited by Miguel Herrero García. Madrid: Consejo Superior de Investigaciones Científicas, Instituto Miguel de Cervantes, 1983.

Correa, Gustavo. 'El doble aspecto de la honra en el teatro del siglo de oro'. *Hispanic Review* 26, no. 1 (January 1958): 99–107.

Cotarelo y Mori, Emilio. *Bibliografía de las controversias sobre la licitud del teatro en España*. Madrid: Revista de archivos, bibliotecas y museos, 1904.

Covarrubias Orozco, Sebastián de. *Tesoro de la lengua castellana o española*. Madrid: Luis Sánchez, 1611. Fondo Antiguo, Universidad de Sevilla. http://fondosdigitales. us.es/fondos/libros/765/36/tesoro-de-la-lengua-castellana-o-espanola/

Crapotta, James. *Kingship and Tyranny in the Theater of Guillén de Castro*. London: Tamesis Books, 1984.

Dekker, Rudolf, and Lotte C. van de Pol. *The Tradition of Female Transvestism in Early Modern Europe*. Translated by Judy Marcure and Lotte Van de Pol. London: Macmillan Press, 1989.

Donnell, Sidney. *Feminizing the Enemy: Imperial Spain, Transvestite Drama, and the Crisis of Masculinity*. Lewisburg: Bucknell University Press, 2003.

Dopico Black, Georgina. *Perfect Wives, Other Women: Adultery and Inquisition in Early Modern Spain*. Durham: Duke University Press, 2001.

Dunn, Peter N. 'Honor and the Christian Background'. *Bulletin of Hispanic Studies* 37 (1960): 75–105.

Durán, D. Agustín, (ed.). *Romancero de romances caballerescos é históricos anteriores al siglo XVIII, vol. II*. Madrid: Imprenta de don Eusebio Aguado, 1832.

Eco, Umberto. 'Semiotics of Theatrical Performance'. *The Drama Review* 21, no. 1 (1977): 107–17.

Elliott, J. H. *Imperial Spain: 1469–1716*. London: Penguin Books, 1990.

Erauso, Catalina de. *Lieutenant Nun: Memoir of a Basque Transvestite in the New World*. Edited by Michele Stepto and Gabriel Stepto. Translated by Michele Stepto and Gabriel Stepto. Boston: Beacon Press, 1996.

Erauso, Catalina de. *La Monja Alférez, doña Catalina de Erauso: dos manuscritos inéditos de su autobiografía conservados en el Archivo de la Santa Iglesia Catedral de Sevilla*. Edited by Pedro Rubio Marino. Sevilla: Cabildo Metropolitano de la Catedral de Sevilla, 1995.

Erickson, Martin E. 'A Review of Scholarship Dealing with the Problem of a Spanish Source for *Love's Cure*'. In *Studies in Comparative Literature*. Edited by Waldo F. McNeir: 102–19. Baton Rouge: Louisiana State University Press, 1962.

Fausto-Sterling. *Sex/Gender: Biology in a Social World*. New York: Routledge, 2012.

Fausto-Sterling. *Sexing the Body: Gender Politics and the Construction of Sexuality*. New York: Basic Books, 2000.

Finucci, Valeria. *The Manly Masquerade: Masculinity, Paternity, and Castration in the Italian Renaissance*. Durham: Duke University Press, 2003.

Fothergill-Payne, Louise. 'Labyrinthine Questions: Gender Ambivalence and Its Mythological Antecedents in Lope's *El laberinto de Creta* and *La prueba de los ingenios*'. In *Gender, Identity, and Representation in Spain's Golden Age*. Edited by Anita K. Stoll and Dawn L. Smith, 61–85. Lewisburg: Bucknell University Press, 2000.

Fox, Dian. 'Performing Masculinity, Nationalism, and Honour in Early Modern Spain: Calderón de la Barca's *El pintor de su deshonra*'. In *The Poetics of Masculinity in Early Modern Italy and Spain*. Edited by Gerry Milligan and Jane Tylus, 293–316. Toronto: Centre for Reformation and Renaissance Studies, 2010.

Frenk, Margit, (ed.). *Lírica española de tipo popular: Edad Media y Renacimiento*. Madrid: Cátedra, 2004.

Fuchs, Barbara. 'Border Crossings: Transvestism and "Passing" in *Don Quijote*'. *Cervantes: Bulletin of the Cervantes Society of America* 16, no. 2 (1996): 4–28.

Ganelin, Charles, and Howard Mancing (eds). *The Golden Age Comedia: Text, Theory, and Performance*. West Lafayette: Purdue University Press, 1994.

Garber, Marjorie. *Vested Interests: Cross-dressing and Cultural Anxiety*. New York: Routledge, 1992.

García Lorenzo, Luciano. *El teatro de Guillén de Castro*. Barcelona: Planeta, 1976.

Gaylord, Mary Malcolm. 'How to Do Things with Polimetría'. In *Approaches to Teaching Early Modern Spanish Drama*. Edited by Laura R. Bass and Margaret R. Greer, 76–84. New York: Modern Language Association of America, 2006.

Gracián, Baltasar. *Agudeza y arte de ingenio*. Edited by Evaristo Correa Calderón. 2 vols. Madrid: Castalia, 2001.

Green, Otis H. 'New Documents for the Biography of Guillén de Castro y Bellvís'. *Revue Hispanique* 81, no. 2 (1933): 248–60.

Greer, Margaret Rich. 'The Development of National Theater'. In *The Cambridge History of Spanish Literature*. Edited by David Thatcher Gies, 238–50. Cambridge: Cambridge University Press, 2004.

Greer, Margaret Rich. *María de Zayas Tells Baroque Tales of Love and the Cruelty of Men*. University Park: Pennsylvania State University Press, 2000.
Greer, Margaret Rich, director. Manos teatrales: base de datos de manuscritos teatrales. http://manosteatrales.org.
Halberstam, Judith. *Female Masculinity*. Durham: Duke University Press, 1998.
Hamilton, Edith. *Mythology*. Boston: Little, Brown and Company, 1998.
Heise, Ursula K. 'Transvestism and the Stage Controversy in Spain and England, 1580–1680'. *Theatre Journal* 44, no. 3 (1992): 357–74.
Hotchkiss, Valerie R. *Clothes Make the Man: Female Cross-dressing in Medieval Europe*. New York: Garland, 1996.
Huarte de San Juan, Juan. *Examen de ingenios para las ciencias*. Edited by Guillermo Serés. Madrid: Cátedra, 1989.
Jeffs, Kathleen. 'Gender Politics in Guillén de Castro's *La fuerza de la costumbre*'. In *On Wolves and Sheep: Exploring the Expression of Political Thought in Golden Age Spain*. Edited by Aaron Kahn, 147–76. Newcastle upon Tyne: Cambridge Scholars Publishing, 2011.
Jeffs, Kathleen. 'The Power of Transformation in Guillén de Castro's *El caballero bobo* (1595–1605) and *La fuerza de la costumbre* (1610–1615): Translation and Performance'. In *The Reinvention of Theatre in Sixteenth-Century Europe*. Edited by T. F. Earle and Catarina Fouto, 161–83. London: Modern Humanities Research Association and Maney Publishing, Legenda, 2015.
Jeffs, Kathleen. *Staging the Spanish Golden Age: Translation and Performance*. Oxford: Oxford University Press, 2018.
Juliá Martínez, Eduardo. 'Observaciones preliminares' to *Obras de don Guillén de Castro Y Bellvis*, Vol. 1, by Guillén de Castro, vii–xcv. Madrid: Real Academia Española, 1925.
Juliá Martínez, Eduardo.'Observaciones preliminares' to *Obras de don Guillén de Castro Y Bellvis*, Vol. 3, by Guillén de Castro, v–xxxix. Madrid: Real Academia Española, 1927.
Jones, C. A. 'Honor in Spanish Golden-Age Drama: Its Relation to Real Life and to Morals'. *Bulletin of Hispanic Studies* 35 (1958): 199–210.
Jones, C. A. 'Spanish Honour as Historical Phenomenon, Convention and Artistic Motive'. *Hispanic Review* 33, no. 1 (1965): 32–39.
Laquer, Thomas. *Making Sex: Body and Gender from the Greeks to Freud*. Cambridge: Harvard University Press, 1990.
Larson, Donald R. *The Honor Plays of Lope de Vega*. Cambridge: Harvard University Press, 1977.
Loftis, John. 'La comedia española en la Inglaterra del siglo XVII'. In *La comedia española y el teatro europeo del siglo XVII*. Edited by Henry W. Sullivan, Raúl A. Galoppe and Mahlon L. Stoutz, 101–19. Rochester: Tamesis, 1999.
Luis de León, Fray. *A Bilingual Edition of Fray Luis de León's* La perfecta casada:

the Role of Married Women in Sixteenth-Century Spain. Edited by John A. Jones and Javier San José Lera. Lewiston: Edwin Mellen Press, 1999.

Luis de León, Fray. *La perfecta casada; Cantar de los cantares; Poesías originales*. Edited by Joaquín Antonio Peñalosa. 9th edn. México, D.F.: Porrúa, 1999.

Madroñal Durán, Abraham. 'Glosario de voces comentadas relacionadas con el vestido, el tocado y el calzado en el teatro español del Siglo de Oro'. In *El vestuario en el teatro español del Siglo de Oro*. Edited by Mercedes de los Reyes Peña, 229–301. Madrid: Compañía Nacional de Teatro Clásico, 2000.

Maravall, José Antonio. *La cultura del barroco: análisis de una estructura histórica*. Esplugues de Llobregat: Ariel, 1975.

Martí Grajales, Francisco. *Ensayo de un diccionario biográfico y bibliográfico de los poetas que florecieron en el reino de Valencia hasta 1700*. Madrid: Tipografía de la Revista de archivos, bibliotecas y museos, 1927.

McKendrick, Melveena. *Identities in Crisis: Essays on Honour, Gender and Women in the Comedia*. Kassel: Edition Reichenberger, 2002.

McKendrick, Melveena. *Theatre in Spain, 1490–1700*. Cambridge: Cambridge University Press, 1989.

McKendrick, Melveena. *Woman and Society in the Spanish Drama of the Golden Age: a Study of the Mujer Varonil*. London: Cambridge University Press, 1974.

Mendieta, Eva. *In Search of Catalina de Erauso: the National and Sexual Identity of the Lieutenant Nun*. Reno: Center for Basque Studies, 2009.

Mercader, Gaspar. *El prado de Valencia*. Edited by Henri Mérimée. Paris: Bibliothèque Méridionale, 1907.

Mesonero Romanos, Ramón de (ed.). *Dramáticos contemporáneos a Lope de Vega: colección escogida y ordenada, con un discurso, apuntes biográficos y críticos de los autores, noticias bibliográficas y catálogos*. Vol. 1. Madrid: M. Rivadeneyra, 1857.

Milligan, Gerry and Jane Tylus (eds). *The Poetics of Masculinity in Early Modern Italy and Spain*. Toronto: Centre for Reformation and Renaissance Studies, 2010.

Moll, Jaime. 'Diez años sin licencias para imprimir comedias y novelas en los reinos de Castilla: 1625–1634'. *Boletín de la Real Academia Española* 54 (1974): 97–103.

Montaner, Alberto (ed.). *Cantar de mio Cid*. Barcelona: Crítica, 2000.

Montemayor, Jorge de. *La Diana*. Edited by Juan Montero. Barcelona: Crítica, 1996.

Navarro Tomás, Tomás. *Métrica española: reseña histórica y descriptiva*. Barcelona: Labor, 1986.

Oleza, Joan. 'Introduction' to *Obras completas*, vol. 1, by Guillén de Castro. *Obras completas*, ix–xxxv. Madrid: Fundación José Antonio de Castro, 1997.

Ovid. *Metamorphoses*. Translated by Frank Justus Miller and revised by G. P. Goold. Vols. 3 (Books I–VIII) and 4 (Books IX–XV) of Ovid. 3rd edn. 1977. Reprint, Cambridge: Harvard University Press, 2004.

Pérez de Montalván, Juan. *La monja Alférez*. Edited by Luzmila Camacho Platero. Newark: Juan de la Cuesta, 2007.
Pérez Díez, José. 'What the Quills Can Tell: the Case of John Fletcher and Philip Massinger's *Love's Cure*'. *Shakespeare Survey* 70 (2017): 93–102.
Perry, Mary Elizabeth. 'From Convent to Battlefield: Cross-dressing and Gendering the Self in the New World of Imperial Spain'. In *Queer Iberia: Sexualities, Cultures, and Crossings from the Middle Ages to the Renaissance*. Edited by Josiah Blackmore and Gregory S. Hutcheson, 394–419. Durham: Duke University Press, 1999.
Perry, Mary Elizabeth. *Gender and Disorder in Early Modern Seville*. Princeton: Princeton University Press, 1990.
Petra Ramet, Sabrina (ed.). *Gender Reversals and Gender Cultures: Anthropological and Historical Perspectives*. London: Routledge, 1996.
Petrarch, Francesco. *Petrarch: The Canzoniere, or, Rerum vulgarium fragmenta*. With translation, notes and commentary by Mark Musa. Bloomington: Indiana University Press, 1996.
Pitt-Rivers, Julian. *The Fate of Shechem; or, The Politics of Sex: Essays in the Anthropology of the Mediterranean*. Cambridge: Cambridge University Press, 1977.
Plato. *Republic*. Translated with an Introduction and notes by Robin Waterfield. Oxford: Oxford University Press, 1998.
Poska, Allyson M. 'When Love Goes Wrong: Getting Out of Marriage in Seventeenth-Century Spain'. *Journal of Social History* 29, no. 4 (Summer 1996): 871–82.
Ramos, Juan Luis. 'Guillén de Castro en el proceso de la comedia barroca'. *Cuadernos de Filología III: Literaturas, Análisis* 3 (1983): 169–98.
Reyes Peña, Mercedes de los. *El vestuario en el teatro español del Siglo de Oro*. Madrid: Compañía Nacional de Teatro Clásico, 2000.
Romera-Navarro, M. 'Las disfrazadas de varón en la comedia'. *Hispanic Review* 2, no. 4 (1934): 269–86.
Rubin, Gayle. 'The Traffic in Women: Notes on the "Political Economy" of Sex'. In *The Second Wave: A Reader in Feminist Theory*. Edited by Linda Nicholson, 27–62. New York: Routledge, 1997.
Ruiz de Conde, Justina. *El amor y el matrimonio secreto en los libros de caballerías*. Madrid: M. Aguilar, 1948.
Salamon, Gayle. *Assuming a Body: Transgender and Rhetorics of Materiality*. New York: Columbia University Press, 2010.
Stroud, Matthew D. *Plot Twists and Critical Turns: Queer Approaches to Early Modern Spanish Theater.* Lewisburg: Bucknell University Press, 2007.
Stroud, Matthew D. '"Y sois hombre o sois mujer?": Sex and Gender in Tirso's *Don Gil de las calzas verdes*'. In *The Perception of Women in Spanish Theater of the Golden Age*. Edited by Anita K. Stoll and Dawn L. Smith, 67–82. Lewisburg: Bucknell University Press, 1991.

Taddeo, Sarah. '"Ahógame este vestido": la amazona y la mujer-paje en *La fuerza de la costumbre* y *Love's Cure*'. In *Vidas paralelas: la comedia española y el teatro isabelino, 1580–1686*. Edited by Anita K. Stoll, 63–76. Madrid: Tamesis, 1993.

Tárrega, Francisco Agustín. *El prado de Valencia*. Edited by José Luis Canet Valles. London: Tamesis, 1985.

Thacker, Jonathan. *Role-play and the World as Stage in the* Comedia. Liverpool: Liverpool University Press, 2002.

Tirso de Molina. *Don Gil de las calzas verdes; La Prudencia en la mujer; El condenado por desconfiado*. Introduction and notes by D. Amando Isasi Angulo. Barcelona: Bruguera, S. A., 1969.

Tirso de Molina. *Don Gil of the Green Breeches*. Trans Sean O'Brien. Unpublished production script, 2013, 122–23.

Valverde, José María. *El barroco: una visión de conjunto*. Barcelona: Montesinos, 1981.

Vega Carpio, Lope Félix de. *Comedias de Lope de Vega*. 28 Vols. Directed by Alberto Blecua and Guillermo Serés. Lleida: Milenio, 1997–2012.

Vega Carpio, Lope Félix de. *La prueba de los ingenios*. Edited by Julián Molina. In *Comedias de Lope de Vega*, Vol. 21, Part 9:1, series directed by Alberto Blecua and Guillermo Serés, Part 9 coordinated by Marco Presotto, 39–164. Lleida: Milenio, 2007.

Vega Carpio, Lope Félix de. *New Art of Writing Plays at This Time*. Trans. Victor Dixon, Biblioteca Digital Artelope, http://emothe.uv.es/biblioteca/textosEMOTHE/EMOTHE0116_NewRulesForWritingPlaysAtThisTime.php, 2009, Accessed 8 August 2017.

Vega, Garcilaso de la. *Obra poética y textos en prosa*. Edited by Bienvenido Morros. Barcelona: Crítica, 2001.

Velasco, Sherry M. *The Lieutenant Nun: Transgenderism, Lesbian Desire & Catalina de Erauso*. Austin: University of Texas Press, 2000.

Velasco, Sherry M. *Male Delivery: Reproduction, Effeminacy, and Pregnant Men in Early Modern Spain*. Nashville: Vanderbilt University Press, 2006.

Vélez-Quiñones, Harry. '"Templa, pequeño joven, templa brío": Pretty Boys and Queer Soldiers in Miguel de Cervantes's *Numancia*'. In *The Poetics of Masculinity in Early Modern Italy and Spain*. Edited by Gerry Milligan and Jane Tylus, 241–65. Toronto: Centre for Reformation and Renaissance Studies, 2010.

Villegas, Francisco de. *Lo que puede la crianza*. In *Comedias nuevas, y escogidas de los mejores ingenios de España*. Madrid: Domingo García Morras, 1666.

Vives, Juan Luis. *The Education of a Christian Woman: A Sixteenth-Century Manual*. Edited and translated by Charles Fantazzi. Chicago: University of Chicago Press, 2000.

Vollendorf, Lisa. *The Lives of Women: a New History of Inquisitional Spain.* Nashville: Vanderbilt University Press, 2005.
Weiger, John G. 'Another Look at the Biography of Guillén de Castro'. *Bulletin of the Comediantes* 10, no. 1 (1958): 3–5.
Weiger, John G. 'Forced Marriage in Castro's Theatre'. *Bulletin of the Comediantes* 15, no. 1 (1963): 1–4.
Weiger, John G. '"Monstruo de Naturaleza": Castro's Ironic Use of Cervantes' Epithet for Lope de Vega'. *Hispania* 65, no. 1 (March 1, 1982): 39–44.
Weiger, John G. 'Sobre la originalidad e independencia de Guillén de Castro'. *Hispanofila* 31 (1967): 1–15.
Weiger, John G. *The Valencian Dramatists of Spain's Golden Age.* Boston: Twayne Publishers, 1976.
Wilson, William E. *Guillén de Castro.* New York: Twayne Publishers, 1973.
Wilson, William E. 'A Note on Fifteen Plays Attributed to Guillén de Castro'. *Modern Language Quarterly* 8 (1947): 393–400.
Wilson, William E. 'Guillén de Castro and the Codification of Honor'. *Bulletin of the Comediantes* 19 (Spring 1967): 24–27.
Wilson, William E. 'Two Recurring Themes in Castro's Plays'. *Bulletin of the Comediantes* 9, no. 2 (1957): 25–27.
Zayas, María de. *Novelas amorosas y ejemplares.* Edited by Julián Olivares. 3rd edn. Madrid: Cátedra, 2007. Edited and translated by Margaret R. Greer and Elizabeth Rhodes as *Exemplary Tales of Love and Tales of Disillusion* (Chicago: University of Chicago Press, 2009).

TRANSLATOR'S NOTE

At its best, translation is a refusal to accept that we are born into and live in little worlds of our own, worlds that border only on silence. It is a celebration of that same journey into otherness that lies at the heart of the experience of theatre, perhaps above all other forms.

Out of the Wings translation team[1]

This play takes us on a journey into otherness that is one of the most personal yet collectively experienced differences between human beings: sexuality and gender. Castro examines the performative aspects of gender, placing them in a specific, 17th-century scenario: 'Is gender learned or innate? This controversial play asks the question: what happens if you raise a boy to sew and behave as a girl, and raise his sister to fight as a soldier?'[2] This translation was born during the inception of Out of the Wings: Spanish and Spanish American Theatres in Translation, an Arts and Humanities Research Council-funded project spearheaded by Catherine Boyle, Jonathan Thacker, and David Johnston. My colleagues Gwynneth Dowling and Gwendolen MacKeith and I served as post-doctoral research assistants, translating and curating excerpts of Spanish plays with contextual material for free use on the web resource. Jonathan Thacker, who had published on *La fuerza de la costumbre* and been interested in the play for some time, suggested that we take a look at its translation and performance potential. That potential has only begun to be glimpsed.

Since the play has undergone a staged reading (2011) and two full productions (2013 and 2015), I have come to see that this work is not 'just' about nature *vs* nurture, or about the pressure that performing gender puts on men and women in our society, but it is also a damning commentary on the choices parents make in bringing up children. The parents here are: Pedro, a domineering soldier-father determined to re-enter civilian society and straighten out the children his actions have cross-gendered; and his wife, Costanza, who resists conformity but has very limited scope for action once her husband returns to the house. Her efforts to raise her son as a daughter bear life-long consequences, only some of which are seen in the play itself,

---

1 http://www.outofthewings.org/approaches/translation/
2 Quoted from my 'Pitch' for this play on the Out of the Wings site, http://outofthewings.org/db/play/la-fuerza-de-la-costumbre.

the rest skilfully hinted at by Castro. Children and their parents push and pull in a war of independence and control, with poignant moments of seeking approval and desperation to meet impossible expectations. The pressures are those of gender, but they are also those of family, a drama that plays out in households across cultures and generations.

When I first directed this translation as a staged reading in Washington, DC at the Association for Theatre in Higher Education conference in August 2011, the cast was drawn from experts in Golden Age drama and the *comedia* in particular, so we made many changes in rehearsal and worked the text for clarity and meaning. When I directed the full production in February 2013 at Gonzaga University in Spokane, Washington, with a cast of students, we tested the script, and because the actors playing Félix and Hipólita were close to the characters' ages, they were able to suggest insightful emendations to bring the struggle of gender's rigidity in the play to a young audience (and their parents). See production photos from p. 96 onwards.

The third time the play met production was under the direction of Sara Freeman at the University of Puget Sound in October 2015, where it received an edit by our dramaturg Hannah Ferguson, who read it for accuracy and closeness to the Spanish. That production benefited again from the precious time spent working the text with the actors. The University of Puget Sound is a campus with a particularly progressive stance toward issues of gender and sexuality, a place where a growing number of students identify as non-binary in gender or employ the use of non-gender-specific pronouns (referring to themselves as 'they' or 'them' instead of 'he/she', 'him/her'). Rehearsing and performing the play there, with those actors, for their audience steeped in contemporary trends and gender theory, brought on another complete edit of this play from another place and time. Finally, preparing the text for publication in facing pages with the Spanish for this edition has brought the translation one step closer to Castro's play, as Melissa Machit and I have re-drawn the lines closer to the Spanish than the scripts for production. It is my intention that this version here provides an experience of the play for readers interested in it on the page and for the stage, as it is very much a living, breathing text that has been tested in the crucible of performance.

Practical note about the translation

I am using British spelling, including 'honour' throughout and 'practising' at I. 719.

1. Pedro: "I have changed her name and thoughts, / if not her being, into those of a man." (l. 248–249). Hipólita (Erin Fitzgerald), Pedro (Connor Brenes), Costanza (Devin Devine). Photo by Summer Berry, Gonzaga University, 2013.

2. Hipólita: "*Oh, my sword! Even as you lose / your place at my side. […]*" (l. 581–582). Hipólita (Sophie Schwartz), Pedro (Darrin Schultz), Tutor (Parker Simpson). Photo by Kurt Walls, University of Puget Sound, 2015.

3. ("*Félix helps his sister with the shoes.*") (l. 722). Félix (Patrick Ostrander), Costanza (Devin Devine), Hipólita (Erin Fitzgerald). Photo by Summer Berry, Gonzaga University, 2013.

4. Félix: "You've made more stitches / there than you should." (II. 240–241). Hipólita (Sophie Schwartz), Félix (John Miller Giltner). Photo by Kurt Walls, University of Puget Sound, 2015.

100   Illustrations

5. Hipólita: "Can there be such malice? / Like the eye of the storm / I am suspended in calm shock." (III. 362–364). Galván (Ben Yee), Hipólita (Erin Fitzgerald). Photo by Summer Berry, Gonzaga University, 2013.

6. Galván: "*(Aside) That's right, rage with jealousy, / and you will understand what it means / to box such an honourable nose.*" (III. 368–370). Galván (Mariah Prinster), Hipólita (Sophie Schwartz). Photo by Kurt Walls, University of Puget Sound, 2015.

7. Hipólita: "*but listen to my sword, / it will say what I cannot.*" (III. 594–595). Luis (Taylor Pedroza), Hipólita (Erin Fitzgerald). Photo by Summer Berry, Gonzaga University, 2013.

8. Luis: "Wait, my lady, by God! / Do not kill me, I will surrender; / though you strike with the sword / you wound with the eyes;" (l. 783–786). Hipólita (Sophie Schwartz), Luis (Justin Brush). Photo by Kurt Walls, University of Puget Sound, 2015.

9. Otavio: "You are nothing, / and this is the prize that I want." (ll. 788–789). Félix (Patrick Ostrander), Otavio (Andrew Garcia). Photo by Summer Berry, Gonzaga University, 2013.

10. Otavio: "I have a thousand things to say / about its unfathomable force" (II. 77–78). Luis (Justin Brush), Otavio (Robbie Diaz). Photo by Kurt Walls, University of Puget Sound, 2015.

11. Pedro: "*you whine like a woman, / go avenge yourself!*" (ll. 341–342). Pedro (Connor Brenes), Félix (Patrick Ostrander). Photo by Summer Berry, Gonzaga University, 2013.

12. Hipólita: "you said the eyes are traitors, / [...] What will I do? / Mother, my eyes have killed me!" (III. 801, 805–806). Hipólita (Sophie Schwartz), Costanza (Bobbijo Katagiri). Photo by Kurt Walls, University of Puget Sound, 2015.

LA FUERZA DE LA COSTUMBRE

THE FORCE OF HABIT

INTERLOCUTORES

DOÑA COSTANZA
DON FÉLIX
DON PEDRO DE MONCADA
DOÑA HIPÓLITA
UN VIEJO AYO de Don Félix
GALVÁN, lacayo
DON LUIS
DOÑA LEONOR
OTAVIO
MARCELO
INÉS, criada
UN CRIADO
UN CAPITÁN
[UN MAESTRO DE ARMAS]+
[JUSTICIA Y GENTE; entre ellos un ALGUACIL y un CORCHETE]

---

lacayo: 'lackey' *alguacil*: 'sheriff' *corchete*: 'bailiff'.
+ The characters listed in brackets are not mentioned in the 'Interlocutores' list of P.

DRAMATIS PERSONAE

DOÑA COSTANZA
DON FÉLIX
DON PEDRO DE MONCADA
DOÑA HIPÓLITA
TUTOR to Don Félix
GALVÁN, servant
DON LUIS
DOÑA LEONOR
OTAVIO
MARCELO
INÉS, servant
A SERVANT
CAPTAIN
FENCING MASTER
OFFICERS, a BAILIFF, and OTHERS

JORNADA PRIMERA

Salen DOÑA COSTANZA, y DON FÉLIX en hábito largo de estudiante.*

FÉLIX	¿Qué novedades son estas,	[romance a–a]
	mi señora? ¿Qué mudanzas?	
	¿Del hábito de sayal,	
	monjil pardo, tocas largas,	
	al enrizado cabello,	5
	trenzas de oro, entera saya?	
	¿Del rosario a la cadena,	
	de los lutos a las galas?	
	¿Ayer desnudas paredes	
	de tristeza apenas blancas,	10
	y hoy de brocados y sedas	
	tan compuestas y entoldadas;	
	ayer pesares, hoy gustos?	
	Todo en fin, todo en tu casa,	
	cuanto vi llorar de triste,	15
	veo que de alegre canta;	
	¿qué es esto?	
COSTANZA	Ay, ¡hijo don Félix!	
FÉLIX	Hasta en mi nombre hay mudanza:	
	¿ayer Feliciano, y hoy	
	don Félix?	
COSTANZA	Oye la causa:	20
	mi padre don Juan de Urrea,	

---

* *hábito largo de estudiante*: clergy and students wore long cassocks and a full-length cloak.

4–6 *hábito de sayal*: clothing made of an unrefined, course wool; "tela muy basta labrada de lana burda", (*DRAE*, 1st def.); typical of peasant characters in the theater (see Madroñal Durán, p. 290); *monjil*: nun-like, austere; *pardo*: greyish-brown color of undyed wool, and as Covarrubias states, a color and fabric worn by humble people ("el vestido pardo es de gente humilde" ('pardo')); *tocas largas*: veil worn over the head, usually long enough to hang over the body; *entera saya*: a full-length overgown worn over an undershirt and petticoat.

8 *galas*: formal attire worn on special occasions. Cov: "es el vestido curioso y de fiesta alegre y de regozijo […] la gala hermosea y adorna al que la trae" (882).

19 *Feliciano*: 'Feliciano' sounds more rustic, pastoral, than 'Félix'.

ACT ONE

SCENE 1.1

Enter DOÑA COSTANZA, and DON FÉLIX dressed in the long robes of a student.

FÉLIX	What new ways are these,
	my lady? What are these changes?
	From a sackcloth habit,
	long dark veils like a nun,
	to curls in your hair, 5
	golden braids, and this full flouncy skirt?
	From rosaries to necklaces,
	the blacks of mourning to fine gowns?
	Yesterday these naked walls
	stood sadly, bare and white, 10
	and today they are hung with silk sheets
	and lovely scenes in brocades;
	yesterday was sorrows, today pleasures?
	Everything, everything in your house,
	as much as it wept from sadness, 15
	now sings with joy;
	what is happening?
COSTANZA	Oh, my son, Don Félix!
FÉLIX	Even to my own name there are changes:
	yesterday 'Sweet Little Félix',
	and today 'Don Félix'?
COSTANZA	It's time you heard the reason: 20
	my father, Don Juan de Urrea,

que con su nobleza honraba
esta ciudad a quien César
honró con nombre y con armas,
en doña Inés de Bolea, 25
que a tres años de casada
pagó la deuda que todos
temen más y mejor pagan,
tuvo a mi hermano y a mí;
que con su amparo y crianza 30
crecimos en Zaragoza
entre envidias y alabanzas;
él de honrado y gentilhombre,
bravo en amores y en armas,
y yo con fama de hermosa 35
¡(debió de mentir la fama)!
Sucedió que un caballero
de la casa de Moncada,
que desde la gran Valencia
iba por la posta a Italia, 40
yendo a oír misa y a ver
la primera insigne casa
que en España edificó
el santo patrón de España,

23–24 *esta ciudad…*: Zaragoza, the capital city of the province of Aragon, in Northeastern Spain. In the first century BCE, the Romans occupied this city, formerly called Salduba, making it a colony of the Roman Empire. In honor of the emperor, Augustus Caesar, it was renamed Caesaraugusta, from which the current name 'Zaragoza' derives.

38 *casa de Moncada*: there was, in fact, a Moncada family in Valencia during Guillén de Castro's lifetime. In 1590 the playwright attended the wedding of Francisco de Palafox to Lucrecia de Moncada. Guillén de Castro was related to Francisco through his paternal grandmother, Juana Palafox.

39 *Valencia*: the capital city of the Province of Valencia, located on the east coast of the Iberian peninsula, and the native city of Guillén de Castro.

40 *posta*: 'with haste', by way of a calvary relay; *Italia*: In Spanish poetic rhyme schemes the weak vowel of a dipthong is ignored, making words such as 'Italia', 'causa', and 'gracia' function in the assonant rhyme scheme of *romance* in a–a.

41–44 Santiago el Mayor, known in English as James the Greater, the patron saint of Spain, is famous for receiving a pillar from the Virgin Mary, who appeared to the apostle while he was evangelizing in present-day Zaragoza. The saint then built a small chapel in honor of the Virgin on the banks of the Ebro River, which later became the site of larger churches, such as the Basílica de Nuestra Señora del Pilar.

whose nobility honoured
this city that Caesar
honoured in name and with defences,
with Doña Inés de Bolea, 25
who after three years of marriage
paid the debt that everyone
dreads to pay but knows will be collected,
had my brother and me;
and with her protection and care 30
we grew up in Zaragoza
where we were praised and envied;
he, an honoured and noble man,
brave in love and in fighting,
and I, with a reputation for beauty 35
(we know reputations can lie)!
It happened that a gentleman
of the house of Moncada,
who from the great city of Valencia
came by post horses to Italy, 40
coming to hear Mass and to see
the first great house of God
that was built in Spain
by our Spanish patron saint,

La fuerza de la costumbre: Jornada primera

hallome en la iglesia a mí; 45
y vi que en él, cuando entraba,
cuerdamente competían
la prudencia y la arrogancia.
Llevaba un jubón de tela,
ligas y medias⁺ de nácar, 50
y sobre zapatos negros,
de lo mismo, dos lazadas;
de refino vellorí
calzones, ropilla y capa;
con puntas una valona, 55
y una cadena por banda;
gallardamente ceñida,
cubierta de oro la espada,
y al otro lado, pendiente
de otra cadena, la daga; 60
de falda larga el sombrero,
vuelta a la copa la falda,⁺
con muchas plumas azules,
y algunas garzotas blancas.
Llegó al salir de la misa, 65
y yo que en la misa estaba
más compuesta que devota
y más curiosa que santa,

45 *hallome*: in the 17th century this kind of enclitic pronoun placement was common, even with conjugated verbs that would favor proclitic placement in modern Spanish.
+ 50 *medias* A B C : *media* P.
49–52 *jubón*: 'doublet', 'jerkin'; a tightly fitted button-up jacket; *de tela*: 'of fabric'; *ligas*: 'garters' *medias de nácar*: 'pearl-colored stockings'; *y sobre zapatos negros, / de lo mismo, dos lazadas*: 'and two pearl-colored bows over black shoes'.
53–54 *vellorí*: a medium weight grey wool; *calzones*: 'pants'; *ropilla*: a short garment worn over the doublet, often with loose sleeves; *una valona*: 'a collar'.
55–56 *puntas*: decorative semi-circles of lace; *cadena por banda*: a *banda* was a sash strung across the body from shoulder to waist. Differences in color and style of these sashes indicated different military offices. Costanza describes Pedro wearing a chain, instead of a piece of fabric, across his chest as a sash.
+ 62 *vuelta a la copa la falda* B C : *buelta la copa a la falda* P.
61–64 *de falda larga el sombrero*: a wide-brimmed hat; *vuelta la copa a la falda*: 'with the brim tilted up toward the bowl [of the hat]'; *garzotas blancas*: 'egrets', 'herons', known for their long, white feathers.

he found me in the church; 45
and I saw, from the moment he entered,
that prudence and arrogance
were wisely competing in him.
He wore a doublet of cloth, garters
and stockings the colour of pearl, 50
and on his black shoes,
in the same colour, two bows;
and in a fine grey wool were
his breeches, a shirt and cape;
with a lace collar, 55
with a chain across as a sash;
and so handsomely at his side,
he wore his golden sword,
and on the other side, hung
on another chain, his dagger; 60
he topped it off with a large,
wide-brimmed hat at a jaunty angle,
with many blue feathers,
and a few white egrets.
He came up as he left Mass, 65
and I who at that Mass was
more dressed up than devoted
and more curious than holy,

La fuerza de la costumbre: Jornada primera

 mirele con atención:
 pareciome que arrojaba   70
 el corazón por la boca,
 y por los ojos el alma.
 Llegose al descuido, y dijo
 una razón poco clara,
 porque se tragó, al decilla,   75
 la mitad de las palabras.
 Quise excusar la respuesta,
 pero no pude excusalla,
 porque hay en los ojos niñas
 que nunca en la iglesia callan.   80
 A lo que supe después
 esta fue bastante causa
 para no lograr entonces
 los fines de su jornada;
 detúvose en Zaragoza,   85
 y pasando con más gracia
 de las galas soldadescas
 a las cortesanas galas,
 sirvió, festejó, obligando
 con suspiros y con ansias   90
 de mi calle las esquinas,

75 *decilla*: it was common to assimilate the consonant in an infinitive followed by lo, la or le, thus changing into -llo, -lla or -lle.

77 *excusar la respuesta*: 'avoid responding'; this use of 'excusar' is also found in verse 291.

80 *hay en los ojos niñas*: there is a play on the two meanings of 'niña' here, both referring to the anatomy of the eye, 'pupil', and 'niña' as the 'little girl' who can't keep quiet in church.

87–88 *las galas soldadescas* are in chiasmus with the next clause, '*las cortesanas galas*'. 'Galas' here means 'gallantry', 'charm', specifically 'courting'. Costanza explains that, in delaying his departure from Zaragoza, Pedro traded the activities of soldier life for those of courtship.

89–96 *sirvió*: 'to serve' in this context has to do with the rituals through which the courtier displays his affection for and devotion to his lady. Cov: "Vale obedecer a otro, y hazer su voluntad, y unos siruen libremente dando gusto a otros" ('servir'). *obligar*: here, with a connotation of ingratiating oneself to someone; *Aut. 1737*: "Vale también adquirirse y atraher la voluntad, o benevolencia de otro, con beneficios o agasajos, para tenerle propicio quando lo necessitate" ('obligar', 2nd def.).

looked at him with attention:
it felt like my heart 70
jumped out of my mouth,
my soul leapt from my eyes.
Both of us forgetting ourselves, he said
something barely intelligible,
he swallowed half the words 75
in trying to get them out.
I did not want to respond,
but I could not avoid it,
with so many eyes on me, like young girls
who titter to one another in church. 80
From what I learned later
that was reason enough
for him not to complete
the rest of his journey;
he lingered in Zaragoza, 85
happily passing his time
as he traded his soldierly duties
for the charms of courtship,
wooed me, made merry, promising
with sighs and with pleas, 90
he hung around the corners of my street,

La fuerza de la costumbre: Jornada primera

los umbrales de mi casa,
venerando como altares
del ídolo que adoraba
las verjas de mis balcones   95
y puertas de mis ventanas.
Viendo, en fin, que el padre mío,
por su condición extraña,
al trato del casamiento
tuvo las puertas cerradas,   100
obligada en mi aposento
por una estrecha ventana,
ancha puerta le di yo
para lograr su esperanza;
por ella entró muchas veces   105
teniendo para escalalla
por amigas las tinieblas
y por enemiga el alba.
Destas esperadas horas,
desta voluntad pagada,   110
destos logrados deseos,

99–100 The issue of the legality of Pedro and Costanza's marriage is complex. After the Council of Trent (1545–1563), marriage had to be performed publicly by a priest. Prior to this decree, clandestine marriage, consisting of the consent of both parties, their promise of marriage to each other, and consummation was considered legally binding (see Justina Ruiz de Conde, *El amor y el matrimonio secreto en los Libros de Caballerías*). However, *La fuerza de la costumbre* takes place after the Council of Trent, given that the historical backdrop of the play is the war in Flanders, which began in the mid 1560s. Even after the Council of Trent, a promise of marriage was still considered legally binding and disputes were resolved in the courts (see Allyson M. Poska, 'When Love Goes Wrong: Getting out of Marriage in Seventeenth-Century Spain'). The *Siete Partidas*, the book of laws written by the Castilian King Alfonso X, stated that if a woman married a man without her family's consent the marriage was still valid but the daughter could be disowned by her family (Ruiz de Conde 1948, p. 17).
107–108 This was a common friend/enemy pair for clandestine lovers in medieval lyric. The dawn, the time of day when the lovers must part ways, was the enemy, while darkness, which allowed lovers to keep their affair secret, was a friend. Consider the following examples: "Ya cantan los gallos, / buen amor, y vete, / cata que amanece" (in Frenk 2004, '112', p. 94); "Púsoseme el sol, / salióme la luna: / más me valiera, madre, / ver la noche escura" (Frenk, '365', p. 173). See also Dronke 1996, Ch. 5, 'The *Alba*', pp. 167–85.
109 *Destas*: 'De estas'. The contraction of 'de' with demonstrative pronouns was common.

and the doorstep of my house,
venerating, as if they were holy altars
to the idol he worshipped,
the railings of my balconies 95
and the shutters on my windows.
Seeing, finally, that my father,
because of his strange condition,
had closed all the doors to
the business of my marriage, 100
forcing me to stay in my room
where by way of a narrow window
I gave him a wide door
to attain his hopes;
in this way he entered many times 105
and in scaling the house
darkness was his friend
and dawn was his enemy.
From those anticipated hours,
from those wishes spent, 110
from those desires achieved,

	destas tinieblas amadas,	
	una niña salió a luz,	
	mas no para todos clara.	
	Sabe Dios lo que costó	115
	de cautelas y de trazas.	
	Al cabo de otros seis meses,	
	oye la mayor desgracia	
	que se ha visto ni se ha oído,	
	pero fue mía, que basta:	120
	acertó a pasar mi hermano	
	cuando a subir empezaba	
	por la escalera don Pedro,	
	que así mi esposo se llama.	
	Reparó, llegose, y viendo	125
	quien le ofende y quien le agravia,	
	los dos lucientes aceros	
	atrevidamente sacan,	
	gallardamente se tiran,	
	y yo mirándolo estaba	130
	tan sin aliento, que agora	
	para decillo me falta.	
	Diole mi esposo a mi hermano	
	en el pecho una estocada,	
	que dejó bastante boca	135
	por donde saliese el alma.	
	'¡Jesús!,' dijo, '¡que me han muerto!	
	¡Confesión, Jesús me valga!'	
	Pienso que le miro agora,	
	estribando con la espada,	140
	arrimarse a las paredes	
	y caer.	
FÉLIX	¡Desdicha extraña!	
COSTANZA	Reconocida su voz,	
	alborotó calle y casa;	
	dejole don Pedro y fuese,	145

116 *cautelas ... trazas*: Cov: 'Cautela': "el engaño que vno haze a otro ingeniosamente, vsando de terminos ambiguos, y de palabras dudosas y equiuocas." Cov: 'trazar': "dezimos dar traza a vn negocio, concertarle, y dar medio para que se efetue."

	from those beloved nights,	
	a little girl was born,	
	but we kept her hidden.	
	God knows the risks we took	115
	in tricks and sneaking around!	
	Six months later there occurred	
	the greatest disgrace	
	ever seen or heard,	
	but it was mine, and that's the worst:	120
	my brother happened to pass by	
	when who was just starting to come up	
	the ladder but Don Pedro,	
	which is my husband's name.	
	He noticed, realising, and seeing	125
	the man who offends and dishonours him,	
	they bravely draw	
	their bright steel swords,	
	and they fight nobly,	
	and I was watching it	130
	so breathlessly, that even now	
	in telling it, I have none.	
	My husband dealt my brother	
	a stab to the chest,	
	which opened up a wide mouth	135
	for his soul to escape.	
	'Jesus!,' he said, 'they have killed me,	
	give me confession, Jesus save me!'	
	I can still see him clearly now	
	leaning on his sword,	140
	lunging at the walls	
	and falling.	
FÉLIX	What strange misfortune!	
COSTANZA	Recognizing his voice,	
	the street and the house were in an uproar;	
	Don Pedro left him, and fled,	145

La fuerza de la costumbre: Jornada primera

	y yo quedé tan turbada, tan sin alma, tan sin mí que no retiré la escala arrimada a mis paredes y asida de mis ventanas. Salió mi padre al ruido, donde vio a la luz de un hacha su hijo en su sangre envuelto y, a mi vergüenza, colgada la delincuente escalera.	150 155
FÉLIX	¡Válame Dios, qué desgracia!	
COSTANZA	No pude ver sus extremos, que un criado y dos criadas me sacaron medio muerta. Huyendo de su amenaza, entregueme a la justicia y estuve depositada en casa de una señora de mi madre prima hermana. A Flandes se fue don Pedro; dijéronme que llevaba la casi recién nacida pedazo de mis entrañas. Otra prenda dejó en ellas, y eres tú, que de mis ansias fuiste consuelo en naciendo, aunque te callé la causa. Veinte años ha que tu padre sirve al Rey, y en Flandes manda un tercio de infantería	160 165 170 175

168 *pedazo de mis entrañas*: fig., 'child', 'baby'. A literal translation ('piece of my entrails') does not fully capture the fact that in Spanish this is a term of endearment; cf Covarrubias, 'entrañas': "suele ser termino de regalo, como vida mia, entrañas mias, y coraçon mio, &c".

173–175 *Flandes*: the military occupation of Flanders by Spanish troops began as a response to the Calvinist revolt of 1566. The conflict would go on for another seventy years, until the signing of the Treaty of Münster in October, 1648, with a twelve year truce halting the fighting between 1609 and 1621. For more on this subject see Elliott's *Imperial Spain: 1469–1716*, pp. 232–351.

	and I was left there so upset,
	so without my soul, so beside myself,
	that I did not put away the ladder
	leaning against my wall
	and anchored to my window.
	My father came out, hearing the noise,
	and there he saw by the light of a torch
	his son covered in his own blood,
	and, to my shame, hanging outside
	was the guilty ladder.
FÉLIX	My God, what a disgrace!
COSTANZA	I could not see then the extent of it,
	since a servant and two serving girls
	carried me away half-dead.
	Fleeing from the threat of him,
	I turned myself in to the police,
	and I was deposited
	in the house of a lady,
	my mother's first cousin.
	Don Pedro left for Flanders;
	they told me that he took with him
	my newborn baby girl,
	a piece of my heart.
	He left another treasure in my womb,
	and that is you, in my sorrows
	your birth was a comfort to me,
	although I kept the truth from you.
	For twenty years your father has
	served the King, and in Flanders commands
	a regiment of the infantry

con méritos y esperanzas,
y otros tantos que tu abuelo,
con malicia dilatada,
ni bajó de la querella,
ni depuso la venganza. 180
Pero murió habrá seis meses,
y (aunque siempre en su desgracia)
quedé yo sola heredera
de su hacienda y de su casa.
Avisé al esposo mío 185
para que venga a gozalla,
y estoylo esperando agora;
mas ya el corazón señala
que es sin duda aquel ruido
que en el zaguán se levanta 190
precursor de su venida
y fin de mis penas largas.
¡Abrázame, Félix mío!
(Abrázanse.)
FÉLIX Con más gusto que palabras
te responderé, señora, 195
que aun más cerca que pensabas
tienes la gloria que esperas.
COSTANZA Matarame por ser tanta.

Sale DON PEDRO DE MONCADA con barba entrecana, y DOÑA HIPÓLITA en hábito de hombre, y un viejo AYO de don Félix.

PEDRO ¿Señora, no me abrazáis? [redondillas]
¿O es que no me conocéis? 200
¿Callando me respondéis?
(Abrázanse.)
¿Qué tenéis? ¿Por qué lloráis?
    Aunque me veis tan mudado,
(que tanto el tiempo ha podido)
mi pecho, que vuestro ha sido, 205
siempre está en el mismo estado.

	with merit and ambition,	
	and your grandfather for all those years,	
	with protracted malice,	
	never withdrew his case for retribution,	
	nor ceased his vow for vengeance.	180
	But he died six months ago,	
	and (although he saw me as disgraced)	
	I remain the sole heir	
	to his estate and to his house.	
	I wrote to my husband,	185
	that he may come and enjoy it,	
	and I await him now;	
	but already my heart signals	
	that no doubt that sound	
	we can hear from outside	190
	heralds his arrival	
	and the end of my long suffering.	
	Embrace me, my Félix.	
	(They embrace.)	
FÉLIX	With more pleasure than words	
	I will reply to you, my lady,	195
	that even closer than you thought	
	is the joy you await.	
COSTANZA	The anticipation is killing me.	

SCENE 1.2

Enter DON PEDRO DE MONCADA, with a greying beard, and DOÑA HIPÓLITA, in man's attire, and an old man, DON FÉLIX'S TUTOR.

PEDRO	My lady, won't you embrace me?	
	Or don't you know me?	200
	Is silence your answer?	
	(They embrace.)	
	What is it? Why are you crying?	
	Although I must look different to you,	
	(for time has done its work on me)	
	my heart, which was yours,	205
	still belongs to you.	

COSTANZA	Mi don Pedro, por ser tanta	
	esta gloria vuestra y mía,	
	de terneza el alegría	
	puso un nudo a la garganta,	210
	y cayera en mayor mengua	
	si entre amorosos despojos,	
	reventando por los ojos,	
	no desatara la lengua.	
PEDRO	Mi bien, otra vez llegad	215
	a darme tiernos abrazos.	
	(Abrázanse.)	
COSTANZA	¿Que os vuelvo a ver en mis brazos?	
PEDRO	¡Con cuán diferente edad!	
	De las canas, que os confieso,	
	¿qué os parece? Pero ¿a quién	220
	las canas parecen bien?	
COSTANZA	Diréos lo que siento en eso.	
PEDRO	¿Qué sentís?	
COSTANZA	Vilas, señor,	
	y como con todo efeto	
	de las canas el respeto	225
	hacen más tierno el amor,	
	contémplolas con decoro,	
	con respeto las admiro,	
	piadosamente las miro,	
	y tiernamente las lloro.	230
PEDRO	De vuestro ingenio despojos	
	fue la respuesta, señora;	
	pero bien será que agora⁺	
	miréis con serenos ojos	
	este gallardo mancebo,	235
	y abrazalde como a mí.	
COSTANZA	¿Quién es? ¿Qué siento? ¡Ay de mí!	

224   *efeto*: efecto.
+ 233   agora A B C : agota. Since 'agora' makes more sense here, I am rejecting P's reading, which is likely a printing error.
235   *gallardo mancebo*: note that Hipólita is introduced as a 'dashing young man'.
236   *abrazalde*: 'abrazadle'; metathesis of the l and d were common.

COSTANZA	My Don Pedro, the abundant	
	joy that we both share,	
	the tenderness and happiness	
	put a lump in my throat,	210
	and it would be even worse	
	if with love's bounty	
	streaming through our eyes,	
	the tongue was also not freed.	
PEDRO	My love, come again	215
	to embrace me tenderly.	
	(They embrace.)	
COSTANZA	Can you really be in my arms again?	
PEDRO	And how we've aged!	
	I confess I've a few more grey hairs,	
	how do they look? Then again,	220
	who likes grey hairs?	
COSTANZA	I will tell you how I feel about that.	
PEDRO	How do you feel?	
COSTANZA	I saw them, sir,	
	and as always,	
	grey hair calls for respect	225
	but they make my love more tender,	
	and I prudently contemplate them,	
	respectfully admire them,	
	piously look on them	
	and softly … weep for them.	230
PEDRO	Your answers are the spoils	
	of your ready wit, my lady;	
	but now it will be better if you	
	look with your serene eyes	
	upon this handsome youth,	235
	and embrace him as you did me.	
COSTANZA	Who is it? What's this? Oh, my!	

130   *La fuerza de la costumbre: Jornada primera*

PEDRO   Deste tronco es un renuevo,
             mas ya para vos venía
             bien sobrescrito el papel.   240
COSTANZA   Un retrato miro en él
             de lo que yo ser solía.
HIPÓLITA*   *(Arrodíllase DOÑA HIPÓLITA.)*
             Dame.
COSTANZA   El alma te daré
             hija, hija de mi vida.
HIPÓLITA   Madre, y señora.
COSTANZA   ¿Vestida   245
             en este traje, y por qué?
PEDRO   Desde que el pecho dejó,
             si no el ser, le mudé el nombre,
             y con pensamientos de hombre
             el hábito se vistió,   250
                   por ser más desenfadado
             para una y otra jornada,
             y como si fuera espada,
             nunca la perdí del lado.
                   Criose en la guerra, y vio   255
             vencer, herir, y matar,
             y agora puede enseñar
             lo que entonces aprendió.
                   Asiéntale un coselete
             como si el Cid se le armara;   260
             juega una pica y dispara
             un arcabuz y un mosquete;

---

* *HIPÓLITA*: this name carries resonances of warrior women from classical mythology. According to Greek mythology, Hipólita (in English, Hippolyta or Hippolyte) was the daughter of the god of war, Ares, and the Queen of the Amazons, a race of fierce female warriors.

259 *coselete*: 'shield'.

260 *el Cid*: the eleventh-century Spanish hero, Rodrigo Díaz de Vivar (more commonly known as 'el Cid Campeador'), whose tribulations and military feats were immortalized in the epic poem, *El cantar de mio Cid* (composed between 1140 and 1207). Guillén de Castro takes this celebrated figure as the protagonist of two plays, *Las mocedades del Cid* (*Primera* and *Segunda parte*), which incorporate many *romances* about the Cid.

262 *arcabuz*: 'harquebus', a long barreled gun dating from the 14th or 15th century.

PEDRO	He's a chip off the old block all right,	
	but he is an image of you which I have	
	written over with quite new material.	240
COSTANZA	He is the very picture of	
	how I used to look.	
HIPÓLITA	*(HIPÓLITA kneels.)*	
	Give me your hands.	
COSTANZA	I'll give you my soul,	
	my daughter, my precious daughter.	
HIPÓLITA	My mother and my lady.	
COSTANZA	You're dressed	245
	as a man? And why is that?	
PEDRO	Since she left the breast,	
	I have changed her name and thoughts,[1]	
	if not her being, into those of a man.	
	I dressed her in male attire	250
	in order to embolden her	
	in our many campaigns in the war,	
	and just as if she were my sword,	
	I have kept her always at my side.	
	She grew up in the war and she saw	255
	how to fight, wound, and kill,	
	and now she could teach	
	the lessons she learned as a child.	
	A breastplate suits her well, as if	
	El Cid had dressed her in armour;	260
	she can wield a pike and fire	
	a harquebus and a musket.	

---

1 See p. 96, Fig. 1, for a photograph of this scene in production.

	pues pelea, yo lo fío,	
	y como yo se aventura,	
	si no con tan gran cordura,	265
	a lo menos con más brío.	
	Y cáusale pesadumbre	
	verse en efeto mujer;	
	milagros que suele hacer	
	la fuerza de la costumbre.	270
COSTANZA	Mil años la guarde Dios.	
HIPÓLITA	Para empleallos en ti.	
COSTANZA	Esta prenda quedó en mí	
	cuando yo quedé sin vos.	
PEDRO	¿Es mi don Félix?	
COSTANZA	Él es.	275
PEDRO	Ya os quería preguntar	
	por él.	
FÉLIX	Déjame besar	
	(Arrodíllase DON FÉLIX.)	
	tu mano, si no tus pies.	
PEDRO	Mano y brazos te daré.	
	(Abrázale, y levántase DON FÉLIX.)	
	Hijo, ¡sucesos extraños!,	280
	mas teniendo ya veinte años,	
	¿hábito largo, y por qué?	
	¿Es devoción bien fundada?	
	¿Quiere ser de iglesia?	
COSTANZA	No,	
	mas por no obligalle yo	285
	a que se ciñera espada,	
	por no perdelle del lado,	
	por tenelle a mi contento	
	las noches en mi aposento	

281–284 Pedro is surprised that Félix would still be wearing long clothing, which is either childish, effeminate, or indicates that he is interested in a career in the church. See introductory essay for more on the implications of Félix's clothing.

	She fights and attacks	
	just like I do, I tell you,	
	if not with as much wisdom,	265
	at least with more manly spirit.	
	And it causes her distress	
	to see herself as a woman;	
	these are the miracles performed	
	by the force of habit.	270
COSTANZA	May God protect her all her life.	
HIPÓLITA	Only to spend it serving you.	
COSTANZA	And this precious one was left with me	
	while I was left without you.	
PEDRO	Is this my Don Félix?	
COSTANZA	It is he.	275
PEDRO	I was going to ask	
	about him.	
FÉLIX	Let me kiss	
	(DON FÉLIX kneels.)	
	your hand, if not your feet.	
PEDRO	My hand and my arms I give to you.	
	(They embrace, and FÉLIX stands up.)	
	Son, this is strange,	280
	for you are now twenty years old,	
	yet you're in this long dress? Why?	
	Is this some kind of devotion?	
	Does he intend to join the church?	
COSTANZA	No,	
	but to keep him	285
	from taking up the sword,	
	to never lose him from my side,	
	to have him for company	
	by night in my chambers	

	y los días en mi estrado,	290
	por excusar deste modo	
	ocasiones de pesar,	
	y, en fin, por no aventurar	
	en él mi consuelo todo,	
	nunca su ánimo dispuse	295
	a que mudara el vestido,	
	y el hábito largo ha sido	
	grillos que a los pies le puse,	
	sin que le den pesadumbre	
	el no pasear, ni ver;	300
	milagros que suele hacer	
	la fuerza de la costumbre.	
PEDRO	No se ha visto imaginada	
	tan nueva y extraña cosa,	
	fuistes mujer temerosa.	305
COSTANZA	Madre soy, y escarmentada.	
PEDRO	Don Félix sabrá mejor	
	vencer con brío y con gala	
	esa costumbre tan mala,	
	que disminuye el valor.	310
	Y tan mal me han parecido	
	en un lego esas pihuelas	
	que antes que yo las espuelas,	
	se ha de quitar el vestido.	
	En corto le ha de mudar,	315
	y luego, que así conviene.	
	¿Tiene vestidos?	
COSTANZA	Sí tiene,	
	mas no se los dejo usar.	

---

291 *excusar*: as in l. 77, excusar meaning 'evitar', 'avoid'.
306 *escarmentada*: 'punished', 'taught a lesson'. Corominas: "castigo ejemplar", "desengaño adquirido con la experiencia" (CE–F, 'escarmiento').
312 *pihuelas*: 'shackles'. Pedro equates the long cassock with leg irons.
317a *vestidos*: here the word is gender neutral and means 'clothing'.

	and by day in my sitting-room,[2]	290
	this was our way of life	
	in difficult times,	
	so that I would never have to risk	
	losing him, my one consolation,	
	I never encouraged him to	295
	change his way of dressing,	
	and this long habit has been like	
	shackles I placed on his feet,	
	so as not to disturb him	
	with going out and seeing;	300
	these are the miracles performed	
	by the force of habit.	
PEDRO	No one has ever seen or imagined	
	such a novel and strange thing –	
	you have acted as a cowardly woman.	305
COSTANZA	I'm a mother, and I've paid dearly for it.	
PEDRO	Don Félix will learn	
	with manly spirit and elegance	
	to overcome this terrible habit	
	which diminishes his valour.	310
	I think it is terrible for a layman	
	to be fettered by these robes;	
	he'll have to take off that dress	
	before I can take off my spurs.	
	Put him in something shorter now,	315
	that's the best thing to do.	
	Does he have any clothes at all?	
COSTANZA	Yes he does,	
	but I don't let him wear them.	

---

2 'sitting-room' or 'drawing room': quoting from Cruickshank and Page, 'the *estrado* was a dais where ladies sat on cushions to receive visitors (Covarrubias). This eastern custom was one of many that survived the eight centuries (711–1492) of Moorish presence in the Iberian peninsula. The correct English word in the circumstances was 'divan': "A continued step, or raised part of the floor, against the wall of a room, so as to form a sofa or couch" (*OED*)'. See *No hay burlas con el amor* note 321 p. 21, also note 1634–40 p. 104, Calderón de la Barca, ed. Cruickshank and Page, Warminster: Aris and Phillips, 1994.

PEDRO	Y a Hipólita le poned	
	largo vestido y tocado,	320
	y en aposento y estrado	
	para consuelo tened.	
	Yo a don Félix llevaré	
	de ordinario al lado mío,	
	porque aprenda a tener brío,	325
	y sí tendrá, yo lo sé;	
	pues mudará pareceres	
	en ciñéndose la espada;	
	que la casa de Moncada	
	no consiente hombres mujeres.	330
	Y ansí podremos hacer,	
	para que el mundo se asombre,	
	vos una mujer de un hombre,	
	yo un hombre de una mujer.	
	En los hombres cosa es cruel	335
	faldas largas de doncella;	
	id luego, y ponelde a ella	
	las que le quitáis a él.	
	Quedaré con esperanza	
	de trocar con el vestido	340
	las costumbres que ha tenido.	
HIPÓLITA	Reniego de tal mudanza.	
COSTANZA	Por dejaros satisfecho	
	voy luego.	
PEDRO	Guárdeosme Dios.	
HIPÓLITA	¡Qué buenos vamos los dos!⁺	345
	Vil fortuna, ¿qué habéis hecho?	
FÉLIX	La pérdida será mucha	
	si a mi madre he de dejar.	
PEDRO	¿Quién os ayudó a criar	
	a Félix?	

---

325 *porque*: 'para que', 'in order that'.
+ 345 *dos!*: dos? P.

PEDRO	And as for Hipólita, put her	
	in a long dress and do her hair;	320
	in your chamber and sitting-room	
	you will console yourself with her.	
	I will take Don Félix	
	to keep always at my side,	
	so that he can learn to show spirit,	325
	and he will, I know it,	
	he will change his appearance	
	when he puts on his sword;	
	for the House of Moncada	
	does not allow any girly men.	330
	That is the way we will do it,	
	for the amazement of the world,	
	you will make a woman of this man,	
	and I will make a man of this woman.	
	It is cruel to force men to wear	335
	long skirts like girls –	
	go now, and put on her	
	the clothes you take off him.	
	I will wait here, hopeful	
	that we can change habits	340
	by exchanging clothes.³	
HIPÓLITA	I refuse to change.	
COSTANZA	To do as you wish,	
	I'll go right now.	
PEDRO	God help me.	
HIPÓLITA	It's going very well for the two of us!	345
	Vile fortune, what have you done?	
FÉLIX	It will be even worse for me	
	if I have to leave my mother.	
PEDRO	Who was it that helped you	
	to raise Félix?	

---

3   Ambiguity in the Spanish pronouns is harder to capture in English here. I have elected to leave the pronouns out, but one could say, 'hopeful that we can change their habits by changing their clothes'. Pedro is, as usual, more concerned with changing Félix's habits, so it is also possible to render this as 'hopeful we can change his habits by changing his clothes'.

138   La fuerza de la costumbre: Jornada primera

AYO　　　　　Yo soy.

Vanse DOÑA COSTANZA, DON FÉLIX y DOÑA HIPÓLITA.

PEDRO　　　　　Escucha:　　　　　　　　　　350
 dime tú, que le has criado,
 si el quedar así encogido
 don Félix, mi hijo, ¿ha sido
 naturaleza o cuidado?
  ¿Nace de su mismo ser　　　　　355
 lo que en él su madre ha hecho?
 ¿Tiene valor en el pecho
 que revienta sin querer?
  ¿Por qué pasión se lastima?
 ¿De qué temores se espanta?　　　360
 ¿Qué pensamientos levanta?
 ¿Con qué inclinación se anima?
 Y di verdad.　　　　　　　　[romance i–a]
AYO　　　　　　Yo, señor,
 serví a tu suegro hasta el día,
 o la noche desdichada,　　　　　365
 causa de tantas desdichas,
 porque yo fui aquel criado
 que hasta en casa de su tía
 acompañé a mi señora,
 previniendo a la justicia;　　　　370
 y desde entonces, sus cosas
 las más importantes fía
 de mí, sirviéndola yo
 con el alma y con la vida.
 Serví a tu hijo también,　　　　375
 desde su menor puericia,
 de quien diré la verdad
 que me mandas que te diga.
 En su niñez dio señales
 de naturaleza altiva,　　　　　　380

354　*cuidado*: 'care'; Pedro is asking whether Félix's effeminacy comes from his nature or his upbringing.
376　*puericia*: 'boyhood'.

| TUTOR | It was me. |

Exit COSTANZA, FÉLIX and HIPÓLITA.

PEDRO Listen. 350
You tell me, since you raised him,
if these cowardly qualities
in Don Félix, my son, are due to
his nature or upbringing?
Is it born of his own nature, 355
this way his mother has made him?
Has he any valour in his heart
that bursts out unexpectedly?
By what passion is he stirred?
What frightens him? 360
What does he think about?
What interests excite him?
And tell the truth.

SCENE 1.3

TUTOR I, sir,
served your father-in-law until the day,
or rather that unfortunate night, 365
the cause of so many misfortunes,
for I was the servant who
accompanied my lady
to the house of her aunt,
protecting her from the force of law; 370
and from that time, she entrusted
her most important affairs
to me, and I serve her
with my soul and with my life.
I also served your son 375
from the time he was a little boy,
and now I will tell you the truth
that you ask me to reveal.
In his childhood he showed signs
of a noble nature, 380

de caballeroso brío,
que causara honrada envidia;
pero su amorosa madre,
femenilmente encogida,
previniendo los peligros 385
y temiendo las desdichas,
con diligencias piadosas,
(prudencia mal entendida)
sus acciones reformaba
y su natural vencía. 390
Cuando a varoniles cosas
inclinarse pretendía,
divertíale con otras,
de afeminadas, indignas.
Por los estrados andaba 395
entreteniendo los días,
viendo labrar las doncellas,
o jugando con las niñas.
Si encontrando una almohada,
sobre el estrado caía; 400
de triaca y cordiales⁺
agotaba las boticas.
Siempre a su cuello colgado
entre alcorzadas caricias,
con regalos lo enviciaba, 405
con temores le ofendía.
En invierno y en verano
soles y vientos temía,
y todo el año el sereno.
Al fin, en toda su vida 410

401–402 *triaca*: 'antidote' to poison or venom or more generally, 'medicine' (Cov. 'atriaca'). *cordiales*: also a medicinal term, in this case a drink given to the sick to strengthen them, fortifying the heart in particular (*Aut. 1729* 'cordial', 2nd and 3rd defs). *boticas*: 'pharmacies'.
+ 401 This line is short one syllable.
409 *sereno*: humidity and wind which appear after sundown; Cov.: "Comunmente llamamos sereno el ayre alterado de la prima noche, con algun vapor que se ha levantado de la tierra" ('sereno').

of gentlemanly spirit,
worthy of honourable envy;
but his loving mother,
fearful, as women are,
trying to prevent danger 385
and fearing misfortune
with pious diligence,
(and misunderstood prudence)
she altered his actions
and overcame his nature. 390
When manly occupations
drew his attention
she distracted him with others,
effeminate and unworthy of him.
Through the rooms he wandered, 395
whiling away his days,
observing the serving-maids
and playing with the little girls.
If he tripped over a cushion
and fell on the floor; 400
he would apply every antidote
and potion in the pharmacy.
He always hung his arms
around her neck for sweet caresses,
she spoiled him with gifts 405
and instilled her own fears.
In winter and in summer
he feared the sun and winds,
and was afraid of the dark all year round.
So, he has spent his whole life 410

	le ofendió el viento, ni el sol,	
	oyendo en su casa misa,	
	o en la iglesia alguna vez,	
	si era muy templado el día.	
	Si pasaba un corredor	415
	dentro de su casa misma,	
	como si pasara un puerto,	
	la cabeza le envolvían.	
	A cualquier rumor de espadas	
	tiernamente al hijo asida	420
	diciendo a voces, '¡Jesús!	
	¡En la calle se acuchillan!'	
	Todas las puertas cerraba,	
	y parece que le abría	
	las de su medroso pecho.	425
	Pues, ¿qué, cuando la estampida	
	de un arcabuz resonaba?	
	Con tocas, ropa y vasquiña	
	le guardaba todo el cuerpo,	
	todo el rostro le cubría.	430
	Pues, ¿si un trueno retumbaba,	
	o un relámpago lucía?	
	Temblaban casi debajo	
	del altar de la capilla.	
PEDRO	Ese solo es miedo honrado,	435
	que, advirtiendo su justicia,	
	temer a Dios es virtud,	
	y a los hombres cobardía.	
AYO	Creció con esta crianza,	
	y cuando aprender podría	440
	varoniles ejercicios	
	los poderes le limita;	

---

428 *vasquiña*: 'skirt'; when she heard the blast of a harquebus, Costanza would wrap Félix up in her clothing to shield him.

	in fear of the wind, or the sun,	
	listening to Mass at home,	
	rarely venturing to church,	
	and only if the weather was perfect.	
	If he was walking down a corridor	415
	in his own house,	
	as if he was passing a port,	
	they would turn his head away.	
	At any sound of swords,	
	tenderly clinging to her son	420
	she would yell, 'Lord!,	
	they are fighting in the street!'	
	She would lock all the doors of the house,	
	though it seemed that she opened	
	the doors to his faint heart.	425
	But, what about when the shot	
	of a harquebus rang out?	
	With her veil, clothes, and skirt	
	she would cover his body	
	hiding his whole face.	430
	And if thunder rumbled	
	or a lightning bolt struck?	
	They trembled and would	
	hide under the chapel altar.	
PEDRO	That alone is honourable fear;	435
	for, recognizing His justice,	
	to fear God is virtue,	
	but to fear men is cowardice.	
TUTOR	This is how he was brought up,	
	and whenever he would try	440
	his hand at manly occupations,	
	she limited his abilities;	

	ni espada blanca jamás	
	dejó ponelle en la cinta,	
	ni tomar negra en la mano.	445
	Y así, si una piedra tira,	
	es con aire de mujer,	
	y pudiera despedilla,	
	según es fuerte, y metella	
	en el tronco de una encina,	450
	pero el cuchillo en la mesa	
	hoy de la mano le quita,	
	temiendo que ha de ofendelle.	
PEDRO	¡Válgame Dios, qué desdicha!	
AYO	Y así, como esta costumbre	455
	tan dilatada y seguida	
	convirtió en naturaleza,	
	tiene condición muy tibia;	
	es encogido, es medroso…	
PEDRO	Y es, en efeto, gallina.	460
	Siendo Moncada, ¡por Dios!,	
	que es una cosa inaudita.	
	Menester será volvelle	
	su naturaleza misma.	
	Pondré fuego en sus acciones,	465
	hirviendo la sangre mía	
	en sus venas y en su pecho.	
	Será honrada, pues es limpia,	
	o sacarésela toda;	
	que el que con una sangría	470
	la mala sangre derrama,	
	a la buena purifica.	

443–445 *espada blanca*: the '*blanca*' is the steel sword carried and used by nobles, with a sharp tip and blade, while a '*negra*' ('foil'), used for fencing, was unsharpened and darker in color because it was made of unpolished iron (*DRAE* 'espada blanca', "espada de esgrima / espada negra"; also Cov. 'espada').

453 *ofendelle*: 'harm him'.

460 *gallina*: lit. 'hen', fig. 'chicken'; *Aut. 1734*: "Por analogía se llama al que es cobarde, pusilanime y timido. Dixose assi aludiendo à la cobardia que tiene esta ave" ('gallina', 2nd def.).

470 *una sangría*: a medical procedure, 'bloodletting'.

	no steel blade would ever	
	be hung around his belt,	
	nor would he take the foil in his hand.	445
	So now if he throws a stone,	
	he throws it like a girl,	
	and he would be able to throw it,	
	since he is strong enough, lodging it	
	into the trunk of an oak;	450
	and even the table knife	
	she now takes out of his hand	
	for fear that it may cut him.	
PEDRO	God help me, what a disgrace!	
TUTOR	And so, since these habits	455
	he followed are by now so ingrained,	
	it became his nature;	
	his condition is very timid,	
	he is shrunken, he is fearful.	
PEDRO	He is, in short, a chicken.	460
	And for a Moncada, by God,	
	this is unheard of.	
	It will be necessary to change him	
	back to his own nature.	
	I will put a fire under his actions;	465
	boiling my own blood	
	in his veins and in his heart.	
	It will be honoured, for it is pure,	
	or I will shed it all myself;	
	for the bloodletter	470
	who spills bad blood	
	purifies the good.	

Sale GALVÁN lacayo.

GALVÁN	Toda tu gente está aquí.	[redondillas]
AYO	Tu hijo viene galán.	
PEDRO	Falta me has hecho, Galván.	475
GALVÁN	Mayor me la hizo a mí	
	la mula que no me han dado	
	para caminar.	

Sale DON FÉLIX vestido de corto, mal puesto cuanto lleva, y él muy encogido.

PEDRO	Bien viene;	
	razonable talle tiene,	
	aunque tibio y desairado.	480
	Bueno vienes, Félix mío,	
	pues ya sin trabas estás,	
	alarga los pasos más,	
	(Alarga el paso descompasada y ridículamente.)	
	asienta los pies con brío.	
FÉLIX	Servirte en todo deseo.	485
PEDRO	Caiga con más desenfado	
	el ferreruelo a este lado;	
	advierte que no es manteo;	
	imita a los cortesanos.	
	(Pone los dos dedos pulgares asidos de la pretina.)	
	Esa es postura frailesca;	490
	¡quita, quita! No parezca	
	que te embarazan las manos.	
	Párate varonilmente…	
	(Pone los pies juntos.)	
	…¡qué mal te paraste aquí!	

---

487   *ferreruelo*: a hoodless cape with a collar, commonly worn hanging off to one side. According to Covarrubias, the garment is thought to be of German origin.
488   *manteo*: 'cloak'; this garment was associated with students or those in the ecclesiastic profession.
490   *postura frailesca*: again, effeminacy and religious office are compared; Pedro relates Félix's effeminate stance to that of a friar holding his habit.

SCENE 1.4

Enter GALVÁN, a servant.

GALVÁN	All of your people are here.	
TUTOR	Your son comes dressed as a gentleman.	
PEDRO	I missed you, Galván.	475
GALVÁN	And I missed the mule you didn't lend me, it's a long walk.	

Enter DON FÉLIX, dressed in a short jacket, with his male clothes ill-fitting, and he is uncomfortable and ashamed.

PEDRO	He looks well; he has a decent figure, though timid and graceless. You look well, my Félix, and now that you are unshackled, lengthen your stride, *(He lengthens his steps out of rhythm and ridiculously.)* and step firmly, with manly spirit.	480
FÉLIX	I will serve your every wish.	485
PEDRO	Allow your short cape to fall casually to one side; look, it's not a friar's cloak; wear it like they do at court. *(FÉLIX puts his thumbs in his waistband.)* No, that is a monk's posture; stop, stop, do not allow your hands to get in the way. Stand up like a man… *(FÉLIX puts his feet together.)* …the way you are standing looks terrible!	490

GALVÁN	Es un hombre puesto así	495
	un cántaro propriamente.	
PEDRO	Haz ballesta de los pies	
	y huye siempre de juntallos,	
	que si es malo en los caballos,	
	en los hombres bueno es.	500
	Ponte el sombrero, y advierte	
	que es gracia aparte también	
	sabérsele poner bien;	
	no va airoso desa suerte.	
	Nunca respetes al cuello,	505
	y llévale, ¡qué tibieza!,	
	encajado en la cabeza,	
	no encomendado al cabello.	
GALVÁN	Más diadema que sombrero	
	parecerá dese modo.	510
FÉLIX	Mal a sufrir me acomodo	
	esas burlas; no las quiero.	
PEDRO	¿También te corres?	
FÉLIX	Desprecio	
	me parece.	
PEDRO	¿Aún no has sabido	
	que al hombre que está corrido	515
	le tienen todos por necio?	
FÉLIX	Suplícote me perdones	
	el no sufrir burlas tales.	
AYO	Esto es hombres principales	
	criados por los rincones.	520

Sale DOÑA HIPÓLITA vestida de mujer, y DOÑA COSTANZA tras ella, y un CRIADO que saca su espada y daga.

505–508 Pedro critiques Félix's womanish way of elongating his neck, as if the neck were 'at the service of' (*'encomendado al cabello'*, lit. 'entrusted to') his hair, instructing him instead to 'insert his neck into his head', i.e., shorten it.

GALVÁN	A man standing like that	495
	looks more like a little teapot.	
PEDRO	Make like a crossbow with your feet	
	and never allow them to come together,	
	for even though it is a flaw in a horse,	
	this stance is becoming for a man.	500
	Put your hat on, see how	
	it is part of a man's grace	
	to know how to wear it well;	
	don't go swanning about in that way.	
	Never stretch out your neck,	505
	but let it (what meekness!)	
	firmly hold up your head	
	without stretching to show off your hair.[4]	
GALVÁN	His hat looks more like a tiara	
	sat on his head in that way.	510
FÉLIX	I am not accustomed	
	to being laughed at; I do not like it.	
PEDRO	Are you ashamed?	
FÉLIX	When it seems I	
	am scorned, yes.	
PEDRO	You still don't see	
	that the man who is ashamed	515
	is taken by everyone for a fool?	
FÉLIX	I beg of you to pardon me	
	as I do not suffer such ridicule.	
TUTOR	This is what happens when fine men	
	are raised in corners.	520

Enter DOÑA HIPÓLITA, dressed as a woman, and DOÑA COSTANZA after her, and a SERVANT who carries her sword and dagger.

---

4 Pedro implies that a feminine posture would be to stretch the neck out in order to call attention to the hairstyle.

HIPÓLITA	Que no acierto, te confieso,	
	a dar paso.	
	(Tropieza con los chapines y arrójalos.)	
COSTANZA	Escucha, espera.	
HIPÓLITA	Sobre cosa tan ligera	
	¿cómo irá seguro el seso?	
	¿Cómo puede una mujer,	525
	destos corchos⁺ sostenida,	
	viéndose toda la vida	
	ir cayendo, no caer?	
	Reniego de los chapines,	
	del vestido y del tocado;	530
	impertinente cuidado	
	de tan mal seguros fines.	
PEDRO	¿Qué hay, Hipólita? Qué ha sido?	
	Linda estás.	
HIPÓLITA	A ti, señor,	
	apelo deste rigor;	535
	ahógame este vestido.	
	Deste postizo cabello	
	a mi cabeza apretado,	
	sospecho que el más delgado	
	sirve de lazo a mi cuello.	540
COSTANZA	Hija, repórtate agora.	
	¡Jesús mío, qué extrañeza!	
PEDRO	Monstros de naturaleza	
	son nuestros hijos, señora.	
GALVÁN	Dele las barbas su hermano,	545
	y ella infúndale el valor	
	en cambio, y así, señor,	
	quedará el negocio llano.	

+ 526   *corchos*: A B C: corches P.
535   *rigor*: *Aut. 1737*: "se toma tambien por la crueldád ò excesso en el castigo, pena ò reprehension" ('rigór', 6th def.).
543   *Monstros de naturaleza*: Covarrubias on 'monstro': "qualquier parto contra la regla y orden natural, como nacer el hombre con dos cabeças, quatro braços, y quatro piernas."

HIPÓLITA	I confess, I am not skilled at walking this way. *(She trips in the high-heeled shoes, takes them off, and throws them.)*	
COSTANZA	Listen, wait.	
HIPÓLITA	Walking on such flimsy things how will I keep my head safe? How can a woman, perching on these cork sandals, spend her entire life on the verge of falling, and not fall? I refuse to wear these shoes, this dress and this headpiece; frivolous adornments that are sure to come to a bad end.	525

530 |
| PEDRO | What's wrong, Hipólita? What is it? You look pretty. | |
| HIPÓLITA | To you, sir, I appeal this punishment; this dress is drowning me. As for this false hair piece squeezing on to my head, I can feel the finest strand serving as a noose around my neck. | 535

540 |
COSTANZA	Daughter, stop this right now. Jesus! How strange!	
PEDRO	Monsters of nature are our children, my lady.	
GALVÁN	Have the brother give her his beard, and the sister lend him her bravery in exchange, and then, sir, you will have the business all fixed up.	545

COSTANZA	La sangre se le ha subido	
	al rostro. ¿Si se ha enojado?	550
PEDRO	De haberle tan mal criado	
	le nace el vivir corrido.	

(Toma la espada de las manos del criado.)

HIPÓLITA	La espada me he de volver	
	al lado, y quedar exenta	
	de lo que tan mal me asienta.	555
PEDRO	Paciencia, que eres mujer,	
	y al lado quiero ponella	
	de tu hermano.	
HIPÓLITA	¡Injusta calma!	
	Déjame que con el alma	
	pueda despedirme della.	560

(Saca la espada.)

    Ay, espada, adorar quiero   [décimas]
por una y otra razón
la cruz de tu guarnición
y de tu hoja el acero.
Ceñirte otra vez no espero,   565
pues sería ser cruel,
poco honrada y poco fiel,
si poniendo, a mi pesar,
una rueca en tu lugar,
volviese a ponerte en él.   570
    Con más honroso caudal
mirara, valiente espada,
en tu acero una celada,
que el tranzado en un cristal;

---

563   *guarnición*: 'cross guard', the part of a sword which separates the grip from the blade and protects the hand.

569   *rueca*: 'distaff', 'spinning wheel'; specifically referred to as the shameful counterpoint to the glory of wearing a sword; see Cov. on 'espada': "la comun arma de que se usa, y los hombres la traen de ordinario ceñida para defensa, y para ornato y demostración de lo que son: y a los que no estan tenidos en esta reputación, les dizen que traen ruecas."

573   *en tu acero una celada*: looking into the polished blade like a mirror.

574   *tranzado*: a hair accessory which began at the crown of the head and then was braided into the hair.

COSTANZA	The blood has all rushed	
	to his face. Is he angry?	550
PEDRO	Having been raised so badly	
	has caused him to live in shame.	
	(He takes the sword from the hands of the servant.)	
HIPÓLITA	I must return my sword to my side	
	and be freed from this,	
	which does not suit me at all.	555
PEDRO	Patience, as you are a woman,	
	and I want to put this sword	
	at your brother's side.	
HIPÓLITA	What injustice!	
	Please allow my soul	
	to say goodbye to it properly.	560
	(She draws the sword.)	
	Oh, sword! You deserve my adoration	
	for your many merits,	
	the insignia of your cross guard	
	and the steel of your blade.	
	I do not hope to wear you again,	565
	because that would be to act cruelly,	
	with scant honour and little loyalty,	
	if having hung a distaff, against my will,	
	at the place of your sheath,	
	I returned you to my side.	570
	It would grant me greater esteem,	
	valiant sword, to look into your steel	
	and see a helmet reflected there,	
	rather than my braided hair in a mirror,	

	mas hízolo el tiempo mal;	575
	que, pues, tan bien me acomodo	
	a ser varón, diera modo	
	con que acertara mejor,	
	y como mudo el valor,	
	mudara el género y todo.	580
	¡Ay, mi espada! Pues perdistes	
	mi lado, mostrad siquiera	
	un sentimiento de cera,	
	aunque tan de acero fuistes;	
	y volveos donde estuvistes	585
	tan bien pegada, y ceñida;	
	pues, espada de mi vida,	
	sabe el cielo soberano	
	que de mi cinta a mi mano	
	jamás salistes corrida.	590
	Y así, si no me obligara	
	la obediencia que me incita,	
	él que de mi lado os quita	
	de mi mano no os quitara.	
	Yo os defendiera y guardara,	595
	y al mismo que me obligó	
	pongo por testigo yo	
	de que, obediente y honrada,	
	os dejo por desdichada,	
	pero por cobarde, no.	600
	(Tómale la espada DON PEDRO.)	
PEDRO	Baste, hija, bueno está.	
	Y vos agora, hijo mío,	
	recebilda con el brío	
	que vuestra hermana os la da;	
	y escuchadme a lo que está	605
	obligado un caballero	
	que ciñe el luciente acero;	
	que el que no le lleva al lado	

	but fate has gotten this one wrong;	575
	for, though it suited me so well to be	
	a young man, now I exchange my ways	
	for those which will be better suited,	
	and as I change my valour, my gender	
	and everything will change.	580
	Oh, my sword! Even as you lose[5]	
	your place at my side, you show	
	that your feelings are soft as wax,	
	although you were of such hard steel;	
	and you return to where you were	585
	so proudly worn, so tightly girded;	
	for, sword of my life,	
	sovereign heaven knows that	
	from my waist to my hand	
	you were never drawn in vain.	590
	If it were not for my obedience	
	that forces me to take this action,	
	he who would take you from my side	
	would never take you from my hand.	
	I would defend and guard you,	595
	and it is that obedience that forces me	
	to offer myself as witness	
	to the fact that, obedient and honourable,	
	it is my misfortune to leave you,	
	but I do not do so out of cowardice.	600
	(PEDRO takes the sword from her.)	
PEDRO	Enough, daughter, you've done well.	
	And you now, my son,	
	receive it with the manly spirit	
	with which your sister gives it to you,	
	and listen to me tell you that	605
	a gentleman is obliged	
	to wear a shining sword;	
	for he who does not wear one at his side	

---

5 See p. 97, Fig. 2 for a photograph of this scene in production.

vive menos obligado,
pero vuela más terrero. 610
　Es la espada, al lado asida,
en el que tiene valor,
un respeto del honor
y un resguardo de la vida.
Y no ha de darla rendida, 615
aunque vea peligrar
la vida que ha de guardar,
porque aunque no le convenga
a la vida, es bien que tenga
la honra el primer lugar. 620
　Por su fe primeramente,
sirviendo a su rey cristiano,
debe ponella en la mano,
protestando eternamente
que entre la herética gente 625
se ofrece a morir por ella,
sin mudalla ni ofendella;
pues les toca, para honralla,
a la boca confesalla
y a la espada defendella. 630
　Por causas ligeras no
debe salir a ofender;
mas si sale, ha de volver
menos limpia que salió.
Sangrienta la estimo yo, 635
porque el dar muestras de honrada
es al revés en la espada;
pues aunque atropelle o venza,
está con mayor vergüenza
desnuda y no colorada. 640
　Y más si contra un villano
sacarla, obligado, debe,
porque altivo se le atreve
cuerpo a cuerpo y mano a mano;

610　*pero vuela más terrero*: lit. 'but he flies closer to the earth', meaning, he has a lower status, is more humble.

lives with fewer responsibilities, though
he flies a little closer to the ground. 610
The sword, at a man's side,
is where his valour is,
a sign of his honour
and a safeguard of his life.
And he does not give it up 615
even if he sees put at risk
the life it has to guard,
because although it may cost
his life, it is better for him to put
his honour first. 620
With his faith primarily,
serving his Christian king,
he should place it in his hand,
proclaiming eternally
that when confronted by heretics 625
he offers himself to die for it,
never wavering or offending it,
for they are obliged to honour it,
to confess it with their mouths
and defend it with their swords. 630
For lesser causes
do not draw it to fight;
but if it is drawn, it must return
less clean than when it came out.
Bloody is how I admire it most, 635
since to give proof of honour
is the opposite in the case of the sword;
though you may stumble or be victorious,
it is more shameful
bare than coloured with blood. 640
And still more if you are obliged
to draw it against a peasant, you should,
since he will dare you to fight
man to man, and hand to hand,

entonces es caso llano 645
que un caballero en rigor
quedará siempre peor
si, con valiente aspereza,
lo que le lleva en nobleza
no le aventaja en valor. 650
 Que, en osando resistir
el vulgar al principal,
anda corto y queda mal
sin matar o sin morir,
o al menos hacelle huir, 655
por no andar en opiniones.
Y así, por estas razones,
pudiendo disimular,
el hidalgo ha de excusar
con el villano ocasiones. 660
 Más te pudiera decir, [redondillas]
mas poco a poco sabrás
lo que hay que decirte más.
(Ciñe la espada DON PEDRO a DON FÉLIX.)
Ya te la puedes ceñir;
 oirás misa, y allí 665
los evangelios dirán
sobre ella, y bendecirán
a ti y a ella; y así,
 harate el cielo un varón
cual yo se lo pido agora. 670
Llegad a dalle, señora,
brazos, mano y bendición.
(Besa las manos DON FÉLIX a DON PEDRO
y a DOÑA CONSTANZA.)

---

646 *en rigor*: 'when left with no alternative', 'forced [to fight]'; *Aut. 1737*: "se toma assimismo por el ultimo término à que pueden llegar las cosas" ('rigór', 7th def.).
656 *andar en opiniones*: 'put one's honor at risk' by being at the center of a scandal; *Aut. 1737*: "Vale ponerse en duda el crédito ò estimación de alguno" ('andar en opiniones', 3rd entry on 'opinion').

and it will be plain to see 645
that a gentleman who has no choice but to fight
is always worse off
if, with valiant intent,
the nobility he bears
is not matched with his valour. 650
For, if the peasant
challenges the nobleman,
the nobleman comes up short and looks foolish,
if he does not kill or die
or at least scare him off, 655
to not risk his reputation.
And so, for these reasons,
if he is discreet,
the nobleman should be able to
avoid any fights with commoners. 660
I could tell you more;
but little by little you will learn
what else I have to teach you.
(PEDRO puts the sword around FÉLIX's waist.)
Now you can wear this sword;
you will hear Mass, and there 665
the Gospels will proclaim
about the sword, and bless
both it and you; like this,
Heaven will make a fine man of you,
which I pray it will do right now. 670
Come to give him, my lady,
your arms, hand, and blessing.
(FÉLIX kisses the hands of PEDRO and COSTANZA.)

FÉLIX	Déjeme el cielo pagarte	
	el nuevo ser que me has dado.	
PEDRO	Eso para ser honrado	675
	no será la menor parte.	
COSTANZA	Con el alma que te di,	
	te doy bendición y mano.	
HIPÓLITA	¡Qué envidia te tengo, hermano!	
FÉLIX	Y yo te la tengo a ti;	680
	que tengo celos de quien	
	con mi madre podrá estar;	
	y porque te veo andar	
	sin cuello, y puños también,	
	que es una mala invención.	685
PEDRO	Acostúmbrate a traellos.	
FÉLIX	Más gustara de rompellos.	
GALVÁN	Por Dios, ¡que tiene razón!	
	Son los puños inhumanos,	
	y el curioso que se ofrece	690
	a conservallos parece	
	que lleva a vender las manos.	
PEDRO	Que no los guarda, verás,	
	sino un galán adamado;	
	que las galas sin cuidado	695
	en los hombres lucen más.	
	La espada en medio del lado	
	ha de ir, y tú la has torcido;	
	(Compónele la espada.)	
	así ha de ir.	
FÉLIX	Estoy corrido	
	de que nunca la he llevado.	700

684 *cuello*: 'ruff', a circular collar made of linen or lace, gathered into folds, the size of which determined the thickness of the ruff. A large one would be big enough to cover the neck entirely. *puños*: cuffs, made in the same fashion as the ruff.
694 *adamado*: 'effeminate', via the word 'dama', 'lady.'
695 *sin cuidado*: the adornments of male clothing look better when worn 'carelessly', it is unbecoming for a man to be noticeably concerned with his clothing.

FÉLIX	May Heaven allow me to repay you	
	for the new being that you have given me.	
PEDRO	On the path to becoming honourable	675
	this is no small step.	
COSTANZA	With the soul which I gave you,	
	I give you my blessing and my hand.	
HIPÓLITA	How I envy you, brother!	
FÉLIX	And I envy you;	680
	for I am jealous of you who	
	is allowed to stay with my mother,	
	and because I see you walking around	
	without this ruff, and cuffs as well,	
	which are a terrible innovation in fashion.	685
PEDRO	Accustom yourself to wearing them.	
FÉLIX	I'd prefer to rip them to shreds.	
GALVÁN	By God, he's right!	
	Cuffs are inhumane,	
	and the unusual man who wears those	690
	old-fashioned things seems to be	
	decorating his hands as if they're for sale.	
PEDRO	You'll see, he who takes too much care	
	over them is nothing but a womanish man;	
	fine finishing touches suit men	695
	best when they appear effortless.	
	Wear the sword squarely on your hip,	
	you've got it all twisted;	
	(PEDRO arranges FÉLIX's sword.)	
	there, that's how it goes.	
FÉLIX	I'm ashamed	
	that I've never worn one before.	700

162   *La fuerza de la costumbre: Jornada primera*

PEDRO   Llévala, y no te amohínes.
COSTANZA ¿Hipólita?
HIPÓLITA   ¡Mi señora!
COSTANZA Ya me toca el darte agora
          lición de llevar chapines;
          vuelve a ponellos.
          (Pruébase DOÑA HIPÓLITA a ponerse los chapines
          y no acierta.)
HIPÓLITA   Sí haré,   705
          pero estoy mirando el cómo;
          si en la mano no los tomo,
          (Sacando la pierna descompuestamente, toma el chapín
          en la mano y quiéresele poner, y tiénela su madre.)
          y los pongo, no podré.
COSTANZA ¿Qué haces, hija?
PEDRO   Bien, por cierto.
GALVÁN   ¿Es zapato, por ventura?   710
COSTANZA ¿Con tan gran descompostura
          el pie y pierna has descubierto?
HIPÓLITA Si no los cubrí jamás,
          y ha veinte años que nací,
          ¿por qué me culpas que aquí   715
          los descubra?
          (Vuelve a querer ponerse los chapines y no acierta.)
COSTANZA   Buena estás.
HIPÓLITA ¿¡Cuándo no puedo?!
COSTANZA   ¿No ves...
GALVÁN   En vano otra vez se ensaya.
COSTANZA ...que debajo de la saya
          son más lascivos los pies?   720

---

704 *chapines*: see note to the stage direction at line 522.
707 *Sacando la pierna descompuestamente*: in this period, legs were considered seductive and provocative. Hipólita's lack of modesty about showing her legs as she tries to put her shoes on would have been risqué.
710 *¿Es zapato, por ventura?*: Galván's joke implies that the chapines are so different from other footwear as to be difficult to recognize as such.

PEDRO	Wear it and do not sulk.
COSTANZA	Hipólita?
HIPÓLITA	My lady!
COSTANZA	Now it is my turn to give you
	lessons in wearing high-heels;
	put them back on.
	(HIPÓLITA tries to put the shoes on, but she cannot.)
HIPÓLITA	Yes, I will, 705
	but I cannot see how;
	if I don't take them in my hands
	(Uncovering her leg haphazardly, she takes the shoe in her hand and tries to put it on, but her mother stops her.)
	and try to put them on, I cannot.
COSTANZA	What are you doing, daughter?
PEDRO	They look good, certainly.
GALVÁN	Is that a shoe, by chance? 710
COSTANZA	With such discomposure
	you have shown your foot and your leg?
HIPÓLITA	If I have never covered them
	in all the twenty years of my life,
	why do you blame me for 715
	showing them now?
	(She goes to put the shoes on again, but she cannot.)
COSTANZA	You look nice.
HIPÓLITA	When I can't do it?!
COSTANZA	Don't you see…
GALVÁN	She's practising again in vain.
COSTANZA	…that below a skirt,
	the feet are more enticing? 720

	Haz tú, Félix, del galán; ayúdale allí.	
FÉLIX	*(Cálzale don Félix los chapines.)* Yo voy.	
PEDRO	¡Como suspendido estoy destas cosas!	
FÉLIX	Bien están.	
GALVÁN	¡A sacar tan bién⁺ la espada como ha metido el chapín!	725
PEDRO	Sí sacará, que es, en fin, sangre de Urrea y Moncada.	
COSTANZA	Ven, que es bien que se disponga para visitas mi estrado, y pondraste un verdugado.	730
HIPÓLITA	Un verdugo se le ponga, ¡voto a Cris…!	
COSTANZA	¡Jesús! No he visto tal cosa; ¡terrible estás!	
GALVÁN	Pues por dos letras no más le gastas el nombre a Cristo.	735
PEDRO	Ruido es aquel; ve a ver qué es aquello.	

Vase GALVÁN.
Suena ruido de espadas y DOÑA CONSTANZA se pone delante de DON FÉLIX.

FÉLIX	Espadas son.
COSTANZA	¡Ay, hijo del corazón!
HIPÓLITA	¿Iré allá?

721 *del galán*: 'like a handsome man'; the irony here is that Costanza is asking Félix to demonstrate how to put on *women's* shoes.
723 *suspendido*: lit. 'frozen [in place]', fig. 'shocked', 'taken aback'.
+ 725 *tan bien* A C : tambien P B. P uses 'tambien' for 'también' and 'tan bien'.
731 *verdugado*: 'farthingale', an underskirt fitted with stiff hoops, providing a frame which shaped a woman's dress, giving the lower half of the body a fuller appearance. The hoops themselves were called '*verdugos*' and were sometimes sewn directly into a dress or skirt.
732 *verdugo*: 'executioner'. Here playing on 'verdugado' from line 731. Hipólita connects her skirt with a method of execution.

	Félix, play the gentleman, and help her there.	
FÉLIX	*(FÉLIX helps his sister with the shoes.)*[6] I'll help.	
PEDRO	I can't believe these things I am seeing!	
FÉLIX	They look good.	
GALVÁN	If only he could handle a sword as well as a lady's shoe!	725
PEDRO	Yes, he will, since he is, after all, of the blood of Urrea and Moncada.	
COSTANZA	Come, it is time to get you ready for visiting in the sitting-room, and you'll put on a farthingale.	730
HIPÓLITA	Locked in an iron maiden,[7] I swear to Chri…	
COSTANZA	Lord! I've never seen such a thing; you are terrible!	
GALVÁN	With two letters more you would have used Christ's name in vain.	735
PEDRO	That's a noise; go to see what that is.	

Exit GALVÁN.
There is the sound of swordfighting, and COSTANZA places herself in front of FÉLIX.

FÉLIX	They're swords.
COSTANZA	Oh, my precious boy!
HIPÓLITA	Shall I go out there?

---

6 See p. 98, Fig. 3 for a photograph of this scene in production.
7 Hipólita plays on the idea of *verdugado* (farthingale) and *verdugo* (executioner) here, making a link between women's fashion and instruments of torture. An iron maiden is a metal enclosure fitted with spikes, into which the victim was tightly locked.

PEDRO	*(Quiere ir DOÑA HIPÓLITA, y tiénela DON PEDRO.)*	
	Tente, mujer.	740
HIPÓLITA	El nombre me ha reportado,	
	afrentoso para mí.	

Vuelve GALVÁN, y desnuda la espada.

GALVÁN	¡Aquí, aquí, señor, aquí!	
	Que hasta en tu casa han entrado,	
	y acuchillan, a canalla,	745
	tus criados; son perdidos.	
	Hay entre muertos y heridos	
	más de setecientos.	
PEDRO	¡Calla!	
	¿De qué te alborotas, vil?	
	Con cólera reportada,	750
	déjame sacar la espada	
	y mataré siete mil.	
	(Vase DON PEDRO metiendo mano.)	
HIPÓLITA	¿Cómo no mueves los pies?	
	¿No vas con tu padre, hermano?	
FÉLIX	Turbado estoy.	
HIPÓLITA	¡Mete mano!	755
	Mas tu espada rueca es;	
	(Sácale DOÑA HIPÓLITA la espada del lado a DON FÉLIX y vase, dejando los chapines.)	
	dámela a mí, maricón,	
	y desos chapines ten	
	cuidado.	

---

741 *me ha reportado*: 'has restrained me', 'has reined me in'.
745 *a canalla*: 'like scoundrels'. *DRAE*: 'a': "denota el modo de la acción. A pie. A caballo. A mano. A golpes; [...] Da principio a muchas locuciones adverbiales. A bulto. A oscuras. A tientas. A regañadientes. A todo correr" (10th and 22nd defs.).
750 *cólera*: the humor associated with a dry and hot composition, synonymous with rage.
755b *¡Mete mano!*: 'Get your hand on your sword!' i.e., 'Get ready to fight!'
756–759 See note on '*rueca*' at l. 569. The material objects which symbolize their genders are reversed again. The feminine implement is again contrasted with the male sword.

PEDRO	*(HIPÓLITA wants to go, but PEDRO detains her.)*	
	Stop, woman.	740
HIPÓLITA	That name holds me back;	
	I despise it.	

GALVÁN returns, his sword drawn.

GALVÁN	Here, here, sir, here!	
	They've entered the house,	
	and they're duelling, vile scoundrels,	745
	with your servants; they're lost.	
	There are, among the dead and wounded,	
	more than seven hundred.	
PEDRO	Quiet!	
	Why are you fussing, peasant?	
	With my resounding rage	750
	let me draw my sword,	
	and I'll kill seven thousand.	
	(He goes, ready to fight.)	
HIPÓLITA	Why are you just standing there? Won't	
	you go with your father, my brother?	
FÉLIX	I'm frightened.	
HIPÓLITA	Get ready to fight!	755
	Your sword is more like a knitting needle;	
	(HIPÓLITA draws FÉLIX's sword from his side, and runs	
	out, leaving the high-heeled shoes behind.)	
	give it to me, you weakling,[8]	
	and take care of these	
	high heels.	

---

8   This word in the Spanish, *maricón*, is a homophobic invective, such as 'faggot'. It is used three times in the play: here by Hipólita at I. 757, and twice by Pedro, at II. 841 and II. 886. Covarrubias defined it: "El hombre afeminado que se inclina a hacer cosas de mujer, que llaman por otro nombre marimaricas; como el contrario decimos marimacho la mujer que tiene desenvolturas de hombre" ["An effeminate man who inclines himself to things that pertain to women, who is called also by the name 'marimaricas'; like his opposite whom we call 'marimacho', a woman who has the characterisitcs of a man"].

FÉLIX   ¡Señora, ven!
COSTANZA   Mis temores grandes son.   760

Vanse y salen DON LUIS y DON PEDRO con las espadas desnudas, y DOÑA LEONOR deteniendo a DON PEDRO.

PEDRO   Fue atrevimiento; ¡¿en mi casa,   [romance e–e]
              y con mis criados?!
LEONOR   ¡Tente!
LUIS   Tengo a tus canas respeto.
PEDRO   No son tan del todo nieve
              que hielen la sangre mía,   765
              y a mi espada se le tienen
              en Italia, Francia, y Flandes.
              ¡Suplícote que me dejes,
              señora!
LEONOR   ¡Señor, espera!
PEDRO   Y advierte que a las mujeres   770
              les tengo respeto yo;
              ¡no me obligues a perdelle!

Salen DOÑA HIPÓLITA, DOÑA CONSTANZA, [y] DON FÉLIX; y DOÑA HIPÓLITA acomete a DON LUIS.

HIPÓLITA   Prueba conmigo la espada
              que con los demás valiente
              se ha mostrado.
COSTANZA   *(DOÑA CONSTANZA tiene a DON PEDRO asido.)*
                          Espera, hija…   775
LEONOR   *(Desmáyase DOÑA LEONOR en los brazos de DON FÉLIX.)*
              ¡Muerta estoy! ¡Jesús mil veces!
FÉLIX   Tente a mis brazos, señora.
COSTANZA   …si he de volver a perderte
              tan presto, infelice soy.
PEDRO   ¿No riñe gallardamente   780
              nuestra hija?
COSTANZA   Dios la guarde.

---

779   *infelice*: 'infeliz'.

FÉLIX	Come, my lady!	
COSTANZA	I am greatly afraid.	760

SCENE 1.5

Exit ALL, and enter DON LUIS and DON PEDRO, with their swords drawn, and DOÑA LEONOR trying to hold back DON PEDRO.

PEDRO	That was some daring; in my house and with my servants?	
LEONOR	Wait!	
LUIS	I show respect for your white hair.	
PEDRO	My hair is not yet all so snow-white that it freezes my blood, and my sword is known throughout Italy, France, and Flanders. I beg you to unhand me, my lady…	765
LEONOR	My lord, wait!	
PEDRO	…let it be known that for women I have great respect; do not force me to lose it!	770

Enter HIPÓLITA, COSTANZA and FÉLIX, and HIPÓLITA rushes over to LUIS.

HIPÓLITA	Test me with the sword that has proven its valour with the others.	
COSTANZA	*(COSTANZA attaches herself to PEDRO.)* Wait, daughter…	775
LEONOR	*(LEONOR faints in the arms of FÉLIX.)* I am lost! Oh, God!	
FÉLIX	Take my arms, my lady.	
COSTANZA	…if I lost you again so soon, it would be my sorrow.	
PEDRO	Does our daughter not fight gallantly?	780
COSTANZA	God protect her.	

PEDRO	El miralla me suspende.	
LUIS	Tente, señora, ¡por Dios!	
	No me mates, rendireme;	
	que aunque con la espada tiras,	785
	pero con los ojos hieres,	
	con mucha ventaja riñes.	
HIPÓLITA	Con lo bien que te defiendes	
	sin ofender, has mostrado	
	que eres animoso y fuerte,	790
	y por eso no he querido	
	ni matarte, ni ofenderme.	
LUIS	Ya me ha muerto tu hermosura,	
	pero ha sido dulcemente.	
HIPÓLITA	Deja dulzuras aparte,+	795
	que me cansan y me ofenden,	
	y riñe sin cortesías.	
PEDRO	Déjame, que gente viene.	

Salen OTAVIO y MARCELO.

OTAVIO+	*(Esto dice a DOÑA COSTANZA.)*	
	Mi señora, ¿qué es aquesto?	
MARCELO	*(Mete paz MARCELO.)*	
	Ténganse vuesas mercedes.	800
HIPÓLITA	Valor es la cortesía.	
FÉLIX	No se ha visto en el oriente	
	con más hermosura el sol.	
LEONOR	Poco resplandor le debes,	
	pues está puesto en tus brazos.	805

786   *con los ojos hieres*: it was believed that love was caused by 'spirits' which emanated from the eyes, and entered the soul of the viewer through his eyes. Beauty in particular wounded the eyes, which is what Luis refers to here as even more dangerous than the sword in Hipólita's hand (Herrera 2001, 335). Herrera on eyes and love: "Entre los grandes efetos i maravillas de Amor, es la más grande i más poderosa la que procede de la vista de los que se aman, […] porque es un recordamiento i renovación del afeto amoroso; i de la suerte que el fuego junto a la materia, assí aquel mirar inflama el sentido" (2001, 300–301).

+ 795   *aparte* C: a parte P. This spelling will not be noted henceforth.

+ 799   *OTAVIO*: in this instance, P spells this 'Octa', deviating from the usual spelling 'Otauio' (usually abbreviated as 'Ota.'). This also occurs at I. 866 and I. 879.

PEDRO	Watching her takes my breath away.	
LUIS	Wait, my lady, by God![9]	
	Do not kill me, I will surrender;	
	though you strike with the sword	785
	you wound with the eyes;	
	you fight with a great advantage.	
HIPÓLITA	With your skill at defending yourself	
	without offending, you have shown	
	that you are spirited and strong,	790
	and because of this I have decided	
	neither to kill you nor to take offence.	
LUIS	Your beauty has killed me	
	but it has been a sweet death.	
HIPÓLITA	Leave these sweetnesses aside,	795
	for they tire me and offend me,	
	and fight without flattery.	
PEDRO	Leave me, people are coming.	

Enter OTAVIO and MARCELO.

OTAVIO	*(Addressing COSTANZA.)*	
	My lady, what is all this?	
MARCELO	*(Halting the commotion.)*	
	Wait, your graces.	800
HIPÓLITA	Valour is courtesy.	
FÉLIX	The sun in the east has never	
	appeared with more beauty.	
LEONOR	You owe your own glow to it	
	for it is placed in your arms.	805

---

9 See p. 103, Fig. 8 for a photograph of this scene in production.

FÉLIX	Y en mis ojos amanece.	
LUIS	Si escucháis disculpas mías, veréis que sola mi suerte tiene culpa en vuestro enojo.	
COSTANZA	Señor don Luis, no puede errar quien es de mi casa tan conocido pariente. ¿Señora doña Leonor?	810
LEONOR	¿Mi señora?	
FÉLIX	*(Aparte)* ¡Oh, quién pudiese en los brazos y en el alma recogella otras mil veces!	815
LUIS	Venía yo con mi hermana en un coche, y como hubiese impedimento en la calle de acémilas y de gente, pidió lugar el cochero de la manera que suelen. Respondiéronle tan mal como suelen respondelles. Hableles con cortesía, y obligáronme de suerte que hube de sacar la espada, y, por Dios, sin que supiese que criados vuestros eran; porque yo, inviolablemente, hubiera guardado entonces el respeto que se debe a esta casa, aunque tuviera solo desnudas paredes; cuánto más estando en ella	820

825

830

835 |

---

820 *acémilas*: Arabism for 'mule', commonly used in the Golden Age.
826–827 Luis recounts that he was 'obliged', 'forced' to unsheath his sword because of an honor issue; he asked in a civil and gracious manner if the men in the street could make way for his carriage to pass, but they responded to him with disrespect. He is also enacting Pedro's instructions to Félix on the proper comportment of a man of honor given at I. 631–660.

FÉLIX	And it dawns in my eyes.	
LUIS	If you will hear me out,	
	you will see that only my bad luck	
	is to blame for your anger.	
COSTANZA	My lord Don Luis, one cannot	810
	err in my house	
	when they are a close relative.	
	My lady Doña Leonor?	
LEONOR	My lady?	
FÉLIX	*(Aside)* Oh, to be the one	
	whose arms and soul	815
	would hold her a thousand times more!	
LUIS	I came with my sister	
	in a carriage, and as	
	the street was clogged	
	with mules and people,	820
	the coachman asked to get through	
	in the way they usually do.	
	They responded to him so rudely,	
	in the way they usually reply.	
	I spoke to them with courtesy,	825
	and they challenged me right then	
	so I was forced to draw my sword	
	and, by God, without realising	
	that they were your servants;	
	since I, of course,	830
	would not have done so,	
	out of the respect that is owed	
	to this house, even if it had	
	only bare walls;	
	all the more as it is so honourably	835

	el blasón que la engrandece,	
	y honrándola mi señora	
	doña Constanza, que tiene	
	tantas causas de mandarme.	
	Y aún no sabía que hubiese	840
	llegado el señor don Pedro	
	de Moncada, solamente	
	por el nombre conocido	
	de mí, que estimo el tenelle	
	por señor y por amigo.	845
PEDRO	Vuestras razones corteses,	
	señor don Luis, obligan	
	a que yo os estime, y bese	
	las manos y dé los brazos.	
LUIS	Son excesos tus mercedes.	850
PEDRO	Ya os estoy aficionado	
	por galán y por valiente.	
HIPÓLITA	Todo lo tiene, por Dios.	
LUIS	Pues tú, señora, me vences;	
	alabándome te alabas.	855
HIPÓLITA	Tú te rindes cortésmente,	
	habiendo usado conmigo	
	lo que con otras mujeres	
	que se precian de hermosas,	
	y no estiman el ser fuertes.	860
PEDRO	Es Hipólita hija mía.	
LUIS	En el valor lo parece.	
LEONOR	Dadme las manos, señora.	
HIPÓLITA	Las vuestras es bien que bese.	
FÉLIX	*(Aparte)* ¡Ay, qué hermosura tan grande!	865
OTAVIO	Contento de conocerte;	
	dame las manos, señor.	
MARCELO	Y a mí también me las debes,	
	por lo que a tu fama y nombre	
	he sido inclinado siempre.	870
PEDRO	De todos merced recibo,	
	que me honráis sobradamente.	

	emblazoned by your esteemed presence,	
	and honouring it is my lady	
	Doña Costanza, at whose	
	command I am fully disposed.	
	And still I did not know that	840
	my lord Don Pedro	
	de Moncada had arrived,	
	only known to me by name,	
	and I greatly value him	
	as my lord and as my friend.	845
PEDRO	Your courteous statements,	
	my lord Don Luis, oblige	
	me to hold you in high regard, and to kiss	
	your hands, and embrace you.	
LUIS	Your favours are excessive.	850
PEDRO	I admire you, for your	
	gallantry and for your bravery.	
HIPÓLITA	He has it all, by God.	
LUIS	And you, my lady, defeat me;	
	in praising me you praise yourself.	855
HIPÓLITA	You surrender with empty flattery,	
	trying it on with me	
	as if I were like other women	
	who value themselves as pretty things	
	and are not esteemed for being brave.	860
PEDRO	This is Hipólita, my daughter.	
LUIS	She takes after you, in valour.	
LEONOR	Give me your hands, my lady.	
HIPÓLITA	It is right that I should kiss yours.	
FÉLIX	*(Aside)* Ah, what spectacular beauty!	865
OTAVIO	I am delighted to meet you;	
	it is a pleasure to take your hands, sir.	
MARCELO	You also owe them to me,	
	for I have always bowed in awe	
	to your reputation and name.	870
PEDRO	I am pleased to receive you all,	
	you honour me so greatly.	

COSTANZA	Mal estamos en la calle; en mi casa, si os parece, tomará doña Leonor, por el espanto que tiene, un jarro de agua si quiera.	875
LEONOR	Justo será que lo acete.	
OTAVIO	Vamos todos a serviros.	
LUIS	*(Aparte)* Ardiendo el alma, apetece su honesta desenvoltura.	880
HIPÓLITA	*(Aparte)* ¿Qué me buscan, qué me quieren ojos que tanto me miran?	
LEONOR	*(Aparte)* Mucho me mira don Félix.[+]	
FÉLIX	*(Aparte)* Esto sin duda es amor, pues me regala y me ofende.	885
COSTANZA	Mirad, señor, vuestro hijo; sospecho que se enternece mirando a doña Leonor.	
PEDRO	Pluguiera a Dios que así fuese, porque en siendo enamorado, fuera cierto el ser valiente.	890

---

878 *acete*: acepte.
+ 884 This line slightly departs slightly from the e–e rhyme scheme, with a rhyme in e–i.
886 *me regala*: this could mean either 'it delights me' or 'it melts me' (*Aut. 1737*, 'regalar', 3rd def.; 'regalarse', 2nd def.).

COSTANZA	It's not right for us to stand in the street;	
	into my house, if you please,	
	you will take Doña Leonor,	875
	and for the fright she has suffered,	
	a glass of water if she would like one.	
LEONOR	It would be right to accept it.	
OTAVIO	Let us all go to serve you.	
LUIS	*(Aside)* My soul is burning,	880
	her chaste manner is very enticing.	
HIPÓLITA	*(Aside)* Why do they search me, what	
	do they want, eyes that look at me so?	
LEONOR	*(Aside)* Don Félix is staring at me.	
FÉLIX	*(Aside)* This, no doubt, is love,	885
	for it delights and wounds me.	
COSTANZA	Look, my lord, at your son;	
	I suspect that he looks	
	tenderly at Doña Leonor.	
PEDRO	God I wish that he would,	890
	because if he falls in love,	
	being brave will surely follow.	

JORNADA SEGUNDA

Salen OTAVIO y MARCELO.

MARCELO	Bueno está el templo.	[redondillas]
OTAVIO	Extremado	
	de hermosura y devoción.	
MARCELO	Imágenes vivas son.	
OTAVIO	¡Y qué dellas se han juntado!	
MARCELO	Siempre en San Francisco es	5
	como divino lo humano.	
OTAVIO	¿Vistes misa?	
MARCELO	Aún es temprano.	
OTAVIO	Pues verémosla los tres,	
	que ya viene allí don Luis.	
MARCELO	Por amante se pregona	10
	desta entre Marte y Belona.	
OTAVIO	¿Es hermosa?	

Sale DON LUIS.

LUIS	¿Qué decís?	
	¿De quién murmuráis los dos?	
OTAVIO	De vuestro nuevo cuidado.	
MARCELO	Muy recién enamorado	15
	estáis.	
LUIS	Y mucho, ¡por Dios!	
	Hasta el alma me penetra,	
	con ser tan niño este amor.	
MARCELO	Por vos se dirá mejor	
	aquello, de que la letra	20
	con sangre entra.	

---

11 *Marte*: Ares (Mars), the god of war; *Belona*: a Roman war goddess, identified in the Middle Ages with Minerva, the goddess of wisdom.

14 *cuidado*: *Aut. 1729*: "Se llama también la persona a quien se tiene amor" ('cuidado', 4th def.).

20–21 *la letra / con sangre entra*: a proverb; *Aut. 1732*: "ref[rán] que dá à entender que el que quiere saber ha de trabajar y sudar: y que con dificultad se adquieren los bienes y excelencias de las virtudes" ('la letra con sangre entra', in 'entrar').

ACT TWO

SCENE 2.1

Enter OTAVIO and MARCELO.

MARCELO	Nice church.	
OTAVIO	It is the pinnacle	
	of beauty and devotion.	
MARCELO	The icons are very lifelike.	
OTAVIO	They are arranged with subtle perfection!	
MARCELO	Always in St. Francis's church	5
	the divine appears human.	
OTAVIO	Were you here for Mass?	
MARCELO	It's still too early.	
OTAVIO	Then the three of us can go together,	
	for here comes Don Luis.	
MARCELO	He has declared his love of	10
	she who is half Mars and half Bellona.	
OTAVIO	Is she good-looking?	

Enter DON LUIS.

LUIS	What was that?	
	Who are you two murmuring about?	
OTAVIO	About your new love interest.	
MARCELO	As recently lovestruck	15
	as you are.	
LUIS	So much so, by God!	
	It pierces me right through my soul,	
	even though this love is so young.	
MARCELO	For you it would be better, as they say,	
	to keep slogging away at it,	20
	no pain no gain.	

OTAVIO	Sí, que ha entrado con gentiles cuchilladas.	
LUIS	Y a no ser bien reparadas, mucha me hubieran sacado; pero sus divinos ojos hicieron más sangre en mí que la espada, a quien rendí toda el alma por despojos.	25
OTAVIO	De aquel coche salen.	
LUIS	¿Quién?	
OTAVIO	Don Pedro y doña Costanza.	30
LUIS	¡Qué bien lograda esperanza!	
MARCELO	Y vuestra dama también; ¡qué salto+ ha dado al bajar! Enojado se ha.	
OTAVIO	¿Qué dijo?	
MARCELO	A los chapines maldijo.	35
LUIS	Aún no los sabe llevar.	

Salen DON PEDRO, y DOÑA COSTANZA, y DON FÉLIX, y DOÑA HIPÓLITA, y el AYO.

PEDRO	Qué buen tiempo aquel, señora, que yo os esperaba aquí que entrárades.	
COSTANZA	Es así, pero más quiero el de agora, pues que, como esposo mío, os llevo con libertad de la mano.	40
PEDRO	Así es verdad. ¡Don Félix, pisa con brío!	

---

22 *gentiles cuchilladas*: 'courteous stab wounds'; love was often referred to as a 'wound' in courtly lyric. Otavio is making a joke about Luis's courtship of Hipólita, in which the reference to 'stab wounds' is a literal, not only poetic threat.
25 *divinos ojos*: see note at I. 786.
28 *despojos*: 'spoils [of battle]'.
+ 33 *salto* A B C : saltò P.

OTAVIO	He takes that literally	
	and lets his lady stab him sweetly.	
LUIS	And if her aim hadn't been so true,	
	her jabs would have taken much more	
	of me, but her divine eyes	25
	have shed more of my blood	
	than her sword, to which I yielded	
	my entire soul as the spoils of love.	
OTAVIO	They're coming out of that carriage.	
LUIS	Who?	
OTAVIO	Don Pedro and Doña Costanza.	30
LUIS	It is just as I have hoped!	
MARCELO	And your lady is there as well;	
	she really jumped out of that coach!	
	She looks angry.	
OTAVIO	What did she say?	
MARCELO	She swore at her shoes.	35
LUIS	She doesn't have the hang of them yet.	

Enter PEDRO and COSTANZA, FÉLIX and HIPÓLITA, and FÉLIX'S TUTOR.

PEDRO	What happy memories I have, my lady,	
	of waiting for you to come through	
	this church door years ago.	
COSTANZA	Yes,	
	but I prefer now to then,	40
	now that, as my husband,	
	I can walk with you freely	
	hand in hand.	
PEDRO	How right you are.	
	Don Félix, walk with manly spirit!	

FÉLIX   Aún no acierto; enseñareme 45
        (Aparte) porque no me aflijas tanto.
COSTANZA ¿Como ferreruelo el manto,
        Hipólita?
HIPÓLITA   Descuideme.
LUIS   *(Aparte)* Con toda el alma la quiero.
PEDRO   Cuidado nos dais los dos.⁺ 50

Salúdanse, y DOÑA HIPÓLITA hace como que se va a quitar el sombrero. Vanse, y quedan los tres.

MARCELO ¡Oh, qué donaire, por Dios;
        que iba a quitarse el sombrero!
LUIS   Es que se le van las manos
        donde saben el camino.
OTAVIO   ¿No es extremo peregrino 55
        los contrapuestos hermanos?
            Causa admiración el verlo.
MARCELO Es notable cosa el ver,
        él pareciendo mujer,
        y ella no acertando a serlo. 60
            Ni al uno viene la espada,
        ni al otro el manto le viene.
LUIS   Todas esas fuerzas tiene
        la costumbre dilatada.
OTAVIO   Fuertemente es poderosa; 65
        más que papas, más que reyes;
        divinas y humanas leyes
        puede hacer.

---

47 *como ferreruelo el manto*: the 'ferreruelo' is a male garment (which Pedro admonished Félix for not wearing properly in Act I 487–488), while 'manto' is a 'shawl', a garment for women.

+ 50 In P, this line appears after the two stage directions. Pedro is offstage, however, after the stage direction "Vanse, y quedan los tres," therefore the line should precede the stage directions. A has Otavio as the speaker of this line. In C, the stage direction reads, "vanse, queda otavio / y marse y don luys."

55 *¿No es extremo peregrino…?*: 'Isn't it the rarest of oddities?' (lit. 'Isn't it a rare extreme?').

FÉLIX	I still haven't mastered it; I will learn	45
	(Aside) so that you'll stop tormenting me.	
COSTANZA	You wear your shawl as a cape, Hipólita?	
HIPÓLITA	I forgot.	
LUIS	*(Aside)* I love her with my entire soul.	
PEDRO	You are both very worrying to us.	50

They exchange greetings, and HIPÓLITA makes as if she is going to doff her cap, forgetting she isn't wearing one. They exit, leaving the three men.

MARCELO	Oh, how gallant, my God, she was trying to doff her cap!	
LUIS	Her hands go where they're used to going.	
OTAVIO	Aren't the cross-dressed siblings a rare sight to behold? They're quite shocking to look at.	55
MARCELO	It's an extremely odd thing to see, he seeming so like a woman, and she not knowing how to be one. One can't handle a sword, and the other can't master the shawl.	60
LUIS	These are the many forces of long-held habit.	
OTAVIO	It is strong and powerful; more than popes, more than kings; it can make divine and human laws.	65

MARCELO	Extraña cosa:	
	dicen que por solo un mes	
	que un hombre, por cierto antojo,	70
	se puso un parche en un ojo,	
	se le halló ciego después.	
	A tan extraño poder	
	¿qué cosa habrá que resista,	
	pues basta a quitar la vista	75
	la costumbre del no ver?	
OTAVIO	Mil cosas hay que decir	
	de su fuerza inaccesible.	
	¿Hay cosa más imposible	
	que, no bebiendo, vivir?	80
	Pues hidrópico ha de haber	
	tanto a curarse inclinado	
	que de beber ha dejado,	
	y ya vive sin beber.	
MARCELO	Es un hechizo, un encanto	85
	la costumbre.	
LUIS	En conclusión	
	tiene mucho de ocasión,	
	y por eso puede tanto.	
MARCELO	Mas, ¿qué mayores grandezas	
	della se pueden contar	90
	que vella en éstos trocar	
	tan varias naturalezas?	
	Son efetos sobrehumanos,	
	por quien sus fuerzas dilata.	
OTAVIO	Ya en el lugar no se trata	95
	sino de los dos hermanos.	
MARCELO	Dellos he oído contar	
	extremadas, os prometo,	
	muchas cosas; en efeto	

---

81 *hidrópico*: one who suffers from dropsy, a condition defined by swelling and retention of fluid.
98 '*extremadas*' can mean 'notable', 'unique', 'admirable'; or '*chistoso*', 'funny' (*Aut. 1732*, 'extremado, da', 2nd and 3rd defs.).

MARCELO	A strange thing: they say that for only one month a man, on some whim, put a patch over one eye, and found himself blind afterwards. To such a strange power what could possibly be immune, if a man can lose his sight simply by making it a habit not to see?	70 75
OTAVIO	I have a thousand things to say[10] about its unfathomable force. Is there anything more impossible than to live without a drop to drink? Well there was once a dropsy patient who so wanted to be cured, that he gave up drinking altogether, and to this day he lives without drinking.	 80
MARCELO	It's witchcraft, a spell cast by habit.	85
LUIS	In conclusion it has many opportunities to affect us, that's why it can do so much.	
MARCELO	But, what greater claims can be made about it than to see it in these two switching such opposite natures? These are superhuman effects, in them their forces are revealed.	 90
OTAVIO	Nobody around here talks about anything other than that brother and sister.	95
MARCELO	I have heard tales told about them, amazing, I swear, many of them; indeed	

---

10 See p. 105, Fig. 10 for a photograph of this scene in production.

	son fábula del lugar,	100
	y don Luis entra en ella.	
LUIS	Y no es poca suerte mía.	
MARCELO	Háblase mucho del día	
	que os vimos reñir con ella.	
LUIS	Es como la misma espada.	105
MARCELO	Talle me tiene en rigor	
	que por daros un favor,	
	os dará una cuchillada.	
LUIS	Sabe ya cómo las doy	
	y estimará mi cuidado.	110
MARCELO	¿Estáis muy enamorado?	
LUIS	¿Queréis ver cuánto lo estoy?	
	A la sangre y al valor	
	de don Pedro de Moncada,	
	y a su estimación honrada	115
	tengo envidia y tengo amor,	
	y el recogimiento estrecho,	
	calidad, fama, opinión	
	de doña Costanza son	
	nobles hechizos del pecho;	120
	con esto, después de ver	
	que es como la luz del día,	
	quiero mujer para mía	
	que nunca lo supo ser,	
	y amor que a tantos alcanza	125
	mucho ha de ser.	
OTAVIO	Bien decís.	
MARCELO	¿De don Félix qué sentís?	
LUIS	Eso dejo a la esperanza	
	del tiempo, que aunque criado	

---

100 *fábula del lugar*: *Aut. 1732*: "El rumór y hablilla del Pueblo, y lo que comunmente se dice y habla de algun particular" ('fabula', 1st def.).

106 *Talle*: an unusual spelling of 'tale', an archaic variant of 'tal' still used in sixteenth century ballads. The change from l to ll is likely an influence of the assimilation of the r in infinitives accompanied by a pronoun (see I. 75).

125 *amor que a tantos alcanza*: 'love for so many people' (lit. 'love which reaches so many'); Luis loves Hipólita and her parents, which multiplies his love.

	they are the talk of the town	100
	and Luis's name also comes up.	
LUIS	Such is my good fortune.	
MARCELO	They talk constantly about that day	
	we all saw you swordfighting with her.	
LUIS	She is one with her sword.	105
MARCELO	She holds me in such low regard,	
	that just to do you a favour,	
	she'll give you a poke.	
LUIS	She now knows how I give them myself	
	and she loves that I'm highly skilled.	110
MARCELO	Are you very much in love?	
LUIS	Would you like to know how much?	
	The blood and valour	
	of Don Pedro de Moncada,	
	as well as his honourable reputation	115
	inspire my envy and admiration,	
	and the protected seclusion,	
	nobility, reputation, and good name	
	of Doña Costanza are	
	noble enchantments of the heart;	120
	with all that, after seeing that she	
	is light to my day, she who never	
	even knew how to be a woman	
	is the one I want for my wife,	
	love that includes her whole family	125
	is truly great.	
OTAVIO	Well said.	
MARCELO	And how do you feel about Don Félix?	
LUIS	That one I leave to the hope	
	of passing time, for though he was raised	

	entre regalos tan mal,	130
	él es de tan buen metal	
	que lucirá bien templado.	
OTAVIO	¿No tenéis más que decir?	
LUIS	¡Ni más que saber los dos!	
	Allá voy, adiós.	
OTAVIO	Adiós.	135

(Vase LUIS.)

	Algo debes de sentir,	
	porque hablaste apasionado;	
	la dama fuerte también	
	te habrá parecido bien.	
MARCELO	Y tiéneme tan picado	140
	como a ti doña Leonor.	
OTAVIO	Allí viene, voy a vella.	
	Queda en paz.	
MARCELO	Y ve con ella;	
	todo en el mundo es amor.	

Vanse, y salen DOÑA COSTANZA y DOÑA HIPÓLITA.

COSTANZA	Muy libres tienes los ojos,	145
	que no arguye honestidad.	
HIPÓLITA	Criéme con libertad,	
	pero miro sin antojos.	
COSTANZA	Yo lo creo, y no he topado	
	en que tal pudiera ser;	150
	pero la honesta mujer	
	mira con menos cuidado;	
	con descuido y gentileza	
	cuánto quisiere verá.	

131–132 *metal*: 'material', 'stock' (lit. 'metal'); there is wordplay here with '*metal*' both referring to lineage, and as a metaphor of a sword used to talk about Félix's development. As in the making of a sword, in which the metal has to be forged and tempered, Félix has the necessary 'raw materials', but needs to be shaped and polished.

145 *libres*: 'free', 'lacking in modesty'; *Aut. 1734*: "Vale tambien licencioso, poco modesto, atrevido y desvergonzado" ('libre', 6th def.). It was not considered ladylike for a woman to look men in the eyes.

	spoiled by such poor playthings,	130
	he is of such good metal that he will	
	ultimately shine when polished.	
OTAVIO	That's all you have to say?	
LUIS	Nothing more that you both should know!	
	I'm off, goodbye.	
OTAVIO	Goodbye.	135
	(Exit LUIS.)	
	You must feel something,	
	because you spoke so passionately;	
	that fearsome lady has also	
	made an impression on you.	
MARCELO	And she has me as transfixed	140
	as Doña Leonor has you.	
OTAVIO	There she is, I'm going to see her.	
	Peace be with you.	
MARCELO	And go with her;	
	everything in the world is love.	

They exit, and enter COSTANZA and HIPÓLITA.

SCENE 2.2

COSTANZA	You are too free with your eyes,	145
	it's not the look of a chaste woman.	
HIPÓLITA	I was raised freely,	
	but I can see clearly without glasses.	
COSTANZA	I believe it, and I would have never	
	thought that it could go so far;	150
	but a chaste woman	
	lifts her eyes politely;	
	casually and courteously	
	she sees all she could want to see.	

La fuerza de la costumbre: Jornada segunda

HIPÓLITA	Crieme en Flandes, y allá	155
	se trata con más llaneza;	
	más de los hombres se fía;	
	pero haré lo que tú mandes.	
COSTANZA	Advierte, hija, que Flandes	
	es una tierra muy fría.	160
HIPÓLITA	Y yo también lo seré,	
	porque eso mismo me obliga.	
COSTANZA	¡Ay, hija! Ninguno diga	
	'desta agua no beberé;'	
	que de otros hielos mayores	165
	he visto arder los despojos.	
	No te fíes de los ojos,	
	que son amigos traidores;	
	ellos las vidas maltratan,	
	ellos las almas fatigan;	170
	como curiosos obligan,	
	y como atrevidos matan.	
	Son regalados abismos	
	de cautelas y traiciones,	
	buscando siempre ocasiones	175
	de matar sus dueños mismos.	
	Los enemigos mayores	
	que tenemos las mujeres	
	son los ojos.	
HIPÓLITA	Pues tú quieres	
	que los tenga por traidores,	180
	guardareme dellos cuanto	
	baste para que te admires.	
COSTANZA	No digo yo que no mires,	
	pero que no mires tanto.	
	A don Luis has mirado,	185
	por cierto, excesivamente.	

163–164 *Ninguno diga / 'desta agua no beberé'*: a *refrán*, or popular saying, documented in Gonzalo Correa's 1627 *Vocabulario de refranes y frases proverbiales* meaning roughly 'never say never'.

177–179a See note I. 786, 'con los ojos hieres'.

HIPÓLITA	I was raised in Flanders, and there	155
	it is more straightforward;	
	you can put your trust in the men;	
	but I will do as you command.	
COSTANZA	You see, daughter, Flanders	
	is a very cold land.	160
HIPÓLITA	And I will have to be cold too,	
	because that fact itself commands it.	
COSTANZA	Oh, my daughter! Never say	
	'from that water I will not drink;'	
	for within greater blocks of ice	165
	I have seen burn the spoils of love.	
	Do not trust the eyes,	
	for they are treacherous friends;	
	they are the ruin of lives,	
	the downfall of souls;	170
	as curiosities they entice us	
	and as daredevils they kill.	
	They are abysmal gifts	
	for secret tricks and treacheries,	
	always looking for occasions	175
	to kill their own masters.	
	The greatest enemies	
	that we have as women	
	are the eyes.	
HIPÓLITA	As you command me	
	to treat them like traitors,	180
	I will protect myself from them	
	so completely, you won't believe it.	
COSTANZA	I'm not saying you can't look at all,	
	just don't look quite so much.	
	You've certainly been looking	185
	excessively at Don Luis.	

HIPÓLITA	Como le vi tan valiente,	
	tan cortés y tan honrado…	
	vile barrer una calle	
	de hombres con tal destreza,	190
	tanto brío y fortaleza,	
	que aficionaba el miralle.	
	Vile a mi padre tener	
	tan hidalga cortesía;	
	vile de la espada mía	195
	defenderse y no ofender.	
	Cobrele afición, y así	
	quise miralle mejor,	
	porque es imán el valor,	
	a lo menos para mí;	200
	mas no, por Dios, con cuidado	
	de mujer.	
COSTANZA	Así lo creo;	
	mas siempre empieza el deseo	
	con presupuestos de honrado,	
	pero luego es atrevido.	205
HIPÓLITA	Pues conmigo no lo crea.	
COSTANZA	Plega a Dios que no lo sea.	
HIPÓLITA	¿Cómo, si jamás lo ha sido?	
	Porque en mi buena intención	
	todas mi acciones fundo.	210
COSTANZA	Mas ya no basta en el mundo	
	limpieza de corazón,	
	pues juzga por lo exterior	
	y éste ha de ser ejemplar;	
	pero siéntate a pasar	215
	adelante en tu labor.	

211–214 See Fray Luis, *La perfecta casada*: "a la castidad cristiana no le basta ser casta, sino parecer también que lo es; porque ha de ser tan cumplida, que del ánima mane el vestido, y del secreto de la consciencia salga a la sobrehaz, para que se vean sus alhajas de fuera" (1999, 188).
216 *labor*: 'embroidery'.

HIPÓLITA	Because I saw that he was valiant,	
	so courteous and so honourable…	
	I saw him clear a street	
	full of men with such skill,	190
	so much spirit and strength,	
	I had to just stare at him in awe.	
	I saw him treat my father	
	with such noble courtesy; I saw	
	him defend himself from my sword	195
	without a single offence to me.	
	I have come to admire him, and so	
	I wanted to take a closer look,	
	because valour is a magnet,	
	at least for me; but never,	200
	by God, did I look at him the way	
	a woman would.	
COSTANZA	That's right;	
	desire always starts out	
	masquerading like it's honourable,	
	but soon it turns to recklessness.	205
HIPÓLITA	Not with me.	
COSTANZA	I hope to God it doesn't.	
HIPÓLITA	How, if it has never happened before?	
	My good intentions	
	are the root of all my actions.	210
COSTANZA	Still, it isn't enough anymore	
	to just have a pure heart in this world,	
	as you will be judged by what is visible	
	therefore you must be exemplary;	
	but sit down, let's pass the time	215
	as you progress in your work.	

¡Hola!, traime una almohadilla,
siéntate en esta almohada.

Siéntase HIPÓLITA y traen una almohadilla de labor, y no acierta a sentarse como mujer, descubiertos los pies y piernas, y su MADRE llegue y cubrala.[+]

HIPÓLITA	Nunca estaré bien sentada,	
	¿No es mejor en una silla?	220
COSTANZA	Recoge los pies.	
HIPÓLITA	Reniego	
	de quien me puso a mujer.	
COSTANZA	Aprenderás a tener	
	en los ojos más sosiego.	
HIPÓLITA	Estoy con gran pesadumbre.	225

(Alarga las piernas descompuestamente.)

COSTANZA ¡Jesús!
HIPÓLITA ¿Cómo están sentadas,
y algunas sin almohadas?
COSTANZA Eso puede la costumbre.

Salen DON FÉLIX y GALVÁN.

GALVÁN	Ya tu padre me ha mandado	
	que te sirva, y lo he de hacer.	230
FÉLIX	Mucho gusto de tener,	
	buen Galván, tan buen criado.	
	Dame, mi madre, la mano.	

(Besa la mano.)[+]

COSTANZA	Hijo, con el alma entera.	
	Ya está grande labrandera	235
	tu hermana.	
HIPÓLITA	¡No acierto, hermano!	
	Para esto no nací,	

---

218 Women generally sat on cushions on the floor, instead of in chairs. Hipólita is not used to sitting this way, and thus exposes her legs.
+ *218* This stage direction is taken from B.
+ *233* This stage direction is taken from B.
235 *labrandera*: 'embroiderer'.

The Force of Habit: Act Two

          You there! Bring me a sewing pillow.
          Sit down here on this cushion.

HIPÓLITA sits, and they bring her an embroidery pillow, and she is not able to sit like a lady, uncovering her feet and legs, and her mother comes and covers them.

HIPÓLITA	I will never sit comfortably,	
	isn't it better on a chair?	220
COSTANZA	Tuck your feet under you.	
HIPÓLITA	I disown	
	the one who made me a woman.	
COSTANZA	You will learn to show	
	more softness in your eyes.	
HIPÓLITA	I feel like I'm in mourning.	225
	(She splays out her legs indecorously.)	
COSTANZA	Jesus!	
HIPÓLITA	How do they sit like this,	
	some even without cushions?	
COSTANZA	This is the custom.	

Enter DON FÉLIX and GALVÁN.

GALVÁN	Your father has ordered me	
	to serve you now, and I shall do it.	230
FÉLIX	It gives me great pleasure, good Galván,	
	to have such a good servant.	
	Dear mother, give me your hand.	
	(He kisses her hand.)	
COSTANZA	My dear boy, with my entire soul.	
	Already, your sister is quite the	235
	seamstress.	
HIPÓLITA	I can't figure it out, brother!	
	I was not born to do this,	

	que es cosa muy enfadosa	
	y me ofende.	
FÉLIX	Pues es cosa	
	de ingenio.	
HIPÓLITA	De flema, di.	240
FÉLIX	Más hilos cogiste agora	
	de lo justo.	
HIPÓLITA	Matarame.	
FÉLIX	¿Quieres que te enseñe? Dame;	
	con tu licencia, señora.	
	(Toma el almohadilla DON FÉLIX, como mujer, a labrar.)[+]	
GALVÁN	Tú labras cosa escogida.	245
HIPÓLITA	¿Qué haces? ¡Válame Cristo!	
GALVÁN	¡Qué bien te sientas!	
HIPÓLITA	¿Has visto?	
GALVÁN	Hazte sastre, por tu vida;	
	que vales todo dinero	
	para sastre.	
HIPÓLITA	¿Hay tal rigor?	250
	Para dama eres mejor	
	que no para caballero.	
	Quita allá, ¡cuerpo de Dios;	
	con el hombre y con la nada!	
	(Levántase HIPÓLITA y arroja la almohadilla.)[+]	
COSTANZA	Esa es libertad sobrada.	255
HIPÓLITA	Ten valor.	
GALVÁN	¿Hay tales dos?	
FÉLIX	No entendí que le perdía	
	con esto.	

---

240 *de flema*: 'flema' is one of the four bodily humors, associated with a cool and humid constitution. It was believed to cause a sluggish and lazy nature.

+ **244** This stage direction is taken from B.

+ **254** Stage direction from B.

255 *libertad*: 'audacity', 'brashness'; *Aut. 1734*: "la licencia exorbitante, desenvoltúra y desvergüenza de los que abusan de la verdadera libertád" ('libertad', 4th def.).

257 *le*: this is an example of *leísmo*, causing 'le' to be used in place of 'lo', the direct object pronoun referring to 'valor' mentioned by Hipólita in 256a.

	it's an infuriating thing to do
	and I hate it.
FÉLIX	It is only a question of
	a little ingenuity.
HIPÓLITA	You mean it's exasperating. 240
FÉLIX	You've made more stitches[11]
	there than you should.
HIPÓLITA	This will be the death of me.
FÉLIX	Would you like me to show you? Here;
	with your permission, of course, my lady.
	(FÉLIX takes the little pillow, like a lady, and sews.)
GALVÁN	Your embroidery is exquisite. 245
HIPÓLITA	What are you doing? Holy Christ!
GALVÁN	How elegantly you sit!
HIPÓLITA	Have you seen this?
GALVÁN	Become a tailor, by your life;
	you're worth a fortune
	as a tailor.
HIPÓLITA	Outrageous! 250
	You make a better lady
	than a gentleman.
	Stop that, oh my God,
	you are nothing of a man!
	(HIPÓLITA stands and throws the pillow.)
COSTANZA	Now this is taking it too far. 255
HIPÓLITA	Show some valour.
GALVÁN	Have there ever been two like them?
FÉLIX	I didn't realise I was losing
	any by sewing.

---

11 See p. 99, Fig. 4 for a photograph of this scene in production.

HIPÓLITA	Si no lo sabes,	
	empléate en cosas graves	
	y sabrás de cada día	260
	lo que hiciera yo por ti	
	a no ser mujer. ¡Ah, Dios!	
	¡O muda el ser de los dos,	
	o dame la muerte a mí!	
COSTANZA	Mudar de estilo conviene.	265
HIPÓLITA	Perdona.	
FÉLIX	Estimo y adoro	
	que me digas lo que ignoro.	

Salen el AYO y el MAESTRO DE ARMAS.

AYO	El maestro de armas viene.	
COSTANZA	Siéntate, y más reportada	
	procede de aquí adelante.	270
HIPÓLITA	Esto a matarme es bastante.	
	¡Ah, quién tomara la espada!	
MAESTRO	*(El MAESTRO DE ARMAS con espadas de esgrima.)*[+]	
	¿Gusta de tomar lición	
	vuesamerced?	
FÉLIX	Sí maestro,	
	deseo mucho el ser diestro.	275
MAESTRO	Aprende con afición:	
	pon la espada deste modo;	
	sácala briosamente.	
	Saca el pie… no tanto… tente.	
	([FÉLIX] saca mucho el pie y estiende todo el brazo.)[+]	
	Tiende el brazo, no del todo;	280
	aunque en esto hay opiniones,	
	ésta es la buena.	

+ 272 Stage direction from C.
+ 279 Stage direction from B.

HIPÓLITA	If you don't know, apply yourself to some serious matters, and you will know every day what I would gladly do in your place, if I weren't a woman. Oh, God! Either swap our souls with one another, or just kill me!	260
COSTANZA	You should change your tone.	265
HIPÓLITA	Sorry.	
FÉLIX	I admire and adore how you are teaching me what I do not know.	

Enter FÉLIX'S TUTOR and the FENCING MASTER.

TUTOR	The Fencing Master is coming.	
COSTANZA	Sit here, and keep yourself in check from here on out.	270
HIPÓLITA	This is enough to kill me. Oh, to take the sword in my hand again!	
FENCING MASTER	*(Holding out the fencing swords.)* Would you like to take a lesson, sir?[12]	
FÉLIX	Yes, teacher; I very much want to be skilled.	275
FENCING MASTER	Learn with zeal: hold the sword like this; unsheathe it with a flourish. Advance your foot ... not that much ... wait. *(FÉLIX thrusts out his feet and extends his whole arm.)* Bend your arm, no, not all the way; there are different opinions about this, but this is the best way.	280

---

12 The Fencing Master's language in the Spanish characterizes him as a non-native speaker, a comic foreigner who speaks Spanish awkwardly and with an accent.

HIPÓLITA	¡Ay, hermano!
	¡Qué tibio metiste mano!
	¡Qué desairado te pones!
	Dame la espada, y yo fío 285
	que te enseñe a batallar
	tan bien⁺ como tú a labrar
	y hacer vainillas: con brío.
	(Toma la espada negra HIPÓLITA.)
	Se mete mano a la espada,
	mostrando ferocidad 290
	en el rostro.
MAESTRO	Así es verdad,
	y es la postura extremada.
HIPÓLITA	Batallemos.
MAESTRO	Sea así,
	pues que tú gustas, señora.
HIPÓLITA	Pero dejémoslo agora, 295
	que viene mi padre allí.
GALVÁN	Fuiste dichoso.
MAESTRO	¿Qué dices?
GALVÁN	Que si hubiera batallado
	contigo, hubieras quedado
	sin ojos o sin narices. 300

Sale DON PEDRO.

PEDRO	Hipólita, ¿qué es aquello?
	¿Siempre insistes en querer
	ser hombre, siendo mujer?
HIPÓLITA	Siempre me pesa de sello.
PEDRO	Dale la espada a tu hermano. 305
HIPÓLITA	Y fuera bien empleada
	si, como le doy la espada,
	pudiera dalle la mano.

+ **287** tan bien B C : tambien P.
288 *vainillas*: a delicate fringe, sometimes used at cuffs or hems. "Entre las costureras significa aquellos menudos, y sutiles deshilados, que se hacen à la orilla junto à los dobladillos" (*Aut. 1739*, 'vainica ò vainilla').

HIPÓLITA	Oh, brother!	
	How weakly you draw the sword!	
	You have no noble bearing at all!	
	Give me that sword, and I swear	285
	I will teach you how to do battle	
	as well as you can embroider and	
	make your little lace doilies: with gusto.	
	(HIPÓLITA takes the foil.)	
	Grip the sword, showing ferocity	290
	in your face.	
FENCING MASTER	That's right,	
	and her posture is excellent.	
HIPÓLITA	Let's battle.	
FENCING MASTER	All right,	
	if it will please you, my lady.	
HIPÓLITA	Oh no, let's leave it for now,	295
	my father's coming.	
GALVÁN	You're a lucky man.	
FENCING MASTER	What do you mean?	
GALVÁN	If she had fought with you,	
	you would have been left	
	with no eyes, or nose.	300

Enter DON PEDRO.

PEDRO	Hipólita, what's all this?	
	You still insist on wanting	
	to be a man, though you're a woman?	
HIPÓLITA	It still pains me to be one.	
PEDRO	Give the sword to your brother.	305
HIPÓLITA	And that would be a good move,	
	if, as I give him the sword,	
	I could also give him my hand to use it.	

PEDRO	Enseñalde a ser valiente,	
	maestro; digo, a reñir;	310
	que el jugar o el esgrimir	
	es cosa bien diferente.	
	No vuelva con pocos bríos	
	un paso atrás, por mil vidas;	
	sirvan sus mismas heridas	315
	de reparos y desvíos.	
	Saque briosa la espada,	
	lleve compás en los pies,	
	y aprenda a tirar después	
	tajo, revés y estocada.	320
	Y decilde en qué ocasiones	
	debe usar destas tres cosas;	
	que estas serán provechosas	
	y no prolijas liciones.	
	Y ésta, si tiene de acero	325
	el ánimo y fortaleza,	
	será bastante destreza	
	para cualquier caballero.	
	Ea, Maestro, comenzad;	
	mas antes saber conviene	330
	qué naturaleza tiene;	
	reñid con él, batallad.	
	Don Félix, dale al maestro	
	una herida muy bien dada.	
FÉLIX	No acierto a regir la espada.	335
COSTANZA	¡Ay, señor, que es poco diestro!	
HIPÓLITA	¡No te retires, hermano!	
	¡Jesús, qué espada tan floja!	
PEDRO	Dalde, veré si se enoja.	

---

320 *tajo, revés y estocada*: in fencing, the '*tajo*' is a stroke made holding the foil in the right hand, moving the sword across the body from right to left, while a '*revés*' moves from left to right. "En la Esgrima es el corte, que se dá con la espada, ù otra arma cortante, llevando el brazo desde la mano derecha à la izquierda: y se dice assi, à distinción del que llaman revés, que vá al contrario desde la izquierda à la derecha" (*Aut. 1739*, 'Tajo', 5th def.). The '*estocada*' is a direct thrust, or riposte. "El golpe que se dá de punta con la espáda ò estoque, de cuyo nombre es formada esta voz" ('Estocada', *Aut. 1732*).

PEDRO	Teach him how to be valiant,	
	master; I mean, to fight;	310
	play fighting and learning the sword	
	for battle are two very different things.	
	Don't shrink back	
	or cower away, no matter what;	
	he must learn by his own wounds	315
	the art of parrying and thrusting.	
	Draw the sword with spirit,	
	keep a firm stance with the feet,	
	learn to thrust after	
	you strike, slash, and riposte.	320
	And tell him on which occasions	
	it is appropriate to use those three moves;	
	for they will be useful to him,	
	more than giving him a long lecture.	
	And this, if he has the steel	325
	of spirit and strength,	
	he will be skilled enough	
	to take on any gentleman.	
	So, teacher, begin;	
	it is better to find out soon	330
	what nature has given him;	
	fight with him, attack.	
	Don Félix, give the teacher	
	a wound he won't soon forget.	
FÉLIX	I don't have control of the sword.	335
COSTANZA	Oh sir, he doesn't know how to do it yet!	
HIPÓLITA	Don't draw back, brother.	
	God, what a limp sword!	
PEDRO	Let him have it, I'll see if he can be riled.	

FÉLIX (Dale el MAESTRO un golpe [a FÉLIX] y quéjase.)⁺
 ¡Ay, Jesús!
PEDRO Hijo villano, 340
 quéjaste como mujer,
 ¡ve a vengarte!

Toma la espada doña HIPÓLITA y aporrea el MAESTRO.⁺

COSTANZA ¡Ay, desdichada!
HIPÓLITA Vuelve a mi mano la espada;
 direte lo que has de hacer,
 y veremos si el maestro 345
 se excusará destos palos.
MAESTRO ¡Detente, señora!
HIPÓLITA Dalos
 tú mejor, pues eres diestro.

Vase el MAESTRO.⁺

GALVÁN Poco importa su destreza.
PEDRO Baste, ¡ay, hija de mis ojos! 350
GALVÁN No le comerán los piojos
 al maestro en la cabeza.
PEDRO Tú, cobarde, ¿no te afrentas?
 ¿Que te encoges? ¿Que te extrañas?
 ¿De qué tienes las entrañas? 355
 ¿Es posible que no sientas
 que una mujer te avergüence?
 Estoy…
COSTANZA ¡Ay, Jesús; aguarda!
PEDRO ¿Qué vileza te acobarda?
 ¿Qué cobardía te vence? 360

+ *339* This stage direction is taken from B.
+ *342a* This stage direction is taken from B.
+ *348* This stage direction is from A.
350 hija A B C : hijo P. I am rejecting P's reading 'hijo' for A, B, and C's reading 'hija' because it makes more sense that Pedro would be referring to Hipólita here.
351–352 *No le comerán los piojos / al maestro en la cabeza*: Galván makes a joke that Hipólita has given the Maestro such a close shave to the head with her sword that he will not have any trouble with lice.

FÉLIX	*(The FENCING MASTER deals FÉLIX a blow, and he cries out.)*
	Oh, Jesus!
PEDRO	Son, don't be a peasant, 340
	you whine like a woman,[13]
	go avenge yourself!

HIPÓLITA takes the sword and wounds the FENCING MASTER.

COSTANZA	Oh, I'm so ashamed!
HIPÓLITA	The sword returns to my hand,
	I will tell you what you have to do,
	and we will see if the master 345
	can escape a few prods.
FENCING MASTER	Wait, my lady.
HIPÓLITA	Give us
	your best, since you're so great.

Exit the FENCING MASTER.

GALVÁN	His skill didn't do him much good.
PEDRO	Enough; that's my girl! 350
GALVÁN	She gave his head a close shave,
	the lice will have nothing to bite!
PEDRO	You, coward, aren't you ashamed?
	What are you afraid of? You shiver?
	Have you no guts? 355
	Is it possible that you are not appalled
	that a woman puts you to shame?
	I am…
COSTANZA	Oh, Jesus; wait!
PEDRO	What baseness makes you such a coward?
	What cowardice overcomes you? 360

---

13   See p. 106, Fig. 11 for a photograph of this scene in production.

La fuerza de la costumbre: Jornada segunda

¿Tú eres Moncada, y ordenas
vilezas con que me afrentes?
¿No sabes por qué vertientes
llegó mi sangre a tus venas?
    ¿No has visto en tantos papeles 365
dónde y cómo está fundada
la gran casa de Moncada,
que tiene por chapiteles
    que compiten con el sol,
tantos Hugos y Gastones, 370
Pedros, Guillenes, Ramones,
honra del suelo Español?
    Siendo tal, mucho me aflijo
de que tú, con afrentarte,
la derribes por la parte 375
que yo la sustento, hijo.
    Los anales de Aragón
lee, porque en ellos veas
quién son Moncadas y Urreas,
que tus ascendientes son; 380
    y advirtiendo en su valor
tantas hazañas gigantes,
los pensamientos levantes,
y a tu sangre des calor.
    O si es que tu encogimiento 385
nace de alguna virtud
cristiana, tendrás quietud
retirado en un convento.
    Que el quedar sin heredero
será menos daño en mí, 390
que el ver esta mengua en ti.
¿Qué me respondes?

---

368 *chapiteles*: 'column capitals'; 'spires'.
384 *y a tu sangre des calor*: heat is one of the four humors, associated with boldness, bravery and the choleric disposition. Félix refers to the humoral influences of heat as well in his response (v. II 397–402).

You are a Moncada, yet you dare
affront me with this base behaviour?
Do you not know that the blood
of our ancestors runs in your veins?
Have you not read all our histories 365
and learned where and how
the great house of Moncada was founded,
whose spires rise up
to compete with the sun,
men such as the Hugos and Gastons, 370
Pedros, Guilléns, Ramóns,
the honour of the Spanish land?
With this in mind, it afflicts me
that you, bringing shame on yourself,
tear down our great house 375
just as I am trying to build it up, son.
Read the annals of Aragón,
because in them you will learn
about the Moncadas and Urreas,
that they are your ancestors; 380
and as you realize the valour
of their many great deeds,
you will raise up your thoughts, and
feel their heat running through your veins.
Or if your reticence springs 385
from some Christian virtue,
you can go and find peace
hidden away in a convent.
Remaining without an heir
will be less painful for me 390
than to see you as a coward.
What do you have to say to me?

FÉLIX	Que quiero	
	imitar en el valor	
	mis nobles antepasados,	
	y pensamientos honrados	395
	tengo en el alma, señor.	
	Cosquillas la valentía	
	suele⁺ hacerme en la ambición,	
	y acomete al corazón	
	hirviendo la sangre mía,	400
	y ejecutará después	
	su natural influencia;	
	pero mi poca experiencia	
	ata mis manos y pies.	
HIPÓLITA	Eso sí, ya es valentía	405
	el desealla no más.	
PEDRO	Algún consuelo me das.	
COSTANZA	¡Ay, hijo del alma mía!	
PEDRO	Dejalde, señora, el lado.	
COSTANZA	¿Por qué?	
PEDRO	Porque siendo tal,	410
	es contagioso este mal,	
	y vos se le habéis pegado.	
	Llevaos allá esa mujer…	
GALVÁN	¡Qué mal nombre, Dios nos guarde!	
PEDRO	…y enseñalda a ser cobarde.	415
HIPÓLITA	Eso imposible ha de ser.	
PEDRO	Ninguno serlo pudiera,	
	si bien se considerara.	

+ 398   suele A B C : suelo P.

410b–412   *contagioso este mal*: Juan Luis Vives cautioned against women raising children, especially sons, without a husband or substitute male presence in his manual, *On the Education of a Christian Woman*: "We often see it happen that those brought up by a widow are less obedient than they should be to those to whom they owe obedience, spoiled by the excessive indulgence of the widow. Thus, the expression 'a widow's child' has become a proverb among many peoples, especially our own. It is used of young men who are badly brought up, of corrupt, insolent youths who lead a morally depraved life. I should counsel a widow to place the care of the upbringing of her children upon some virtuous and sensible man, for, out of blind love, she thinks she is treating her children too severely, even when she is far too lenient with them" (2000, 315).

FÉLIX	I want to	
	imitate the bravery	
	of my noble ancestors,	
	and I do have honourable	395
	thoughts in my soul, my lord.	
	Twinges of courage	
	often give me little starts of ambition,	
	and they seize my heart,	
	boiling my blood,	400
	which will in turn exercise	
	its natural influence;	
	but my scant experience	
	binds my hands and feet.	
HIPÓLITA	That's it, you already show bravery	405
	just by desiring it.	
PEDRO	That's some consolation.	
COSTANZA	Oh, my precious boy!	
PEDRO	Stand aside, my lady.	
COSTANZA	Why?	
PEDRO	Because it is the case	410
	that this malady is contagious,	
	and it is you who has infected him.	
	Take that woman out of here…	
GALVÁN	Not that name, God protect us!	
PEDRO	…and teach her how to be a coward.	415
HIPÓLITA	That will be impossible.	
PEDRO	No man would be one,	
	if he really considered what it meant.	

AYO	Si su padre le criara,	
	mejor ejemplo nos diera.	420
PEDRO	Para infundirte osadía,	
	dejando el honor aparte,	
	que es en todo, he de probarte,	
	dañosa la cobardía.	
	Fundallo quiero en razón	425
	para que no te acobardes;	
	¿qué fin tiene el ser cobardes	
	en los que cobardes son?	
GALVÁN	Guardar la vida no más;	
	deso están los libros llenos.	430
PEDRO	Pues éstos la guardan menos.	
FÉLIX	¿Menos?	
PEDRO	Oye, y lo verás.	
	Toma, tiéndete hasta darme	
	esta espada a mi despecho.	
	Puesto a la vista o al pecho,	435
	¿podré herirte sin matarme?[+]	
	Pues si es tan cierto el saber	
	que está el peligro en la ofensa	
	y que es la misma defensa	
	de la vida el ofender,	440
	al que se encoge y retira,	
	cierto será y ordinario	
	el matalle su contrario,	
	porque a su salvo le tira.	
	Y si huye, que en los buenos	445
	es una gran desventura,	
	huyendo, ¿quién le asegura	
	de que el otro corra menos?	
	Pues si es más, ¿le alcanza y hiere?	
	Mas, ¡qué infelice habrá sido	450
	el que por la espalda herido	
	vergonzosamente muere!	

434 *a mi despecho*: 'to my displeasure'; 'against my will' (Covarrubias gives the meaning, "A despecho mio, contra mi voluntad" ('despecho', 661).

+ 436 matarme A B C : matarm P (printing error).

TUTOR	If his father had raised him,	
	he'd have turned out a model son.	420
PEDRO	In order to fill you with courage,	
	leaving honour aside, since it	
	infuses all, I must impress upon you,	
	cowardice is damaging.	
	I must make you understand	425
	so that you are not afraid;	
	what purpose does it serve to be cowards	
	for those who are cowards?	
GALVÁN	Just trying to stay alive is all;	
	storybooks are full of examples.	430
PEDRO	Cowards protect their lives even less.	
FÉLIX	Less?	
PEDRO	Listen, and you will see.	
	Take this sword and hold it out to me,	
	showing that you have the advantage.	
	If it points at my face or at my chest,	435
	can I wound you without killing myself?	
	So if it is known for certain	
	that it is dangerous to attack	
	and that the effort to defend	
	may endanger life itself,	440
	he who cowers and retreats	
	will surely be killed by	
	his opponent every time,	
	because he strikes at him safely.	
	And if he flees, which in noble men	445
	is a great disgrace,	
	running away, how can he be sure	
	that his enemy will run more slowly?	
	What if he catches up and strikes?	
	And, how unhappy he would be	450
	to get a knife in the back	
	and die in shame!	

	Y así, si bien se imagina,	
	aunque nunca hubiera honor,	
	hubiera sido en rigor	455
	necedad el ser gallina.	
AYO	¿Qué más se puede decir?	
GALVÁN	Apelo desa sentencia;	
	que es grande la diferencia	
	que hay del correr al huír.	460
HIPÓLITA	Eso en ti debe de ser,	
	que el que de nobleza arguye,	
	de corrido de que huye,	
	suele dejar de correr.	
PEDRO	Hijo mío, ten valor;	465
	mira que en peligro pones	
	nuestra honra.	
FÉLIX	Tus razones	
	me animan mucho, señor;	
	verasme hacer cuanto puedo,	
	si dejo de verme atado.	470
PEDRO	*[Aparte]* Con una cosa he pensado	
	que le haré perder el miedo.	
	[A Félix] Hijo, ¿siénteste con brío	
	para solo acompañarme?	
	Pues ¿de quién he de fiarme	475
	mejor que de un hijo mío?	
FÉLIX	Por servirte honrado y fiel	
	ya mi sangre se alborota.	
PEDRO	Pues vestiraste una cota,	
	y tomarás un broquel.	480
	(Aparte) Será una traza escogida.	
	Ven. Adiós, doña Costanza.	
COSTANZA	Adiós.	
PEDRO	Logra mi esperanza.	

---

479 *cota*: a chain mail coat; armor (*Aut. 1729*, 1st def.).
480 *broquel*: a small shield.

	And so, as one can imagine,	
	even if honour had never existed,	
	it would always be extremely	455
	idiotic to be a chicken.	
TUTOR	What more is there to say?	
GALVÁN	I object to this ruling;	
	for there is a big difference	
	between having to run and fleeing.	460
HIPÓLITA	That's true in your case,	
	but a nobleman would argue,	
	once the shame of fleeing hits him,	
	he will stop running.	
PEDRO	My son, be brave;	465
	you must see that you put all our	
	honour at risk.	
FÉLIX	Your reasoning	
	greatly encourages me, my lord;	
	you will see me do all that I can,	
	if I can unbind myself.	470
PEDRO	*(Aside)* I have thought of another way	
	that I can rid him of his fear.	
	(Aloud) Son, could you muster	
	enough spirit to accompany me alone?	
	In whom can I place my trust	475
	more than my own son?	
FÉLIX	To serve you honourably and faithfully	
	my blood is already boiling.	
PEDRO	Well get yourself an armoured coat	
	and you'll also need a buckler.	480
	(Aside) This will be a rare sight.	
	(Aloud) Come on. Goodbye, Costanza.	
COSTANZA	Goodbye.	
PEDRO	Help me attain my hopes.	

FÉLIX	Yo la lograré, por vida de mi madre.	
GALVÁN	Porque notes el grande encarecimiento.	485
HIPÓLITA	¡Qué gracioso juramento para entre tantos bigotes! Si quitárselos pudiera, y ponellos en mi cara, yo juro a Dios que jurara…	490
COSTANZA	Quedo, ten.	
HIPÓLITA	…de otra manera.	

Vanse, y salen OTAVIO y MARCELO.

MARCELO	Divinamente ha cantado.	[quintillas]
OTAVIO	Es ángel doña Leonor en todo; de enamorado, estoy loco.	495
MARCELO	Con menor ocasión lo habéis estado.	
OTAVIO	Para dejallo de estar me valí desta receta; oíd, que vuelve a cantar.	500
MARCELO	Fuera del todo discreta si cantara sin templar.	

Canta en la ventana DOÑA LEONOR.

LEONOR	Ojos negros, ojos tristes, ¿por qué lloráis? ¿Qué tenéis? Pues que la noche os agrada, por algo debe de ser. Si os alumbra el sol de día y no competís con él, ¿por qué, adorando las nubes, a la noche apetecéis? Mas diréisme que es locura,	[canción: romance é] 505 510

484–485a Félix swears on his mother that he will prove his worth as a man. Galván and Hipólita mock Félix for the effeminacy of the oath.

FÉLIX	I will help you, I swear on my mother's life.	
GALVÁN	Because you know that's the most precious thing to him.	485
HIPÓLITA	What a ridiculous oath to swear among these grizzled men! If I could take their beards and put them on my face, I swear I would give you an oath…	490
COSTANZA	Wait, don't…	
HIPÓLITA	…of another kind entirely.	

Exit ALL. Enter OTAVIO and MARCELO.

SCENE 2.3

MARCELO	Her singing is divine.	
OTAVIO	Doña Leonor is an angel in everything; I'm so in love, I'm out of my mind.	495
MARCELO	With less cause, you've been this way before.	
OTAVIO	To bring me to my senses her song is my prescription; listen, she's singing again.	500
MARCELO	She'd be truly amazing if she sang without tuning up.	

LEONOR sings at the window.

LEONOR	Black eyes, sad eyes, why do you cry? What is it? For the night pleases you, so it must be something else. If the sun lights you by day and you do not compete, why, in love with the clouds, do you prefer the night? You will tell me this is madness,	505

510 |

	y es sin duda que lo es,	
	hacer que os pregunte el alma	
	lo que del alma sabéis;	
	pero pues os pregunta quien no ignora,	515
	enmudeciendo agora	
	lenguas del alma mía,	
	llorad de noche, pues habláis de día.	
MARCELO	Cosa es del cielo, por Dios.	[romance o–o]
OTAVIO	Los ángeles en sus coros	520
	su música habrán dejado,	
	y la suya escuchan todos.	
MARCELO	¿Si seréis vos por quien hizo	
	las preguntas a los ojos?	
OTAVIO	Pluguiera a Dios que así fuera,	525
	pero no soy tan dichoso.	
MARCELO	Ya la ventana han cerrado.	
OTAVIO	Ya en el alma me congojo.	

Sale a la ventana INÉS, criada.

INÉS	*[Aparte]* Pues mi señora se ha ido,	
	despedirme destos tontos	530
	quiero. *[Alto]* Adiós, adiós, galanes.	
OTAVIO	Espera, ¿para tan poco	
	subiste?	
INÉS	Señora llama.	
	[A dentro] Yo voy, al momento torno;	
	[Alto] que ya mi señora espera.	535
MARCELO	Extremado humor.	
OTAVIO	Donoso.	
	Gente viene, vamos.	
MARCELO	Vamos.	

Vanse y salen DON PEDRO, GALVÁN y otro CRIADO.

PEDRO	Ya las calles no conozco.
GALVÁN	En aquesta vive Fabio,
	y es sin salida.

	and without a doubt it is,	
	that you ask my soul what	
	only the soul can know; but	
	the one who asks you already knows,	515
	muting again	
	the voices of my soul,	
	cry by night, since you speak by day.	
MARCELO	She's straight from heaven, by God.	
OTAVIO	The angels in their choirs	520
	have left their music,	
	and everyone listens to hers.	
MARCELO	And if it were you for whom she asked	
	her eyes all those questions?	
OTAVIO	I wish to God it were for me,	525
	but I'm nowhere near that lucky.	
MARCELO	Now they've shut the window.	
OTAVIO	Now my soul torments me.	

Leonor's maidservant, INÉS, appears at the window.

INÉS	*(Aside)* Since my lady has gone,	
	I can now say goodbye to these fools.	530
	(Aloud) Goodbye, goodbye, gentlemen.	
OTAVIO	Wait; you came out	
	just for that?	
INÉS	My lady is calling.	
	(to inside) I'm coming, this instant,	
	(Aloud) for my lady is waiting.	535
MARCELO	Strange humour.	
OTAVIO	Amusing.	
	People are coming, let's go.	
MARCELO	Let's go.	

Exit ALL and enter DON PEDRO, GALVÁN, and another SERVANT.

SCENE 2.4

PEDRO	I don't recognise these streets anymore.
GALVÁN	Fabio lives on that one,
	and it's a dead end.

PEDRO	Vosotros,	540

pues venís bien advertidos,
en viendo a don Félix solo,
asegurad sus espaldas.
¿Preveniste a Fabio?

GALVÁN   Y como;
las dos puertas tiene abiertas,   545
la principal sale al Coso,
y ésta aquí.

PEDRO   Entraré por ésta,
y desconocido en todo,
saldré por allá a buscar
aquí a don Félix; dichoso   550
seré si le quito el miedo.

Sale DON FÉLIX con espada y broquel.

FÉLIX   ¡Válgame Dios poderoso,
qué horror ponen las tinieblas!

PEDRO   Él es, retiraos vosotros.
[A Félix] ¿Hijo?

FÉLIX   Señor.

PEDRO   Esta boca   555
de calle donde te pongo
has de guardarme esta noche.

FÉLIX   Por servirte todo es poco.
(Vase DON PEDRO.)
En aquella casa ha entrado,
confieso que estoy medroso.   560
Como en mi vida he salido
de noche, apenas conozco
si estoy en cielo o en tierra.
Si el infierno es pedregoso,
el infierno debe ser   565

---

546 *Coso*: a main street in Zaragoza. Castro also references this part of the city of Zaragoza in his play *Los mal casados de Valencia*. See http://www.outofthewings.org/db/play/los-mal-casados-de-valencia/sample-translations.

PEDRO	You two,	540

you know what to do,
when you see Félix alone,
watch his back.
Have you filled Fabio in on the plan?

GALVÁN	And how to do it;	
	the two doors are open,	545

the main door opens right onto the Coso,
and this one is right here.

PEDRO   I'll go in this one,
and, fully disguised,
I'll come out there to find
Don Félix here; if I'm lucky   550
it will scare the fear right out of him.

Enter FÉLIX with a sword and buckler.

FÉLIX   Powerful God, protect me,
everything looks frightening at twilight.
PEDRO   There he is; get back, you two.
My son?
FÉLIX   My lord.
PEDRO   Your post   555
is the opening to this street,
where you must stand guard tonight.
FÉLIX   To serve you, every task is small.
(Exit DON PEDRO.)
He's gone into that house,
I confess I feel faint.   560
As I've never gone out at night,
I scarcely know whether I'm
in heaven or on earth.
If hell is rocky,
this is probably hell,   565

                    donde tantas piedras topo,
                    y de estar acostumbrado
                    a pisar estrados solos,
                    casi me dejan sin pies.
                    Como ciego o como loco   570
                    tropiezo con las esquinas,
                    no acostumbrados⁺ mis ojos
                    a ver entre las tinieblas,
                    como suelen hacer otros.
                    Cuántos hombres encontré;   575
                    deslumbrado y temeroso
                    me pareció que traían
                    un gigante en cada hombro.
                    Pero ¿qué veo?

Sale DON PEDRO mudado de capa y con un pañuelo en la boca, y mete mano.

PEDRO   *[Aparte]*   Si salgo
             buen maestro, no haré poco.   580
FÉLIX   ¡Jesús mío! ¡Padre, padre!
PEDRO   *[Aparte]* De serlo tuyo me corro.

Salen al ruido a la ventana DOÑA LEONOR e INÉS.

LEONOR   ¡Cuchilladas! ¿Si es mi hermano?
             ¡Ay cielo, selde piadoso!
FÉLIX   ¿Por dónde podré escapar?   585
             Ya con las espaldas topo
             en la pared; ¿matarame?
             Reñir por remedio escojo.
PEDRO   *[Aparte]* Ya vale la industria mía.

Vase retirando DON PEDRO y éntrase huyendo.

FÉLIX   Reviento de puro enojo.   590
             ¿Huís, cobarde? ¡Esperad!
LEONOR   No le sigáis.

+ 572   acostumbrados   A B C: acombrados P (printing error).

for I've tripped over so many stones,
and as I'm only accustomed
to walking on floorboards,
they've just about left me without feet.
Like a blind man or a madman, 570
I trip at every corner,
as my eyes are not accustomed
to seeing in these shadows,
as other men's eyes might be.
I seem to see so many men; 575
I am blind and fearful,
they look as though they carry
a giant on each shoulder.
But what do I see?

Enter DON PEDRO, covered over with a cape and with a handkerchief over his mouth, sword in hand.

PEDRO	*(Aside)* If I teach him a lesson,	
	it will be no small feat.	580
FÉLIX	My God! Father, father!	
PEDRO	*(Aside)* I'm ashamed to say I am yours.	

Drawn by the sound of fighting, LEONOR and INÉS come to the window.

LEONOR	Swordfighting! Is it my brother?	
	Oh heavens, be merciful!	
FÉLIX	*(Aside)* Where can I escape?	585
	Oh god, my back's up	
	against the wall; will I be killed?	
	I choose to fight to save myself.	
PEDRO	*(Aside)* Now my plan is working.	

DON PEDRO flees across the stage as if pursued, and exits.

FÉLIX	I'll have to show a burst of pure fury.	590
	You flee, coward? Wait!	
LEONOR	Do not pursue him.	

FÉLIX	¿A quién oigo?	
LEONOR	Oíd, señor, por mi vida.	
FÉLIX	Ya vuestra voz reconozco.	
LEONOR	¿Sois don Félix?	
FÉLIX	Sí, señora.	595
LEONOR	¿Estáis herido?	
FÉLIX	Y quejoso	
	de que no me hayáis curado,	
	pues me hirieron[+] vuestros ojos.	
LEONOR	No es muy mortal esa herida.	

Sale GALVÁN y otro CRIADO.

GALVÁN	Lleguémonos poco a poco.	600
LEONOR	Más gente viene, don Félix.	
FÉLIX	Ya vuelvo a estar temeroso.	

Sale DON PEDRO, y lléganse GALVÁN y el otro CRIADO.

GALVÁN	Pues, ¿con la espada desnuda,	
	señor? Acá estamos todos.	
PEDRO	¿Has reñido?	
FÉLIX	Sí, señor;	605
	un hombre me tuvo en poco,	
	pero ya llevó el castigo.	
PEDRO	Huelgo de verte animoso.	
FÉLIX	Dile muchas cuchilladas,	
	y huyó en fin.	
GALVÁN	¡Valiente mozo!	610
	Como gato ha procedido,	
	que apretado es valeroso.	
PEDRO	¿Perdiste sombrero o vaina?	
	Búscalo.	
FÉLIX	Ya lo recojo.	
PEDRO	Que no ha de ir con pieza menos	615
	el que es valiente del todo.	
LEONOR	El padre es gran caballero;	
	de su valor me enamoro.	

+ 598   hirieron   A B C: hicieron P.
615   *con pieza menos*: 'missing anything'; without being completely put together.

FÉLIX	Who's there?	
LEONOR	Hear me, sir, for my life!	
FÉLIX	Now I recognize your voice.	
LEONOR	Are you Don Félix?	
FÉLIX	Yes, my lady.	595
LEONOR	Are you injured?	
FÉLIX	And offended that you have not come to heal me, for it was your eyes that wounded me.	
LEONOR	It doesn't look fatal.	

Enter GALVÁN with ANOTHER SERVANT.

GALVÁN	Let's sneak up on him.	600
LEONOR	Someone's coming, Don Félix.	
FÉLIX	My fearfulness returns.	

Enter DON PEDRO, while GALVÁN and the OTHER SERVANT come closer.

GALVÁN	You come with your sword drawn, sir? We're all here.	
PEDRO	Have you been fighting?	
FÉLIX	Yes, sir, a man dared to underestimate me, so he bore the punishment.	605
PEDRO	It is good to see you in fighting spirit.	
FÉLIX	I gave him a few good thrusts, and in the end he ran away.	
GALVÁN	Courageous young man! He's just like a cat, brave when getting out of a tight spot.	610
PEDRO	Did you lose your hat, or your scabbard? Find it.	
FÉLIX	I'll recover it.	
PEDRO	Only he who is completely put together can be fully valorous.	615
LEONOR	His father is a fine gentleman; I'm quite enamoured of his valour.	

INÉS	¿Y de su hijo?	
LEONOR	También	
	me le inclino y aficiono.	620
PEDRO	Sosiégate.	
FÉLIX	Sí, señor,	
	que voy muy contento.	
PEDRO	¿Cómo?	
FÉLIX	De que mi dama me ha visto	
	en el trance peligroso.	
PEDRO	Esa ambición es honrada.	625
FÉLIX	Ya a tenella me acomodo.	
PEDRO	Si yo curo cobardías	
	seré médico famoso.	

Vanse y salen MARCELO y OTAVIO.

OTAVIO	Ya es don Félix declarado	[quintillas]
	galán de doña Leonor.	630
MARCELO	Podrán jugar al trocado	
	los hermanos.	
OTAVIO	No es amor	
	tan medido y concertado.	
MARCELO	¿Celos tienes?	
OTAVIO	Bien podría.	
	¿Y los tuyos no lo son?	635
MARCELO	Son los mismos que tenía,	
	porque me dio la ocasión	
	celos y amor en un día:	
	primero estuve celoso	
	que enamorado.	

639–640a Marcelo admits that he felt jealousy before love: seeing that Luis was pursuing Hipólita made him jealous, and then he also began to pursue Hipólita.

INÉS	And that of his son?	
LEONOR	Yes, him as well,	
	I feel drawn to him, he is endearing.	620
PEDRO	Be proud of yourself.	
FÉLIX	Yes, sir;	
	I'm very content.	
PEDRO	Why's that?	
FÉLIX	Becuase my lady has seen me	
	in the thick of danger.	
PEDRO	That is an honourable ambition.	625
FÉLIX	Ambition is starting to suit me.	
PEDRO	If I can cure cowardice,	
	I could be a famous doctor.	

SCENE 2.5

Exit ALL, and enter MARCELO and OTAVIO.

OTAVIO	Now Don Félix is declared	
	the suitor of Doña Leonor.	630
MARCELO	I guess the siblings will be able to play	
	their game of switching places.	
OTAVIO	Unrequited	
	love is not so harmonious.	
MARCELO	You're jealous?	
OTAVIO	And well I should be.	
	Are you not, as well?	635
MARCELO	Still the same as always,	
	I have been afflicted	
	by love and jealousy in the same day:	
	I was jealous even before	
	I knew I was in love.[14]	

---

14 This is a common theme found in Golden Age works; one notable example is from Lope de Vega's *El perro del hortelano* [*The Dog in the Manger*], in which the principal couple exchange letters on this subject. In the first letter (I. 551–564), Diana states that it is mere envy to fall in love based only upon seeing the object of love being adored by someone else, and that to feel such jealousy before being in love is impossible. Teodoro's letter, in response, adds that when love is felt prior to the onset of jealousy, the symptom of jealousy is but one in love's long list of signs.

OTAVIO	Es verdad.	640
MARCELO	Y así, aunque el daño es forzoso, como en mí no es novedad, aun no puedo estar quejoso, y en ti al revés viene a ser.	
OTAVIO	Al que es hombre en solo el nombre mi dama no ha de querer.	645
MARCELO	Como yo mujer que es hombre, querrá hombre que es mujer.	
OTAVIO	Es género más perfeto, y así es más apetecible el nuestro.	650
MARCELO	Pero en efeto, en amor todo es posible.	
OTAVIO	Que son las dos te prometo.	

Salen a la ventana DOÑA LEONOR y DOÑA HIPÓLITA.

OTAVIO	A doña Leonor visita sin duda doña Costanza.	655
MARCELO	Grande hermosura, infinita.	
OTAVIO	Su belleza en mi esperanza lo imposible facilita.	
LEONOR	Galanes hay en la calle.	
HIPÓLITA	Ellos ocupan lugar que me holgara de pisalle.	660
LEONOR	No te puedes consolar de ser mujer.	
HIPÓLITA	Aunque calle, te lo dirá este vestido	

647–648 *Como yo…*: Marcelo contradicts Otavio's previous statement that Leonor will not be interested in Félix because he lacks manliness by drawing a parallel between his attraction to Hipólita and thus Leonor's to Félix.

649–651a For more on the Renaissance concept of male perfection and superiority, see section II of the introductory essay, 'Masculine Perfection: Theorized and Performed', where the political importance of the concept of masculinity in this time period is explored.

660–661 *Ellos ocupan…*: Hipólita laments her newfound confinement. As a woman, it would be improper for her to be on the street, especially in the presence of men. This is another instance of Hipólita deploring the loss of the privileges of masculinity.

OTAVIO	It's true.	640
MARCELO	Although it's a heavy blow, for me this is nothing new, I'm not going to complain, though it's quite the reverse for you.	
OTAVIO	He who is a man in name only could never earn the love of my lady.	645
MARCELO	As I desire a woman who is a man, she will desire a man who is a woman.	
OTAVIO	Our gender is the more perfect of the two, and therefore is more desirable.	650
MARCELO	But you know, with love, everything is possible.	
OTAVIO	It's bound to be our ladies up there now.	

Enter at the window LEONOR and HIPÓLITA.

OTAVIO	Doña Costanza[15] has no doubt come to visit the lady Leonor.	655
MARCELO	Her beauty is infinite.	
OTAVIO	Her beauty makes my impossible hope seem easy.	
LEONOR	There are gentlemen in the street.	
HIPÓLITA	They occupy the space where I yearn to walk free.	660
LEONOR	You still cannot console yourself with being a woman.	
HIPÓLITA	Although it cannot speak, this dress will tell you,	

---

15 In rehearsing this scene we noted that Otavio is probably referring to the fact that Costanza and Hipólita are both visiting Leonor, as Marcelo's next line about 'her beauty' certainly refers to Hipólita.

	que me tiene congojada;	665
	notable desdicha ha sido.	
LEONOR	¡Ay, cómo estás extremada!	
	Mil donaires has tenido.	
MARCELO	Pienso que amanece agora.	
OTAVIO	Soles son luces tan bellas.	670
HIPÓLITA	¡Qué cansada está el aurora,	
	el sol, la luna y estrellas	
	destos requiebros, señora!	
LEONOR	Son muy añejos.	
MARCELO	Recelo,	
	que eres en todo feroz.	675
HIPÓLITA	Toda al menos soy de hielo.	
MARCELO	Como es su centro la voz	
	de tu boca, sube al cielo.	
LEONOR	Y no baja donde estás;	
	ya es este nuevo.	
HIPÓLITA	Y valiente,	680
	pues que tú valor le das.	
OTAVIO	Si la hablas tiernamente,	
	no responderá jamás.	
MARCELO	Si no es que la desafío,	
	¿qué he de hacer?	
OTAVIO	Quizá saldrá	685
	al campo, que tiene brío.	
HIPÓLITA	Y ¿si saliese, quizá…?	
MARCELO	Me matarás, yo lo fío.	

671 *el aurora*: note the archaic use of 'el' instead of 'la' with 'aurora'.

671–673 Hipólita rejects the flirtatious compliments of Marcelo and Otavio, who reference frequently used poetic tropes such as dawn and the sun, by retorting that the sun, moon and stars are tired of such amorous remarks.

677–678 *Como es su centro la voz / de tu boca, sube al cielo*: Marcelo compliments Leonor's heavenly voice.

679–680a *Y no baja donde estás; / ya es este nuevo*: 'and it [my voice] won't descend to where you are; that's a new one.' Leonor responds with a jab at Marcelo, though she gives him credit for at least coming up with something new to say (she had previously called attention to the men's lack of originality at 674a, describing their "requiebros" as "muy añejos", "very aged").

	how it distresses me;	665
	this is all a great misfortune.	
LEONOR	Oh, how can you complain!	
	You look so graceful.	
MARCELO	Dawn is breaking now.	
OTAVIO	Two suns radiate beautiful light.	670
HIPÓLITA	How tired are the dawn,	
	the sun, the moon, and the stars	
	of these blandishments, my lady!	
LEONOR	They are quite stale.	
MARCELO	It pains me	
	that you are always so ferocious.	675
HIPÓLITA	In every last detail I am made of ice.	
MARCELO	Your voice rises to heaven,	
	where it finds its true home.	
LEONOR	It does not come down to where you are;	
	though you finally said something new.	
HIPÓLITA	And courageous,	680
	since her voice lends you bravery.	
OTAVIO	If you try to sweet talk her,	
	she'll never speak to you again.	
MARCELO	If not to challenge her to a fight,	
	what else can I do?	
OTAVIO	Maybe you can get her	685
	out to the duelling ground, she's so tough.	
HIPÓLITA	And if we go, maybe, what?	
MARCELO	You will kill me, I'm sure.	

OTAVIO	Dicha sería el matarte tales manos.	
LEONOR	No han mostrado pocos deseos de honrarte.	690
MARCELO	Con todo, me has obligado y estoy por desafiarte.	
HIPÓLITA	Pues el miedo no me ataja; al campo saldré segura.	695
MARCELO	Si eres tan valiente, baja, pero deja la hermosura para reñir sin ventaja.	
OTAVIO	Y pues yo a su lado espero, puédesla tú acompañar; y aunque es en todo de acero, no te obligaré a dejar la hermosura, que esa quiero.	700
LEONOR	¿Soy cobarde, porque tratas de honrarte con mis despojos?	705
OTAVIO	El matarme no dilatas, porque hay rayos en tus ojos con que desde lejos matas.	

Salen DON FÉLIX y DON LUIS.

LUIS	Galanteemos un poco nuestras hermanas.	
FÉLIX	Lleguemos; *(Aparte)* la suya me tiene loco; ¡qué extremados dos extremos!	710
LUIS	*[Aparte]* Celos tengo, brasas toco.	
LEONOR	Más mujer me has parecido en lo tierno que has mirado a mi hermano.	715
HIPÓLITA	Si eso ha sido, por valiente y por honrado podrá habello merecido,	

697–698 *pero deja la hermosura / para reñir sin ventaja*: as at I. 784–787, beauty is referred to as a dangerous weapon (see note at I. 786).
706–708 *hay rayos en tus ojos / con que desde lejos matas*: see note at I. 786.

OTAVIO	It would be a blessing for you to die	
	at such lovely hands.	
LEONOR	They certainly haven't	690
	held back in their show of admiration.	
MARCELO	All right then, you've provoked me	
	and I'm ready to challenge you.	
HIPÓLITA	Well, fear doesn't stop me;	
	I'll go to the battlefield right now.	695
MARCELO	If you are so brave, come on down;	
	but leave the weapon of your beauty	
	in order to fight without unfair advantage.	
OTAVIO	And since I will wait by his side,	
	you could accompany her down;	700
	and though it is as mighty as steel,	
	I will not oblige you to leave behind	
	your beauty, for that is what I love.	
LEONOR	Am I a coward, since you try to	
	honour yourself with my plunder?	705
OTAVIO	Do not draw out my death, my lady,	
	because there are rays in your eyes	
	that can kill from far away.	

Enter DON FÉLIX and DON LUIS.

LUIS	Let's flirt a little	
	with each other's sisters.	
FÉLIX	Here we go;	710
	(Aside) his sister drives me wild;	
	what an extraordinary pair!	
LUIS	*(Aside)* I feel the hot coals of jealousy.	
LEONOR	You seem more like a woman now	
	in the tender way you looked	715
	at my brother.	
HIPÓLITA	If that is true,	
	it is only because he deserves to be	
	admired for his bravery and honour,	

	y agradecí los favores	
	que le hiciste con mirar	720
	a mi hermano.	
LUIS	Pues señores,	
	¿de qué se trata?	
MARCELO	El tratar	
	donde hay damas es de amores.	
FÉLIX	Pues que la plática es tal,	
	proseguid.	
LUIS	Para que quiera	725
	esta la baza cabal.	
OTAVIO	No nos estuviera mal	
	que sin los dos estuviera.+	
FÉLIX	Luego ¿pudiéraisla hacer	
	con las damas?	
LUIS	Bien, por Dios,	730
	ese juego viene a ser	
	proprio nuestro, que en las dos	
	tenemos más que perder.	
LEONOR	¿Ya lo tenéis acabado	
	con nosotras?	
LUIS	He tenido	735
	de necio el ser confiado.	
HIPÓLITA	Por valiente lo habéis sido.	
LUIS	Vos me habéis acreditado.	
FÉLIX	Y yo de la valentía	
	de mi hermana confié.	740
MARCELO	Cosa posible sería.	
OTAVIO	Cosa es llana, pues, ¿en qué?	
FÉLIX	En muchas cosas podría;	
	porque, supuesto que alguno	
	pueda ser merecedor	745
	desta gloria, ¿quién mejor?	

726 *baza cabal*: a good hand in a game of cards.
+ 728 dos estuviera A B C : dos lo estuviera P: since there are eight syllables without 'lo' and there is no logical antecedent for 'lo' to refer to, I have opted for the manuscripts' reading, which omits 'lo'.
732 *proprio*: archaic spelling of 'propio'.

	and I am thankful to you	
	for doing a favour for my brother	720
	by looking at him too.	
LUIS	Well, gents,	
	what's that whispering all about?	
MARCELO	Where there are women,	
	the conversation is always about love.	
FÉLIX	Well if that's the subject,	
	please continue.	
LUIS	For this game,	725
	you have a stacked deck.	
OTAVIO	We wouldn't be doing so poorly	
	if those two had not arrived.	
FÉLIX	Well, are you going to speak	
	to the ladies?	
LUIS	Indeed so, by God;	730
	this round is going to be	
	ours alone, for between the two of us	
	we have much more to lose.	
LEONOR	So have you finished	
	with us now?	
LUIS	I must be a fool	735
	for I feel so confident.	
HIPÓLITA	You have earned it by being brave.	
LUIS	You do me credit.	
FÉLIX	And I was confident	
	in the courage of my sister.	740
MARCELO	I can believe that.	
OTAVIO	Yes, obviously, but why?	
FÉLIX	She is capable of anything;	
	since, supposing that anyone	
	was capable of deserving	745
	her hand, who better?	

OTAVIO	Alguno.	
LUIS	No más.	
HIPÓLITA	¡Ninguno!	
	Ni en linaje, ni en valor.	
OTAVIO	Eso tiene para ser…	
	decillo vos.	
HIPÓLITA	Defender-	750
	lo sabré.	
MARCELO	Nadie os replica.	
HIPÓLITA	¿Que no me canse una pica	
	y me ofenda un alfiler?	
LEONOR	La trenza del puño es,	
	que está asida de un corchete.	755
HIPÓLITA	Átame manos y pies	
	este traje.	
LEONOR	Librarete	
	deste lazo; espera, pues.	
HIPÓLITA	Congójame el esperar.	
	Más de Alejandro ha tenido	760
	el romper, que el desatar.	
	(Cáesele el puño.)	
LEONOR	Cayó.	
HIPÓLITA	¡Que hubiera caído	
	como en la calle, en la mar!	
LUIS	Dame.	
MARCELO	Primero llegué.	
HIPÓLITA	Ya me pesa.	
LEONOR	Ya recelo.	765
LUIS	Dame ese puño, Marcelo.	

752–762a At this point the cuff of Hipólita's sleeve gets stuck in a pin on her dress, tethering her arm to her side. Leonor explains that a braid detail on her sleeve is caught in a hook or pin on the dress and tries to help untangle the sleeve, but Hipólita, already exasperated with the restrictions of female clothing, rips the cuff off completely, invoking the spirit of Alexander the Great, the famed military leader, who 'untied' the Gordian knot by slashing it apart with his sword (Hamilton 1998, 483–84). The cuff falls down to the street below. *corchete*: hook.

763 *la mar*: archaic gender of 'mar.'

OTAVIO	Someone.
LUIS	No one else.
HIPÓLITA	No one!
	Not in bloodline or in valour.
OTAVIO	You could meet that criterion…
	tell her.
HIPÓLITA	I know how to defend 750
	my honour.
MARCELO	No one will dispute that.
HIPÓLITA	How is it I am not wearied wielding a pike
	yet I'm done in by these pins?
LEONOR	It's the braid of your cuff,
	trapped in the clasp of your sleeve. 755
HIPÓLITA	This outfit binds me by the hands
	and feet.
LEONOR	I will free you
	from this knot; wait, please.
HIPÓLITA	Waiting is killing me. Like Alexander,
	I'll cut through this Gordian knot, 760
	rather than wait to be untied.
	(The cuff falls to the ground.)
LEONOR	It fell.
HIPÓLITA	If only it hadn't fallen
	down to the street, but into the sea!
LUIS	Give it to me.
MARCELO	I got here first.
HIPÓLITA	What a mistake.
LEONOR	I am already suspicious. 765
LUIS	Give me that cuff, Marcelo.

MARCELO	¿Por qué quieres que te dé	
	lo que a mí me ha dado el cielo?	
LUIS	Porque su dueño lo espera.	
MARCELO	Y qué, ¿yo no tengo pies?	770
LUIS	Mas no para la escalera	
	de mi casa, ¿no lo ves?	
MARCELO	Cuando esa razón lo fuera,	
	cumpliera yo con tomar	
	licencia tuya.	
LUIS	No quiero.	775
MARCELO	Pues no te le quiero dar.	
LUIS	Quitarétele.	
MARCELO	Ya espero,	
	si me le sabes quitar.	
HIPÓLITA	Si es mío, ¿qué hacéis los dos?	
MARCELO	Para defendelle empuño	780
	la espada.	

Vase MARCELO empuñando la espada y DON LUIS suéltase de OTAVIO y vase tras MARCELO.[+]

LUIS	Soltadme vos,	
	que a puñadas, vive Dios,	
	tengo de quitalle el puño.	

Vanse.

HIPÓLITA	Hermano, ¡llega!	
LEONOR	¡Ay, cuitada!	
	(Cáesele el guante, y tómale DON FÉLIX.)	
	¡El guante!	
FÉLIX	Dicha he tenido.	785
OTAVIO	A venir yo sin espada,	
	dicha, y grande, hubiera sido.	
	(Quítasele de las manos.)	
FÉLIX	Mira que soy…	

+ *781a* Stage direction taken from B.

MARCELO	Why should I give you heaven's gift to me?	
LUIS	Because its owner is waiting for it.	
MARCELO	And what, do I not have feet?	770
LUIS	Not feet that will come up the stairs of my house, don't you see?	
MARCELO	If that was really the reason, I would comply by forcing your approval.	
LUIS	Denied.	775
MARCELO	Well then I deny you this.	
LUIS	Then I'll take it.	
MARCELO	I'm waiting, let's see if you can get it.	
HIPÓLITA	If it's mine, what are you two doing?	
MARCELO	I will draw my sword in its defence.	780

Exit MARCELO with his sword drawn, and DON LUIS frees himself from OTAVIO and exits after MARCELO.

LUIS	Unhand me, so that with my fists, by God, I will take that cuff!

They exit.

HIPÓLITA	Brother, come on!	
LEONOR	Oh, dear! *(She drops her glove, and FÉLIX picks it up.)* My glove!	
FÉLIX	It's my good fortune.	785
OTAVIO	If I had come here without my sword, it would have been your greatest fortune. *(He snatches it from his hands.)*	
FÉLIX	See here that I am…	

238 *La fuerza de la costumbre: Jornada segunda*

	(Quiere meter mano DON FÉLIX y no puede.)[+]	
OTAVIO	Eres nada,	
	y esta prenda yo la quiero.	
FÉLIX	¡Espera!	
OTAVIO	Harás maravillas.	790
FÉLIX	No puedo…	
HIPÓLITA	¡Oh, vil caballero!	
OTAVIO	Ten envainado el acero	
	y trata de hacer vainillas,	
	o lleva siempre un criado	
	que tire para poder	795
	sacalla; mas he pensado	
	que el valor debe de ser	
	el que tienes envainado.	
FÉLIX	No puedo…	
OTAVIO	En pudiendo acuda,	
	amigo, a herirme con ella;	800
	mas no podrá, pues sin duda	
	tendrá espada tan doncella	
	vergüenza de andar desnuda.	

Sale DON PEDRO a la puerta.

PEDRO	¿Qué le pudo suceder?	
LEONOR	Tente, por mi vida.	
FÉLIX	Harelo.	805
HIPÓLITA	Guante y puño he de traer,	
	pues que por hermano el cielo	
	me dio un hombre ques mujer.	
	(Éntrase.)	
LEONOR	Bien quedamos, por mi vida;	
	pero con todo, no hay duda	810
	que queda menos corrida	
	en mí la mano desnuda	
	que en vos la espada vestida.	
	Si saliera a defender	
	mi guante, los dos hermanos	815

+ **788a** Stage direction taken from B. In B it appears as a second stage direction after the one at 781a.

	(He tries to draw his sword, but cannot do it.)	
OTAVIO	You are nothing,[16]	
	and this is the prize that I want.	
FÉLIX	Wait!	
OTAVIO	I'm sure you'll do something amazing.	790
FÉLIX	I cannot…	
HIPÓLITA	Oh, unworthy gentleman!	
OTAVIO	Keep your sword in its scabbard	
	and go back to your knitting,	
	or bring a servant everywhere with you	
	who can get it out for you;	795
	I've always thought that	
	courage is what you've got	
	stuck there in that sheath.	
FÉLIX	I cannot…	
OTAVIO	If you can, then do it,	
	my friend, wound me with it;	800
	but you will not, for doubtless	
	such a shy, maidenly sword	
	will be ashamed to be seen naked.	

DON PEDRO comes to the door.

PEDRO	What could have happened?	
LEONOR	Wait, please.	
FÉLIX	I will do it.	805
HIPÓLITA	I'll get the glove and cuff back myself,	
	since heaven gave me for a brother	
	a man who is a woman.	
	(She exits.)	
LEONOR	Well, I guess that's it;	
	after all, there is no doubt	810
	that there is less disgrace	
	in my gloveless hand	
	than in your sheathed sword.	
	If it came out to defend	
	my glove, the two siblings	815

---

16 See p. 104, Fig. 9 for a photograph of this scene in production.

>   vuestros merecieran ser,
>   pero quien no tiene manos,
>   ¿qué guantes ha menester?
>   No habrá más entre los dos,
>   prenda ni vuestra, ni mía,   820
>   ni ajena, ¡válame Dios!
>   ¿Qué gran cobarde sería
>   el que anoche huyó de vos?
>   Ya os aborrezco, y no en vano
>   por vileza semejante;   825
>   y advertid que fuera llano,
>   si defendierais el guante,
>   quizá el merecer la mano.
>   Con todo, favorecido
>   habéis de ir a vuestro modo,   830
>   que es falta el no haber tenido
>   plumas para ser del todo
>   lo que veo que habéis sido.
>   *(Dale una pluma que se quita del tocado.)*
>   Estas os podéis poner,
>   aunque a ser yo más curiosa,   835
>   para vos habían de ser
>   de otra ave menos hermosa,
>   pero mejor de comer.
>   *(Vase.)*
> FÉLIX   Darete satisfacción;
>   ¡espera, señora, tente!   840

Vase a entrar, y sale DON PEDRO.

831–833 *falta*: in this context, meaning 'defect', 'shortcoming'. Covarrubias: "Poner falta en alguna cosa, es dar a entender que no está caval" ('Falta', p. 831). Her discussion of his lack of feathers is both literal (thus she takes feathers from her outfit and gives them to him to wear in his hat) and a symbol of his failure to adequately perform manliness.

837 *otra ave menos hermosa / pero mejor de comer*: the 'less beautiful bird' Leonor refers to is the 'gallina', 'hen', which has the connotation of 'chicken', 'wimp'.

would be rightfully yours,
but for someone who has no hands,
what good are gloves?
There will be nothing more between us,
no token of yours, or mine, 820
or anyone's, by God!
What kind of extraordinary coward was
the man who fled from you last night?
Now I detest you, and not for nothing,
but for this disgusting cowardice; 825
and see that it would be right
that if you were to fight for my glove,
maybe you could deserve its hand.
Despite everything, still favoured,
you'll go out in your own silly way, 830
and it is a pity you have not worn
feathers so you can be completely
what I see that you have been.
(She drops a feather from her headpiece.)
You could put these pretty plumes on,
but if I were to be more precise, 835
you would be better off wearing
those of another bird, less pretty
but much better to eat.
(She exits.)
FÉLIX   I will see that you are satisfied.
Wait, my lady, wait! 840

He starts to exit, but is stopped by the entrance of DON PEDRO.

PEDRO	¿Qué ha de esperar, maricón? Errar tan infamemente yerros sin enmienda son; por mi mano he de matarte.	
FÉLIX	Escucha, escapar querría por volver después a honrarte.	845
PEDRO	¡Vive Dios que he de sacarte cuanta sangre tienes mía!+	

Vase DON PEDRO tras él con la daga y sale DOÑA COSTANZA teniendo a HIPÓLITA, [sale GALVÁN] y al balcón doña LEONOR y el AYO.+

COSTANZA	¿Viose tal desenvoltura?	[romance ó]
HIPÓLITA	No es esto sino valor.	850
COSTANZA	Tente, hija.	
HIPÓLITA	¡Suelta, madre!	
COSTANZA	Llegad, tenelda los dos.	
HIPÓLITA	¡Aparta, viejo!	
AYO	Las tuyas fuerzas invencibles son.	
GALVÁN	¡Por un puño que te falta!	855
HIPÓLITA	¿Tú me tienes, picarón? *(Dale una puñada.)*	
GALVÁN	¡Pese al sol! Pluguiera al cielo que te faltaran los dos; no me hicieras las narices…	
HIPÓLITA	¡Que una espada! Infames sois, que no me dais una espada, ¡pues tomarémela yo! *(Saca la espada de un criado.)*	860

+ **844–848** This closing *quintilla* presents an abaab rhyme scheme, which does not follow the pattern, ababa, used from II. 629 to here.
+ **848** This stage direction from A is used here because it contains more information about the scene than the one in P: "Vanse y salen doña Costanza, doña Hipólita, el ayo y Galván." However we have added the entrance of Galván back into this stage direction, since he appears in this scene.
849–872 Costanza has caught and is restraining Hipólita, who ran offstage after lines 806–808 to attack Otavio in defense of her brother's honor, after Félix failed to defend Leonor's glove.
855 *¡Por un puño que te falta!*: *puño* is a play on words, meaning both 'cuff' and 'fist'.

PEDRO	What did you expect, sissy?[17] Your errors are so dreadful they are mistakes that can't be remedied; I'll kill you with my own hand.	
FÉLIX	Listen, I wanted to escape, to come back later to do you honour.	845
PEDRO	By God, I'll spill whatever blood of mine is in your veins!	

SCENE 2.6

Exit DON PEDRO in pursuit of FÉLIX with his dagger and enter COSTANZA trying to hold back HIPÓLITA, enter GALVÁN, and up at the balcony are LEONOR and FÉLIX'S TUTOR.

COSTANZA	Have you ever seen such chaos?	
HIPÓLITA	It's no such thing, but valour.	850
COSTANZA	Leave it, daughter.	
HIPÓLITA	Let go, Mother!	
COSTANZA	Come here, hold her, you two.	
HIPÓLITA	Get away from me, old man!	
TUTOR	Your forces are invincible.	
GALVÁN	Even with one cuff missing!	855
HIPÓLITA	You think you can stop me, lowlife? *(She punches him.)*	
GALVÁN	Heavens above! I wish to God you had lost both your cuffs; so you wouldn't have busted my nose...	
HIPÓLITA	If I only had a sword! You're ruffians, and if you won't give me a sword, I'll take one for myself. *(She takes a sword from a servant.)*	860

17 See the note to line I. 757.

COSTANZA Mira, hija, que me matas.
(Sale DOÑA LEONOR.)
Tenelda, doña Leonor.
LEONOR ¡Tente, señora!
HIPÓLITA   ¡Ay amiga,   865
reviéntame el corazón!
Venganza me pide el alma.

Sale DON FÉLIX huyendo de DON PEDRO, y él con la espada desnuda tras él.

FÉLIX   Señor, ¿qué haces? ¡Señor!
PEDRO   ¡He de quitarte la vida!
COSTANZA   ¡Ay, hijo! ¿Y por qué razón?   870
PEDRO   Y tú, ¿dónde vas, mujer?
HIPÓLITA   A vengar mi hermano voy.
PEDRO   ¿Qué hijos me ha dado el cielo,
tan varios en condición?
Pues al uno pongo freno   875
cuando al otro espuelas doy.
Esa venganza que dices
bien pudiera hacella yo,
pero mano propria pide,
y si alguno de los dos   880
la hiciese, imposibilita
el poder cobrar su honor.
Mas que troquéis de vestidos
pienso que será mejor;
pondrele una rueca a él,   885
para que así el maricón
esté como a la vergüenza.
Mas él no la tiene, no;
pues mancha la mejor sangre

877–882 The rules of honor required that Félix vindicate himself. If another were to intervene on his behalf, the intervention itself would dishonor him. According to Pitt-Rivers, "the possibility of being represented by a champion in the judicial combat was restricted to those who were judged unable to defend their honour personally: women, the aged or infirm, or persons of a social status which prohibited them from responding to a challenge, in particular, churchmen and, of course, royalty" (1977, 7–8).

COSTANZA	Look, daughter, you're killing me.	
	(Enter LEONOR.)	
	Leonor, stop her.	
LEONOR	Stop, my lady!	
HIPÓLITA	Oh, my friend,	865
	my heart bursts!	
	My soul is crying for vengeance.	

Enter FÉLIX, fleeing from PEDRO, who has his sword drawn against his son.

FÉLIX	My lord, what are you doing? Sir!	
PEDRO	I am going to take your life!	
COSTANZA	Oh, my son! For what reason?	870
PEDRO	And you, where are you going, woman?	
HIPÓLITA	I'm going to avenge my brother.	
PEDRO	What children has heaven given me,	
	so different in their condition?	
	On the one I put a bridle	875
	and the other I give spurs.	
	This vengeance you speak of,	
	I'd happily take it for you;	
	but it has to be from his own hand,	
	and if either of us two	880
	were to do it, it would be impossible	
	for him to reclaim his own honour.	
	But changing your clothes back	
	I believe would be better;	
	give to him a distaff,	885
	so that the wimp[18]	
	can look suited to his disgrace.	
	But no, he has no shame;	
	though he stains the world's noblest	

---

18 See the note to line I. 757.

	del mundo. ¡Infelice soy!	890
	Estoy por matalle.	
LEONOR	Espera.	
COSTANZA	¡Hijo mío!	
PEDRO	Y aun a vos,	
	causadora desta afrenta.	
FÉLIX	Muerto de afrentado estoy.	

Sale DON LUIS con el puño bañado en sangre.

LUIS	Este, señora, es el puño	895
	que de tu brazo cayó,	
	y perdona si esta sangre	
	pudo mudalle el color;	
	pues por quitalle a la mano	
	que atrevida le llevó,	900
	la corté, y su sangre roja	
	el blanco lienzo manchó.	
	Y a estar, como en ella estuvo,	
	en las garras de un león,	
	en la boca de un infierno	905
	o en su abismo, vive Dios,	
	que por ponelle en tus manos	
	de allí le sacara yo.	
	Tómale y tenle por tuyo.	
HIPÓLITA	Tómole, y por él te doy	910
	mil gracias, mil alabanzas,	
	y añadiera a tu blasón,	
	si fuera rey, este puño	
	con esta sangre.	
LUIS	Mejor	

	bloodline. What misery!	890
	I'm going to kill him.[19]	
LEONOR	Wait.	
COSTANZA	Oh, my little boy!	
PEDRO	And you as well,	
	you are the cause of this outrage.	
FÉLIX	I am dead already from the shame.	

Enter LUIS with the cuff soaked with blood.

LUIS	This, my lady, is the cuff	895
	that fell from your arm,	
	and pardon me if this blood	
	has changed its colour;	
	for to recover it from the hand	
	that dared to take it,	900
	I cut his hand, and his red blood	
	stained the white fabric.	
	Even if it had been (and it was)	
	in the claws of a lion,	
	in the mouth of Hell	905
	or in the abyss, by God,	
	to return it safely to your hands	
	even from there I would have rescued it.	
	Take it, and have it for your own.	
HIPÓLITA	I receive it, and in return I give you	910
	a thousand thanks, a thousand praises,	
	and if I were the King, I would add	
	this cuff to your coat of arms,	
	with this blood.	
LUIS	Who better	

---

19 This speech is fascinating because of the two sentences that start with 'Mas', where Pedro seems to give up on his own project and suggest that the siblings just go back to the way that they were raised. It is, I think, the only place he doubts his ability to reform them. It is also worth noting that he does not speak to Félix in the 'tú' form, but can't even bring himself to speak directly to him, and refers to him in the third person. This builds the plot by having this speech be directed at Hipólita, reminding her of the importance of letting Félix fight his own battle.

	podrá mandar en mis cosas	915
	quien reina en mi corazón.	
PEDRO	¡Oh, cuánto agrada un buen trato!	
	¡Oh, cuánto luce un valor!	
	¿Por qué este ejemplo no tomas?	
	Esta honrada emulación,	920
	¿cómo no te mueve el alma	
	y te revienta en la voz?	
	Pues, vive Dios, hijo indigno	
	deste nombre que te doy,	
	que has de cortalle la mano	925
	con que el guante te quitó,	
	o has de dejar en las mías	
	pedazos del corazón.	
FÉLIX	Padre, no me afrentes más,	
	porque ya de suerte estoy	930
	que habré de empezar en ti	
	a cobrar nueva opinión.	
	Ya el agravio recebido,	
	esta invidia, este dolor,	
	de tantas afrentas juntas,	935
	me ha convertido en león;	
	ya de la vergüenza mía	
	el encendido color	
	retirado en mis entrañas,	
	esta mina reventó.	940
	Seré otro Martín Peláez,	
	que cobarde se corrió	
	de que le quitó el escaño	
	el famoso Campeador,	
	y fue un asombro después.	945
	Por el divino Hacedor,	
	que he de ser rigor del cielo,	
	y en su esfera a todo el sol	

941 *Martín Peláez*: famed coward turned ferocious hero of the ballads of the Cid (see Agustín Durán's *Romancero de romances caballerescos é históricos anteriores al siglo XVIII, Parte II,* "Romances" 26–30).

	to rule my affairs	915
	than she who reigns in my heart.	
PEDRO	Oh, proper accord is so pleasing!	
	Oh, how valour shines!	
	Why do you not follow this example?	
	This honourable emulation,	920
	why does it not move your soul	
	and burst forth in your voice?	
	By God, you are unworthy	
	for me to call you my son,	
	for you must cut the hand	925
	that took the glove from you,	
	or you will have to leave in my hands	
	the shreds of your heart.	
FÉLIX	Father, do not insult me further,	
	because I am now in such a state	930
	that I am going to inspire in you	
	a better opinion of me.	
	The grievance I have suffered,	
	the envy, the pain	
	of so many offences together	935
	have changed me into a lion;	
	now from my shame	
	the smouldering ember lying dormant	
	within me bursts flames to the surface	
	like an exploding mine shaft.	940
	I will be another Martín Peláez,	
	the coward who was ashamed	
	of being knocked off his seat by	
	the famous champion, El Cid,	
	and he was a terror after that.	945
	By the divine maker,	
	I must be Heaven's scourge,	
	and from the sky up to the sun,	

	pondré nubes coloradas,	
	siendo de sangre el vapor.	950
	Mil víboras me han picado;	
	todo de veneno soy.	
	Adiós, padre.	
AYO	Señor, tente.	
PEDRO	Ten reportado el valor;	
	espera consejos míos.	955
COSTANZA	Tenelde, señora, vos.	
LEONOR	Ya no le tengo en el alma	
	hasta volver vencedor.	
GALVÁN	No hayan miedo que le tenga.	
LUIS	Valdrele, pues tuyo soy.	960
FÉLIX	Nadie me siga, dejadme.	
HIPÓLITA	Eso sí, cuerpo de Dios,	
	comenzad a tener brios,	
	pues los voy perdiendo yo.	

| | I will paint the clouds |
| | by turning his blood to mist. | 950
	A thousand vipers have bitten me;
	I am all poison.
	Goodbye, father.
TUTOR	Sir, wait.
PEDRO	Restrain your valour for just a moment;
	wait for my advice.	955
COSTANZA	You stop him, my lady.
LEONOR	I will not hold him in my soul
	until he returns victorious.
GALVÁN	Now they're afraid of him, not for him.
LUIS	I'll go with him, for I am yours.	960
FÉLIX	No one follow me, leave me.
HIPÓLITA	That's it, by God,
	start to show some manly spirit,
	just as mine is starting to fade.

JORNADA TERCERA

Salen DON PEDRO y DON FÉLIX.

PEDRO	El dilatar la venganza [redondillas]	
	para tomarla mejor	
	no disminuye el valor;	
	antes logra la esperanza.	
	Tu contrario ha estado ausente,	5
	y hasta hoy no ha paseado.	
FÉLIX	Tendrame por descuidado.	
PEDRO	No te estima por valiente.	
FÉLIX	Pues, ¿qué debo hacer? ¡Que rabio	
	por cobrar nueva opinión!	10
PEDRO	El que tiene más pasión	
	da el consejo menos sabio,	
	y así no quiero fiallo	
	de mí.	
FÉLIX	Pues, ¿de quién te vales?	
PEDRO	Para en ocasiones tales,	15
	de pocos es bien tomallo;	
	que el juntar gran cantidad	
	de parientes, cosa es llana,	
	que es tocar una campana	
	que alborota una ciudad,	20
	y entre tantos imagina	
	que habrá siempre (y es forzoso)	
	algún viejo escrupuloso	
	o algún mancebo gallina.	
	Éste revela el secreto,	25
	y por la justicia alcanza	

1–190 This scene reveals a great deal about the rules of engagement for honor disputes, as Pedro, Luis and the Captain discuss the best way for Félix to regain his honor after his humiliating conflict with Otavio at the end of Act II.

+ 27 quede A B C : que de P.

25–30 Pedro is careful about who he asks to help them plan Félix's retribution because he does not want anyone to reveal their intentions to the law, who would then try to prevent Félix from attacking Otavio. Pedro wants to avoid such an intervention because he does not want the opportunity for Félix to vindicate the family's honor to be lost.

ACT THREE

SCENE 3.1

Enter PEDRO and FÉLIX.

PEDRO	Taking one's time for revenge	
	in order to do it properly	
	does not show any less valour;	
	but rather ensures success.	
	Your opponent has not been seen;	5
	he has not come around here.	
FÉLIX	He isn't bothered about me.	
PEDRO	He does not consider you a threat.	
FÉLIX	Well, what should I do? I'm chomping	
	at the bit to build my new reputation!	10
PEDRO	He who is emotionally invested	
	in a situation gives the poorest advice,	
	and so, I will not entrust that task	
	to myself.	
FÉLIX	Who then would you trust?	
PEDRO	On occasions such as this	15
	it is better to keep it close;	
	for involving a gaggle	
	of relatives, it's plain to see,	
	is like ringing a bell	
	that wakes up the entire city,	20
	and among them, you can imagine	
	there will always be (you can count on it)	
	some scrupulous old man	
	or some timid youngster.	
	That one gives the game away,	25
	allowing the lawmen to prevent the duel	

	que se quede⁺ una venganza	
	como causa sin efeto,	
	y quiero yo que le tenga	
	esta que toca en mi honor.	30
FÉLIX	¿Y a quién llamaste, señor,	
	para que a valernos venga?	
PEDRO	A don Luis he llamado,	
	que se halló entonces contigo	
	y le toca el ser tu amigo,	35
	y a un capitán, gran soldado,	
	que fue de mi tercio en Flandes;	
	con su consejo podrás	
	hacer lo que importe más.	
FÉLIX	Haré yo lo que tú mandes.	40
PEDRO	Tú solamente guiado	
	de tu honor, piensa atrevido	
	solo en que te han ofendido	
	si quieres quedar vengado.	
	Pues si das en discurrir,	45
	en temeroso has de dar,	
	y nunca acierta a matar	
	quien teme que ha de morir.	
	Siempre a tu contrario trata	
	como cortés y valiente;	50
	que el que habla cortésmente	
	atrevidamente mata.	
	Y si riñes, mejor es	
	asille, estando afirmada,	
	al enemigo la espada	55
	para matalle después;	
	que aunque teniéndole asida,	
	cortarse una mano es llano;	
	bien perdida va una mano	
	cuando asegura una vida.	60
	Y al que es poco diestro o nada,	
	de treta usar le conviene	

---

37 *tercio*: 'regiment', 'military unit'.

	so that the vendetta remains	
	like a cause without effect,	
	and I'd rather that a matter of revenge	
	that touches my honor be resolved.	30
FÉLIX	And who did you call, sir,	
	to come and help us?	
PEDRO	I have called Don Luis,	
	for he was with you when this all started,	
	and he is inclined to be your friend,	35
	and also a Captain, a great soldier,	
	who was in my regiment in Flanders;	
	with their advice you will be able	
	to do what is best for you.	
FÉLIX	I will do as you command.	40
PEDRO	Guided by your honour alone,	
	you must bravely think only	
	on the fact that you have been shamed	
	if you want to be avenged.	
	Because if you start to overthink it,	45
	you will find yourself giving way to fear,	
	and it is impossible to kill	
	if you are afraid to die.	
	Always treat your opponent	
	with courtesy and bravery;	50
	for he who speaks courteously	
	kills daringly.	
	And if you agree to fight	
	with him, it is better to take	
	your enemy's sword from him,	55
	and kill him later only if you have to;	
	for even if you have him defenseless,	
	you can just cut his hand;	
	because it is better to lose a hand	
	and safeguard a life.	60
	And for he who has little or no skill,	
	it is better to use a trick	

	(que para ser buena, tiene	
	haber sido poco usada);	
	que en el no diestro, el querer	65
	regatear es locura,	
	pues si la pendencia dura	
	le han de matar o vencer.	
	Y así, en tal peligro puesto,	
	nunca ha de ir regateando,	70
	sino aventurar cerrando,	
	en un lance todo el resto.	
	Pero los que hemos llamado	
	vienen ya, sosiégate.	
FÉLIX	En la memoria tendré	75
	las liciones que me has dado.	

Salen DON LUIS y el CAPITÁN.

CAPITÁN	Ya vengo a servirte; ordena.	
PEDRO	Sillas, hola. A darme honor	
	venís.	
LUIS	Yo vengo, señor,	
	porque es más propria que ajena	80
	la causa, porque a mi lado	
	tu hijo entonces tenía,	
	y por ser de hermana mía	
	el guante que le han quitado,	
	y el que yo fuera a cobrar	85
	cuando por ti no esperara	
	que don Félix se vengara.	
PEDRO	El cómo se ha de vengar	
	agora saber querría.	
LUIS	Matar su contrario haga	90

---

66   *regatear*: 'dodge', 'swerve'; the unskilled dueler will not be able to dodge the blows of the opponent.
71–72   The recommendation is to take a risk and end a duel quickly, in one shot, rather than prolong a fight with a more skilled opponent. *en un lance*: 'quickly', 'in one shot', 'all at once'; *Aut. 1734*: "ocasion, tiempo y coyuntúra para hacer, ù decir alguna cosa" ('lance', 5).
85–87   See note II. 877–882 about the rules of vindicating one's honor oneself.

	(which in order to work,	
	has to be one which is not well-known);	
	for if he has no skill, the desire	65
	to duck and dive his way out is madness	
	because if the fight is drawn out,	
	they will either kill or defeat him.	
	And so, placed in such danger,	
	he should not try to go dodging about,	70
	but just attack with one quick move,	
	and stake his chances on one fatal blow.	
	But the men we have called	
	are coming now, take heart.	
FÉLIX	In my memory I will keep	75
	the lessons you've taught me.	

Enter DON LUIS and the CAPTAIN.

CAPTAIN	I come to serve you; I await your orders.	
PEDRO	You there, bring chairs. You both honour	
	me by coming here.	
LUIS	I come, sir,	
	because it is more close than distant	80
	this matter, because your son was	
	by my side when it happened,	
	and because it was my own sister	
	whose glove they took from him,	
	and I would have gone to reclaim it	85
	if for your sake I did not have to wait	
	for Don Félix to take his revenge first.	
PEDRO	He now wants to learn	
	the art of vengeance.	
LUIS	Kill your opponent	90

	de noche con una daga,	
	o con un palo de día.	
FÉLIX	¿Y podré cobrar así	
	yo la opinión que he perdido?	
LUIS	¿No puede el que está ofendido	95
	vengarse a su salvo?	
CAPITÁN	Sí,	
	pero a él no le ofendieron;	
	que el guante que no cobró	
	mengua fue que él se causó,	
	mas no afrenta que le hicieron.	100
	Y es cierto que está obligado	
	a otra venganza el que ha sido	
	más por su culpa corrido	
	que por la ajena afrentado;	
	y así debe, en conclusión,	105
	no con término villano	
	cobrar con su propria mano	
	con el guante, la opinión.	
LUIS	Esa razón es bastante.	
PEDRO	Y es la que en el blanco da.	110
FÉLIX	Pues, ¿cómo y dónde será	
	la cobranza deste guante?	
CAPITÁN	El cobralle en el lugar	
	que le perdistes sería	
	una gentil bizarría,	115
	y más si acertase a estar	

94 *opinión*: here, equivalent to 'honor'.
97–104 The Capitán explains that Félix cannot just murder Otavio for revenge because it is Félix's fault that he lost the glove, so to regain his honor Félix must challenge Otavio and recover the glove in a fair fight.
106 *término*: 'comportment'; *Aut. 1739*: "forma, ò modo de portarse, ù hablar en el trato comun" ('termino' 3); *villano*: ill-mannered *Aut. 1739* "ruin, indigno, ù indecoroso" ('Villano' 3).
110 *en el blanco da*: 'dar en el blanco' meaning 'acertar', 'to get it right'.
113–118 The retribution for the loss of the glove should reflect the original conflict, so it would be ideal for Félix to challenge Otavio in the place where he took the glove from Félix, and even better if Leonor is present to witness Félix's recovery of her lost glove.
115 *gentil bizarría*: 'elegant gallantry' *Aut. 1726*: "Generosidád de ánimo, gallardía, denuedo, lozanía y valor" ('bizarria' 1).

	by night with a dagger,
	or with a spear by day.
FÉLIX	And by doing that can I restore
	my lost reputation?
LUIS	Isn't the one who has been offended
	entitled to take his own revenge?
CAPTAIN	Yes,
	but they did not in fact offend him;
	it was Félix's own fault
	that the glove was not recovered,
	they did not affront him by taking it.
	And it is certain that he is obligated
	to enact his own vengeance all the more
	if he has been defeated by his own fault
	than if he was affronted by another;
	and so, he should, in conclusion,
	not in the manner of a peasant
	recover it with his own hand,
	and with the glove, his reputation.
LUIS	That about sums it up.
PEDRO	He's right on target.
FÉLIX	So, how and where will the
	retrieval of the glove occur?
CAPTAIN	Getting the glove back in the place
	where you lost it will show
	a touch of class for all to see,
	and even more so if she

Line numbers: 95, 100, 105, 110, 115

	allí, por testigo fiel,	
	la señora cuyo ha sido.	
FÉLIX	¿Y si le ha dado o perdido?	
CAPITÁN	Cobraréis el precio dél	120
	con las manos valerosas,	
	que una vida es su valor.	
PEDRO	Mira, hijo: ¡el pundonor,	
	cuánto encarece las cosas!	
	Mas por lo mismo que es cuánto	125
	por él se puede pagar,	
	no es razón aventurar	
	cobranza que importa tanto.	
	Considerémoslo bien;	
	veréis que no es bien cobralle	130
	en la calle, que en la calle	
	por milagro falta quien	
	meta paz, sigue o alcanza;	
	con piedad o con malicia	
	la justicia es la justicia,	135
	émulo de la venganza.	
	Y siendo así, ¿quién ignora	
	que entonces, a bien librar,	
	don Félix vendrá a quedar	
	de la suerte que está agora?	140
	Y aun peor, que habrá quedado	
	con agravio más sabido,	

123   *pundonor*: 'honor', 'pride'; Pedro laments the high price one pays for honor.
130–136   As at III. 25–30, Pedro wants to avoid Félix being impeded by the law, or any other interruption. These comments show the conflict between the legal system and the honor code. No man of honor would place the resolution of an honor conflict in the hands of the courts (Pitt-Rivers 1977, 9). *émulo de la venganza*: 'the rival of [true] vengeance.'
141–144   If the law intervenes and commands Félix to make peace with Otavio, preventing him from attacking Otavio to restore his honor, Félix will be in an even worse position because the offence will have been made even more public. The shame of a dishonor is multiplied by the degree to which it is publicized or widely known. Furthermore, the involvement of the law increases the shame the offended person: "to go to the law for redress is to confess publicly that you have been wronged and the demonstration of your vulnerability places your honour in jeopardy, a jeopardy from which the 'satisfaction' of legal compensation at the hands of a secular authority hardly redeems it" (Pitt-Rivers 1977, 9).

	is there, as a faithful witness,	
	the lady whose glove it was.	
FÉLIX	And if it has been given away or lost?	
CAPTAIN	You will collect its ransom	120
	with your own brave hands;	
	valour is worth as much as life itself.	
PEDRO	Look, son: the price of honour	
	is the highest of all things!	
	But because of the very high price	125
	that can be paid for honour	
	it is not right to take risks	
	with a retrieval that matters so much.	
	Let us consider it well;	
	you see it is not good to recover it	130
	in the street, for it would be a	
	miracle if there was not someone there to	
	keep the peace, follow you, catch you;	
	despite their good or malicious intentions	
	the police are the police,	135
	the rival of revenge.	
	That being the case, who can ignore	
	that in this situation, at best,	
	Don Félix will land himself right back	
	in the same state he is in right now?	140
	And even worse, because he will bear	
	an offence even more well-known,	

	públicamente ofendido,	
	lejos de verse vengado.	
	Y así es mejor que el pedir	145
	el guante sea en lugar	
	donde le pueda cobrar,	
	vencer, matar, o morir.	
LUIS	Pues emplace un desafío,	
	y podrá con un billete	150
	obligalle a que lo acete.	
PEDRO	Poco de papeles fío.	
CAPITÁN	Llevarele yo un recado,	
	y haciendo lo que es razón,	
	pondrele en obligación	155
	de que salga acompañado.	
	Saldré con don Félix yo,	
	que importará mi presencia	
	para su poca experiencia.	
PEDRO	No Capitán, eso no;	160
	que habiendo de ser, yo fuera	
	el que a eso se obligara.	
LUIS	Y si a ti no te tocara,	
	yo también lo pretendiera.	
FÉLIX	Hacéisme todos favor,	165
	pero no es consejo sabio	
	que para vengar mi agravio	
	pida prestado el valor.	
PEDRO	Dice bien.	
CAPITÁN	Haga una cosa	
	con que queden escusados	170
	los billetes y recados,	
	buscando ocasión forzosa	
	de que tenga cierto efeto	
	su buena o su mala suerte.	
FÉLIX	Ya la espero.	

165–168 Despite the offers of Pedro, the Capitán, and Luis to provide back up for Félix, he wants to go alone because he can only restore his honor by defeating his enemy without assistance.

	so he will be publicly offended,	
	and far from seeing himself avenged.	
	It will be better for him to demand	145
	the glove in a place	
	where he can recover it by	
	winning, killing, or dying.	
LUIS	Then he should fix a place for the duel,	
	and could, with a note,	150
	compel him to agree to it.	
PEDRO	I place little faith in bits of paper.	
CAPTAIN	I will bring him the message,	
	and following protocol,	
	I will place him under obligation	155
	to arrive accompanied by a second.	
	I will go out with Don Félix,	
	my presence will be important	
	because he has so little experience.	
PEDRO	No, Captain, that's not right;	160
	if it comes down to it, I would be	
	the one who is obliged to do that.	
LUIS	And if it didn't fall to you,	
	I would also offer myself.	
FÉLIX	You all do me favours;	165
	but it would not be a wise idea for me	
	to take my revenge by	
	relying on borrowed valour.	
PEDRO	Well said.	
CAPTAIN	There is one thing	
	you can do that will excuse you	170
	from all the notes and messages,	
	that will be an irresistible opportunity	
	for him to end this once and for all	
	whether it be for better or for worse.	
FÉLIX	Tell me what it is.	

La fuerza de la costumbre: Jornada tercera

CAPITÁN	Pues advierte:	175
	como valiente y discreto,	
	con tal disimulación,	
	en hallando a tu enemigo	
	le saca al campo contigo,	
	que no impidan tu intención;	180
	y en un lugar apartado	
	donde ninguno lo impida,	
	quítale el guante o la vida.	
PEDRO	Así volverás honrado,	
	y pues eres bien nacido;	185
	hijo, con el pecho abierto,	
	sepa de ti que te han muerto,	
	pero no que te han vencido.	
	Y con un abrazo estrecho	
	esta bendición te toca.	190
FÉLIX	El aliento de tu boca	
	ánimo infunde en mi pecho.	
CAPITÁN	¿Hay tal padre?	
LUIS	Tierno escucho	
	en los dos razones tales.	
PEDRO	Ay, santo honor, mucho vales,	195
	pero también cuestas mucho.	
	Adiós, hijo.	
FÉLIX	Padre, adiós.	

Vanse DON PEDRO y el CAPITÁN, diciendo:

PEDRO	Tú que no eres conocido,	
	Capitán…	
CAPITÁN	Ya está entendido.	
PEDRO	Perdonadme, señor, vos…[+]	200

186–188   Félix can restore his honor either by defeating Otavio, or by being killed by his rival while fighting to defend his honor.

198–199   Pedro goes against the wish Félix expressed at III. 165–168 and asks the Capitán to follow his son.

+ 200   After this line, the stage direction 'Vase' appears in P. I have omitted it since Pedro and the Captain are walking offstage talking to one another, leaving Luis alone until Hipólita appears at III. 205.

CAPTAIN	Take note:	175
	with boldness and discretion,	
	and with a bit of acting,	
	once you find your enemy	
	draw him to the duelling ground with you,	
	don't let the law intrude;	180
	and in an isolated place	
	where no one can stop you,	
	you take the glove or his life.	
PEDRO	That way you will return with honour,	
	rightly since you are well-born;	185
	my son, with your chest wide open,	
	let it be known that even if they've killed	
	you, they did not defeat you.	
	And with my outstretched arms	
	I give you my blessing.	190
FÉLIX	The breath from your mouth	
	infuses strength in my heart.	
CAPTAIN	Has there ever been such a father?	
LUIS	I hear such tenderness	
	in their words to each other.	
PEDRO	Oh sainted honour, you're worth	195
	everything, yet you cost so dearly.	
	Goodbye, son.	
FÉLIX	Father, goodbye.	

Exit DON PEDRO and the CAPTAIN, saying:

PEDRO	Since you are not known around here,	
	Captain…	
CAPTAIN	I already understand.	
PEDRO	Excuse me, sir, you…	200

LUIS	El cuidado le divierte
	tanto que me deja aquí.
PEDRO	Pero advierte, escucha.
CAPITÁN	Di.

Vanse y queda solo DON LUIS.[+]

LUIS	Buena ocasión, buena suerte.	

Sale DOÑA HIPÓLITA.

HIPÓLITA	¿Dónde voy? ¿Dónde me llevan?	205
LUIS	¿Quién tuvo dichas mayores?	
HIPÓLITA	¿Qué cuidados, qué temores	
	en mis entrañas se ceban?	
	¿Dónde está el valor pasado?	
	Corazón, ¿qué le habéis hecho?	210
	¿Yo, ternuras en mi pecho?	
	¿Yo temores, yo cuidado?	
	¿Viose mudanza mayor?	
LUIS	¿Viose más dichosa suerte?	
HIPÓLITA	Pues ha herido en lo más fuerte,	215
	sin duda es rayo el amor.	
	¡Ay cielo, el alma me abrasa!	
	Pues, ¿vos en este lugar?	
	Voces, voces quiero dar,	
	ladrones hay en mi casa.	220
LUIS	No es ladrón el que ha venido	
	tiernamente interesado	
	a buscar quien le ha robado	
	y cobrar lo que ha perdido;	
	según esto, a mí me hacéis	225
	el ladrón, y soislo vos.	
HIPÓLITA	¿Yo os robé? ¡Válame Dios!	
	¿Tanto perdido tenéis?	
LUIS	Tenéisme el alma y la vida,	
	no perdida, mas ganada,	230
	porque tan bien empleada,	
	no es bien llamarla perdida.	

+ *203b*   Stage direction taken from B.

LUIS	He is so preoccupied,
	he just left me standing here.
PEDRO	But see here, listen.
CAPTAIN	Speak.

Exit, leaving behind DON LUIS.

LUIS	Here's a good opportunity, what good luck.

SCENE 3.1b

Enter HIPÓLITA.

HIPÓLITA	Where am I going? Where are they taking me?	205
LUIS	Who was ever luckier than this?	
HIPÓLITA	What disturbance, what fears	
	are turning over in my stomach?	
	Where is my old valour?	
	Heart, what have you done to it?	210
	Me, tenderness in my heart?	
	Me, fears, me, concerns?	
	Has there ever been such great change?	
LUIS	Has there ever been such great fortune?	
HIPÓLITA	This has been the fiercest wound,	215
	without a doubt love is a thunderbolt.	
	Oh, heaven! My soul scorches me!	
	But what are you doing here?	
	Shout, I want to shout,	
	there are thieves in my house.	220
LUIS	It is not a thief who has come	
	so tenderly concerned	
	to search for the one who stole from him	
	in order to claim back his loss;	
	though you have called me	225
	a thief, in fact, the thief is you.	
HIPÓLITA	I have robbed you? God save me!	
	Have you really lost so much?	
LUIS	You have stolen my soul and my life,	
	yet they are not lost, but gained,	230
	as they are in such lovely custody,	
	it cannot be right to call them lost.	

HIPÓLITA	La lisonja os agradezco.	
LUIS	Mucho gusto de saber	
	que sepáis agradecer.	235
HIPÓLITA	Luego ¿tan necia os parezco	
	que admitir la voluntad	
	y después no agradecella	
	nace de no conocella?	
	¡Que viene a ser necedad!	240
LUIS	El alma quiero adorar	
	desas divinas razones.	
HIPÓLITA	Quien ignora obligaciones	
	es difícil de obligar;	
	con lo que digo te arguyo	245
	que te quiero honestamente.	
LUIS	Tuyo seré eternamente,	
	y dichosamente tuyo.	
HIPÓLITA	En la guerra me he criado,	
	y basta para saber	250
	que tengo, aunque soy mujer,	
	resolución de soldado.	
	Bien te quiero, soy leal,	
	pero advierte…	
LUIS	¿Tal te escucho?	
HIPÓLITA	…que vendría a sentir mucho	255
	que tú me pagases mal.	
LUIS	Primero el cielo veremos	
	sin luz, y sin agua el mar,	
	que yo deje de adorar	
	tus adorados extremos.	260
HIPÓLITA	¿Quién ha entrado? Vete, quedo,	
	tente.	

Salen INÉS y GALVÁN.

GALVÁN	¿No me escuchas?
INÉS	No.

256 *tú me pagases mal*: 'you treat me badly'.
262a From the entrance of Inés and Galván here and line 276, Inés and Galván are on stage but still out of earshot of Luis and Hipólita.

HIPÓLITA	I thank you for the compliment.	
LUIS	I am very pleased to see	
	that you know how to say thank you.	235
HIPÓLITA	So, do I seem so foolish to you	
	as to accept your affection	
	and afterward not be thankful	
	as if I did not notice it?	
	That would be mere foolishness.	240
LUIS	I want to worship her soul,	
	the source of this divine logic.	
HIPÓLITA	He who is ignorant of obligations	
	is difficult to oblige;	
	which is to say I'm telling you	245
	that I love you, chastely.	
LUIS	I will be yours, eternally,	
	and I am blessed to be yours.	
HIPÓLITA	I was raised in war,	
	and suffice it to say	250
	that I have, even though I am a woman,	
	the iron will of a soldier.	
	I love you, I am loyal,	
	but you should know…	
LUIS	Am I hearing this?	
HIPÓLITA	…that I would take it very badly	255
	if you do not return my love.	
LUIS	First we would see the sky	
	without light, the sea without water,	
	before I would fail to adore	
	your adorable extremes.	260
HIPÓLITA	Who has come in? Go, I'll stay,	
	get back.	

Enter INÉS and GALVÁN.

GALVÁN	You won't hear me out?
INÉS	No.

HIPÓLITA	¿Cómo es posible que yo,
	(A solo DON LUIS se lo dice.)
	¡ay don Luis!, tenga miedo?
	Mucho por mi hermano os debo. 265
LUIS	A más estoy obligado.
GALVÁN	*(Aparte)* De razones han mudado;
	pues a mí, que los entrevo.
LUIS	Señora, adiós; disponed
	de mi persona y mi espada. 270
	[Vase.]
GALVÁN	*(Aparte)* Llega, y darás tu embajada.
	Cayó el pájaro en la red;
	si vengase mis narices
	por este camino yo,
	que me las desternilló 275
	de una puñada.
HIPÓLITA+	¿Qué dices,
	Inés?
INÉS	*(A ella sola se lo dice.)*
	Señora me envía
	a visitarte y a darte
	este recado;
	(Dale un papel.)
	de parte
	de su hermano le traía, 280
	pero ya tú le has hablado.
HIPÓLITA	Hame obligado infinito.
GALVÁN	*(Aparte)* ¿Hijuelas tiene el palmito?
	Bien, por Dios.

268 *entrevo*: this is an alternative conjugation of the verb 'entrever', meaning 'to catch sight of', or 'to have an eye on'. Galván is on stage but hidden from Hipólita and Luis, whom he is watching without them knowing.

+ 276b–333a This conversation between Hipólita and Inés was likely added to the play during revisions for publication, given that it does not appear in any of the manuscript witnesses.

283 *Hijuelas tiene el palmito*: 'my plan is coming to fruition'.

HIPÓLITA	How is it possible that I,
	(Speaking only to DON LUIS.)
	(oh, Don Luis!), am afraid?
	I owe you for helping my brother. 265
LUIS	That and more I am obliged to do.
GALVÁN	*(Aside)* They've changed the subject;
	as for me, I have my eye on them.
LUIS	My lady, goodbye; at your disposal
	are my body and my sword. 270
	(He exits.)

SCENE 3.1c

GALVÁN	*(Aside to INÉS.)*
	Come, and deliver your message.
	The bird has fallen into the net;
	my nose will have its revenge
	if I pursue this path,
	since she shattered it 275
	with just one blow.
HIPÓLITA	What are you muttering,
	Inés?
INÉS	*(She speaks only to her.)*
	My lady sent me
	to visit you and to give you
	this message;
	(Giving her a note.)
	she sent it
	on behalf of her brother, 280
	but you have already spoken to him.
HIPÓLITA	He has obliged me infinitely.
GALVÁN	*(Aside)* Can this plot hold up?
	Good, by God.

HIPÓLITA	¿Y cómo ha estado⁺	
	desde ayer doña Leonor?	285
INÉS	Siempre con algún temor	
	nacido de aquel cuidado;	
	y hoy ha salido temprano	
	de casa, que la obligaron	
	estas paces que firmaron	290
	entre Marcelo y su hermano,	
	que tú mejor las sabrás,	
	y mi señora es tan llana	
	que, con su madre y hermana,	
	quiso asegurarlas más.⁺	295
HIPÓLITA	¿Qué hermana tiene Marcelo?	
INÉS	Tan bella que su arrebol	
	causar puede envidia al sol	
	puesto en la mitad del cielo,	
	y don Luis solía ser	300
	muy grande su apasionado,	
	pero de ti enamorado	
	mudó con el alma el ser.	
HIPÓLITA	*(Aparte)* ¿Válame Dios, ¿qué he sentido?	
GALVÁN	*(Aparte)* ¿Ya mudamos de color?	305
	celuchos son.	
HIPÓLITA	*[Aparte]* ¿Qué temor	
	tan cobarde me ha ofendido?	
	[Alto] ¿Que es tan hermosa?	
INÉS	Pues, no.	
HIPÓLITA	*(Aparte)* Arder mis entrañas siento.	

+ One *redondilla* is short here. The word "estado" in line 284b rhymes with both line 281 and 287. It does not appear that there is a line missing, since the lines are coherent as written. It seems that Castro mistakenly counted v. 284b as both the end of the preceding stanza and the beginning of the next one.
293 *llana*: 'pleasant', 'good-natured'; *Aut. 1734*: "afable, apacible..." ('llano', 2nd def.).
294–295 Inés plants the beginning of the lie Galván has cooked up to punish Hipólita for hitting him in the nose (II. 856–859), telling Hipólita that Marcelo has a sister who Luis used to court and had expressed intention to marry.
305a *celuchos*: alternative form of 'celos'.

HIPÓLITA	And how has she been since yesterday, the lady Leonor?	285
INÉS	She is always with some concern awoken by her feelings; and today she has left early from the house, for she is obliged to uphold the peace agreement signed between Marcelo and her brother, but surely you know all about it, and my lady is so clever at these things that, through his mother and sister, she bolstered the peace even more.	290 295
HIPÓLITA	Marcelo has a sister?	
INÉS	So beautiful that her glow could inspire envy even in the mid-day sun in the sky, and Don Luis used to be in a grand passion for her, but by falling in love with you, he changed his soul and his very being.	300
HIPÓLITA	*(Aside)* By God! What am I feeling?	
GALVÁN	*(Aside)* See how she changes colour? Such jealousy.	305
HIPÓLITA	*(Aside)* What fear challenges me now so timidly? *(Aloud)* Is she really so beautiful?	
INÉS	Of course.	
HIPÓLITA	*(Aside)* I feel my insides burning.	

INÉS	Tratábase el casamiento	310
	pero no se concluyó,	
	que por ti lo habrá dejado.	
HIPÓLITA	¿Tanto con él he podido?	
INÉS	Por tu amor está perdido.	
	(Aparte) Parece que se ha turbado.	315
	[Alto] Pues, mi señora, qué dices?	
HIPÓLITA	Después llevarás respuesta.	
GALVÁN	*(Aparte)* ¡Qué brava ocasión es ésta	
	para vengar mis narices!	
HIPÓLITA	Ve, Inés, y a tu ama di…	320
	mas no sé lo que me digo.	
	Después hablaré contigo.	
INÉS	Tus manos beso.	
	(Vase INÉS.)⁺	
HIPÓLITA	¡Ay de mí!	
	Pero ¿por qué me congoja	
	esta pena, este cuidado?	325
	Lo que es cierto que ha pasado,	
	si no ofende, ¿por qué enoja?	
	Mas bien se puede temer,	
	supuesto que no ha ofendido,	
	que entre amantes lo que ha sido	330
	muchas veces vuelve a ser.	
	Pero ¿a mí me ha de engañar	
	un caballero?	
GALVÁN	Señora,	
	deja tristezas agora	
	y apercíbete a bailar.	335
HIPÓLITA	¿Bailar? ¿Y a qué bodas?	
GALVÁN	Bueno,	
	¿no sabes que se ha casado	
	don Luis?	
HIPÓLITA	*(Aparte)* ¡Ay, que me has dado	
	por los oídos veneno!	

+ **323a** This stage direction has been moved to here from the previous line, where it appeared in P (after line 322), since Inés is the speaker of line 323.
335 *apercíbete*: 'get ready'; *Aut. 1726*: "Prevenir, disponer, aparejar" ('apercebir', 1st).

INÉS	The marriage was all arranged,	310
	but it never came to fruition,	
	he must have left her for you.	
HIPÓLITA	Could I have changed him so much?	
INÉS	He is lost for love of you.	
	(Aside) Looks like that got to her.	315
	(Aloud) But, my lady, what do you say?	
HIPÓLITA	I will bring you my response later.	
GALVÁN	*(Aside)* What a perfect occasion this is	
	for my nose to have its revenge!	
HIPÓLITA	Go, Inés, and say to your mistress…	320
	but I don't know what I am saying.	
	I will speak with you later.	
INÉS	I kiss your hands.	
	(Exit INÉS.)	
HIPÓLITA	Oh, my!	
	But how can I be tormented	
	by this pain, this anguish?	325
	That which is in the past, if it does not	
	slight me, why would it anger me?	
	Perhaps I should be on my guard,	
	even if he has not yet betrayed me,	
	for between old lovers the past	330
	has a habit of returning.	
	But could I have been deceived	
	by a gentleman?	
GALVÁN	My lady,	
	leave all troubles behind,	
	and get ready to dance.	335
HIPÓLITA	Dance? What, a wedding?	
GALVÁN	Well,	
	don't you know that Don Luis	
	has married?	
HIPÓLITA	*(Aside)* Oh, this is	
	poison to my ears!	

GALVÁN	Pues ¿él razón no te dio,	340
	habiendo estado contigo	
	de su gusto?	
HIPÓLITA	*(Aparte)* ¡Ay, falso amigo!	
	[Alto] ¿Que se ha casado?	
GALVÁN	Pues no.	
HIPÓLITA	¿Con quién Galván? *(Aparte)* ¿Que tal hizo?	
GALVÁN	Con doña … *[Aparte]* no le sé el nombre.	345
HIPÓLITA	*(Aparte)* ¡Vil caballero; mal hombre!	
GALVÁN	*[Aparte]* Por doña Ana la bautizo.	
	[Alto] Con doña Ana.	
HIPÓLITA	¿Qué doña Ana?	
GALVÁN	Una hermana de Marcelo,	
	a quien dio la herida.	
HIPÓLITA	*[Aparte]* ¡Ay, cielo!	350
GALVÁN	Que porque quedase llana	
	su amistad, se trató así.	
	¿Agora a sabello vienes,	
	cuando cien mil parabienes	
	le dan?	
HIPÓLITA	¿Tú lo viste?	
GALVÁN	Sí,	355
	y él los recibe…	
HIPÓLITA	*[Aparte]* ¿Hay tal cosa?	
GALVÁN	…con mucho gusto.	
HIPÓLITA	*[Aparte]* ¡Oh, traidor!	
GALVÁN	Su hermana doña Leonor	
	fue a visitar a su esposa.	
HIPÓLITA	*[Aparte]* Ello es cierto.	
GALVÁN	Está contenta;	360
	que debes a su amistad	
	alegrarte.	

343b *Pues no*: 'of course', 'indeed'; *Aut. 1737*: "Usado solo, y como separado de la oración, se usa para preguntar lo que se duda, y para responder afirmando lo que se pregunta: y de este modo se le suele añadir la particular 'No', para darle mas viveza en la respuesta, y la particular 'Que' en la pregunta" ('Pues' 8th def.).

GALVÁN	But, did he not tell you,	340
	I thought you enjoyed	
	each other's company?	
HIPÓLITA	*(Aside)* Oh, false friend!	
	(Aloud) He is married?	
GALVÁN	Indeed so.	
HIPÓLITA	To whom, Galván? *(Aside)* Did he really do this?	
GALVÁN	To Doña … *(Aside)* I don't know her name.	345
HIPÓLITA	*(Aside)* Vile gentleman; despicable man!	
GALVÁN	*(Aside)* I'll christen the bride Doña Ana.	
	(Aloud) Doña Ana.	
HIPÓLITA	What Doña Ana?	
GALVÁN	A sister of Marcelo,	
	the man whom Luis wounded.	
HIPÓLITA	*(Aside)* Oh, heavens!	350
GALVÁN	In order to preserve	
	their friendship, they made this deal.	
	This is the first you've heard of it,	
	when a hundred thousand congratulations	
	are being given to them?	
HIPÓLITA	You saw it?	
GALVÁN	Yes,	355
	he is receiving his guests…	
HIPÓLITA	*(Aside)* Can this be?	
GALVÁN	…with such pleasure.	
HIPÓLITA	*(Aside)* Oh, traitor!	
GALVÁN	His sister Doña Leonor	
	went to visit the bride.	
HIPÓLITA	*(Aside)* That I know is true.	
GALVÁN	Be content;	360
	you owe it to your friendship	
	to be happy for them.	

HIPÓLITA	*[Aparte]* ¿Hay tal maldad? Como corriendo tormenta suspendida estoy en calma.	
GALVÁN	Mamola.	
HIPÓLITA	*(Aparte)* ¿Hay tan gran traición? Muerto tengo el corazón y entre los dientes el alma.	365
GALVÁN	*(Aparte)* Eso sí, rabiad de celos, y sabréis qué es dar puñadas en narices tan honradas.	370
HIPÓLITA	*[Aparte]* Hado injusto; justos cielos; ¿que yo sufra estos agravios?	
GALVÁN	¿Mandas algo?	
HIPÓLITA	Déjame.	
GALVÁN	*(Aparte)* Buena queda; yo vengué las narices con los labios. *(Vase GALVÁN.)*	375
HIPÓLITA	¿Si sueño? ¿Que tal hizo? ¿Que pretendiese de mi amor la palma, y con tan tierno hechizo me abriese el pecho y me llevase el alma, teniendo otra intención, otro cuidado, y en fin, que se ha casado? Estas traiciones, soberanos cielos, afrentas son, aunque parecen celos. ¿Agora, aquí no estaba, tratando de servirme y de obligarme? ¿Para qué me engañaba, si pensaba ofenderme con dejarme? Pero burlose con engaño injusto del honor y del gusto; pues esto en mi valor, ¿qué ha sido? ¡Cielos! Afrentas son, aunque parecen celos.	[estrofa alirada] 380 385 390

365a *Mamola*: literally 'drank it down like mother's milk', figuratively, 'she bought it'; Galván is pleased with the success of his lie.
385 *obligar*: see note at I. 89–96.

HIPÓLITA	*(Aside)* Can there be such malice?[20]	
	Like the eye of the storm	
	I am suspended in calm shock.	
GALVÁN	*(Aside)* Drank it down like mother's milk.	
HIPÓLITA	*(Aside)* Can there be such treachery?	365
	My heart is dead,	
	and my soul is grinding in my teeth.	
GALVÁN	*(Aside)* That's right, rage with jealousy,[21]	
	and you will understand what it means	
	to box such an honourable nose.	370
HIPÓLITA	*(Aside)* Unjust fate; fair heaven;	
	am I to suffer this outrage?	
GALVÁN	Is there anything I can do?	
HIPÓLITA	Leave me.	
GALVÁN	*(Aside)* I've come out on top; I have	
	avenged my nose with my lips.	375
	(Exit GALVÁN.)	

SCENE 3.1d

HIPÓLITA	Am I dreaming? Could he have done this?	
	Could he have won the prize of my love,	
	and then with such tender trickery	
	opened my heart, carried away my soul,	
	while having another intention, another concern,	380
	and really, could he be married?	
	These treacheries, powerful heavens,	
	are insults, though they look like jealousy.	
	Just now, did he not stand right here,	
	vowing to serve me and to please me?	385
	Why did he deceive me,	
	if his plan was to insult me by leaving me?	
	But he mocked me with an unfair trick	
	against honour and pleasure;	
	and as for my valour… Heavens!	390
	It is an insult, though it looks like jealousy.	

---

20   See p. 100, Fig. 5 for a photograph of this scene in production.
21   See p. 101, Fig. 6 for a photograph of this scene in production.

              Como no me engañara
           con alma burladora y fementida,
           aunque más le adorara,
           quedara enamorada y no ofendida;   395
           pero viendo pender tan en mi daño
           mi ofensa de su engaño,
           ¿qué he de pensar que sea? Justos cielos,
           afrentas son, aunque parecen celos.
              Que estoy loca sospecho;   400
           ¿que un hombre tenga atrevimiento y brío
           de escudriñarme el pecho
           y verme el alma, para no ser mío?
           ¿Y quizá por jactarse de que ha sido
           de mi favorecido?   405
           ¿Esto qué viene a ser? Piadosos cielos,
           afrentas son, aunque parecen celos.
              Pues ¿qué espero a matalle,
           y sacar a mi honor de inconvenientes?
           El alma he de sacalle,   410
           cuando no con las manos, con los dientes;
           leona soy, que la cuartana tengo;
           ya bramando prevengo
           el cómo he de vengarme, que estos duelos
           afrentas son, aunque parecen celos.   415

Vase DOÑA HIPÓLITA, y salen OTAVIO y MARCELO con una banda.

MARCELO   En esta mano traía   [redondillas]
            el puño, y no revolví
            la capa al brazo; y así
            la mala fortuna mía
               guió la espada inclemente,   420
            y como en ella me hirió,
            cayome el puño. Llegó

---

393 *fementida*: 'false', 'dishonest'.
412 *cuartana*: a fever which recurs every fourth day, accompanied by chills (*Aut. 1737*: "Especie de calentura, que entra con frio de quatro en quatro dias, de donde parece tomó el nombre" ('quartana')). According to Greer and Rhodes, this illness was common in the seventeenth century, and had a rhythm similar to that of malaria (2008, 54n).

As he wouldn't have deceived me
with a deceitful, lying soul,
no matter how much I would have loved him,
I'd have remained in love and unoffended; 395
but seeing that the pain of the insult hangs on
the fact that it was all just a trick,
what could I think it is? Justice of heaven,
it is an insult, though it looks like jealousy.
I suspect I have lost my mind; 400
for a man to have the daring and rash spirit
to look into my heart
and to see into my soul, to not be mine?
Perhaps only to boast
that I have favoured him? 405
What will come of this? Merciful heavens,
it is an insult, though it looks like my jealousy.
But why hesitate to kill him,
to remove the stain from my honour?
I will rip out his soul, 410
not with my hands, but with my teeth;
I am a lioness, I have the quartan fever;
bellowing my warning that I am to be
avenged, that this heartache is an insult,
though it looks like my jealousy. 415

SCENE 3.2

Exit HIPÓLITA, enter OTAVIO and MARCELO, with a bandage around his arm.

MARCELO   In this hand I held
her cuff, and I did not throw
my cape to the side; in that way
my bad fortune guided
my inclement sword, 420
for when he wounded me,
her cuff fell to the ground.

	de improviso mucha gente,	
	y él tuvo suerte y lugar	
	de poder alzar del suelo	425
	el puño. Llevole, ¡ay cielo!,	
	y dejésele llevar,	
	porque me vi luego asido	
	de la justicia. Fui preso	
	y él se escapó; que hasta en eso	430
	fue dichoso y yo ofendido.	
	Firmé paz, que multiplica	
	la ofensa, mas no se escusa,	
	porque quien la paz rehusa	
	más el agravio publica;	435
	pero por justicia es	
	forzada y no valedora,	
	y así disimulo agora	
	para vengarme después.	
OTAVIO	¿Y cómo estás?	
MARCELO	Casi sano.	440
OTAVIO	No ha sido poca ventura.	
MARCELO	Con facilidad se cura	
	herida que está en la mano;	
	aunque estoy casi sin vida	
	de que don Luis la tiene;	445
	pero voyme, que allí viene,	
	y está muy fresca la herida.	

Vase MARCELO, y sale DON LUIS y un CRIADO; DON LUIS leyendo un papel.

OTAVIO	Leyendo viene un papel,	
	y no se ha vuelto a mirar	
	donde estoy; quiero excusar,	450
	si puedo, el hablar con él.	

432–433 See note III. 141–144 on the increased damage to one's honor due to being forced by the law to make peace.
436–437; 451a According to Pitt-Rivers, "an oath which is not made freely is not binding, nor is a word of honour which is not intended as such" (1977, 12).
450 *excusar*: see note I. 291.

	Suddenly there were people all around,	
	and he had the luck and opportunity	
	to snatch up the cuff from the ground.	425
	He took it, oh heavens,	
	and I let him take it,	
	because at that moment I was in the grip	
	of the authorities. I was arrested	
	and he escaped. For even in that	430
	he was blessed and I was cursed.	
	I signed a pledge of peace, multiplying	
	the offense against me, but it is not over	
	because he who refuses peace	
	serves to publicize his misdeeds;	435
	but since the law has forced	
	this agreement, it is invalid,	
	so I will lay low for now	
	in order to ensure my revenge later.	
OTAVIO	How are you?	
MARCELO	Almost healed.	440
OTAVIO	You have taken no small risk.	
MARCELO	It is easy to remedy	
	a wound to the hand;	
	but what is really killing me	
	is the fact that Don Luis has her;	445
	but I'm off, for he's coming here,	
	and my wound is still too fresh.	

Exit MARCELO, and enter DON LUIS and a SERVANT; DON LUIS is reading a piece of paper.

OTAVIO	He comes reading a letter,	
	and he has not turned to see	
	I am here; I will avoid	450
	speaking to him if I can.	

LUIS	*(DON LUIS lee el papel:)*[+]	
	'Sin embargo de las paces que	[451a]
	tenemos firmadas, pues por justicia no obligan a los	
	ofendidos; te espero a las espaldas de Santa Engracia	
	con una capa y una espada.	
	—Marcelo.'	
	Vete en paz, y esta te doy	
	por las nuevas que me has dado.	
	(Dale una cadena.)	
OTAVIO	Una cadena a un criado	
	no es sin causa.	
CRIADO	Alegre voy.	455
	(Vase el CRIADO.)	
LUIS	Esto me obliga a dudar,	
	a pensar y a prevenir;	
	mas si al fin he de salir,	
	¿de qué me sirve el pensar?	
	Que estas cosas, sin temellas,	460
	es razón ejecutallas,	
	porque el pararse a pensallas,	
	no ponga en duda el hacellas.	
	(Vase DON LUIS.)	
OTAVIO	Ya se fue; que le haya dado	
	por el papel la cadena	465
	no deja de darme pena;	
	pero ya me la ha quitado	
	de su hermana la hermosura,	
	sol bello en mis ojos puesto.	

Sale DOÑA LEONOR a la ventana.

LEONOR	¿No es éste Otavio? ¿Qué es esto?	470
	¿Tan sin miedo se aventura?	
	No osará el medio mujer	
	llegar a pedille el guante.	
	Tan poco atrevido amante	
	mejor es para no ser.	475

+ **451a** The note at line 451a is written in prose and does configure into the rhyme scheme.
451a *Santa Engracia*: a basilica in Zaragoza.

LUIS	*(Reading.)* 'In spite of the peace pledge that we have signed, the authorities cannot force me to forget your offence against me; I await you at the back of Saint Engracia with a cape and a sword.	
	–Marcelo.'	
	Go in peace, and take this	
	for the news you have given me.	
	(Giving him a chain.)	
OTAVIO	One does not give a chain to a servant	
	without good reason.	
SERVANT	I'm off happily.	455
	(Exit the SERVANT.)	
LUIS	This forces doubt into my mind;	
	I must hold back and think;	
	but if I will have to go out to fight in the end,	
	what good will come of thinking about it?	
	At a time like this, banishing fears,	460
	it is best to do it now,	
	so that to stop to think	
	does not cast doubt on the need to act.	
	(Exit DON LUIS.)	
OTAVIO	Now he's gone; he has traded	
	the letter for a chain,	465
	which continues to worry me,	
	but now my cares have been lifted	
	by the beauty of his sister,	
	the shining sun, the light to my eyes.	

Enter LEONOR at the window.

LEONOR	Is that not Otavio? What is this?	470
	He dares to come here so shamelessly?	
	Yet the half-woman will not even dare	
	to come to ask for the glove.	
	A lover showing so little courage would	
	be better to not be a lover at all.	475

OTAVIO	Hablarele, porque agrada	
	a veces la libertad.	
	[A Leonor] Si obligase la humildad	
	del respeto acompañada	
	a que me oyeses agora,	480
	señora, te obligaría.	
LEONOR	Obliga la cortesía	
	a lo que pides.	
OTAVIO	Señora,	
	esta prenda, que no en vano	
	tengo por lugar del alma,	485
	(pues llevo en ella una palma,	
	cuando menos de tu mano)	
	defendí con tanto brío	
	porque era la causa suya,	
	mas fue, sin licencia tuya,	490
	grande atrevimiento mío.	
	Pero, pues entonces viste	
	la disculpa en la ocasión,	
	merezca con el perdón	
	más favor del que me hiciste.	495
	Y para darme renombre	
	de dichoso con tal bien,	
	dame licencia también[+]	
	para guardalla en tu nombre.	

Salen el CAPITÁN por una puerta y DON FÉLIX por otra. Aparte todos.

CAPITÁN	A esta esquina estoy mejor.	500
LEONOR	Este es don Félix.	
FÉLIX	¡Ay, cielos!	
OTAVIO	No importa.	
LEONOR	Con dalle celos	
	quizá le daré valor.	
	[A Otavio] Bien parece, siendo amante;	

---

477   *libertad*: see note II. 255.
+ 498   también B C : tan bien A P.

OTAVIO	I will speak to her, because sometimes taking a little liberty is a good thing. *(To Leonor)* If humility obliges you accompanied by respect to listen to me now, my lady, I would oblige you.	480
LEONOR	Courtesy obliges me to do what you ask.	
OTAVIO	My lady, this treasure, which for no small reason I now hold close to my heart, (I bring it as a palm of victory, especially being from your hand) I defended it with such brio because it was in the name of your glove, though I took a great risk doing so without your permission. But, since you saw my excuse as it occurred, perhaps I deserve, along with your forgiveness, more favor than you showed me then. And if you now see fit to honour me with such a boon as your favour, grant me permission as well to keep it safe, in your name.	485

490

495 |

Enter the CAPTAIN by one door, and FÉLIX by another. They speak apart to one another.

CAPTAIN	I'm better off at this corner.	500
LEONOR	That is Don Félix.	
FÉLIX	Oh, heavens!	
OTAVIO	So what.	
LEONOR	By making him jealous perhaps I can inspire him to be brave. *(Aloud to Otavio)* It is attractive for	

	que enfermo de mal de amores,	505
	estás pobre de favores,	
	pues los pides con un guante;	
	y así, aunque le hayas llevado	
	sin mi licencia, atrevido,	
	pienso que le has merecido	510
	por lo bien que le has guardado:	
	tuyo es ya.	
OTAVIO	Dichoso soy.	
FÉLIX	*(Aparte)* Abrásase el alma mía.	
LEONOR	*[Aparte]* Dalle, pienso, valentía	
	con los celos que le doy.	515
OTAVIO	Y pues me das tanto brío,	
	ponelle quiero en lugar	
	donde más me pueda honrar.	
LEONOR	Defiéndele en nombre mío.	
OTAVIO	Quien le quisiere, de aquí,	520
	(Pónele en el sombrero.)	
	después de rendir mi espada,	
	con mi cabeza cortada,	
	le ha de llevar.	
LEONOR	Eso sí.	
FÉLIX	*(Aparte)* Rabiando estoy; ¡oh mujer!	
	¡Oh enemiga!	
LEONOR	*[Aparte]* Está furioso;	525
	yo que le hago celoso	
	valiente le quiero hacer.	
OTAVIO	Ya competir con los cielos	
	puedo en tu nombre, señora.	
FÉLIX	*(Aparte)* Estoy por matalle agora,	530
	que no hay flema donde hay celos.	
LEONOR	Estimo tal confianza.	
CAPITÁN	*(Aparte)* ¡Qué arrogancia, y qué paciencia!	
FÉLIX	*[Aparte]* Mas es bien con la prudencia	
	asegurar la venganza.	535

531 *no hay flema donde hay celos*: see note II. 240; the sluggishness and clumsiness associated with *flema* are the opposite nature of *cólera*, which results from heat and dryness and causes rage and passion. Jealousy was believed to increase humoral heat.

	a lover to suffer from lovesickness,	505
	but you must be short of favours,	
	if you ask for just one glove;	
	and although you have taken it	
	without my permission, daringly,	
	I think that you have deserved	510
	the token by guarding it so well.	
	It is yours now.	
OTAVIO	I am a lucky man.	
FÉLIX	*(Aside)* My soul is burning.	
LEONOR	*(Aside)* I hope to make him valiant	
	by pricking his jealousy.	515
OTAVIO	And as you buoy up my spirit,	
	I would like to put it in the place	
	where it may do me the most honour.	
LEONOR	Defend it in my name.	
OTAVIO	Whosoever may desire it, from here	520
	(Putting the glove in his hat.)	
	he will only be able to take it after	
	conquering my sword, and cutting	
	off my head.	
LEONOR	That is perfect.	
FÉLIX	*(Aside)* I am raging; oh, woman!	
	Oh, enemy!	
LEONOR	*(Aside)* He is furious;	525
	now that I have made him jealous,	
	I will make him brave.	
OTAVIO	I am ready to compete with heaven itself	
	in your name, my lady.	
FÉLIX	*(Aside)* I'll kill him right now;	530
	there's no composure where there's jealousy.	
LEONOR	I admire such confidence.	
CAPTAIN	*(Aside)* What arrogance; what patience!	
FÉLIX	*(Aside)* It is better to proceed prudently	
	in order to ensure my revenge.	535

La fuerza de la costumbre: Jornada tercera

	[Alto] ¡Otavio!	
OTAVIO	¿Qué quieres?	
	(Hace amago de meter mano a la espada.)	
FÉLIX	Quedo,	
	no tengas miedo, que estoy	
	muy de paz, oye.	
OTAVIO	No soy	
	hombre yo que tengo miedo.	
LEONOR	¡Don Félix!	
FÉLIX	De ti me espanto;	540
	tan poco estimo tu nombre	
	que pierda el respeto a un hombre	
	que tú favoreces tanto.	
LEONOR	Con eso me has obligado.	
FÉLIX	Y tú, ingrata, me has perdido.	545
LEONOR	*(Aparte)*⁺ ¿Si disimula ofendido,	
	y quiere vengarse honrado?	
FÉLIX	Dejemos este lugar,	
	que muy solo quiero hablarte.	
OTAVIO	Aquí y en cualquiera parte	550
	sabré hacer y sabré hablar.	
FÉLIX	En otra parte mejor	
	desenvainar se podrá	
	mi espada; pues tengo ya	
	desenvainado el valor,	555
	y para pedirte el guante	
	no ha de haber inconveniente.	
	Ven, si tienes de valiente	
	lo que muestras de arrogante.	
OTAVIO	Allá te quiero decir	560
	lo que soy.	
FÉLIX	Ven a mi lado.	
CAPITÁN	Ellos se habrán concertado;	
	sus pasos quiero seguir.	
LEONOR	Desafiole; no hay más,	

+ 546 '*(Aparte)*' moved from after line 544, since in both 544 and 545, Félix and Leonor are speaking to each other.

OTAVIO	*(Aloud)* Otavio! What do you want? *(He traces a movement in the air as if getting out his sword.)*
FÉLIX	Hold, do not be afraid, for I come in peace. Listen.
OTAVIO	I am not the sort of man to be afraid.
LEONOR	Don Félix!
FÉLIX	You shock me; 540 so poorly do I esteem your name that I have no respect for a man whom you favor so much.
LEONOR	You leave me no choice.
FÉLIX	And you, ungrateful, have lost me. 545
LEONOR	*(Aside)* Is he pretending to be offended, and wants to avenge himself honourably?
FÉLIX	Let us leave this place, for I want to speak with you quite alone.
OTAVIO	Here or wherever you like, 550 I will know what to do and say.
FÉLIX	It will be better for me to unsheathe my sword in another place; as I have now already unsheathed my valour, 555 and when I ask you for the glove there we will be undisturbed. Come, if you have as much bravery as you have shown in arrogance.
OTAVIO	In that place I will be glad to tell you 560 what I am made of.
FÉLIX	Let us go together.
CAPTAIN	They have made an agreement; I'll follow them and see what happens.
LEONOR	He has challenged him; that's it, he

	bien hizo. ¡Valelde, cielos!	565
	Quien no es valiente con celos,	
	no espere serlo jamás.	

Vanse, y sale DON LUIS solo.

LUIS	¿Qué descubro desde aquí?	
	Asegurarme no puedo.	
	¿Es esto miedo? No es miedo,	570
	pero sobresalto, sí.	

(Sale DOÑA HIPÓLITA en hábito de hombre, cubierto el rostro con la capa o con una banda.)

	Bravo talle; ¡ah, caballero!	
HIPÓLITA	*(Aparte)* Terrible cólera tengo.	
LUIS	¿Qué buscáis?	
HIPÓLITA	Rabiando vengo.	
LUIS	¿Qué queréis?	
HIPÓLITA	Mataros quiero.	575
LUIS	¿Qué escucho? Yo me guardara	
	de vos solo, mas sospecho	
	que hay traiciones en el pecho	
	de quien me encubre la cara–	
	¿quién sois? ¿Envíaos Marcelo?	580
HIPÓLITA	*(Aparte)* ¡Furiosa y cobarde estoy!	
	[Alto] Un rayo del cielo soy.	

(Descúbrese DOÑA HIPÓLITA.)

LUIS	No sois sino el mismo cielo.	
	Señora, pero ¿por qué,	
	enojado y ofendido	585
	me castigas?	
HIPÓLITA	Porque has sido	
	quebrantador de una fe,	
	por inventor de un mal trato,	
	siendo a costa de mi amor.	
	¡Villano, infame, traidor,	590
	falso amigo, amante ingrato,	

---

573 *cólera*: 'fury', 'rage'; See note I. 750.

	did well. Heavens, grant him courage!	565
	He who is not valiant when jealous,	
	cannot ever expect to be brave.	

They exit.

SCENE 3.3

Enter DON LUIS, alone.

LUIS	What is this I discover from here?	
	I cannot be sure.	
	Is this fear? No, it is not fear,	570
	but a shock, yes.	
	(Enter HIPÓLITA in man's clothes, covering her face with her cape or with a cuff.)	
	What a manly figure! Hey, gentleman!	
HIPÓLITA	*(Aside)* I feel a terrible rage!	
LUIS	What are you looking for?	
HIPÓLITA	I come in fury.	
LUIS	What do you want?	
HIPÓLITA	I want to kill you.	575
LUIS	What? I would defend against	
	you by myself; but I suspect	
	treachery in the heart	
	of a man who hides his face from me –	
	who are you? Marcelo sent you?	580
HIPÓLITA	*(Aside)* I am both furious and cowardly!	
	(Aloud) I am a lightning bolt from the sky.	
	(Uncovering herself.)	
LUIS	You are nothing but heaven itself.	
	My lady, but why,	
	infuriated and offended,	585
	do you come to punish me?	
HIPÓLITA	Because you have been	
	the breaker of faith,	
	the inventor of abuse,	
	and the price is my love.	
	Villain, infamous traitor,	590
	false friend, ungrateful lover,	

	mal caballero! Estoy loca	
	de corrida y de enojada;	
	pero escucha de mi espada	
	lo que no cabe en mi boca.	595
LUIS	¡Tente, por Dios, que no entiendo	
	la mala estrella que sigo!	
	¿Yo te enojo, que te obligo,	
	yo que te adoro te ofendo?	
	¿Yo traidor y yo villano,	600
	siendo en mí, señora mía,	
	la lealtad y la hidalguía	
	privilegios de tu mano?	
	¿Yo malos tratos consiento?	
	¿Yo infame, yo falso amigo?	605
	¿Yo ingrato, siendo contigo	
	el mismo agradecimiento?	
	Señora ¿por qué te extrañas,	
	me afliges y me congojas?	
HIPÓLITA	De nuevo agora me enojas	610
	porque de nuevo me engañas.	
	¿Haste casado y preguntas,	
	después de engañarme, ¡ay, triste!,	
	por qué te digo que fuiste	
	todas estas cosas juntas?	615
LUIS	¿Yo casado?	
HIPÓLITA	Tú casado.	
LUIS	¿Con quién?	
HIPÓLITA	Con una doña Ana,	
	que de Marcelo es hermana.	
LUIS	Hante engañado.	
HIPÓLITA	¿Engañado?	
	Recebiste desde ayer	620
	los parabienes…	
LUIS	Espera,…	
HIPÓLITA	…traidor.	
LUIS	…aunque yo lo fuera,	
	eso no pudiera ser.	

	you are no gentleman! My mind reels	
	with shame and fury;	
	but listen to my sword,[22]	
	it will say what I cannot.	595
LUIS	Wait, by God, I do not know	
	what terrible star leads me here!	
	I enrage you, I force you to fight?	
	I adore you, yet you say I offend you?	
	You call me a traitor, me, a villain,	600
	when I am the one, my lady,	
	who enjoys the noble privileges	
	of loyalty to your hand?	
	I, take part in double-dealing?	
	I, infamous, I, a false friend?	605
	I, ungrateful, when being with you	
	I am gratitude itself?	
	My lady, do you act against your own	
	nature, to afflict me and make me suffer?	
HIPÓLITA	Afresh you offend me	610
	as afresh you deceive me.	
	You were married and yet you ask	
	after deceiving me, oh, with such pain,	
	why I say to you, that you are	
	all these things at the same time?	615
LUIS	I, married?	
HIPÓLITA	You, married.	
LUIS	To whom?	
HIPÓLITA	To some 'Doña Ana',	
	the sister of Marcelo.	
LUIS	You have been deceived.	
HIPÓLITA	Deceived, me?	
	Since yesterday you received	620
	congratulations…	
LUIS	Wait…	
HIPÓLITA	…traitor.	
LUIS	…even if I was,	
	this could not be the case.	

22 See p. 102, Fig. 7 for a photograph of this scene in production.

HIPÓLITA	¿Cómo?	
LUIS	Escucha: si es la hermana	
	dese Marcelo sin duda,	625
	si no es que el nombre se muda,	
	doña Elvira y no doña Ana;	
	en esto echarás de ver	
	que te engañaron a ti.	
HIPÓLITA	*[Aparte]* En lo presto que creí	630
	conozco que soy mujer.	
LUIS	Y si no basta en un hombre	
	que te adora esta razón,	
	pasa el mismo corazón	
	donde está escrito tu nombre	635
	y tu imagen estampada;	
	pues por hacerte servicio	
	te doy para el sacrificio	
	consentimiento y espada.	
	Matarme será mejor	640
	que verte ofendida.	
HIPÓLITA	*(Aparte)* ¡Ay, cielos!	
	Al fenecer de los celos	
	queda en su punto el amor;	
	mas fingireme quejosa,	
	enojada y ofendida,	645
	porque tengo de corrida	
	lo que tuve de celosa.	
	[Alto] Satisfacción no pretendo;	
	levanta, y toma la espada...	
LUIS	*(Aparte)* Más corrida que enojada	650
	me responde, ya lo entiendo.	
HIPÓLITA	...y haz por defenderte luego,	
	que te alcanzan mis enojos.	
LUIS	Ya los rayos de tus ojos	
	son de sol y no de fuego.	655
	(Aparte) Mas, ¿qué pensamiento vano	
	toda el alma divertía,	

633 *razón*: here, meaning 'proof'.

HIPÓLITA	What?	
LUIS	Listen; if you definitely mean	
	the sister of Marcelo, then unless	625
	she has changed her name, she is known	
	as Doña Elvira, not Doña Ana;	
	now you must see that someone	
	has deceived you.	
HIPÓLITA	*(Aside)* I was so quick to believe it,	630
	I must be a woman.	
LUIS	And if you will not believe the words	
	of the man who adores you,	
	stab through my heart itself,	
	where your name is written	635
	and your image is stamped;	
	for, to serve you,	
	I offer you this sacrifice,	
	my consent and my sword.	
	To kill me will be better	640
	than to see you offended.	
HIPÓLITA	*(Aside)* Oh, heavens!	
	Once jealousy dies down,	
	love is sure to ripen;	
	but I must pretend to be outraged,	
	aggrieved and offended,	645
	because I now feel as ashamed	
	as I was feeling jealous.	
	(Aloud) I am not satisfied by your words;	
	stand and take up your sword…	
LUIS	*(Aside)* Now there is more shame	650
	than outrage in her reply, I think.	
HIPÓLITA	…and defend yourself now,	
	my rage grows higher still.	
LUIS	Now the rays from your eyes	
	are that of sunlight, not fiery anger.	655
	(Aside) But, what light-hearted thought	
	delighted my entire soul,	

	cuando esta gloria, que es mía, se me ha venido a la mano?	
HIPÓLITA	Defiéndete presto, presto.	660
LUIS	Pues tanto me has obligado, siendo yo el desafiado, me toca escoger el puesto y aun las armas; mas serán estas mismas que traemos.	665
HIPÓLITA	*[Aparte]* Él toca en los dos extremos de discreto y de galán. *[Alto]* Eso es justo, y razón es que yo también lo conceda.	
LUIS	Pues tras de aquella alameda te espero.	670
HIPÓLITA	Mueve los pies, y allí que tengo has de ver de mujer no más del nombre.	
LUIS	Allí verás que soy hombre para más de una mujer; has de probar, ¡vive Dios!, de mis fuerzas los extremos.	675
HIPÓLITA	Camina, que allí veremos cuál se rinde de los dos.	
LUIS	*(Aparte)* Y allí, fortuna, ha de ser logrado mi buen deseo.	680
HIPÓLITA	*(Aparte)* Él me engaña, ya lo veo, pero no lo quiero ver.	
LUIS	*(Aparte)* Ella se deja llevar de mi engañosa corriente.	685
HIPÓLITA	*(Aparte)* Engaña discretamente el que se deja engañar.	

Vanse, y antes de irse sale el CAPITÁN.

662–663 Luis has the right, as the party being challenged to the duel, to choose the location and weapons for the confrontation.

670 *aquella alameda*: the 'poplar grove' bears erotic resonances from the medieval lyric tradition; see for example, "De los álamos vengo, madre, / de ver cómo los menea el aire…" (in Frenk 2004, '346', p. 168).

	when this glory, that is mine,	
	has played right into my hand?	
HIPÓLITA	Defend yourself now, come on!	660
LUIS	You oblige me to fight,	
	as you have challenged me,	
	and it thus falls to me to choose the place	
	and the weapons; but, let's	
	use those that we carry with us.	665
HIPÓLITA	*(Aside)* From one extreme to the other,	
	he is crafty and a gent.	
	(Aloud) This is fair, and thus it is right	
	also that I concede it.	
LUIS	I will wait for you behind that	670
	poplar grove.	
HIPÓLITA	Move your feet,	
	and there you will see	
	that only in name am I a woman.	
LUIS	There you will see that I am man enough	
	for one who is more than a woman;	675
	You will taste, by God,	
	the full force of my strength.	
HIPÓLITA	Walk, for there we will see	
	which of us ends up submitting.	
LUIS	*(Aside)* And there, fortune,	680
	I will achieve what I desire.	
HIPÓLITA	*(Aside)* He is deceiving me, I see that,	
	but I do not want to see it.	
LUIS	*(Aside)* She lets herself be carried away	
	in the swift current of my deceit.	685
HIPÓLITA	*(Aside)* One can deceive discreetly	
	by allowing oneself to be deceived.	

They exit, but before they go, enter the CAPTAIN.

CAPITÁN	Perdilos, ¡válame Dios!
	¿Si son los que allí se van?
	¿Serán ellos? No serán, 690
	porque allí vienen los dos.
	Desde aquí veré escondido,
	que valelle no es razón
	si no le viese a traición
	o con ventaja ofendido. 695

Salen OTAVIO y DON FÉLIX.

OTAVIO	Agrádate este lugar?
FÉLIX	Más escondido le quiero.
OTAVIO	Por algún despeñadero
	a un valle puedes bajar,
	que hasta el abismo mayor 700
	te seguiré; que deseo
	verte solo.
FÉLIX	Yo lo creo,
	de tu nobleza y valor.
	Detrás de aquellas paredes
	iremos.
OTAVIO	Iré tras ti. 705
	Ve que aunque me toca a mí
	señalar puesto, bien puedes.
FÉLIX	Que lo estimo te prometo,
	que es mucho para estimar;
	pero si busco lugar 710
	tan escondido y secreto,
	es porque gente no acuda,
	y porque no tenga, al vella,
	una espada tan doncella
	vergüenza de estar desnuda. 715
OTAVIO	Grande la debe tener;
	que es muy doncella sospecho.

705b–707 See note 662–663; here Otavio cedes his right to choose the location.
712–713 *porque*: 'para que'.

SCENE 3.4

CAPTAIN	I lost them, God save me!	
	Can that be them passing by there?	
	Can it be them? No, that's not them,	690
	here, they are coming now.	
	From here I can watch but not be seen,	
	for it would not be right to step in	
	unless I see some treachery or	
	if his opponent gains the advantage.	695

Enter OTAVIO and FÉLIX.

OTAVIO	Does this location suit you?	
FÉLIX	I'd prefer one that is more secluded.	
OTAVIO	Go ahead and jump off a cliff	
	over a deep valley,	
	for even to the deepest abyss	700
	I will follow you; for I only want	
	to see you alone.	
FÉLIX	I have full faith	
	in your nobility and valour.	
	We are just going behind	
	those walls.	
OTAVIO	I'll follow after you.	705
	Although custom dictates	
	that I would choose the spot, you can.	
FÉLIX	I appreciate it, I promise,	
	and it is admirable indeed;	
	but if I seek a place	710
	that is so hidden and secret,	
	it is so that people do not burst in on us,	
	and so that my maidenly sword will not	
	have to show herself to anyone else,	
	she is ashamed to be seen naked.	715
OTAVIO	It must be big;	
	though I suspect it may be a virgin.	

FÉLIX   Yo confío que en tu pecho
             ha de dejallo de ser.
OTAVIO   Ya vienes más alentado;   720
             de que te animes me alegro.
FÉLIX   Y en vez del vestido negro,
             se le pondré colorado.
OTAVIO   Esa es mucha presunción
             para tan flaco enemigo.   725
FÉLIX   Acaba.
OTAVIO   ¿Qué dices?
FÉLIX   Digo
             que tienes mucha razón.

Vanse, y el CAPITÁN desde la puerta mira la pendencia, y va diciendo:

CAPITÁN   Las paredes han saltado;
             por sus resquicios veré
             el suceso, y estaré   730
             escondido arrodillado.
                  Ser yo don Félix querría,
             porque temo el velle muerto.
             ¡Honrado trato, por cierto!
             ¡Qué valiente cortesía!   735
                  Acciones cierto honradas,
             bravamente procedieron.
             Ya los pechos descubrieron,
             ya sacaron las espadas.
                  Bien Otavio se afirmó,   740
             pero arrojósele al vuelo
             don Félix. ¡Válgate el cielo!,
             ¡gallardamente chocó!

Sale OTAVIO herido, de adentro y cayéndose, y DON FÉLIX tras él.

719   *dejallo de ser*: 'ser' refers to 'doncella' (717); Félix does not argue with Otavio's insult about his 'virgin' sword, but rather warns his rival that his sword will lose its virginity in Otavio's chest.
728–743   The Captain narrates the confrontation between Félix and Otavio because the action occurs offstage.
743   *chocó*: 'chocar' meaning 'fight'; *Aut. 1729*: "Por analogía se toma por pelear; ò combatir" ('chocar', 2nd def.).

FÉLIX	I'm confident that she won't be after she thrusts into your chest.	
OTAVIO	Now you are coming to a boil; to see you with such spirit is encouraging.	720
FÉLIX	Though you wear black she will paint you a shade of red.	
OTAVIO	This is great presumption in such a weak enemy.	725
FÉLIX	End it.	
OTAVIO	What do you say?	
FÉLIX	I say that I'm sure you're entirely correct.	

SCENE 3.4b

They exit, and the CAPTAIN at the door sees the fight, and exits saying:

CAPTAIN	They've jumped over those walls; through its gaps I will see what happens, and I will stay hidden here on my knees. I wish I could take Don Félix's place, because I fear to see him dead. An honourable conversation, certainly! What valiant courtesy! Those are honourable moves, they handled themselves bravely. They have uncovered their chests and drawn their swords. Otavio has shown his strength, but he has been thrown into the air by Don Félix. Heaven protect you! He fought gallantly!	730 735 740

Enter OTAVIO, wounded, from offstage, and falling over, and DON FÉLIX after him.

304   *La fuerza de la costumbre: Jornada tercera*

OTAVIO	¿Por qué matas a un rendido?	
CAPITÁN	Que ha de matalle sospecho.	745
FÉLIX	Soy piadoso y tengo el pecho, en fin, como bien nacido.	
[DENTRO:][+]	*(Ruido de gente.)* ¡Llegad, corred!	
CAPITÁN	Cosa brava, ¿no es gente? ¿Qué intento tiene? Ni sé si de lejos viene o si escondida esperaba, pero la justicia es.	750

Sale la JUSTICIA, [UN ALGUACIL] Y GENTE.[+]

ALGUACIL	Prendeldo.	
FÉLIX	¡Qué intentos vanos! Dejad que mueva las manos y habréis menester los pies.	755
CORCHETE	Muerto soy.	
CAPITÁN	¡Qué bien le dio! Aquí estoy.	
FÉLIX	Yo solo sobro.	
CAPITÁN	Don Félix, poneos en cobro mientras que los mato yo.	

Vanse, y sale DOÑA COSTANZA.

COSTANZA	¡Qué confusión tan extraña! ¡Qué desdicha tan cruel!	[romance é]	760

---

744 *matas* a BC: *matas* P.

+ **748a** *¡Llegad, corred!*: though P leaves this as a continuation of Félix's lines with no change in speaker, all manuscripts attribute the line to another speaker. In A and B, 'dentro' appears in the speaker column (meaning 'offstage'); in C 'Justisia/' appears in the speaker column.

+ **752** This stage direction is taken from A, since the stage direction in P is unclear: in the margin next to 754 and 755 in A: "sale la / just[a] [justicia] y jente" : Salen, y un Alguacil. P : salen quarto o çinco como algua / çiles B : omitted in C.

758 *poneos en cobro*: 'save yourself'. *Aut. 1729*: "significa tambien segúro ù seguridád y resguardo: en fuerza de lo cual comunmente se dice Poner algúna cosa en cobro, Ponerse uno en cobro: esto es, assegurarla, ò assegurarse y resguardarse" ('cobro', 3rd def.).

OTAVIO	Why do you kill one who surrenders?	
CAPTAIN	Looks like he is going to kill him.	745
FÉLIX	I am merciful, and I have the heart, ultimately, of a man who is well born.	
VOICES	*(The sound of people approaching.)* Come, run!	
CAPTAIN	Unbelievable, people, here? What do they want? I can't tell if they came from afar, or if they were waiting here, hidden, but it is the lawmen in any case.	750

Enter OFFICERS, a BAILIFF, and OTHERS.

BAILIFF	Arrest him.	
FÉLIX	You will not succeed! Allow me to move my hands and you will certainly need your feet.	755
OFFICER	I'm dead.	
CAPTAIN	How well he struck him! I am here.	
FÉLIX	Alone I am more than enough for him.	
CAPTAIN	Don Félix, get yourself to safety while I kill the rest of them.	

Exit all, and enter COSTANZA.

SCENE 3.5

COSTANZA	What strange confusion! What cruel misfortune!	760

	Todos saben de mi hijo,	
	y yo sola no lo sé.	
	Mi hija falta de casa,	
	no sé lo que pudo ser.	765
	Estas libertades suyas	
	en vano reformaré.	
	Pero allí viene; ¿qué es esto?	
	De plomo tiene los pies.	

Sale DOÑA HIPÓLITA de mujer.

HIPÓLITA	Aunque me di mucha prisa,	770
	pienso que tarde llegué.	
COSTANZA	¿Sin mi licencia saliste?	
	¿Esto es honra? ¡Bien a fe!	
	¿Por qué te cubres la cara?	
	Vergüenza debe de ser.	775
HIPÓLITA	¡Madre de los ojos míos!	
COSTANZA	¿Qué te aflige?	
HIPÓLITA	No lo sé.	
COSTANZA	¿Tú lloras?	
HIPÓLITA	Sí, madre mía.	
	Ya olvido, como mujer,	
	el ser valiente en la guerra	780
	desde que la paz probé.	
	Ya me espanta un arcabuz;	
	ya para mí no ha de haber	
	tratar en cosas de acero,	
	si no es que opilada esté.	785
	Ya me duele si me pica	
	la punta de un alfiler,	

---

769 *Sale DOÑA HIPÓLITA de mujer*: note that Hipólita was last seen on stage dressed as a man, but appears here in her women's clothing (III. 571).

783–785 *ya para mí no ha de haber / tratar en cosas de acero, / si no es que opilada esté*: Cov. defines 'opilación' as an illness common to women, but does not describe it ('opilación'). It has to do with a blockage or lack of menstruation (*DRAE*, 2nd def.). According to *Aut. 1726*, steel was administered to treat such conditions: "Remedio que se dá à los que están opilados, que se compone de acéro, de diversas manéras preparádo" ('Tomar el acéro' 4th entry for 'acero').

Everyone knows how my son is doing,
and I alone have no news of him.
My daughter is missing from the house,
I don't know what could've happened.
I will keep trying, in vain,
to reform this lawless behaviour of hers.
But here she comes; what is this?
Her feet are like lead.

Enter HIPÓLITA, in women's clothes.

HIPÓLITA   Although I took care to hurry,
I think I have arrived late.
COSTANZA   You went out without my permission?
Is this what you call honour? Lovely.
Why do you cover your face?
It must be from shame.
HIPÓLITA   Oh my dear mother!
COSTANZA   What has come over you?
HIPÓLITA   I do not know.
COSTANZA   Are you crying?
HIPÓLITA   Yes, my mother!
I now forget, as a woman,
how to be brave in war
since I have tasted peace.
Now I am frightened of a harquebus;
I shall no longer
deal with things of steel,
if they are not for women's matters.
Now it hurts me if I prick
my finger with a pin,

	y si hay sangre, será cierto	
	el desmayarme después.	
	Todo en mi pecho es ternura	790
	y todo en mi boca es miel.	
	Enferma tengo la voz,	
	y aun el corazón también.	
	Ya tengo palpitaciones,	
	remedios he menester.	795
COSTANZA	Di la causa.	
HIPÓLITA	Tengo miedo.	
COSTANZA	Di qué tienes.	
HIPÓLITA	No osaré,	
	ya cobarde y vergonzosa.	
COSTANZA	No me aflijas.	
HIPÓLITA	Oye, pues.	
	Qué bien me dijiste, madre,	800
	cuando altiva te escuché,	
	que eran los ojos traidores,	
	pues tanto lo saben ser	
	que con estar advertida	
	me engañaron. ¿Qué haré?	805
	Madre, ¡mis ojos me han muerto!	
	¡Atrevimiento cruel!	
	A don Luis inclinados,	
	tanto dellos me fié	
	que por ellos llevó el alma.	810
	¿Quién lo pudiera creer?	
	Y como donde hay amor	
	hay celos, hoy le saqué	
	al campo, muerta de celos,	
	para matarme con él.	815
	Y como al desafiado	
	le tocaba el escoger,	
	por mudarme la intención,	
	mudome el puesto también.	
	Y en un ameno pradillo	820

	and if there is blood, I will certainly
	faint right away.
	My whole heart is softness 790
	and my mouth is full of honey.
	My voice suffers from an illness,
	and my heart is unwell.
	I have palpitations,
	I need remedies. 795

COSTANZA   Tell me the cause.
HIPÓLITA   I am afraid.
COSTANZA   Tell me what's wrong.
HIPÓLITA   I do not dare;
          I am cowardly and ashamed.
COSTANZA   Do not cause me grief.
HIPÓLITA   Listen, then.
          How right you were, mother,   800
          when I so haughtily wouldn't listen,
          you said the eyes are traitors,[23]
          and they are so good at it,
          that, though I had been warned,
          they deceived me. What will I do?   805
          Mother, my eyes have killed me!
          Cruel daring!
          They inclined toward Don Luis,
          I trusted them so completely that
          he took my soul out through them.   810
          Who would have believed it?
          And because where love is found
          there is jealousy, today I took him out
          to the field of battle, dying of jealousy,
          resolved to fight him to the death.   815
          And as he was the one challenged,
          it was up to him to choose the place,
          but to change the purpose of it on me,
          he changed the place as well.
          And in a secluded meadow   820

---

23 See p. 107, Fig. 12 for a photograph of this scene in production.

donde el sol no pudo arder
por las sombras que le hacían
dos álamos y un laurel,
con tantas pintadas flores
que al más curioso vergel 825
causarle pudiera envidia;
y por lo que vi después,
fue un jardín de los de Chipre,
que allí debió de traer
amor, que milagros hace, 830
y este sin duda lo fue.
Dos arroyuelos corrían
y murmuraban; no sé
qué les obligaba entonces;
profetas debieron ser. 835
Allí, madre, allí atrevidos,
que todo amante lo es,
sacamos las dos espadas.
Yo una punta le tiré;
desviola, retirose; 840
tirele segunda vez;
hizo ganancia en mi espada;
metió el brazo, y no excusé
el quedar dél abrazada,
y el abrazarme con él. 845
Forcejamos un gran rato,
cada uno por vencer;
mas es jabón en la yerba
el rocío; resbalé,
y dando traspiés, caí 850
de mi enemigo a los pies.

823   *álamos*: see note III. 670.
828   *Chipre*: birthplace of the goddess of love and beauty, Venus (Aphrodite in the Greek pantheon).
842   *hizo ganancia*: literally, 'he made a gain', fig. 'he got the better of', 'he gained an advantage over'.
848–849   *es jabón en la yerba / el rocío*: 'the dew is like soap on the grass;' meaning that the dew made the grass slippery.

where even the sun could not shine
through the shadows made by
two poplars and a laurel,
with so many colourful flowers,
that even the most splendid orchard 825
would be driven to envy;
and from what I could see afterwards
it was a garden like those in Cyprus,
for that is where love must grow,
love which can do miracles, 830
and this, I have no doubt, is what it was.
Two little brooks ran
and babbled; I do not know
what promises they were whispering;
I'm sure they were prophets of love. 835
There, mother, there, daringly,
for every lover is daring,
both of us drew our swords.
I thrusted at him with my sword;
he parried, he drew back; 840
I thrusted a second time;
he overpowered my sword;
he took hold of my arm, I could not resist
being embraced by him,
and embracing him myself. 845
We wrestled for a long time,
each one the victor in turns;
but the grass was slippery as soap
from the dew; I slipped,
and stumbled, I fell 850
at the feet of my enemy.

                Y aun esto no fuera nada,
                pero después de caer
                hizo, ¡ay, madre!, cierta cosa,
                que nunca la imaginé.   855
                Revolviome toda el alma
                y mudome todo el ser,
                diciendo, 'para que vea,
                pues, es mujer, que lo es.'
                Creí con tal desengaño   860
                que lo soy, y ya no sé
                sino llorar tiernamente
                su ausencia; quiérole bien,
                y en efeto, madre mía,
                desde entonces soy mujer. +   865

Sale DOÑA LEONOR.

                                                                     [octavas reales]

COSTANZA   Hija, no te respondo, porque viene
                    allí doña Leonor.
LEONOR   ¡Cielo divino,
                    qué penas pasa quien cuidados tiene!
COSTANZA   Algo de que tú vengas imagino.
LEONOR   ¿Qué sabes de tu hijo?
COSTANZA   El cielo ordene   870
                    sus cosas y las mías.
LEONOR   ¿Que no vino?
COSTANZA   ¿Sabes algo, señora?
LEONOR   Algo recelo.
COSTANZA   La sangre de mis venas toda es hielo.

Sale[n] DON PEDRO y GALVÁN.

PEDRO   ¿Está el caballo a punto?
GALVÁN   Aparejado
                    está ya en el zaguán, ten confianza.   875

---

860 *desengaño*: 'disillusion', 'opening of one's eyes'. This is a key theme in Baroque Spanish literature.

+ 864–865 In P, lines 864 and 865 appear in reverse order. The lines appear in the correct order in A B and C.

And if that were not enough,
right after I fell
he did, oh mother, something,
that I never could have imagined. 855
He stirred my soul,
and changed my whole being,
saying, 'let the one
who is a woman see that she is.'
I understood, I saw so clearly 860
that I am, and now I do not know
how to do other than weep tenderly
and miss him; I love him so well,
and so, my mother,
since that moment I am a woman. 865

SCENE 3.5b

Enter LEONOR.

COSTANZA   Daughter, I cannot reply to you because
              here comes Leonor.
LEONOR   Divine heavens, why must
              those who love endure such suffering!
COSTANZA   I am just as worried as you.
LEONOR   Do you have any news of your son?
COSTANZA   Heaven ordains 870
              his matters and mine.
LEONOR   Has he not come?
COSTANZA   Do you know something, my lady?
LEONOR   I have a terrible feeling.
COSTANZA   The blood in my veins is all ice.

Enter PEDRO and GALVÁN.

PEDRO   Is the horse ready?
GALVÁN   Rigged for riding and
            in the holding area, you're all set. 875

PEDRO	Soy padre, en fin, y apriétame el cuidado, pero estoy previniendo la venganza si me matan mi hijo. ¡Ay, hijo amado!	
LEONOR	Yo tengo mucha pena.	
HIPÓLITA	Y yo esperanza de velle presto.	
COSTANZA	Mi desdicha es mucha.	880

Sale el CAPITÁN.

PEDRO	¿Qué hay, Capitán?	

CAPITÁN	Alégrate y escucha:
	sacó a Otavio don Félix en campaña,
	que ya de ser tu hijo no se corre,
	hasta pasar las márgenes que baña
	la Guerva humilde, cuando alegre corre.
	Seguilos yo con diligencia extraña,
	y donde las ruinas de una torre
	conservan, a pesar de quien la pierde,
	paredes rotas entre yerba verde,
	    llegaron, y llegué determinado
	no de valelle, porque no lo hiciera,
	ni aun viéndole matar, que soy honrado,
	si no es que con ventaja le ofendiera.
	Pero por esconderme, arrodillado
	quise ver el suceso, y no le viera
	si una abierta pared no me dejara
	sacar la vista y esconder la cara.
	    Llevaba Otavio altivo y arrogante,
	el guante como pluma en el sombrero.
	Pidiósele don Félix. 'Soy bastante
	a defendelle,' dijo, 'y saber quiero
	si me le quitas tú, porque este guante
	bien le puedes llevar, pero no entero;
	pues de faltarme fuerzas en los brazos,
	con la cabeza ha de ir hecho pedazos.'
		885
		
		890
		
		895
		
		900
		
		905

---

885 *Guerva*: this is an archaic spelling of 'Huerva', a tributary of the Ebro River, which passes through Zaragoza.

PEDRO	I am a father, after all; concern for my son grips my heart, but I must prepare myself to take revenge if he is killed. Beloved son!	
LEONOR	I suffer this most strongly.	
HIPÓLITA	And I have great hopes that we will see him soon.	
COSTANZA	My misfortune is great.	880

Enter the CAPTAIN.

PEDRO	What is it, Captain?	
CAPTAIN	Rejoice and listen: Félix took Otavio out to the field, for he is no longer afraid to act like your son, they went past where the shores are bathed by the humble Huerva as it happily runs along. I followed them closely, to where the ruins of a tower are preserved, despite that no one cares for it, where broken walls crumble among green vines, they arrived, and I was determined not to defend him, and I would not do so, even if he were about to be killed, for I am honourable, unless he was endangered by unfair advantage. So in order to hide myself, I was kneeling, and I wouldn't have been able to see but for an opening in the wall that allowed me to watch while still hiding my face. Haughty and arrogant, Otavio wore the glove in his hat, like a feather. Don Félix asked him for it, and he said: 'I believe I can defend it from you, and I would love to see you try and take it from me, you may take the glove, but not in one piece; for only if my arms fail me will the glove, like my head, end up in pieces.'	885 890 895 900 905

    Don Félix dijo entonces: 'así vengo,'
Y a Otavio le mostró el pecho desnudo.
Él replicó: 'Lo mismo te prevengo'
– descubriendo del pecho cuanto pudo –
'dese mismo metal las armas tengo,   910
que noble soy, y a lo que soy acudo.'
Y en un punto les vi desenvainadas,
como si fueran rayos, las espadas.
    Otavio se afirmó gallardamente,
pero asiole la espada, y se le arroja   915
don Félix tan furioso y tan valiente
que por un hombro desvió la hoja,
y con la guarnición, nariz y frente
le hizo pedazos, y su sangre roja,
cuando sobre la yerba dio de espaldas,   920
en rubís convirtió las esmeraldas.
    Perdió sombrero y guante, y aturdido,
perdiendo espada y todo, al cielo invoca,
repitiendo '¡No mates a un rendido!,'
con voz turbada en la sangrienta boca.   925
Don Félix le dejó; que al bien nacido
el ser piadoso por razón le toca.
Pero apenas recoge sus despojos,
cuando un ruido me llevó los ojos.
    Vi por un lado gente, y como estaba   930
atendiendo a los fines del suceso,
viéndola casi al punto que llegaba
alborotada con notable exceso,
dudando en si venía o si esperaba,
temía alguna traición, yo lo confieso.   935
Y así, ya con la sangre alborotada,
calé el sombrero y empuñé la espada.
    Pero, como ministros reconozco
de justicia llegar desalentados
con multitud de villanaje tosco,   940

937 *calé*: Here meaning 'I pulled down'. *Aut. 1729*: "Vale baxar alguna cosa para resguardarse y cubrirse, ò para otros efectos: como calar la viséra, el sombrero, &c" ('calar', 4th def.).

Don Félix then said: 'That is why I am here,'
and he bared his chest to Otavio.
Otavio replied, 'I'll give you the same warning,'
– baring as much of his chest as he could –
'I am made of the same steel as my weapons, 910
for I am noble, and I live up to who I am.'
And right then I saw them unsheathe
their swords as if they were lightning bolts.
Otavio held himself gracefully,
but Félix grabbed his sword, and threw him 915
so furiously and so valiantly,
that one of his shoulders hit the blade,
and with the cross guard he bashed his nose
and forehead into pieces, and his red blood,
when he fell on his back on the ground, 920
jewelled the emerald grasses with rubies.
He lost his hat and the glove, and was stunned,
losing his sword and all, and he invoked heaven,
repeating, 'Do not kill one who surrenders,'
with a broken voice in his bloody mouth. 925
Don Félix left him: for the well-born
are merciful as their code demands them to be.
But he scarcely had collected his spoils,
when a sound caused me to raise up my eyes.
I saw people coming, and since they were 930
watching the end of the event,
seeing the moment when there arrived
a great tumult and all in fury, and I was in doubt
whether they had just come or had been waiting,
I feared some treachery, I must confess. 935
And so, with my own blood boiling,
I pulled my hat down and readied my sword.
But, I recognized them as our justices
of the peace, arriving all out of breath
with a multitude of crude peasants, 940

	a prender a don Félix inclinados,	
	llego, y terrible soy, yo me conozco,	
	pues con solos seis golpes mal tirados	
	maté media docena de corchetes,	
	y huyeron los demás como cohetes.	945
	Escapose don Félix entre tanto,	
	y ya con honra y con salud lo espero.	
	De que llegué más presto no me espanto,	
	que soy más alentado y más ligero.	
	Pero ya viene, por el cielo santo	950
	que ha de ser acertado caballero;	
	bien merece por cosa tan honrada	
	proceder de la casa de Moncada.	
HIPÓLITA	Don Luis viene con él.	[romance u–e]

Salen DON LUIS y DON FÉLIX con el guante, [sombrero] y espada de OTAVIO.[+]

LUIS	Dichoso en hallarte anduve.	955
FÉLIX	La vitoria con que vengo	
	a tu valor se atribuye.	
PEDRO	Entra agora en mis entrañas.	
COSTANZA	Muda estoy, y muerta estuve;	
	¿vienes bueno?	
FÉLIX	Honrado vengo.	960
LEONOR[+]	Mis abrazos no se excusen.	
	Notable gusto me alegra,	

---

944 *corchetes*: 'bailiffs', 'officers'.

949 *alentado*: this usually means "animóso, valiente, resuelto, esforzado, denodado", but in this case the Capitán is saying that he is in better physical shape than Félix (*Aut. 1726*, 'alentado', 2nd def.).

+ 954 Stage direction taken from B instead of P. In P the stage direction reads: "Salen don Felis, y don Luis."

958 *Entra agora en mis entrañas*: as discussed at I. 168, 'entrañas' can be used in terms of endearment. This echoes Costanza's use of "pedazo de mis entrañas". Thus, this phrase signals the end of Pedro's threats to disown his son. Félix is now fully accepted as the true heir of his father's lineage.

+ 961 LEONOR: in all three manuscripts, Leonor is the speaker of this line. In P, this line is spoken by the Ayo. However, P has no stage direction placing the Ayo on stage, therefore the reading from the manuscripts has been adopted here. Leonor's lines 962–963 are omitted in A, B and C.

	they were determined to arrest Félix,	
	I went, I attacked with terrible fury, I know that,	
	for with only six half-formed blows	
	I killed half a dozen bailiffs,	
	and the rest of them took off like rockets.	945
	Don Félix escaped amidst all the action,	
	I expect he did so with honour and with health.	
	That I arrived before him does not worry me,	
	for I have a stronger heart and quicker feet.	
	But here he comes, by holy heaven,	950
	he has become a successful gentleman;	
	he well deserves for such an honourable deed	
	his place in the house of Moncada.	
HIPÓLITA	Don Luis is with him.	

Enter LUIS and FÉLIX with Otavio's glove, hat, and sword.

LUIS	I was fortunate to find you there.	955
FÉLIX	The victory that I achieved	
	was due to your valour.	
PEDRO	Come now into my heart.	
COSTANZA	I am mute, and I was dead with worry;	
	are you well?	
FÉLIX	I am honoured.	960
LEONOR	You'll not be excused from my embrace.	
	This great joy delights me,	

	y no es mucho que me turbe.	
FÉLIX	Este, señora, es tu guante,	
	y hasta el mesmo lugar truje	965
	a donde tú le pusiste,	
	y donde mis celos puse.	
	([FÉLIX le da el guante y] el sombrero de Otavio.)	
	Esta es la espada de Otavio,	
	con quien mi opinión compuse.	
	[FÉLIX le da la espada.]	
	Recíbele de mi mano,	970
	si tus desdenes lo sufren;	
	y perdona si al perdelle	
	tan turbado y corto anduve,	
	pues atado me tenía	
	la fuerza de la costumbre.	975
LEONOR	Con el alma le recibo	
	para ponelle en las nubes.	
	Y perdona aquellos celos,	
	porque con ellos dispuse	
	tu corazón, que era mío.	980
PEDRO	Quien el guante restituye	
	también merece la mano.	
LUIS	Pues mi hermana no la huye,	
	yo soy en ello el dichoso.	
FÉLIX	Y mis dichas se concluyen.	985
COSTANZA	Y don Luis se la dé	
	a Hipólita; pues que supe	
	que por otro desafío	
	la merece; no la excuse.	
GALVÁN	Yo tuve la culpa en eso.	990
HIPÓLITA	Y yo perdonalla pude.	
FÉLIX	¡Dicha grande!	
	¡Grande gloria!	
LEONOR	Yo la tengo.	
HIPÓLITA	Yo la tuve.	
PEDRO	Su naturaleza misma	

973 *corto*: lit. 'short', fig. 'lacking', 'incompetent'.

FÉLIX	and it isn't surprising that I'm overcome. This, my lady, is your glove, I took it from the same place where you left it, at the site of my jealousy. *(Giving her Otavio's glove and hat.)* This is Otavio's sword, and with it I reclaim my reputation. *(Giving her his sword.)* Receive it from my hand, if your disdain will suffer it; and pardon me that when you lost it I was so bewildered and fell short, because I was bound by the force of habit.	965 970 975
LEONOR	With my soul I receive it, and I make it an offering to heaven. And I beg pardon for making you jealous, for with jealousy I awakened your heart, which was mine all along.	 980
PEDRO	He who returns the glove also deserves the hand.	
LUIS	My sister will not flee from it, and I am fortunate in this.	
FÉLIX	My fortune is complete.	985
COSTANZA	And let Don Luis be given to Hipólita; since I know that he has won her in another battle; don't let him refuse.	
GALVÁN	That one was my fault.	990
HIPÓLITA	And I can forgive it.	
FÉLIX	Such blessings!	
LUIS	Great glory!	
LEONOR	I have it.	
HIPÓLITA	I had it.	
PEDRO	To their own nature	

volver a mis hijos pude; 995
de la costumbre, un milagro,
en quien más sus fuerzas lucen;
que una costumbre vencida
con otra, pone en las nubes,
con el fin de la Comedia 1000
La fuerza de la costumbre.

I changed my children back; 995
a miracle of custom,
whose power we have seen shine bright;
with one habit defeated
by another, offered up to heaven,
with the end of the play 1000
The Force of Habit.

INDEX OF VARIANTS

For this index of textual variants I have followed a slightly modified version of the system for marking alterations to the text used by the Prolope team for their editions of Lope de Vega's plays, published by Editorial Milenio at the Universitat Autònoma de Barcelona. I have also consulted Margaret Rich Greer's version of this system in her edition of Calderón's *Basta callar*, published by Dovehouse Editions. The present edition uses the following system:

<-X>	text deleted
<-?>	illegible deleted text
<-XY>	text modified by overwriting
</>	text added in the line
<\>	text added above the line
<\\>	text added in margin
<-X/Y>	deleted text altered by text added in the line
<-X\Y>	deleted text altered by text above the line
<-X\\Y>	deleted text altered by text in the margin

Headings: P is the only source with a title page. On p. 375 the heading, "COMEDIA / De la fuerza de la costumbre. / DE DON GVILLEM / DE CASTRO" appears, before the list of characters ("INTERLOCVTORES"). The First Act heading appears at the top of p. 376 and reads "IORNADA PRIMERA". | In A, the heading (on f. 1r) reads: "Comedia dela fuerça dela costumbre / salen doña costanza y don felis destudian / te–". A wide horizontal line underneath this text divides it from the first lines of the play. Other markings on the page are described in the 'Manuscript Description' section. | The heading on f. 1r in B is: "COMEDIA Famossa de la / #Fuerça de la costumbre=" followed by a wide horizontal line underneath the text, then "Sale dpña constança Y don Felix. / en auitto de estudiantte", followed by a horizontal line with two vertical slash marks in the middle, like this:
——||——
Additional markings are described in the 'Manuscript Description' section. | In C, above all text on f.2r is a short horizontal line with two vertical/ diagonal slash marks through it. The heading reads: "La fuersa de la costumbre primera jornada / felis y costansa solos d. guillen de castro". A

horizontal line across the entire width of the folio divides the heading from the beginning of the play.

Interlocutores: The cast list was omitted from A and C. P presents the following list:

INTERLOCVTORES
    Doña Gostança.
    Don Felis.
    Don Pedro de Moncada.
    Doña Hipolita.
    Vn Viejo Ayo de dõ Felis.
    Galuan lacayo.
    Don Luys.
    Doña Leonor.
    Otauio.
    Marcelo.
    Ines criada.
    Vn criado.
    Vn Capitan.

Juliá Martínez correctly adds "Un MAESTRO de armas", "Un ALGUACIL" and "CORCHETES y gente". In B, the list appears an odd place; on the last folio of the Act I gathering, right before Act II begins. It was probably copied with the first act and then inserted in the wrong place. It is also possible that the copyist created the list of characters by reading the text he was copying, and therefore added it at the end of the act. In B it is titled "figuras" and the 'Ayo' and 'criado' do not appear. A symbol similar to an underlined letter 'v' with a longer stroke on the right appears, underlined, before each character. The characters are listed in the following order:

figuras~
    Doña Costança
    Doña ypolita
    Don feliz
    Don P^o demoncada P.^{e} de don feliz
    galban lacayo
    Don luis
    Doña leonor
    ynes criada

Index of Variants 327

    ottauio
    Marçelo
    Un Capitan

Jornada primera – **Act I Variants**

0	In A and C a version of this stage direction is present but is written with the title of the play, separated by a line from the main text. In B, the title and stage direction are set off separately by lines under the text. | *Salen* : sale B | *en hábito largo*: omitted in A | *largo* : omitted in B | In C the stage direction is very brief: "felis y costansa solos".
4	pardo : largo B : <-pardo\negro> C, correction by another hand.
5	enrizado : herizado A
6	This line crossed out but visible in C. Correction <\\a la ermosa rropa i saya> in a different hand, next to line 5.
10	apenas : peñas B
12	entoldadas : <-entoldadas\adornadas> C, different hand.
13	ayer pesares, hoy gustos : ayer de pesares oy de gustos B
14	Todo en fin, todo en tu casa, : en fin mudada tu casa A
20a	<\\nouedad rrara, no sabre io la ocasion / mi señora"> other hand, C
24	con nombre y con armas, : con letras y armas B
30	que con su amparo y crianza : que en tres años de crianza A
33	gentilhombre : gentil hombre J | él de honrado y gentilhombre : el de hombrado y caballero A : ~el honrado y de gentilhombre B
34	en amores y en armas : entre amores y armas A
45	hallome : me allo C
47	cuerdamente : ciertamente A : juntamente C
50	medias A B C : media P
53	refino : paño fino B
59	al : a A
60	otra : una A| daga : banda A
61	de falda larga el sombrero : aRodillose en la yglesia A
62–65	Omitted in A
62	vuelta a la copa la falda B C : buelta la copa a la falda, P : (Omitted in A)
69–72	Omitted in A
80	que nunca en la iglesia callan : que aun en la yglesia no callan A
91	de mi calle las esquinas : las puertas de mis balcones A

92	los umbrales : las ventanas A
93–96	Omitted in A
97	en fin : pues A | el : al B
99	al : que A
102	estrecha : estraña B
105	veces : noches C
106	teniendo A B C : tiniendo P | escalalla : escala A
107	amigas : amiga A
110–111	Omitted in A
122	a : omitted in B
134	en : por A
135	dejó : deja C | boca : puerta C
136	por donde : para que A C
137	han : ha B
142a	caer : cayo A
142b	FÉLIX : change in speaker omitted in B, such that 142 is not a split line but rather Costanza continues speaking uninterrupted.
143	su : la A
144	Omitted in A
146	y : omitted in B
149	paredes : balcones A
153	su : omitted in B | envuelto : buelto A
156	Válame : Valgame A B
159	sacaron : llevaron A | muerta : muerte B
160	amenaza : benganza A : desgracia B C
163	señora : parienta A
167	la casi : acaso B
170	eres : eras A
172	callé : calle A C P : callo B
173	In A, folio 4r begins with three crossed out lines (l. 204–206) followed by line 173. The copyist must have realized he was copying the wrong lines in the wrong place and corrected himself.
174	y : omitted in A B
176	esperanzas : esperanza A
177	abuelo : A and B attest the alternate spelling 'aguelo'
180	Omitted in A
182	desgracia : des A This incomplete word in A is probably a copyist error

184	su : mi A | su : mi A
186	gozalla : gozallos A
187	estoylo : estoyle A C : omitted in B | esperando agora : esperando lo agora B : esperando aora A
189	que es sin : quesin A
193	*Abraçanse* : Omitted in C
194	gusto : gu<-stasto> <-stas//gusto> A The error "gustas" was crossed out and corrected to "gusto" both above the line and in the right margin.
195	te : <-te> A
197	la : <\la> B
198	Matarame : matareme B
198	*don Pedro de Moncada* : don pedro A | *con* : de A | *entrecana* : cana A | *doña Hipólita* : ypolita su hija A | *de hombre* : de soldado A | *un viejo AYO* el ayo A B; in C the stage direction reads "don pedro viejo muy galan de camino ypolita de ombre y el / aio <-?>". The rest of the line is crossed out and illegible.
200	o : omitted in A
201	¿Callando : llorando A
201	*Abrázanse.* : Omitted in A C. In B, "abraçanse" appears after 200, not 201.
202	¿Por qué : de que A
206	el : un A
210	nudo : A and B use the alternate spelling "ñudo"
216	*Abrázanse* : Omitted in A C. Written a line earlier, after 215, in B.
217	In P, a '9' was type-set upside-down, such that page 379 is mistakenly marked "376."
221	B changes speaker here to Costanza ('d^a. c.'). This is likely a mistake since it makes more sense if Pedro finishes his question.
225	el : al B.
226	hacen : haçe A | el : al A
227	contémplolas : contenpladas A
228	con : y con B : co<\n> C | admiro : miro B
229	Omitted in B
233	pero bien : mas raçon A | agora A B C : agota P
234	miréis : mireyes B
235	este : a este A

236	abrazalde : abraçaldo A : abraçadle B
238	tronco : ronco B | es : omitted in B
240	sobrescrito : sobreescrito A
242	ser solía. : solia ser. B
242	Omitted in A C
245a	señora : señora <-mia> B
246	y : omitted in A C
248	si no : sino A B C P 'si no' is always written as one word in P, so I will not note it henceforth | el nombre : en hom^e [hombre] B. A uses this same abbreviation in line 249.
252	para : y para B : por A
255	vio : bio A B : uio C : yio P
256	vencer : vencer y B | vencer, herir, : herir bençer A
258	lo : la A
259	Asiéntale : y sienta le A
260	le : lo A
261	C changes to the second hand here, at the top of folio 6r.
263	pues : Que es <-?> B | pelea : pelear C | lo : la B
265	tan gran : tanta A
266	más : tal C
267	cáusale : causole C
271	In C there are four lines circled and crossed out between 271 and 272, where the copyist mistakenly copied lines I. 345–348. <-d. Hipo que buenos bamos los dos / vil fortuna que haueys hecho / dpe la perdida sera mucha / si ha mi madre he de dejar> A note in the left margin reads "no es nada lo rayado."
277b	Déjame besar : dexame besar tu mano B | C writes 277b and 278 as one line: "dejame besar tus manos si no tus pies"
277	Omitted in A C
278	tu mano : omitted in B because it was added onto line 277b
279	Omitted in A C | levántase : leuantale B | DON FÉLIX : Omitted in B
282	y : omitted in A C
284a	¿Quiere : quiero B : quieres JM | de : de la B C
285	obligalle : obligar le A : obligarle B JM
288	tenelle : tenerle B
293	en : al C
296	mudara : mudase A | el : omitted in A

Index of Variants   331

298	In A three lines are crossed out after 298, the lines appear to be 299, 296 (on the bottom of f. 6r) and 297 (first line on 6v).
299	den : de C
308	y : q' [que] B
309	esa : y esa B
310	disminuye : desminuye A C
312	lego : ombre C | pihuelas : piguelas B C
314	se ha de quitar : a de quitarse C
315	En : y en B | le : lo A | ha : hazen C
316	y : omitted in B | que : porque B | así : ansi A
318	mas : <-pero\mas> C
319	Y : Omitted in A
323	Yo : y A
328	ciñéndose : mudando se A
331	ansí : asi A | podremos : podemos B
335	los : omitted in A B C | hombres cosa es : hombres cosa B : hombre es cosa C
337	id : y A | y : omitted in B | ponelde : ponedlo B : ponedle C
340	trocar con : mudar en A
341	ha : an B
345	dos! : dos A B C : dos? P
348	In C in the margin next to this line the stage direction "banse quedad. p° / y el ayo" appears.
350a	a Félix : a <-don> felis A
350b	Yo soy. : yo señor A : Yo soy <-escucha> C | In B this line is crossed out and then written again after the stage direction *350b*.
350b	Omitted in A | COSTANZA : constança y B | DOÑA HIPÓLITA : Ypolita B
350c	Escucha : <-escucha/escucha> C In C "escucha" is crossed out, then written again, and a note in the margin reads "esto vale".
352	así : ansi B
358	revienta : rebiente C
363a	di verdad : di la verdad A C
363b	Yo, señor, : <-yo señor/ yo señor> A ("yo señor" is written, crossed out, and written again on the same line in A).
365	o : a B | desdichada : desgraciada B
371	sus : se sus B
373	sirviéndola : sirbiendole A

374	An inkblot obstructs the period at the end of this line in P.
377	la verdad : las verdades A B C
378	mandas : mandes C
381	caballeroso : caballero A B | brío : sobrio A : brioso B | Verse 381 was omitted in C until a corrector added a line in between lines 380 and 382: <\tanto que puedo decir>.
382	causara : causaba A
385	previniendo : pues biniendo a B : previniendo a C
386	y : omitted in B | temiendo : temiendo a C
391	a : omitted in B
394	de : omitted in B | afeminadas : afeminadas y C
397	doncellas : doncel A The last letters of the word were cut off in rebinding.
398	o : y J
395–414	Originally omitted in A. Lines 395–398 and 403–414 were added in the margin of folio 8r with a line indicating where they should be inserted into the text after line 394 by the second hand of A. This hand also adds text in the margin on folios 8r, 10r and 12v, and copies f. 48r–49v, the final pages of the play. It seems likely that the second hand copied from a different source than that of the first hand (for more information, see 'The Present Edition'). Some of the last letters of these additions in the margin were cut off, likely during rebinding. Lines 399–402 are absent both in the main text and the text added in the margin.
400	sobre : en B
401	y cordiales : y de cordiales J
404	alcorzadas : alcorcadas C
405	lo : la B
406	C returns to the first hand here in the middle of a page.
407	En : y en A
409	el sereno : al ser A Last letters of the word cut off in rebinding.
410	Al : y al C
411	ni : y B | el sol : omitted in A or cut off in rebinding.
413	o : y A | alguna vez : algunas veçes A
414	muy : mas A
417	un : el B C
418	envolvían : enboluia C
419	cualquier : cualquiera B

425	las de su medroso pecho. : las de su madre sospecho B	medroso : amoroso A
426	pues : por A	que : omitted in B	la estampida : el estampido B
428	tocas, ropa : ropa saya A	vasquiña : vasquiñas B
429	le guardaba todo el cuerpo : todo el cuerpo le guardaba A B C
431	retumbaba : resonaua B
433	Temblaban : temblaua B
434	haldar : altar A B C
435	Ese solo es : eso es solo el A : eso solo es B
436	que : y C
437	temer : temor A
439–454	Omitted in A
439	con : omitted in B
440	podría : podia C
441	exercicios : peninencias B
442	limita : evita B
447	con : un B
455	así : al fin A	como : tomo B
458	tiene condición muy tibia : tiene la condiçion tibia A
459	es : y B
462	inaudita : inaudita A
463–464	Omitted in A
466	mía : misma B
468	honrada : honrado J
469	toda : todo B
471	la : su A
472	*Sale* GALVÁN *lacayo.* : sale galban lacayo y don felis galan. A : galvan y felis de galan C
475	has : ha B
476	me la hizo : me la a hecho A
477	mula : mucha B
478a	Omitted in A C : sale don Felix bestido de cortto B
480	aunque : aunque es B
483	los : esos A
483	Omitted in A B C
484	los : esos A
488	advierte : adbertid B
489	Omitted in A B C

493	Párate : para mas B
493	Omitted in A C
494	aquí! : aqui? P| te : omitted in B
495	así : ansi C
498	y : omitted in A
500	bueno no es J : bueno es P A B C
503	sabérsele : saberselo A
504	airoso : bueno B	desa : de A
514b	Aún : antes B
515	al : el A
516	le tienen todos : todos le tienen A
518	burlas : cosas B
519	Esto : eso A
520	*Sale doña Hipolita vestida de muger, y doña Gostança tras ella, y vn criado que saca su espada y daga.* : Sale doña costanza y ypolita dama A : Sale doña Hipolita vestida de muger, y doña Gostança tras ella, y vn criado saca una espada y daga y tropieça en los chapines y arrojalos= B : In margin: "ypolita y costansa"; and first line of f. 10v: "ypolita de dama bestida y constansa con ella" C (This line is marked as a stage direction by page-width lines above and below the text).
522a	Omitted in A B C
526	corches : corchos A B C J
529	Reniego : a reniego B
533–540	Originally omitted in A. The second hand of A added lines 533–540 in the margin, though in the wrong place, between lines 544 and 545.
533	¿Qué hay, Hipólita? Qué ha sido? : que ay ypolita linda A
534a	Omitted in A
536	vestido : vestid A Last letter of the word cut off.
537	Deste : este C : y este A
538	apretado : apretada B
539	delgado : del A Last letters of the word cut off.
540	cuello : cue A Last letters of the word cut off.
541	agora : aora A
542	mío : mio y C
543	Monstros : monstruos A B
544	nuestros : vros [vuestros] B

545	C switches back to the second hand here.
546	el : en B
549–552	Omitted in A
552	Omitted in A B C
553	me he : me C (unclear whether this means 'me' or 'me he' via allision of the syllables, though the latter certainly makes more sense in the line).
554	quedar : quedarme B
555	After 555, B adds the following stage direction: "Toma ypolita una espada a un / criado="
560	pueda despedirme : me pueda despedir B
560	*Saca la espada.* : Omitted in A C : =Saca ypolita laspada / y habla con ella= B
566	pues sería ser cruel, : cruel y poco fiel B
567	Omitted in B | y : omitted in A
570	volviese : bolbiera A
574	el trançado : estrado A
576	que, pues : pues que A | tan bien : tambien B C
577	diera modo : <-diera modo\\de otro modo> C correction in other hand.
578	con que : como A : <-con que\\pudiera> C correction in other hand.
579	y : si C
580	mudara : mudare A | género : azero B
581	mi : omitted in A : <\mi> C | perdistes : perdiste J
584	aunque : pues que A
585	y volveos : que volveros B
586	tan bien : tambien B C
591	Y así, si no : y assi sino P : <-y asi si\y si aqui> C
594	os : omitted in B
595	Yo : y B
599	dejo : <\dexo>
600	*Tomale la espada don Pedro.* : Omitted in C : Toma don P° la espada B
601	Baste : basta A B
602	y : omitted in C
603	recebilda : recebidla C
605	escuchadme : adverted A

607	luciente : baliente A
608	le : la A
613	respeto : espejo B
615	darla : dalla A C
616	vea : ve a C
617	vida que A B C : vidaque P, printing error
618	porque : pues A
620	el : en A
621–640	These two *décimas* omitted in A.
629	confesalla : confella B
635–660	Two and a half *décimas* omitted in C, meaning that the change to *redondillas* occurs at line 631, as the first four lines (631–634) of P's *décima* (631–640) serve as the first four lines of *redondilla* in C.
642	sacarla : sacalla A
643	se le atreve : sella ttiene B
645	es : el A
651	en osando : enojando A
652	el : al A | al : el A : o el B
654	matar : matar le A
655	o al : al A : o alo B | hacelle : hacerle B
661	te : omitted in B
662	C changes to the first hand here.
663	hay : oy B
663	Omitted in A B C
664	Ya : bien B | <\\ciñela>
665	oirás : oyras la A C | y : que A
668	ella A B C : elia P, printing error | así : ansi A C
669	harate : hagate A
671	dalle : darle B C
672	brazos, mano : mano braço A
672	Omitted in C : In margin next to lines 672–674: "besa / las ma / nos a su / Padre"
679	HIPÓLITA : <-d. P°\ypol.> | envidia te tengo, hermano : enbidia tengo a mi hermano A
680	Y : Omitted in B
688	tiene : tienes A | razón : valor B
694	adamado : <-amado\adamado> B

696	lucen : luçe A
698	la has : las C; this hand often joins vowels in this way ('la has' runs together into 'las').
698	Omitted in A B C
699a	así : ansi B
702a–b	Omitted in A
703	Ya me toca el darte agora : raçon es que te de agora A
704	llevar : poner B
705a	Omitted in A C : *Pruébase* DOÑA HIPÓLITA *a ponerse los chapines y no acierta.* : =Buelue a ponellos y no acierta= B
707	*Sacando la pierna descompuestamente, toma el chapín en la mano y quiéresele poner, y tiénela su madre.* : Sacando la pierna descompuestamente, prueba a ponellos y tienela su madre= B (In B this stage direction appears after v.708.) : Omitted in A C
709a	¿Qué haces, hija? : que dices A
709b	Bien, por cierto A B C : Bien por / cierto P
712	el : ay A
713–722a	In A these lines were originally omitted and later added in the margin
713	los : le A | cubrí A C : cobri P B
715	culpas que aquí : culpas aqui A B
716a	*Vuelve a querer ponerse los chapines y no acierta.* : Omitted in A C : Buelue a prouar Y no açierta B (This stage direction appears after v. 716b).
716b	Buena : linda A
718	En vano otra vez se ensaya : en vano / otra vez / ensaya A
721	In A the main text repeats line 721, which was also copied in the margin. In the main text the line reads "az efetos del galan". | del : de B
722a	Omitted in A C | *Cálzale* : Ponele B (In B this stage direction appears after line 722b)
722b	Yo : ya A B
725	tan bien A C : tambien P B
727	es en : es al A : <-al\es en>
729	que es bien que se : ques bien ques bien quese (the repeated 'ques bien' is likely a scribe error) A
730	visitas P B C : visitar A
733b–734	Omitted in B

735	Pues : Omitted in B
736	le gastas el nombre a Cristo : llegaste al nombre de Cristo A | In B, written in the margin next to 736: "suena ruydo base galban"
737	Ruido es aquel : que Ruido eraquel B | In margin in C: "espadas dentro"
738a	Omitted in C | *Vase* GALVÁN : Omitted in B | *Suena ruido de espadas y* DOÑA CONSTANZA *se pone delante de* DON FÉLIX. : In margin of A next to line 738b: "suena ruydo despadas dentro" : In B this stage direction appears after 738b: "doña costança se pone delantte de / don Felix y don P⁰ de Ypolita"
740a	¿Iré allá? : yo yre alla C
740a	Omitted in A B C
742	Omitted in A C | *Vuelve* GALVÁN, *y desnuda la espada.* : sale galban B (written in margin in B)
743	Aquí, aquí A B C : A qui aqul P (printing error) | señor : omitted in B
744	en : omitted in A B C | hasta en tu casa han entrado : hasta tu casa an llegado A
746	perdidos : por dios A
748	setecientos : seyçientos A : treçienttos B : sietecientos C
752	*Vase* DON PEDRO *metiendo mano.* : base A : vase don P⁰ B (In margin) : base d. pe C (In margin)
756	Omitted in A B C
760	In margin next to line 760 in C: "banse todos"
760	*Vanse y salen* DON LUIS *y* DON PEDRO *con las espadas desnudas, y* DOÑA LEONOR *deteniendo a* DON PEDRO. : banse y sale don p⁰ y don luys riñendo y doña Leonor metiendo los en paz A : Vanse y salen con espadas desnudas don Luys, y don Pedro y doña Leonor teniendo a don Pedro. B : don pedro don luys doña leonor galuan <-?> / todos las espadas desnudas C
762a	y : oy B
766	le : la A | tienen : tiente B
768	Suplícote : suplicote s^{ra} [señora] B | que : <\que> <\\que> A (In A, 'que' is added above the line and again in the margin)
769a	señora : omitted in B : mi señora C
769b	Señor : tente C
770	Y : Omitted in A

771	les : las C | les tengo : las guardo el A | respeto yo : yo respecto B
772	DOÑA CONSTANZA, *[y]* DON FÉLIX : don feliz y dona costança B : dona Gostança, don Felis, P | *acomete* : arremete con la espada B | *Salen* DOÑA HIPÓLITA, DOÑA CONSTANZA, *[y]* DON FÉLIX; *y* DOÑA HIPÓLITA *acomete a* DON LUIS. : sale ypolita con espada y costanza y don felis A : ypolita con espada desnuda B
773	Prueba : pruebe A
774	que : pues A
775a	Omitted in A C |*asido* : omitted in B
775b	Omitted in A C |*de* DON FÉLIX : de d Pº [de don Pedro] B (This stage direction appears after 776.)
776	estoy : estoy // B (These slash marks likely indicate a pause) : soy C
777–782	Omitted in A C
779	infelice : infelizmente B
786	pero con los ojos : con tus bellos ojos C | ojos : ojos me B
787	con mucha ventaja : y con mil ventajas C
788	Con : en A
792	ofenderme : ofenderte A B C
793	Ya A B C : Y a P (this unneeded space is probably a printing error)
794	pero : mas A | dulcemente : dulce muerte B
795	aparte C : a parte P B : y parte A
796	cansan : cansas A | ofenden : ofendes A
798	*Salen* B : Sale P A | *Salen* OTAVIO *y* MARCELO. : marselo y otabio solos C | *Esto dice a* DOÑA COSTANZA : Omitted in A B C
799	aquesto : aquello J
799	Omitted in C
809	tiene : tubo A | vuestro : este A
814a	Mi señora. : Mi señora? P : mi señora A B C
814b	*Aparte* : Omitted in A B C | Oh : a C
816	otras mil : una dos mil B
818	hubiese : biese A B
825	Hableles : abloles A : hablables B
834	solo : solas A : sola B

835	cuánto : questos (probably an allision of 'que esto es') A : quantto y B | ella : ellas B
836	blasón : balor C | engrandece : guarnece B
839	tantas : tas A | causas : ca<\u>sas <\\causas> A
840	Y aún : que aun que A
843	por : Pero B
844	el tenelle : tenerle A
850	Son excesos tus mercedes : es para mi onor y suerte A B C
851	Ya : yo A
857	usado : hablado B
859	precian de : tienen por C
861	Es Hipólita : ypolita es B
863–864	Omitted in A
863	Dadme : dame B
865	*Aparte* : Omitted in A B C | que : omitted in A
866	Contento : juelgome A
867	señor. A : señor.! P : señor B C
868	también : tanbien C
871–872	Omitted in A
871	todos : todo B
873	COSTANZA : In A the speaker designation is: dp⁰ [don Pedro]
876	por : para A
877	si quiera P A B C : siquiera J
878	acete : acepte B
880–885	*Aparte* : In P most "Aparte"s appear after the preceding line in italics.
885	Esto : este A
886	pues : que A
887	Mirad : mira B
890	Plugiera : plubiera A : plugiese C
891	en : omitted in B
892	fuera : fuese A : sera C
892+	The three manuscripts each have a colophon at the end of the act.
A:	"fin desta jornada / alabado sea el ssantisimo sacramento / amen."
B:	"fin de La Pmrᵃ Jornada".
C:	"fin de la primera jornada / laus deo et mᵉ" There are two small flourishes on the right and left of the colophon.

Index of Variants

In A the folios between Act I and Act II, 16v and 16bis (r and v), are blank except for the words "Don Guillen–J2" on 16bis(v). In B there are two blank folios between Act I and Act II.

Jornada segunda – Act II Variants

Jornada segunda : Jornada 2ª dela fuerça dela costumbre A : 2ª segunda jornada marselo y otauio solos de galanes C

1–12a	In A, Marcelo and Otavio are reversed as the speakers of these lines, for example: 1a: MARCELO : ota [Otavio]; 1b: OTAVIO : mar [Marcelo], etc.
1b–2	In B these lines are divided differently: "estremado de Hermosura / y debocion"
7a	Vistes : Oistes B
8	OTAVIO : Omitted in A. Given the omitted change of speaker, lines 7b–9 are all spoken by Otavio. This was likely an error, however, since line 10 repeats Otavio as the speaker without Marcelo having a line in between. | verémosla : oyeremos la B | los tres : despues C
11	desta : questa A
12a	*Sale* DON LUIS : don luys solo C
12b–13	In B these lines are divided differently: "que deçis de quien murmurais / los dos"
13	quién : que A C
15	Muy recién enamorado : estays muy enamorado A
16a	estáis : don luys A
16b	Y : Omitted in A B
18	niño : nuebo C | este : el A
19	vos : ti A
20	de que : que de C | aquello, de que la letra : deaquello dequella letra A
21b	entrado : enviado J
23	a no : con B
24	hubieran : ubiera A B
26	sangre : fuerça A
27	que la espada, a quien rendí : que en biendo la la rendi A
28	toda : sola B C
29b	LUIS : mar [Marcelo] A
31	lograda : logra la A

32	MARCELO : ota [Otavio] A
33	A adds "mar" [Marcelo] in the speaker column before this line.	salto : saltò P (Printing error).	ha dado : que dio C
34a	Enojado se ha. : enojado se a que digo A
34b	Omitted in A
35	MARCELO : ota [Otavio] A : maldijo : maldigo A
36	DON FÉLIX, *y* DOÑA HIPÓLITA : don felix y doña ypolita B	*Salen* DON PEDRO, *y* DOÑA COSTANZA, *y* DON FÉLIX, *y* DOÑA HIPÓLITA, *y el* AYO. : sale don·felis y ypolita de la mano y de / tras doña costanza y don pedro A : don pedro doña constansa ypolita y don felis y gente C
39a	que entrárades. : que meen trarades A
39b	Es así : ansi A : es ansi C
40	pero más quiero : mas mejor es A	agora : aora <\\agora> A
41	pues que : porque B	como : como a B
45-6	In B these lines are divided differently: "aun no açierto / enseñame (aparte)"
45	enseñareme : enseñame B
46	*Aparte* : Omitted in A C
49	*Aparte* : entranse A : Omitted in B C	toda A B C : to da P
49	Omitted in A B C
50	PEDRO : ota [Otavio] A	In margin in C : "vanse queda otauio / y marse y don luys"
52	quitarse : quitalle A ; <\\lee> A	Between lines 52 and 53, B contains the stage direction "van pasando y dona ypolita haze como q' se ba a quitar el sombrero y banse"
57	verlo : vello A C
60	serlo : sello A C
61	viene : le vien J
63	fuerzas : cosas B C
66	más : ni B
67	y : ni B
68a	puede : puedan B
68b	Extraña cosa : cosa estraña B
71	en un ojo : en<\tre> el ojo A; <\\entre> A ("tre" is written above "en" and "entre" is written in margin to clarify)
72	se le : y se A
77	OTAVIO : Omitted in A. As above, there is no change of speaker

	indicated at this point in A. However, this appears to be a mistake since at line 85 "mar" [Marcelo] is given as the speaker, but this would be redundant if Marcelo had been speaking since v. 68b
79	Omitted in B
80	bebiendo : viniendo B
82	tanto : quanto B | tanto a curarse : tan a hurtarse A
84	y : omitted in B | ya : omitted in A
85	un encanto : encantado B
87	ocasión : baron C
88	eso : esto B
89	MARCELO : Omitted in A
90	della : dellas B : de ella C | pueden : puede A
97	Dellos : de ellos C | contar : decir A
98	extremadas : muchas cosas C
99	muchas cosas : estremadas C
100	fábula : fabulas A | lugar : mentir A
102	Y : yo B
103	Háblase : Hablan J
106	Talle me : talle B : y talle C
107	que por daros un : por daros en un B
108	os dará : en buelta B
109	doy : da B
113	A : q' a [que a] C
117–120	Omitted in A
117	el : al B
121	esto : esto y A
124	que : quien B
125	y : ya A | que a tantos : que <\a> tantos A ; clarification in margin: <\\queatan> A
128	dejo : dexolo B | esperanza : esperiençia A
129	aunque : aun A
130	regalos : criados B | tan mal : bozal A
132	lucirá : bivira A
134	saber : hablar B
135a	voy : bas A | In margin of B: vase don luis : In margin of C: vase luys
135b	Omitted in A B C
137	porque hablaste : pues hablas tan B

139	Omitted in B
143b	Y : Omitted in B
144	amor : amor–banse A | In margin in C: "/vanse los dos"
144	*salen* : sale B | *Vanse, y salen* DOÑA COSTANZA *y* DOÑA HIPÓLITA. : salen ypolita y doña costanza A | constansa y ypolita solos C
146	que : y C
149–184	Omitted in A
154	quisiere verá : quisieres versa B
159	COSTANZA : In B, "d.c." [doña Costanza] was written at line 160. This mistake was corrected with a line from "d.c." to line 159
181	cuanto : tantto B
182	te : omitted B
192	aficionaba : aficionaria B | el : al A
198	quise miralle mejor : es fuerça tenelle amor A
201	mas no, por Dios, con cuidado : mas por dios no lo he mirado A
202a	de : como A
202b	Así : yo A
203	mas : que A
204	presupuestos : presupuesto A
207	Plega : Ruego B
208	si : en mi B
211	Mas ya : si mas C | Mas ya no basta en el mundo : si mas no bale en el mundo A
212	limpieza : pureza A
216	en : omitted in C
217	traime : traedme B : dame A
218	esta : una A | After 218, B adds this stage direction: "sientase ypolita y traen una almoadilla / de lavor ynoaçierta a asentarse como / mug'. descubiertos los pies y piernas / y su madre llegue y cubrala"
221a	Recoge : recoged B | Recoge los pies. : sientate hija A
221b–222	In B these lines are written as one: "a Reniego de quien me pusso a mug"
222	a : omitted in A
225	*Alarga las piernas descompuestamente* : Omitted in A : Buelue a sacar los pies y su madre los tapa B

Index of Variants

226a	¡Jesús! : Jesus no bes asentadas / algunas en almoadas A | In margin of A : "sacanle una almoadilla"
226b-7	Omitted in A
227	y : <-y> C J
228	COSTANZA : ypo [Hipólita] A
228	*Salen* DON FÉLIX *y* GALVÁN. : Sale don Felis, y Galuan. P : sale galban y don felis A : Galban lacayo. B : galban y felis C
229	tu padre : mi s' [señor] B : mi señor C
233	In B, "besa la mano." appears in the margin to the right of line 233
234	Hijo : Omitted in B
237	esto : aquesto C
239	Pues es cosa : pues es cosa <-de yngenio> B
241–264	In A, folio 21v returns to this point a page late because an entire folio was copied out of order. Folio 21r contains lines 265–292, and the following page, 21v, contains 241–264. The first line on 21v (v. 241) is only readable as "ylos cojiste aora" because the corner at the top of the page is torn, leaving part of the line missing. The physical pages do not appear to be out of order, it rather seems that the text was just copied in the wrong order. This could possibly have been the reason for the addition of the half folio here.
241	FÉLIX Más : In A, the speaker designation and first word of this line were lost with the top corner of f.21v or were omitted. | agora : aora A
242a	lo justo : los justos A
244	In B, the stage direction "Toma el almoadilla don Feliz como / mug' a labrar" is added between 244 and 245
246	Válame : balgame A C : valgame B
247a	GALVÁN : Omitted in C | ¡Qué bien te sientas! : así <-?> te asientas C
247b	HIPÓLITA : gal/ [Galván] C
248	GALVÁN : Omitted in C
251	eres : lo es B
253	Quita : quite C
254	nada : ronada B (unclear meaning, likely a mistake)| In B, the stage direction "lebantase ypolita y arroja la almoa / dilla" is added between 254 and 255

258b	Si no lo sabes : saues emplease B
259	empléate : omitted in B
260	de P : omitted in B : mas A C
262	Ah : ay B
264	o : v [u] B
265–267	Omitted in B
266–267	Omitted in A
267	*Salen* : sale B	*Salen el* AYO *y el* MAESTRO DE ARMAS. : Sale un maestro de armas A : Omitted in C
268	Omitted in A
269	This line is divided differently in B and C: sientate / y mas reportada B : costan/sientate / felis/y mas reportada C
272	Between lines 272 and 273, C presents the stage direction "el maestro de armas con espadas desgrima".
273	Gusta : gustas B
274a	vuesamerced : señor B
276	Aprende : aprended A
278	sácala : sacalla B	briosamente : baronilmente C
279	Between lines 279 to 280, B contains the stage direction: "Saca mucho el pie y estiende todo/ el braço"
280	brazo : brasa C
282a	In B, the following stage direction appears between 282a and 282b: "Toma la espada a don feliz / ypolita"
285	y : q' [que] B
287	tan bien como B C: tambien como P : mejor que no A
288	con brío : omitted in B
288	Omitted in A B C
289	Se mete : si metto B
293b	Sea así : seansi [sea ansi] B
296	viene mi padre : mi padre viene C
298	Que : pues A	hubiera : uvieras B
299	contigo : consigo B : con ella C	hubieras : hubiera A
300	*Sale* DON PEDRO. : Pedro solo C
301	aquello : aquesto B
302	insistes : resiste A : asistes C
305–308	This *redondilla* omitted in A
308	pudiera dalle la : le pudiera dar la B
311	o : y C

314	atrás : tras B | mil : mile B
317	briosa : brioso C
321–324	This *redondilla* omitted in A
322	destas : de estas B
323	serán : son B
325	ésta : estas J | si : se A
328	cualquier caballero B C : qualquier Cauallero P : qualquier <-cosa> caballero A
329–332	This *redondilla* omitted in A
332	reñid : Roni B
334	Line broken into two lines in B, between "herida" and "muy".
335	No : Omitted in A | regir : Re<-ferir\gir> B
336	In B between 336 and 337: "Deshase desayradamt^e".
339	Dalde : dale B | veré : bereys A | se : le B | In margin after 339: "dale" A : Between 339 and 340a in B, "dale el maestro un golpe y/ quexase="
342a	¡ve a vengarte! : bengate A | Between 342a and 342b in B: "Toma la espada doña ypolita y / aporrea el maestro"
342b	COSTANZA : ypo [Hipólita] A
346	escusará : librara C
347a	Detente : tente <\mi> C
348	In margin in A: "base el / maestro"
350	ay : omitted in C | hija A B C : hijo P | mis ojos : mi vida B
354	extrañas : estrañes B (this is likely a scribe error since "estrañes" does not fit the rhyme scheme) | ¿Que te encoges? ¿Que te extrañas? : hijo ynfame que te estrañas A
359	PEDRO : Omitted in B | vileza : tristeça B
360	Qué : y con B
362	vilezas con que me afrentes? : tal bileza con que afrentes A
364	llegó mi sangre a : llego a mi sangre A
366	dónde : donde donde C | y : omitted in B
367	gran casa : grandeza A
368	por : sus A
371	Pedros : prados A : <-pedros\\pardos> C, other hand | Ramones : montones B
378	veas : be<-ras\\as> A : This word is unreadable in B due to damage to the bottom corner of folio 13r.
380	tus : sus J | ascendientes : desçendientes A

384 des : de A
385 O : y C
388 retirado en : retirate a B
390 daño : mal B
391 In A, this line added in margin with a line indicating insertion between 390 and 392
398 suele A B C : suelo P
399 al : el A
400 hirviendo : y en biendo B
401 y ejecutará : exercitara B : y executaré J
406 In A, the speaker designation "dPo" [don Pedro] appears at the beginning of 406, changing speaker a line early
409 el : del B
411 es : es tan B
412 le : la B : lo J
414 nos P : me A B C
415 y : omitted in A B
418 se : lo A
419 le : lo A
420 nos : le B
421–424 This *redondilla* omitted in A
421 infundirte : infundirle B
423 todo, he de probarte : todos estos base B
425 Fundallo : fundarlo C
426 In A in margin after 426: "a milanes"
429 GALVÁN : <-gal\ayo> A
430 In A the speaker changes at 430 to "dpo" [don Pedro]. | deso: de eso A B | llenos : <-menos\llenos>, <\\llenos> A ("menos" was originally written instead of "llenos," then crossed out. "llenos" was then written in the same hand both above the crossed out word and in the margin)
431 éstos : eso A : esos B C | la : lo A
432a FÉLIX : <-gal\ayo> A | ¿Menos? : <-oye lo beras/menos> A
432b y : omitted in A | In margin of B: "Toman las espadas"
433 tiéndete : tiende este A
434 esta espada a mi despecho : con esa espada en mi pecho B
435 Puesto : puesta A B C | vista : vida A | al : a el A
436 matarme A B C : matarm P (printing error)

437	Pues : Omitted in B | cierto : facil B
438	peligro en la ofensa : peligro <-el ofensa\\en la ofensa> A
439	y que es la misma : de la bida y que es A
441	al : el B
445–448	This *redondilla* omitted in A
449	si es más : si mas A : si el B | más, ¿le alcanza y hiere? : cosa verdadera C | hiere : <-mira\\yera> A
450	qué : omitted in B
451	la espalda : las espaldas B
452	vergonzosamente : afrentosamente A : vergonçossa muerte B | muere : muera C
454	hubiera : tenga B
457	AYO : ypo./ [Hipólita] C | Qué : si A
458	GALVÁN : speaker designation omitted in A, meaning that in A lines 457–460 would all be spoken by the "Ayo." | desa : de la A : de esa B
461	en ti : entiende B
462	de : omitted in A
463	Omitted in B
466	pones : <-estoy\\pones> A : as puesto B
467a	honra : sangre A
467b	Tus razones : tus razones mucho <-me animan s'> B
468	mucho : omitted in B
469	hacer : fazer B
470	verme : estar C | In margin of B: "aparte"
471	PEDRO A B C : Fed. P (printing error)
472	le haré perder : podre quitarte A
475	he de : puedo B
476	un : vos B
481	*Aparte* : Omitted in A B C : Appears after 480 in P
483b	Logra : logre B
486	el : tan C
488	entre tantos : quien tiene A C
489	quitárselos : quitar çelos B
491	In B, "banse" appears between 491 and 492a.
492b	In margin of A after 492b: "banse"
492b	*Vanse, y salen* OTAVIO *y* MARCELO. : salen otabio y marçelo A : salen marçelo y otauio = mar. B : marselo y otauio solos C

494–496a These lines divided differently in C: " es angel doña leonor en todo / de enamorado estoy loco". C changes to the 2nd hand in the middle of line 494, at "en todo".
496b menor : mayor A
499 valí : valgo B
501 MARCELO : Omitted in A at 501, instead appears at 502.
502 cantara : tañera A
502 Omitted in C | *en la ventana* : omitted in A
503 LEONOR : "Cantan" appears in the speaker column in C, thus specifying that these verses be sung, though not by whom. | negros : bellos A
504 por qué : de que A C
505 agrada : agrauia C
507–518 Omitted in C
508–518 After line 507, A presents 3 lines which do not appear in P and lacks 10 lines of P's version of the song. A's version of 508–510 is as follows: "no es raçon que ansi lloreys / que lagrimas de esos ojos / a un risco pueden mober".
511 Mas : más J
512 y : que B | es : omitted in J
513 hacer : hazed B
515 pero : omitted in J
519 es del cielo : del cielo es C
520 en : con B
522 escuchan : escuchando B
523 seréis : seruis B | por quien hizo : aqui/v/ enotra p^{te}. B
524 ojos : ojos son B
525 que : omitted in A | así : lo C
527–536b Omitted in A
527 cerrado : abierto B
528 en : omitted in B | congojo : encojo B
528 Omitted in C
529–536b Omitted in C
532 poco : poco saliste B
533a subiste : omitted in B
533b Señora llama. : no puedo mas B
534 B deviates from P here, with the following two lines replacing 534: "Mar: escucha / yn al momento torno" ("yn" = Inés)

537a	In A and C, this line is spoken by Marcelo ("mar"). | vamos : omitted in B
537b	MARCELO : ota [Otavio] A C | In margin of A: "–banse"
537b	*salen* : sale B | GALVÁN : Caluan P : y galuan B| *otro* CRIADO : dos criados | *Vanse y salen* DON PEDRO, GALVÁN *y otro* CRIADO. : sale don pedro y criados y galban de noche A : Don Pº y Galban C
539	aquesta : aquella J
544a	Fabio : fabriçio B
547b	ésta : ella J
549	allá : aqui A : ella B J
551	seré : dicho sere A (Given that 'dicho' adds excess syllables to the line, it is likely an accidental repeat of "dichoso" in the previous line.) | In A line 551 is the first on folio 26r, which contains a vertical tag, "La fuerça de la Costumbre = 9011" (or possibly "90CC") which runs lengthwise along the outside edge of the text, written in a different hand.
551	*con espada y broquel* : omitted in A C : con broquel y espada B
556	de : desta B
557	In margin in A: –base : In margin in C: vasse : In B between 557 and 558: vase don Pº [Pedro]
558	Omitted in A B C
561	he salido : e sa<-?/lido> A
563	o : ni A : v [u] B | en tierra : <\en> tierra A
564	pedregoso : peligroso A : pedragoso C
565	el : omitted in A C | debe : debe de A
566	tantas : tan<-?/tas> A
567	de estar : destar A
568	estrados solos : estrados solo A : entre dos soles B
569	casi me : a<-n>si me A : asome B
570	o : u A
571	con : en B
572	acostumbrados A B C J : acombrados P (printing error)
573	entre : en B
575–578	Omitted in A
577	pareció : pareçe B
579a	*pañuelo* : paniçuelo B | y mete mano : mete mano y acuchilla a don felix hasta que el haze arrimar a la pared y sale a la bentana

	doña Leonor ynes criada suya= B | Sale DON PEDRO *mudado de capa y con un pañuelo en la boca, y mete mano*. : sale don p° con capa diferente A : Don pedro solo sale C (This stage direction appears in the margin next to line 579a in C).
579b	Si salgo : sile saco <-buen> B
582	tuyo : suyo B
582	Omitted in A B | *Salen al ruido a la ventana* DOÑA LEONOR *e* INÉS. : sale D. Leonor a la bentana C (This stage direction appears in the margin after line 582).
583–584	Omitted in A
583	Si : Omitted in B
584	cielo : cielos C J | selde : sedle B | piadoso : piadosos C J
585	podré : pode B | ¿Por dónde podré escapar? : balga me el cielo que hare A
587	en : omitted in C | matarame : matareme A
589	Omitted in A C | *Vase retirando* DON PEDRO *y éntrase huyendo*. : Tirale don Felix cuchilladas a don P° como no puede huir y vye don P°= B
591	In A between 591 and 592b appears the stage direction: "sale doña Leonor a la bentana".
593–594	Omitted in A
598	hirieron A B C : hizieron P
599	Omitted in B | *Sale* GALVÁN *y otro* CRIADO. : sale don pedro y criados A : salen P.° y Galban C
600–602	Omitted in A
601	Omitted in B
602	Omitted in A B C
603	Pues, ¿con la espada desnuda, : bes con la espada en la mano A
604	señor : señora A | Acá : aqui B
605b	Sí, señor : s˜ si [señor si] B
608	Huelgo : huelgome B : gusto C | animoso : a<-si moço\nimoso> B
610a	huyó A B C J : huy o P (printing error)
614b	lo : los B
615	no : omitted in A
616	el que : quien A
619a–620	Omitted in A
620	me le : del B

Index of Variants

622a	que voy : questoy A
623	De que : porque C
624	B assigns this line to Pedro ("d Pº")
627	yo : le A
628	Omitted in B | In margin in A: –banse : In margin in C: vansse
628	*Vanse y* : Omitted in A C : vanse B | MARCELO *y* OTAVIO : otabio y marçelo A : octauio y marçelo B
633	medido : medrosso B | concertado : contestado J
634a	tienes : tiene A
634b	podría : podia B
637	la : omitted in B
639	estuve celoso : estube <-?> çeloso A
641	así, aunque : a ti que A
642	como : aunque A
643	aun no puedo : no dejo de A : no puedo B
644	Omitted in A
645	Al : <-a\e>l C | hombre en : ombre-aun C
648	querrá : que era B
651a	el : al A | nuestro : mio B
653–654	OTAVIO : Omitted in A. Since there is no change in speaker in A until verse 657, lines 651b–656 would all be spoken by Marcelo | In P the speaker Otavio ("Ota.") is repeated both in line 653 and 654; this is unnecessary since the lines are only separated by a stage direction.
653	Omitted in A C : Appears in B between lines 655 and 656
655	At this line, A repeats "mar" [Marcelo] even though this is unecessary since he is the speaker of the preceding lines. This suggests that the copyist may have omitted a change of speaker in the preceding verses.
656	MARCELO : Omitted in A (in preceding line) | Grande : gran A B | infinita : omitted in A B | In A, this line is split between Marcelo and Otavio, thus adding "ynfinita" as the first of Otavio's next three lines.
657	Su : <-lo> su C | en : es A
658	In margin of C : "a la bentana Leonor y hipolita" | In A, between 658 and 659: "sale a una bentana ypolita y doña leonor"
661	holgara : holgare A | pisalle : ocupalle A C
664	este : el B

665   congojada : aqui aogada A
666   Omitted in A
669   MARCELO : otab [Otavio] A | C changes back to the first hand at this line.
670   OTAVIO : mar [Marcelo] A
671   el aurora A : el Aurora P : laurora B C
674b–675 These lines are written as one in B.
677   su centro : diuina B
679   baja : baxa a B
680a   ya es este : ya es <-te> es<\te> C
682   la : le B | tiernamente : tier<\na>mente C
688   MARCELO : Speaker designation omitted in A, so Hipólita speaks both lines 687 and 688, which is likely a mistake since 688 makes more sense as a response to 687, as in P.
689   sería el matarte : se<-ria matar\\ria matarte> A | el : omitted in A B
691   pocos deseos : poco desseo B
693   Omitted in B
699   Y : Omitted in B
701   y : omitted in B : que C | y aunque es en : que ese es A
702   te : le C | dejar : dejar <-la ermosura> C
703   esa quiero : es ajena A
706   dilatas : dilates B
707   hay rayos en : son rayos C
708   desde : dasde B
708   *Salen* : sale A | *Salen* DON FÉLIX *y* DON LUIS. : Don Feliz y don Luis salgan B : don luys y don felis solos C
710b   C switches to the 2nd hand here.
711   *Aparte* : Omitted in A B C
712   A and B assign this line to "mar" [Marcelo]
713   brasas toco : omitted in A
718   habello : auella B
719   y : yo A : ya B : omitted in C
720   hiciste : hizistes B
724   FÉLIX : d luy [don Luis] A
725b   LUIS : mar [Marcelo] A
726   esta : este A
728   dos estuviera A B C : dos lo estuviera P

Index of Variants 355

729	FÉLIX : d luy [don Luis] A | pudiéraisla : pudieradesla A : pudierayslo C
730b	LUIS : Omitted in A
732	proprio nuestro : por premio A | las : los A B
734	acabado : alcançado B
735b	He : a A
740	hermana : hermano A
742	es llana : clara C
744	porque : ber que B
748	Ni : Omitted in B
749–750a	In C these lines were written as one. A slash mark '/' divides the line.
749	Eso : ese B
750a	decillo : decirlo C
750b–751a	In B, these two lines are written as one.
751b	MARCELO : ota [Otavio] A | Nadie : nayde B
753	ofenda : canse A | In margin of B: "asesele el puño"
754	trenza : tranca A : traza B | del : de el A
757a	traje : tajo A
759	Congójame : congojeme A : congojome B | el esperar : desperar B
760	ha : e A B C
761	Omitted in A C | *Cáesele el puño.* : quiere desatarlo doña Leonor ypolita / lo rompe y abaxanse por el mar / çelo y don Luis y cogele marçelo= B
763	calle : tierra A | la : el C
765a	HIPÓLITA : d leo [doña Leonor] A
765b	LEONOR : ypo [Hipólita] A | recelo : reciclo C
768	ha dado : dio A
769	lo espera : lespera A : la espera B
770	Y : pues A
773	esa : hera A
775a	tuya : vra [vuestra] A
776	Pues no : ni yo C | le : la B | dar A B C J : da P (printing error)
778	le : lo J | sabes : puedes A
779	Si : y si B
780	defendelle : defender A : defendella B
781a	In margin of C: "vase". | In B, there are two separate stage

	directions between 781a and 781b. The first reads, "Base marçelo enpuñando la espada y / don Luis sueltase de octauio y base / tras marçelo". The second says "caese un guante a doña Leonor y alçala / don feliz y quitasela octauio y / quiere meter mano don felix y no / puede".
781b	Soltadme : dejadme A B
783	tengo de quitalle : quele he de quitar B
783	*Vanse.* : banse los dos A : Omitted in B
784a	Hermano, ¡llega! : llega tu hermano A	C changes to the first hand here.
784b	cuitada : cuytada <-el guante> A
784b	Omitted in A B C
785	Dicha he : d ha B (this may be an abbreviation for something, or may also simply be a mistake).
787	dicha : d ha B	y : omitted in A C
787	Omitted in A B
788b	Eres : no eres B
789	A assigns this line to "d fe" [don Félix] here, instead of changing speaker at 790a.	y : omitted in A B
790a	FÉLIX : Omitted in A
791a	Omitted in A	In margin of B: "no puede sacar la espada"
791b	Omitted in A
795	tire : tiene A	para poder : para<-?> poder A
797	debe : a B
798	Between 798 and 799a in A: "sale don p° y este escuchando"
801	pues : que B C
802	tendrá : tendra la B
803	In margin of A : "–base"
803	*Sale* DON PEDRO *a la puerta.* : Omitted in A : vase octauio sale don P° B : don pedro asomado al paño escuchando lo que a pasado C
804	A designates "ypo" [Hipólita] as the speaker of this line.	Qué le pudo : questo puede A : questo pudo C
805b	FÉLIX : ypo [Hipólita] A
806	HIPÓLITA : Omitted in A
808	In margin of A: "–base ypolita"	In margin of B: "vase"
808	Omitted in A B C
814	saliera : salieras B

Index of Variants 357

815	mi : el A B C
820	ni vuestra : vuestra B
821	válame : balgame A B C
822	cobarde : gallina A
824	Ya : Yo A
827	defendierais : defendierades A B
828	quizá el merecer : que merecierays A
831	que es : Pues B | falta el : culpa A
833	Omitted in A B C
834	Estas : esta B | poner : tener A
835	a ser yo más : yo a ser tan A
836	para vos : aquestas no A
838	Omitted in C | In margin of A: "arrojale unas / plumas y base"
840	tente : detente B
840	Omitted in A B C
848	cuanta sangre tienes mía! : la sangre que tienes mia/vanse C
848	DOÑA HIPÓLITA : ypo [Hipólita] B | *el* : y el B | *Vanse y salen DOÑA COSTANZA, DOÑA HIPÓLITA, el* AYO *y* GALVÁN : base don p° tras el con la daga y sale doña constanza teniendo a ypolita y al balcon doña leonor y el ayo A : costansa y ypolita y galuan y otro C
852	Omitted in B | Llegad : llega A
853a	Aparta : apartad A | viejo : vosottros B : loco C | In B between 853a and 854: "da a galban y al ayo demogicones"
853b	Omitted in B
854	fuerzas invencibles son. : yntolerables son tus fuerças B
855	GALVÁN : Omitted in C
856	Omitted in A B C
857	Pluguiera : y pluguiera B : plubiera A | al cielo : a dios B
859	no : que no B | hicieras : quiebras B
860–863	Omitted in A
860	Omitted in B
861	que : pues C
862	tomarémela yo : tomare mi lacayo B
862	Omitted in C | *un criado* : la çinta ypolita a / galban B
863	Omitted in A C
864	A assigns this line to "dcos" [doña Costanza] | Tenelda, doña Leonor. : tened la señora bos A

358   *Index of Variants*

867   *Sale* DON FÉLIX *huyendo de* DON PEDRO, *y él con la espada desnuda tras él.* : sale don p° tras don felis A : felis y don pedro C
868   Señor, ¿qué haces? ¡Señor! : señor señor que hazes B | In B between 868 and 869: "Recogese don felis con su madre y / dona ypolita en contra con su Padre" B
869   He de quitarte : e te de quitar A
870   Y : Omitted in A B | In B this line is divided into two, with the line break between "hijo" and "por que".
878   hacella : açello A : a ella B : aserla C
879   pide : dije B
880   si alguno : si que alguno J (source unknown)
881   hiciese, imposibilita : que se ynposibilita A : biese ynposibilitada B
882   el : de A B
883   troquéis de : mudeys los A
885   pondrele una : ponerle <-a> B
886   así : ansi B
891b   LEONOR : d fe [don Félix] A
892b   Y : Omitted in A
894   afrentado : afrentadas B
894 *Sale* : Omitted in C | *bañado en sangre* : omitted in A C | *Sale* DON LUIS *con el puño bañado en sangre.* : sale con el puño baynado en sangre / don Luis B
896   brazo : mano A
897   perdona si : perdonaras B
898   mudalle : mudalla B
899   quitalle : quitalla B
900   atrevida : atrevidamente B | le : la A
903   Y a estar : ya estas B | ella : ellas B
905   en : y en A : v en B : <-?> en C | de un : de<-l\un> C
906   o : y A | en : un B
909   Tómale : tomela B | tenle : tenme B : ten<-le\me> C
910   Tómole : tomolo C
912   tu : su A
913   rey : Reyna B C | este puño : esta sangre A
914a   esta sangre : este puño A
917   agrada : bale A

920	Esta : en tu A
921	alma : pecho A
923	indigno : indino C
925	cortalle : cortarle A
927	o has : os he B
934	invidia : en bida A
936	ha : e A : an B
937	vergüenza mía : colera mira A
939	retirado : etirado B | en : a B C
942	que : que de B | corrió : agrabio A
948	a todo el : el mismo A
949	pondré : pondre en A
950	vapor : color A : pauor B
951	picado : <-picado\mordido> C
953b	AYO : d cos [doña Costanza] A | Señor, tente. : Tentte s' [señor] B : tente hijo A
954	reportado : reporta A
956	Tenelde : tenedle A B
959	hayan : aya A B | tenga : tengan B
960	Valdrele : baldrale A | pues tuyo : yo pues tu B | Between 960 and 961 in B is a crossed out line: <-fe Pues tu estoy nay>
961	Nadie : nayde B
963	brios : brio A
964	los : lo A
964	The manuscripts contain end-of-act colophons similar to the ones in Act I. In A: "fin desta jornada / alabado sea el santisimo sacramento / amen." In B: "fin de la 2a / Jornada", followed by a rubric. In C: "fin de la segunda laus deo et m^e" followed by a rubric.

Jornada tercera – Act III Variants

Jornada tercera : Jornada 3ª de la fuerça de la costumbre / salen don pedro y don felis A : Acto Terçero de la Fuerça de la Costumbre = salen don P° y don Feliz B : tersera jornada don pedro y don felis solos C

0	This stage direction appears within the Act heading in the manuscripts.
1	El : Omitted in B
2	tomarla : tomalla A C

3	disminuye : diminuye B : desminuye C
4	antes : que antes A
6	hoy : agora B | ha paseado : se ha hallado B
8	estima : tiene A B C
13	así : ansi A B
18	cosa es : es cosa B
20	alborota : alborote C | una : la A B
24	o algún : <-?\o> algun A; <\\o al> A
25	el : vn B
27	quede A B C : que de P
28	como causa : sin causa y B
30	esta : este A B | en : a A
31	Y : Omitted in A
32	a : omitted in C
39	importe : importa B
40	yo : omitted in C | tú mandes : tu mand<-as\e> <\\des> A : tu me mandas B
41	Tú solamente : de aquese balor C
43	han : a B
44	quedar vengado : bolber homrado A B
45	Pues : que A B C
46	en temeroso has de dar, : es muy claro de alcançar B
47	y : que B | nunca : nadie A
48	quien : si A
49–60	These three *redondillas* omitted in A.
49	tu : su B
53–68	These four *redondillas* omitted in C.
57	teniéndole : tiniendola B
61	al que es : a ti A B
62	le : te A B
65	el querer : querer A B
68	han : a A
69	tal : el B
71	cerrando : heRando A : echando C
74	In B between 74 and 75: "sale don luys y el Capitan".
76	In B appears after 74| *Salen* : sale A | *Salen* DON LUIS *y el* CAPITÁN. : el capitan y don luys C
78–79a	honor : honor benis B (In B 78 and 79a are written on one line).

Index of Variants 361

79a	In A, between 79a and 79b: "sentaos"
80	propria : mia B
81	la : esta A B	porque a mi : que mi A B
87	se vengara : le cobrara A B
88	vengar : cobrar A
89	agora : es lo que A B
99	él : omitted in A
100	mas : que B
101–112	Three *redondillas* omitted in A
107	con : de C	propria : propia C
111	y : v [u] B C
113	El : Y e</l> <\\y el> A
119	Y : Omitted in B	o : y A : v [u] B	perdido : ronpido A B
120	dél : de el C
122	que : omitted in B
126	pagar : cobrar A
133	meta : mete A B
135	justicia : ynjusticia B
138	que : omitted in C
144	lejos : y lejos C	verse : ser C
145	mejor : raçon A B
149	emplace : enplazar A
150	podrá con : llebando yo A B
151	A assigns this line to "d pº" [don Pedro].	acete : acepte B
153–169a	These four *redondillas* are omitted in A
158	presencia : prudencia B
165	C changes to the second hand here.
169b	Haga una cosa : aora bien haga una cosa A
170	que : omitted in A
171	billetes : papeles A
174	In A this line (and line 175a) are assigned to "d po" [don Pedro].
175a	FÉLIX : Omitted in A	la : le C	espero : escucho A B
178	en hallando : biendo solo A : en topando B
179	le saca : sacalle A : La saca C
180	que no impidan : donde encubra A	impidan : sepa B
181	y en un lugar apartado : y alli de tu esfuerço armado A B
182	donde : sin que A B
183	quítale : quitalle A	o : y A

184	PEDRO : Omitted in C | Así volverás : y assi quedaras C
185	C assigns this line to "p"" [Pedro].
186	pecho : pechos C | abierto : ynserto A
187	sepa : sepan C
192	en : omitted in C
193a	CAPITÁN : d lui [don Luis] A : d.L. [don Luis] B
193b	LUIS : cap [Capitán] A B
194	dos : omitted in A
197a	Adiós, hijo. : ea señores a dios A
197b	Omitted in A
197b	Omitted in A B C
199b	está entendido : te entendido (most likely this should be read as [te he entendido]) A C : te he entendido B
200	Perdonadme : perdonad mi A : perdoname B
200	After line 200, P presents the stage direction "Vase," which was omitted in A, B and C.
203b	In B between 203b and 204: "Banse y queda solo don Luis"
204	Buena ocasión : braba ocasion A | buena suerte : braba suerte A : braua suerte B
204	DOÑA : omitted in C | *Sale* DOÑA HIPÓLITA. : banse y queda don luys y sale / ypolita A
209–216	Two *redondillas* omitted in A B
217	Ay cielo, el alma me : ~Jesus el alma se A B
218	Pues : Omitted in B | este : aqueste B
218–219	In A lines 218 and 219 appear in reverse order.
221	venido : bençido A
222	tiernamente : solamente A B
224	cobrar lo : a ber el bien A B
225	esto, a mí : eso bos A B | <-?\\y siendo ansi a mi aseys> C This correction is written in a third hand above an entire line which was crossed out
226	y soislo vos : <-?/soys lo bos> C
227	Válame : balgame A B C
229	Tenéisme el alma y la vida, : tengo os el alma ofrecida A B
230	mas ganada : ni robada A
232	es bien llamarla : se a de llamar A B
233	<-La lisonja estremada> In C this line is crossed out and written correctly on the next line.

Index of Variants

239	nace de : te hace A
245	lo que digo : esto solo A B
250	y : que C | saber : entender B
255	que : Y que B | a : omitted A
256	pagases : tratases A B
260	adorados : deseados B | In A between 260 and 261: "sale galban"
262a	tente. : <-?> tente si me an visto no C
262a	Omitted in A C | *Salen* INÉS *y* GALVÁN. : sale galuan B
262b	¿No me escuchas? : si me an bisto no A B : Omitted in C
262c	Omitted in A B C
263	HIPÓLITA : Omitted in C, though it wouldn't be necessary since Hipólita is the speaker of the previous lines, since 261.
263	Omitted in A B C
264	tenga : tengo A C
266	In B between 266 and 267: "sale galban"
267	*Aparte* : Omitted in A B C
268	los : las C | entrevo : en<-tiendo\trebo> B
270	y mi espada : y espada –base A
271	GALVÁN : Omitted in C until the following line | *Aparte* : Omitted in A C | Llega, y darás tu embajada : la traça a sido estremada A : yo quiero dar mi embaxada B | In margin of C: "vase"
272	C assigns this line to "gal" [Galván]
273	si vengase : tengose B
275	las : los B
276b	Qué dices : In C, after line 276b there are three lines written and crossed out by the first hand.
277a	Omitted in C | Inés : galban A B
277a	Omitted in A B C : In P this stage direction appears after 227b.
277b–333a	A, B and C lack this entire conversation between Inés and Hipólita (v. 277b-333a), meaning that Hipólita's conversation with Galván begins here. The manuscripts each contain two lines between 227a and 333b. In A the first line reads "gal no te haçierto hablar". In B, "gal no te açierto a hablar". In C, "gal/ no se como asierte ablar". In A, B and C the second line reads : "yp que traes amigo".
323	In P this stage direction appeared after line 322, which does not make sense since Inés is the speaker of line 323.
336a	Y : Omitted in B

364 Index of Variants

337	ha : an B
338b	*Aparte* : Omitted in A C
342b	*Aparte* : Omitted in A B C : In P, appears after 342a
344	*Aparte* : Omitted in A B C : In P, appears between 343b and 344
346	*Aparte* : Omitted in A B C : In P, appears between 345 and 346
353	sabello : saberlo A
355a	le : se B
356b	cosa? : cosa! P
357b	Oh : ay A : a B C
362b	maldad? : maldad! P
365b	*Aparte* : Omitted in A B C : In P, appears between 365a and 365b
368	*Aparte* : Omitted in A B C : In P, appears between 367 and 368
371	justos : ynjustos B
373a	In C this line is at the top of folio 39v, after an accidental repeat of line 372 which is crossed out
374	*Aparte* : Omitted in A B C : In P, appears between 373b and 374 | yo : ya A
375	Omitted in C
377	pretendiese : rindiese A
380	teniendo otra intención, otro cuidado, : y para no ser mio A : y me dexase en calma B
381	en : al C | y en fin, que se ha casado? : aquesto en mi balor que a sido çielos A : burlando mi valor q' es esto çielos B
382	Omitted in A B
383	afrentas : agrabios A | parecen : parezcan A
384	Agora : Ahora J
385	servirme : ser me A | de obligarme : obligarme A B C
389	honor : balor A B
391	Afrentas : agrabios A | parecen : parezcan A
392–407	Omitted in A
400–407	Omitted in C
408	Pues : mas A B
409	y : y a A
413	bramando : rauiando B
414	duelos : <-çelos/duelos> A
415	afrentas : agrabios A B | celos : celos / vase C
415	DOÑA HIPÓLITA : omitted in A B | *salen* : sale A | *con una banda.* : omitted in A B | *Vase* DOÑA HIPÓLITA, *y salen*

Index of Variants

	OTAVIO *y* MARCELO *con una banda.* : marselo y otauio C
417	puño : guante B
418	y así : omitted in B
419	la : y ansi la B | mala : corta A B
420–427	Omitted in A
422	Llegó : y llego C
426	ay : a C
428	porque me vi luego asido : ordeno que fuese herido A B
429	de la justicia. Fui preso : y de la justiçia preso A
430	que hasta en eso : a se qeneso [que en eso] A : se q' enesso [que en eso] B
440a	C changes to the second hand here. | estás : esta A : estais B
440b	sano : sana A
443	herida : La herida C
444	aunque estoy casi sin vida : mas mi nobleza ofendida A B
445	de que don Luis la tiene; : la benganza le prebiene A B
446	que allí : porque A B
447	Omitted in A B C
449	mirar : mirar/ a donde estoy C
450	donde estoy : omitted in C | donde estoy; quiero excusar, : desde aqui quiero estorbar A B
451a	*lee el* : leyendo un A | *DON LUIS lee el papel* : Sale don luis con una carta y un criado / lee d. luis = B : sale don luys C | obligan : obliga C | ofendidos : baldores A : valedores B | te espero : pero B | con una capa y una espada : una espada y una capa A B : con capa y espada C
452–453	In B these lines are included with the text block containing the note (451a), instead of being written as separate lines.
452	esta : esto A
453	las nuevas : la nueva A B C
453	Omitted in C
455a	no es : no <-asi> es A
455b	Alegre voy. : yo me voy C | In margin of C, "vasse"
455b	Omitted in A B C
459	el pensar : pensar A : dudar B
460	Que estas : questas C
461	ejecutallas : executa<-llas/llas> A
462	pararse a : parezer C | pensallas : pensa<-llas/llas> A

463	ponga en duda : desminuya A : ponga estoruo B | el : al B | In margin in C, "vasse"
463	*Vase* DON LUIS. : –base A B | In C the "vasse" appears in the margin in the previous line
464	fue : ba A
469	sol bello : sobre ello A
469	*Sale* DOÑA LEONOR *a la ventana.* : a la bentana doña leonor A : sale leonor C
471	se : le A
473	pedille : quitalle A B
475	mejor es : mas bale C
476	Hablarele : ablarela A : Hablaréla J : ablarelo C
477	libertad : boluntad A
478	Si : <-se> si C
481	te obligaría : t<-?>e obligaria A : teo obligaria C
486	una palma : <-la\una> <\\una> A
488–495	Omitted in C
498	también B C : tan bien A P
499	guardalla : guardallo A
499	C switches to the first hand here. | *Salen el* CAPITÁN *por una puerta y* DON FÉLIX *por otra.* : salen el capitan y don felis A : sale don felix y el capitan B : el capitan y don felis C | *Aparte todos.* : Omitted in A B C
500	estoy : soy A
501a	Félix. : Felis ay çielos B
501b	FÉLIX : Omitted in A
504	parece : <-para/pareçe> A
505	enfermo : el enfermo B | amores : amor C
506	favores : fabor C
507	los : le C
511	le : lo A
512a	tuyo es ya. : mucho obligada te estoy A : muy obligada te estoy B
512b	Omitted in A B
513	*Aparte* : Omitted in A B : In P, appears between 512b and 513
514	Dalle : darle C
515	doy : das B
517	quiero : pienso A B
519	Defiéndele en : defiendale el A

520	Omitted in A B C
522	mi : la A B
524	*Aparte* : Omitted in A B C : Appears in margin after 525a in P. | oh : a A B C | mujer : mujeres A
525a	Oh : a A B : Omitted in C
530	*Aparte* : Omitted in A B C | matalle : matarle B
531	flema : orden A B C
533	y : omitted in C
536b	Omitted in A C
540a;b–543	Julía Martínez adds question marks to 540a and 540b–543
541	estimo : mas B
544	obligado : satisfecho A
554	pues : que B | ya : yo B
555	valor : onor A
559	muestras : tienes A B
560	Allá te quiero decir : camina bien puedes yr A B
561a	lo que soy : que otabio te seguira –banse A B
561b	Omitted in A B because in A and B 561 is a full line : In margin of C next to this line: "vanse los tres"
562	concertado : desafiado le a. A : concertado se an B
563	quiero : quiere A | In margin of A and B: "–base"
567	In margin of A: "base". In margin of C: "vase"
567	*Vanse, y* : Omitted in A | *solo* : omitted in A B | *Vanse, y sale* DON LUIS *solo.* : don luys por una puerta y ypolita por otra C
570	esto : este A B
571	Sale DOÑA HIPÓLITA *en hábito de hombre, cubierto el rostro con la capa o con una banda.* : salga de hombre ypolita A : sale doña Ypolita de capa y espada B : Omitted in C
573	*Aparte* : Omitted in A B C | Terrible : Zelos y B
574a	¿Qué buscáis? : benis a reñir A
574b	Rabiando : si A : çelosa B
576	guardara : guardare B
578	Omitted in B
579	me : mi A
581	*Aparte* : Omitted in A B C
582	*Descúbrese doña* HIPÓLITA : Omitted in A C : Descubrese P B | In P and B, this stage direction appears between 583 and 584.
583	sino : s<-?\si>no A

585	enojado y : enojada y yo C
586a	castigas : castiga A : castigais B
586b	has sido : asido A (It is unclear because of the allision of the syllables whether this would read "ha sido" or "has sido").
589	amor : onor A C
595	boca A B C : toca P
596	por Dios : mi bien A B
598	enojo : agrabio A B
600–607	Omitted in A B
610	De nuevo agora : por que de nuebo A B
611	nuevo : nueb<-?\o> <\\bo> A
619b	Omitted in B
627	doña : de doña B | y no : en B
628	en : y en C | esto : eso B C
634	pasa : pase A C
640	será : y sera B
641b	*Aparte* : Omitted in A B C
646	tengo : tube A
650	LUIS : A mistakenly writes "d lu" [don Luis] at line 651, instead of 650. However, these two lines make more sense together, and spoken by Luis. | *Aparte* : Omitted in A B C : In P, appears in margin after line 649.
651	lo : la A
652	y : omitted in C | y haz por defenderte : ea defiendete A
656	*Aparte* : Omitted in A B C
657–659	Omitted in A B
660	presto, presto : presto A
661	LUIS : Omitted in B until the following line.
662	siendo : d. lu. siendo B
663	escoger : elegir B
664	aun : hazen B
668–669	Omitted in A B
670	Pues tras : detras A B
671a	In A and B, the lack of v. 668–669 means that v. 670 is the beginning of the next *redondilla*. In order to complete the *redondilla*, A and B add two and a half lines not shown in P, before coinciding with P again starting at 672. The lines are as follows: "te espero o me espera a mi / yp yo te yre siguiendo a ti / porque perderte no pueda

Index of Variants

671b	Omitted in A B
674	Allí : y alli A C
676	has : y has B C
677	mis fuerzas : mi fuerça A : mi esfuerço B : mi fuersa<\s> C
679	cuál : quien B
680	*Aparte* : Omitted in A B C
682	*Aparte* : Omitted in A B C
684	*Aparte* : Omitted in A B C
686	*Aparte* : Omitted in A B C
687	engañar : engañar/banse C
687	*Vanse, y antes de irse sale el* CAPITÁN : sale el capitan A : banse y sale el capitan B : el capitan solo C
688	válame : balgame C
689	Si son los : son aquellos B | se : omitted in B
690	¿Serán ellos? : si son ellos B
691	In A and B, there is a stage direction between 691 and 692. In A: "salgan otabio y don felis". In B: "salen otabio y don felis"
692–695	Omitted in A B
695	*Salen* : Omitted in C
697	escondido : apartado A B | le : lo B
699	a un : al C
711	escondido : apartado A B
715	estar : andar A B
722	del : de A
726a	Acaba : In B this text is unclear. It could be "Camoria" or "La moria", though neither of those make much sense
727	In margin of A and B: "–banse". In margin of C: "vanse los dos"
727	Omitted in A B C
728	CAPITÁN A B C : Gapi. P (printing error)
729	por sus resquicios veré : balgame dios que hare A B
730	el suceso, y estaré : aqui aguardare y bere A B
731	escondido : el suceso A B
733	velle : verle B
735	valiente : gallarda B
736	Acciones : acciones por A B C
737	bravamente procedieron. : que bien los dos se pusieron A B
741	arrojósele : arrojoselas A : arrojosela B
742	Válgate : valgame B

743	chocó : enbistio C
743	Omitted in C	*Sale OTAVIO herido de adentro y cayéndose* : sale cayendo otabio A : sale otauio cayendo B	él : del A
744	un : a un B C
746	piadoso : homrrado A : honrado B : onRado C
747	en : al A B C
747	Omitted in A B C
748a	Dentro: : Though P leaves this as a continuation of Félix's lines with no change in speaker, all manuscripts and Julía Martínez attribute the line to another speaker. In A and B, "dentro" appears in the speaker column; in C "Justisia/" appears in the speaker column, and JM chooses "Voces" as the speaker designation.
751	o : ni se A B : ni C	esperaba : mirava C
752	*Sale la* JUSTICIA Y GENTE (Taken from A: in the margin next to 754 and 755: "sale la / just^a [justicia] y jente") : *Salen, y un* ALGUACIL. P : salen quarto o çinco como algua / çiles = B : Omitted in C
753a	ALGUACIL : uno A : Justicia/ C	Prendeldo : prendelde A B C
753b	Qué : Por que B
756a	Corchete: : 2° [segundo] A : Justicia/ C
756b	le : se B
757a	Aquí estoy : aqui es<-toy/to> A
759	los : lo A	In margin of C: "/vanse todos"
759	*Vanse* : vanse todos B	*Vanse, y sale* DOÑA COSTANZA. : Costansa sola C
763	sola : solo A B C
765	pudo : puede A C : pueda B
767	reformaré : refrenare C
768	allí : quien B	viene : en A
769	*Sale* DOÑA HIPÓLITA *de mujer.* : sale ypolita A : salga ypolita B : ypolita sola C
770	prisa : priesa A : priessa B
772	saliste : salistes A
773	Esto : esta A	Bien : bueno A	fe! : fe? P
774	¿Por qué : de que A B
777–796b	Omitted in A B
783	ya : y J
784	en : de C

Index of Variants

790	ternura : ternesa C
791–794	Omitted in C
799a	No me aflijas. : dilo acaba A B
799b	Oye : escucha A B
802	ojos : hombres B
814	muerta de celos : desafiado B
819	mudome : mudando B
821	pudo : puede A
822	las sombras : la sombra B | hacían : asen [hacen] C
824	pintadas : pisadas A
825	al : el B J
827	y : omitted in B : <-y/pues> C | que vi : que en el vi B
832–835	Omitted in C
836	allí atrevidos : de atreuidos C
843	metió el brazo : desbiola A B
846–863	Omitted in C
846	gran : buen B
848	mas : más J
850	traspiés : un traspie A B
852–863	Omitted in A B
864–865	In P, lines 864 and 865 appear in reverse order. The lines appear in the correct order in A B and C.
865	Omitted in A | *Sale* : Omitted in C | In B and C this stage direction appears after verse 867a.
867b	LEONOR : sale d leo [doña Leonor] A ("sale" appears with the character name in the speaker column).
870b	cielo ordene : cielo lo ordene B
873	*Sale* : Salen B | *Sale* DON PEDRO *y* GALVÁN. : sale galban y don pedro A : don pedro <-?> galuan C
875	en el zaguán, ten confianza. : omitted in B
876	en : al A B | y : omitted in B
877	la : la<-s> : en la B
879b	HIPÓLITA : do co [doña Costanza] A : d.c [doña Costanza] B
880a	velle : verlo J
880b	COSTANZA : d p° [don Pedro] A : d.c. [doña Costanza] B – this indication of speaker is redundant in B since Costanza has been the speaker since line 879b.
880b	In A this stage direction appears after line 881a.

881a	In C between 881a and 881b appears the stage direction "el capitan", designated as a stage direction by a line above and below the text, indicating that the Capitán returns to the stage here.
881b	y : omitted in B
882	en : a C
884	pasar las márgenes que : llegar donde los canpos A
885	Guerva : yerba A
886	diligencia : dili<-?>jençia A
887	y : y a A
888	la : las A
894	After 893, A shows a crossed out line which reads <-pero apenas alli ubieron llegado>. This is the last line on folio 47v and the final verse in A written in the main hand; the final four folios (48r–49v) are copied by a second hand (the same hand which added missing lines in the margin on folios 8r, 10r and 12v). The fact that the first copyist's version of v. 894 is crossed out, and that the second hand begins with a different version of the line ("pero por esconderme aRodillado") suggests that the two scribes likely copied from different sources.	Pero por esconderme, arrodillado : al fin se fueron juntos lado a lado B
895	quise ver el suceso, y no le viera : donde los pude ber y no los biera B
896	abierta : rota B
903	le puedes : lo podras B
905	ha : e C	hecho : echa C
906	así : así que B : a eso C
908	Él : y el C	replicó : respondio B
910	dese : de este B
911	soy : deuo C
915	asiole la espada : asiosele al buelo B	le : la B
916	furioso : brioso B
919	su : la C
920	cuando : bertio y C
921	en : y en A C	rubís : rubies B
922	guante : bayna B
923	perdiendo espada y todo, al : pidiendole perdon al B : perdie<-sombrero\ndo> espada todo el C
928	sus : los B

Index of Variants

932	viéndola casi al punto que llegaba : temiendo si benia /o/ si esperaua B (In B line 932 is moved to line 934).
933	alborotada : alborotado B
934	en : omitted in A | venía : temia C | si : omitted in A | dudando en si venía o si esperaba, : biendola casi al puntto que llegaua B
935	temía : temi A B : temí J | yo : y C
943	con : en B
947	lo : le A B C
949	alentado : adelantado B
951	acertado : omitted in B | In C this line is the first on folio 49r, a folio which has a sheet pasted over the middle half of the page.
954	HIPÓLITA : gal/ [Galván] C
954	*Salen* DON LUIS *y* DON FÉLIX *con el guante[, sombrero] y espada de* OTAVIO (Taken from B: salen don luis y don felix con el guante = / y espada de otavio =) : *Salen don Felis, y don Luis.* P : salga don luis y don felix con el guante / y espada de otavio A : don luys y don felis C
957	valor : baler A
960a	¿vienes : d pº/ vienes A ([Don Pedro] is written in the speaker column.)
961	AYO : Leon/ [Leonor] A B C
962–963	Omitted in A B C
964–976	In C these lines are written on the paste-on in the middle of folio 49r, by the first hand. Félix's lines, 964-75, appear out of order and include two additional lines (9641 and 9642) not present in P. The order is as follows, with the symbol marking lines that are modified in C: 9641, 9642, 968, 969, 970, 971, 964, 965, 966, 967, 972, 973, 974, 975:

        felis/   ermosa doña leonor
        suplicote que mescuches
        esta es la espada de otauio
        con que mi opinion conpuse
        rresibela de mi mano
        si tus desdenes lo sufren
        este señora es <-el/tal> guante.
        que asta el mismo lugar truje
        adonde tu le perdiste
        y adonde mis selos tube

	y perdona si al perdelle
	tan couarde y torpe anduue
	pues atado me tenia
	la fuersa de la costunbre
964	señora, es : es sr^a [es señora] B | Este, señora, es tu guante, : esta es señora tu jente A : este señora es <-el/tal> guante. C (Appears after 971)
965	y : que B C | mesmo : mismo B C
966	a : omitted in B | pusiste : perdiste C
967	y : y a A B C | puse : tube C
967	[FÉLIX le da el guante y] [e]l sombrero de OTAVIO : El sôbrero / de Otauio P, in margin next to lines 966 and 967 : Omitted in A B C | I have added the glove into the stage direction since Félix's lines clearly indicate that he presents both items to Leonor.
968–969	Omitted in A B
970	Recíbele : rresibela C
972	al : el A
973	turbado : couarde C | corto : torpe C
976	Con : en A
983	la : las B
984	yo : d fel/ yo [don FÉLIX yo] A In A this speaker designation appears a line early, at 984, instead of 985. | ello : eso A C : esto B
985	FÉLIX : In A, appears in previous line. | Y : oy A B C
989	merece : mereçes A | la : lo C
990	en : de C
991	perdonalla : perdonarle B : perdonalle C
992a	FÉLIX : d luis/ A B | In A and B, the speaker designations of 992a and 992b are switched.
992b	LUIS : do fe/ [don Félix] A B
997	quien : que C | lucen : luçe A
1001	In P after the final line: *Fin de la Comedia de La fuerça de la costumbre.* | In B after the final line: "Fin" | In C a colophon similar to that of the first and second acts appears after the final line, along with a tag from the copyist: "finis laus deo et ^{me} / escribio la osorio y es suya a pesar de uellacos"